Canada . . . Notwithstanding

Canada . . . Notwithstanding

The Making of the Constitution 1976–1982

ROY ROMANOW

JOHN WHYTE

HOWARD LEESON

CARSWELL/METHUEN

Toronto   New York   London   Sydney   Auckland

Canadian Cataloguing in Publication Data

   Romanow, Roy J.
     Canada — notwithstanding

   Includes index.
   ISBN 0-458-98830-8 (bound). – ISBN 0-458-97560-5 (pbk.)

   1. Canada — Constitutional history.　2. Canada —
   Politics and government — 1980–　*I. Whyte,
   John D., 1940–　I. Leeson, Howard A., 1942–
   III. Title.

   JL65.1984 R65 1984　　342.71′029　　C84-098567-3

Printed and bound in Canada

1　2　3　4　　84　　88　87　86　85

This book is dedicated
to all the men and women
who laboured through numerous meetings,
and conferences, to patriate
the Canadian Constitution.

Table of Contents

Detailed Table of Contents

Preface

The authors of this book were participants in the political events surrounding the reform of the Constitution. Like participants in any intense political process, we did not often stop to consider what it all meant. Considering that question at length was impossible given the immediate pressures to give advice, make choices, and take action. Yet, as participants caught up in the events, we sensed that what we were part of was a significant political moment in the nation's history. We knew that what we were doing was somehow of greater stuff than the normal work of minister or official. That sense has not left us and we have, since November 1981, been filled with the belief that the new Constitution and the process by which it came about are worth our exploring. The source of our conviction that the constitutional renewal process counts for much in our history is our belief that the nation's Constitution is ultimately an ethical document; it stands as a major source for discovering the ethos or nature of the country. Belief in the importance to the country of a constitution produced in us an overriding ambition: we wished to describe as fully as possible, recognizing the limitations imposed on us by our experience, the process by which the new Constitution came into being so that, in the endlessly repeated process of national self-discovery, this account, along with others, will mark out this journey.

It is not possible for three people to tell this tale. It requires the aid and persistence of a large number of people whose names do not appear as authors. In particular, we express our appreciation to all of the people who worked with us in the departments of intergovernmental affairs and the attorney general during the period 1976 to 1982. Through their efforts and diligence positions were developed and understanding of the process was enhanced. We benefited greatly from that association. We thank also the researchers directly involved with the project since 1982: John Sutherland in Saskatoon, Kathy Maher-Walbaum in Regina, and Mary Beth Currie in Kingston. Their detailed research was instrumental in ensuring the accuracy of the work.

In particular we extend our gratitude to the law firm of Mitchell, Taylor, Ching for the generous use of their office and facilities at a crucial time in the preparation of the work. And, in conjunction with their office, we specifically thank Sherri Jackson and Charlene Sasko for the long hours of typing and revising. As well, we thank Susan de la Roche in Kingston for her secretarial assistance.

We acknowledge gratefully the University of Saskatchewan, whose appointment of Roy Romanow as visiting scholar enabled him to work on this book, and in particular, Dean Daniel Ish of the College of Law for his support of this project. Our appreciation is also extended to the Law Foundation of Saskatchewan, which provided a generous grant, the Queen's University Research Committee, which provided financial aid, and the University of Regina. We also thank those who took time to read and comment on portions of this manuscript. We wish to acknowledge the contribution of Dr. Peter Meekison and Professor Bryan Schwartz, who in collaborative efforts with Roy Romanow and John Whyte respectively, produced articles, parts of which appear in this book.

Finally, without the patience and understanding of Eleanore Romanow, Tessa Whyte, and Ede Leeson, this work would not have been completed.

Introduction

We are entering a very dangerous decade . . . and many lethal currents are swirling about our shores. . . . These are great dangers, but in a sense the greatest enemy is the enemy within, not the enemy without. . . .

It is this loyalty to the whole country upon which we must build if we want to vanquish this enemy within, this gnawing doubt, this uncertainty as to whether or not we will continue in ten or 20 years to act as a strong, united nation. . . .

We are the only group of men and women in this country who can speak for every Canadian. We are the only group, the only assembly in this country, which can speak for the whole nation, which can express the national will and the national interest. . . .

We in this Parliament have a great duty to try and express as fairly as possible the national will of all Canadians.[1]

The national will. Who could express the national will? For Pierre Trudeau, that expression could come only from the national Parliament. It could not be articulated from a collection of legislative bodies, and it could not emerge from the creative tension among regions and communities or among governments. That would not only lead to disunity but would divide allegiances and, ultimately, destroy the nation. In the final analysis the nation could admit of no competitors; it could tolerate no filtering of the expression of identity. A modern liberal state was based on a direct relationship with its individual citizens, and its citizens, in turn, must in all important respects relate directly to the national government. Anything less would divide allegiances, divide sovereignty, and weaken the nation. The lesson of the sixties and seventies for the prime minister was that the sharing of power led to a desire and need for more power. This, in turn, led to looser and looser association and, ultimately, separation. The modern nation state could brook no enemies, without or within. Trudeau had come a long way from the sign on his door at Harvard, "Pierre Trudeau, Citizen of the World."[2]

Constitution Making in Canada

At Confederation, John A. Macdonald attempted to graft a liberal democratic state onto a set of discrete colonial communities. In part the impetus for his vision of the Canadian state was the lesson learned from the American Civil War: the horrible cost of perpetuating the autonomy of communities within a new federation. In the very decade of the Canadian Confederation, the American union had come apart over the issue of states' rights, notably the right of individual states to maintain slavery. But Macdonald must have sensed that Canada in 1867 was not truly a nation state, but a tenuous community of communities. People had strong loyalties to groups and governments other than the national government. These fundamental loyalties and fundamental cleavages manifested themselves again and again during the first hundred years, including the war years when one might have expected national loyalties to be stronger. Macdonald's attempt to implant a strong centralized government structure in Canada failed neither because of the constitutional arrangement (indeed, at a structural level Macdonald was remarkably successful), nor because the courts systematically confounded the national role; it failed because Canadians had simply not formed the sense of nation which conformed with Macdonald's centralizing, liberal vision of Canada.

The impetus for constitutional reform doubtlessly results from unresolved conflicts between institutional arrangements and notions of identity and allegiance at work in a nation. When, however, there is deep ideological conflict over national identity and political allegiance, constitutional revision is not easily achieved.

Canadians have never, as a whole community, developed a clear idea of themselves as a modern unified liberal state, nor have they clung consistently to the early idea that Canada is the product of its diverse regional identities. Constitutional reform, therefore, has not been easy.

Historically, the constitutional rearrangements Canadians have been able to make have concerned power sharing between political communities—between the provinces and the federal government. They have not concerned the perfection of the relationship between the citizen and the state. Power sharing has also been the focus in the cases which have failed, as between 1927 and 1930 when the two levels of government attempted to find an amendment for altering the allocation of governmental powers. It was again the focus in 1936 and 1950 when attempts were made to patriate the British North America Act and to address the questions surrounding the relationship between political representatives of the two major linguistic communities. Constitutional reform has been viewed predominantly as a sorting out of federal–provincial power relationships.

That pattern has slowly changed. In the last quarter century there has been a movement towards examining the position of individuals in the state. Protection of individual rights, including language rights, has begun to replace argument over respective political responsibility for legislative matters bearing on rights and language. The interest in regional disparities has evolved into concern over protecting economic and mobility rights. Formulae for amending the Constitution based on the number and configuration of governmental consents began to include proposals to let the people alter our basic arrangements directly.

The idea of the nation has been undergoing a profound change. Canada is catching up to Macdonald. Less and less do Canadians see the country's virtue to be its capacity to accommodate and nurture its many local political communities. More and more Canada is seen to be a single political unit which, in its own right, has the responsibility and, now, the will to represent the interests of all.

The New West, Quebec, and Constitutional Reform
The irony of Canada's most recent constitutional agreement is that it was not, in fact, driven by the modern conception of the state as articulated by Pierre Trudeau. On the contrary, the period of constitutional negotiations, which began after 1976, was entirely the product of the older, communitarian impulses. It was the convergence of forces brought about by the OPEC oil cartel and the election of the Parti Québécois in Quebec. The immediate cause of the federal–provincial struggle to produce a new constitution was the conjoining of regional/economic and regional/ethnic forces. Once the struggle was underway, competing visions of Canada met in dramatic collision. The idea of the liberal state clashed with western regionalism and Quebec nationalism and, from our present perspective, liberalism appears to have won. The constitutional battle that concluded in November 1981 was not just another petty intergovernmental wrangle but, rather, the most significant conflict since 1867.

None of this was apparent in the middle and late 1970s. Indeed, for nearly twenty years the national government had been in retreat, fending off growing nationalist forces in Quebec. The shock of the rapid increase in oil prices after 1973 had added a new dimension to the already potent division caused by Quebec nationalism. These were the pressures which were widely understood to be at work.

For over a century the economic destiny of the country had been directed by the "old wealth" of central Canada. In the 1970s it was challenged directly by "regional wealth" of growing importance. That regional wealth was centred in Alberta, and the strength of its political voice was intimately bound up with the rising strength of the Lougheed Conservatives.

Peter Lougheed and his party had built a potent political force during the previous ten years, and this, together with the enormous transfer of wealth caused by OPEC, caused severe distortions in the traditional political and economic structure of Canada. Lougheed had come to office in

1971 by exploiting the new political circumstances of rapid urbanization in Alberta during the 1960s. He appealed to the new middle class in Alberta; he was urban, and urbane, by contrast with the older and more rural Social Credit movement.

The oil industry in Alberta was primarily either local or international. Central Canadians were not heavily involved in energy resource ownership. The provincial government had jurisdiction over the development of oil and gas, as well as the preponderant ownership position, and a natural alliance grew up between the industry and the provincial government. Enormous wealth was generated, and both industry and government were determined that it should stay with them.

In Ontario there was an early recognition that rapid oil price increases posed a threat to the economic dominance of central Canada. This economy was based on manufacturing, which was increasingly less competitive and increasingly burdened by high energy costs. Ottawa and Queen's Park were called upon for help in the situation and the result was a protracted political crisis between 1974 and 1981.

In Alberta, the alliance of the federal and Ontario governments was perceived as an attempt to keep the new Albertan economic base, and the provincial government, in a subordinate position. The battle generated considerable ill feeling toward the East, and a new alienation in the oil industry and the large new entrepreneurial class which arose as a result of the economic vibrancy which had come to Alberta. Lougheed, on the strength of this alienation, moved his party beyond its primarily urban base. He wed the residual rural alienation, the traditional ground of Social Credit strength, with the new urban forces. This produced a powerful political coalition which gave formidable strength to his demands for a new constitutional order which would match the new economic order.

The fight was not restricted to Alberta, however, but included the regional economic elite from the three western-most provinces. It manifested itself, intra-regionally, in organizations such as the Canada West Foundation, a group primarily composed of western Canadian business leaders. Alberta was a natural leader of the private resource groups, which correctly perceived their interests to be intimately bound up with the success or failure of Alberta's fight with Ontario and Ottawa. Regional economic leaders closed ranks behind Lougheed and Alberta in this conflict.

The New Democratic Party in Saskatchewan had few connections with the economic elite of western Canada. Although significantly more regional in its orientation than other NDP governments, it was interested in securing power for the provincial state in order to diversify its economy and redistribute the new economic wealth. Manitoba was only peripherally involved in natural resource extraction and, therefore, did not become involved in the fight with central Canada, at least not on the basis of economic conflict.

British Columbia might have been a leader in advancing western Canada's claim, but, influenced by its inward-looking tendencies, its diversity of interests outside of resources, and the lack of specific focus from its government—a coalition of Liberals and Conservatives, except between 1972 and 1975 when the NDP was in power—it did not consistently act in the regional interest. Alberta was, therefore, at the centre of resistance.

The major new element in constitutional reform after 1973, therefore, was the economic fight waged between the western region and the centre. The fight soon turned into competition over jurisdiction to control resources and collect economic rents; it became intimately bound up with the constitutional struggle and remained a driving force to the process that continued into 1981.

The longer standing impetus for reform was, of course, the need to respond to Quebec's demands for powers which would enable it to create a fully modern, productive francophone community in Canada and North America. Quebec's emergence from the parochialism of the Duplessis era was accompanied by a realization that building links to the wider world could soon lead to the destruction of Quebec society unless its political community were to control cultural and social evolution. It was also soon appreciated that cultural and social autonomy could be eroded without the capacity to direct the economic and political world which sustained the community. The claims of the Quiet Revolution and the *maîtres chez nous* policy had created powerful centrifugal forces within Canada by the early 1970s. This alone necessitated a significant constitutional rearrangement.

These forces were immensely magnified by the election of the Parti Québécois in November, 1976. The election gave Quebec the one card in the constitutional renewal game that the West never enjoyed: the belief by the rest of Canada that Quebec might indeed separate. While highlighting the need for constitutional reform, the election in Quebec provoked conflicting reactions. On the one hand, it was recognized that the struggle for autonomy to be waged by the Parti Québécois could aid the decentralization ambitions harboured by many provinces. On the other hand, there was great uncertainty how far such decentralization should be urged before it assumed undesirable or unmanageable proportions. Moreover, western alienation was exacerbated by Ottawa's increasing tendency to focus reform on the needs of Quebec. In any event, from the time of the 1976 election until the referendum in the spring of 1980, decentralist pressure was intense. There was a general perception that only a looser federation could contain these pressures. Even after the federalist victory in the referendum, the need to demonstrate that Canada could adjust to meet Quebec's nationalist sentiment sent the governments of Canada to the bargaining table again and, then, again.

These forces, of a regional/economic and regional/ethnic character, were of sufficient strength to compel the view that constitutional reform was indispensable to Canada's survival. The shape of the resulting negotiations was moulded by the political contexts in which the actors found themselves. Equally important, however, was the fundamental conflict between the regionalist vision of Canada and the notion of Canada as a single community with one dominant political focus.

At the 1978–79 First Ministers' Conferences the federal government found itself politically weak. It was in the last months of a mandate which had, in any event, slipped away. It was faced by strong provincial governments, in many cases, fresh from electoral victories and armed with a reform agenda bound to enhance their authority. The conference concentrated on the issues of devolution. But it failed. To the next First Ministers' Conference in September 1980 came a humbled Quebec, just defeated in the referendum, and a newly elected federal Liberal government, not only armed with a powerful mandate from Quebec but also with a clear majority and drawing strength from central Canada's rejection of the Clark government and its devolutionist policies. The conference, and the summer-long talks which preceded it, consisted of a vigorous attempt by the federal government to bring confederation back within a more centralist (and from Trudeau's perspective a more cohesive) view of the nation. The provinces, taken by surprise, rejected Trudeau's proposals, and the conference failed.

While the failure of the first conference in 1979 meant the continuance of the old system, the failure of the second conference in 1980 led to the federal government's plan of unilateral patriation. In a bold attempt to defeat the "enemies within" Trudeau moved to create constitutional arrangements which would transform the essential political relationships within Canada. Most provinces fiercely resisted this move; some tried to alter it; two accepted it. In part, the resistance to the Trudeau plan was successful, but the transformation of Canada, it would seem, was inevitable. The outcome of this struggle, the Constitution Act, 1982, which came into force on 17 April 1982, did not respond to the two great impulses which had driven constitutional reform for six years. However, the constitutional agreement put in place an arrangement speaking to that other, much older, conflict which has been at the centre of our nation's formation. The new Constitution, with its charter of rights, forged a pattern of political participation for citizens to vindicate their interests, and forestall majoritarian tyranny, by enforcing standards of political decency. The other means of vindicating political preferences, based on the federal division of power, was weakened.

Whether or not Canadians seize on this new pattern of political participation and embed it within the culture of Canada remains to be seen. Forecasts of political direction, as we learned from the original Canadian compromise, are fraught with difficulty. Clearly, a new direction has been set; a fresh impetus to the aspirations of 1867 has been advanced. It may eventually fail; the inertia of the past may prove too strong. But if it continues, 1982 will become a significant year indeed in the history of this nation.

Notes

1. Excerpts from a speech by Pierre Trudeau, *House of Commons Debates*, 32nd Parliament, 1st Session, 1:32-36 (15 April 1980).
2. R. Gwyn, *The Northern Magus: Pierre Trudeau and Canadians* (Toronto: McClelland and Stewart, 1980), 53.

Chapter 1
The Quest Begins Anew

On 31 March 1976 Prime Minister Trudeau wrote to each of Canada's ten premiers.[1] Attached to the letter was a draft proclamation which detailed the substance of a proposed constitutional agreement. Both the letter and the draft proclamation were based on the assumption that Quebec nationalism was the most important issue behind constitutional reform. However, the context of constitutional reform had changed and the question of Quebec now had to share primacy in constitutional developments. Trudeau seemingly did not recognize the demand for a realignment of powers between federal and provincial governments being made by *all* provinces, especially Quebec and the West. He refused to acknowledge that Canada's constitutional debate had been redirected by new economic, social, and political issues which threatened Canada's ability to survive as a national entity.

Canada's economic, regional, and political differences had been compounded by increased energy costs, rising inflation, mounting deficits, and devastating unemployment which had appeared in the mid and late 1970s. This economic instability, together with the new wealth of western Canada, had created economic and regional tensions and led to serious competition between governments over economic policies. Equally, the rising nationalist tendency in Quebec, dedicated to a radical rearrangement of that province's traditional place within the federal system, exacerbated the new Canadian crisis.

The 1971 Victoria Constitutional Conference[2] marked the last attempt by governments to resolve the nation's long-standing constitutional problems. In the past, this had largely meant a re-definition of Quebec's role within confederation. New centrifugal forces now tugged at the fabric of Canada's unity.

Draft Proclamation, 1976
The draft proclamation, which accompanied the Trudeau letter in March 1976, contained some modifications to the agreed measures of the Victoria

conference, primarily "to take into account the altered circumstances since 1971 and to benefit by some hindsight."[3] The draft proclamation was divided into six parts.

In Part 1 the Victoria Charter amending formula was set out.[4] The measures proposed at Victoria with respect to the Supreme Court of Canada were incorporated in Part 2.[5] Part 3 would have entrenched the French and English languages at the federal level, applicable to courts, Parliament, and certain other federal institutions. The provinces were given the right to "opt in" to this provision.[6] Part 4 of the draft proclamation, which had not been contained in the Victoria Charter, was a general statement of principles which endeavoured to provide the constitutional "guarantees" sought by Quebec's Premier Bourassa. The most important part of this section was a statement that the "fundamental purpose underlying the federation of Canada is to ensure the preservation and the full development of the French language and culture based on it and neither the Parliament nor the Government of Canada in the exercise of their respective powers, shall act in a manner that will adversely affect the preservation and development of the French language and the culture based on it."[7] The details of this guarantee were to be worked out but, politically, it let Bourassa satisfy those who sought to achieve Quebec's objectives within the federal system and, at the same time, it allowed him to adopt an aggressive negotiating posture with Ottawa in order to blunt separatist criticism. Part 5 repeated the basic thrust of the Victoria Charter's commitment to reducing regional disparities and maintaining the principle of equalization. Finally, Part 6, another new provision, dealt with federal and provincial agreements in the fields of immigration, communications, and social policy. Like Part 4, it was intended to respond to Bourassa's demands for greater provincial authority in these fields, even though the government of Quebec and Ottawa had already concluded a number of agreements with respect to these same matters. There was no mention in the proclamation of entrenching a charter of rights.

The prime minister's proposals, developed in part in consultation with Quebec, indicated that the federal government's strategy for constitutional negotiations stressed patriation, an amending formula and minimal enhancement of provincial jurisdiction in the field of language and culture. It did not address federal–provincial squabbles over energy and remained silent on increased western Canadian agitation for reform of the existing division of powers. Although Ottawa proposed that some of Quebec's demands in Victoria on social policy be acknowledged, the initiatives did not meet widened claims for new jurisdictions. In any event, the political situation within Quebec, where the political fortunes of the Parti Québécois were clearly on the rise, eventually made it extremely improbable that Bourassa would agree to something which he had rejected in principle in

1971. Rooted as it was in earlier discussions, the March 1976 federal initiative did not address the new mood of Canada in the mid 1970s.

The Edmonton Conference, 1976

In August 1976 the provincial premiers met in Edmonton in an atmosphere of deepening regional tensions to consider Trudeau's proposals. Wary of the possible direction of the prime minister's plan for constitutional reform, the premiers embarked on the tricky task of reconciling their own conflicting positions so that a united proposal could be articulated and advanced to Trudeau. Pitfalls abounded. Bourassa was faced with two choices, both difficult. On the one hand, his government could attempt to meet demands for increased provincial jurisdiction for Quebec within the framework of the present federal structure of Canada. On the other hand, it could forestall any settlement so as to deny his separatist opponents the opportunity to make the inevitable allegation that the agreement inadequately safeguarded Quebec's special place within confederation. Bourassa apparently toyed with both approaches. The other premiers were sensitive to the looming crisis for the Bourassa government, but they were also aware of the growing resentment in many parts of the country towards the seemingly endless problems and demands of Quebec. For western Canada, that conflict could at least be partially resolved if Quebec endorsed the West's demands with respect to enhanced provincial jurisdiction over natural resources in exchange for its support of Bourassa's demands for cultural "sovereignty."

The Edmonton Premiers' Conference, like all such gatherings of the provinces, was permeated with a strong sense of collegiality. Even where strong differences existed, such as the growing cleavage between the economic objectives of the West and Ontario, there was a strong tendency to subscribe to a position which isolated no one. Although this was partly the result of the understandable desire to forge a united front in order to meet Ottawa at the bargaining table in a position of strength, there was also an objective of assisting each premier with his own local political and economic policies. Bourassa's impending general provincial election was a case in point. It was widely known that Bourassa's election strategy, as part of an economic plan, consisted of, first, attacking the power of the trade unions and, second, juggling the conflicting federalist and separatist solutions to the constitutional dilemma by refusing to agree to any new constitutional proposals. In pursuit of this same strategy, the Quebec premier wanted Trudeau to incorporate a specific reference to achieving patriation in the 1976 speech from the throne; Bourassa would then be able to campaign against the proposal, and at the same time plead for a strong mandate to bargain for a better, more comprehensive, deal for

Quebec within confederation. Seemingly in compliance, the federal government did declare in its speech from the throne in October 1976 that it would "place a very high priority upon the promotion of and better understanding among French-speaking and English-speaking Canadians and upon the achievement of formal constitutional independence."[8] Regardless of their own reservations about Quebec's language and cultural demands, the premiers were not prepared to act in a way which would interfere with Bourassa's election strategy.

Notwithstanding these substantial stumbling blocks, the 1976 Edmonton Premiers' Conference and its follow-up meeting in Toronto in October was the first significant attempt since 1971 to address an expanded agenda of constitutional issues. On 14 October 1976, the premiers outlined their position in a letter from Alberta's premier, Peter Lougheed, to the prime minister. While there was general agreement with the objective of patriation, Lougheed wrote that it should not be done "without a consensus being developed on an expansion of the role of the provinces and/or jurisdiction in the following areas: culture, communications, Supreme Court of Canada, spending power, Senate representation and regional disparities."[9]

The premiers also identified other specific areas upon which they unanimously agreed. First, they proposed that there be a greater degree of provincial involvement in immigration, granting the provinces concurrent power with federal paramountcy. Second, the guarantees for French and English language rights were to be confirmed. Third, provincial legislative jurisdiction with respect to taxation of lands, mines, minerals, and forests was to be strengthened. A complementary provision would have limited the federal declaratory power to circumstances where the province directly affected concurred in its use. Fourth, the premiers urged that a First Ministers' Conference on the Constitution be held at least once a year. Finally, the creation of new provinces was to be made subject to a new amending formula.

While these matters received the unanimous consent of all premiers, other matters such as culture, communications, the Supreme Court, the federal spending power, the Senate, and regional disparities, received only a "high degree of consensus." With respect to culture, the consensus urged that the provinces be granted concurrent constitutional power in the field of arts, literature, and cultural heritage with provincial paramountcy. In particular, the majority of the provinces wished greater provincial jurisdiction over cable television. On the issue of selection of judges for the Supreme Court, most of the provinces wanted a greater role for provincial attorneys general. The provinces also wanted a formal mechanism for consideration of their opinions in those areas where the federal government exercised its spending power in areas affecting provincial jurisdiction. Central to suggestions on restructuring the Senate were British Columbia's proposals that the upper chamber consist of representatives of the provinces and that its composition be based on five regions within Canada. Under British Columbia's proposal that province would, itself, constitute one of the five regions.[10] The last area of consensus related to regional disparities and equalization. However, British Columbia, while not objecting to the idea of equalization payments, objected to placing in the Constitution a commitment to equalization. The clear overall direction of the premiers was to devolve constitutional authority from Ottawa to the provinces.

One issue on which resolution proved to be impossible was the matter of the amending formula. It was the knot which had to be untied if any constitutional agreement was to be forthcoming. Although the western provinces, especially Alberta, had decried the political and economic power of central Canada, they were incapable of rallying around any single specific amending formula which would counterbalance this power. British Columbia favoured an altered Victoria Charter amending formula which would grant it a veto over constitutional change, just like Ontario and Quebec. Alberta, however, insisted that any amending formula be based on the principle of the equality of all provinces. Saskatchewan and Manitoba professed their support for any formula which was acceptable to the other governments and which would be uniformly applied throughout the country.

The election of the Parti Québécois initially threatened the provincial alliance born at Edmonton. But when, at subsequent meetings of premiers, the new Quebec premier, René Lévesque, repeatedly assured the other provincial governments that Quebec would play by the traditional federal and provincial rules until such time as the people of the province determined otherwise, the strength of the alliance was reinforced.

The general tactical position of the other provinces was to promote their devolutionary demands by linking up with Lévesque's. However, the premiers never precisely defined how far in that direction they were prepared to go, even though that question would inevitably present a fundamental point of departure. Moreover, the pervasive sense of suspicion and mistrust about Ottawa's intentions occupied more of the premiers' attention than the motivations of Lévesque, especially when the list of provincial demands was endorsed by the new premier.

In retrospect, the provincial "shopping list" was too unwieldy, general, and unrealistic, especially in light of Trudeau's growing apprehension about the centrifugal forces within Canada. Nevertheless, pushed by Trudeau's resolve to patriate and fuelled by their mistrust of his government, all the premiers in their 1978 meeting in Regina reaffirmed their adherence to the October 1976 position. Rather than hindering the provincial alliance's objective of greater devolution of constitutional authority to the provinces, Lévesque's entry to the circle of premiers boosted both the general aims and intensity of the provinces. However, the most important aspect of the 1976 developments was that, for the first time in Canadian history, the constitutional interests of Quebec were not the only ones on the public agenda.

The Economic Conference:
A Lesson in Cooperative Federalism

The perilous state of the economy, compounded by incessant federal and provincial feuding over the pricing and the development of natural resources, forced governments to consider cooperative mechanisms to overcome the mounting uncertainty left in its wake. Economic issues rivaled the constitutional problems for prominence on the public agenda. Economic forecasts in the fall of 1977 had cautiously predicted a modest recovery in 1978, but it had not materialized. Lingering economic problems forced both orders of government to realize that only genuine consultation and cooperation would yield a positive response to the deepening economic malaise.[11] In an economic Green Paper, *Agenda for Co-operation*, published in May 1977, Ottawa had recommended closer cooperation with the provinces in the orderly dismantling of its wage and price program instituted eighteen months earlier.[12] Most of the provinces had objected to the federal controls program, claiming that they had not been adequately consulted and that the program had proven to be ineffective. Some provinces, clearly unhappy about continuing the federal scheme, took their own steps to terminate the plan at the provincial level. For example, the Lévesque government had withdrawn its public sector employees from the program shortly after assuming office, while Alberta had withdrawn from the program in December of 1977. The question remained, nevertheless, how to wind up the program without inflicting further inflationary damage on the Canadian economy.

In addition to the problem of controls, the growth of the public sector, fiscal and monetary policies, government regulation, energy megaprojects, regional development, and sectoral industrial policy all vied with each other for attention. In February 1978 the premiers and the prime minister met in Ottawa to tackle this panopoly of complex economic problems. A wide divergence of views emerged as to how the economic crisis should be handled. The final communiqué offered only the most tentative and general of statements. The governments agreed to encourage recovery, led by the private sector, by maintaining price stability, reducing public expenditures, eliminating jurisdictional overlap, and ensuring that public sector wages did not exceed those in the private sector. Notwithstanding the general nature of the agreements, the February economic conference was hailed as a success by most of the provincial premiers since it appeared to be based on genuine intergovernmental consultation. This assessment was shared by the federal government. In his closing remarks to the conference, Trudeau declared that the "real condition for the success of this Conference in leading the way towards a better economic future is that it marks the beginning of a process of more complete and purposeful intergovernmental consultation."[13] The newly appointed minister of federal and provincial relations, Marc Lalonde, echoed these sentiments by concluding that ". . . the time when 'the ship of state had watertight compartments' is long past."[14] As a result, another first ministers' conference was arranged for November 1978, at which time economic and constitutional questions would be considered simultaneously.

A Time for Action: New Federal Initiatives

By mid-1978 in a climate of worsening economic recession, however, it was clear that the federal anti-inflation program had not succeeded. In addition, there was the Parti Québécois. The Lévesque government had completed its first eighteen months in power and, although it was making plans for the forthcoming referendum within Quebec, it was withholding any detailed announcement of its intentions until after the next general federal election, due in a matter of months. The timing, the wording, and the rules for the referendum would depend in large measure on the make-up and the philosophy of the new federal government. Quebec ministers privately conceded that the Trudeau administration, led by a native son from Quebec, was its most formidable obstacle to scoring a success in the referendum. Thus, its strategy was clear: participate in federal and provincial constitutional negotiations but agree to nothing until after the next federal election and the outcome of the referendum. Judging from the national opinion polls on support for the three federal parties, the Lévesque government could afford to outwait Trudeau.

For its part, the Trudeau government realized the potential for recapturing political support if it could advance a reasonable policy on the entire unity issue presented by the PQ. In January 1977 the prime minister had responded to the Lougheed letter with a revised draft proclamation which attempted to meet some of the provincial demands.[15] However, the revisions failed to "give in" to the provincial assertion that reconsideration of the division of powers must constitute an integral part of any future constitutional agreement. In effect, Trudeau's position retained its adherence to the original parameters outlined in 1974. Therefore, its January 1977 revised proclamation had failed to gain provincial support, and time was running out. It was essential that something new be tried; something had to be proposed in connection with constitutional reform which would lead to action but which would by-pass the intolerable set of provincial conditions.

In June 1978, five months after the cooperative federalism of the economic conference, the federal government unveiled a new White Paper on the Constitution, *A Time for Action*,[16] and, subsequently, tabled Bill

C-60[17] in the House of Commons to give legislative meaning to its new proposals. *A Time for Action* proposed that constitutional reform be divided into two phases. Under Phase 1 it intended to deal with only those matters which, in the opinion of Ottawa, could be amended by federal legislation without the consent of the provinces. Such consent would be sought, but, if not forthcoming, Ottawa argued that it could act alone. In order to provide the regions with a greater influence at the centre, the main emphasis was placed on the reform of the central institutions, such as the Senate and the Supreme Court of Canada. Phase 1 also embraced an extremely important "new" matter: an entrenched charter of rights more extensive than previous ones. It would be incorporated into the Constitution but made applicable only to the federal government. The provinces could opt into the charter if they so chose. Other issues which were to be dealt with during the first phase included a general statement of aims, identification of those values common to all Canadians, and a redefinition of the role of the governor general. A deadline for the completion of Phase 1 was set: 1 July 1979. Although the provinces would be consulted, their consent was not viewed as essential by the federal government.

The second phase would deal with those matters in which the consent of the provinces was required, particularly reform of the division of powers between the two orders of government. Ottawa did not advance any specific suggestions with respect to this question. Aboriginal rights were also to be discussed during the second stage. Unless an agreement could be reached on the question of patriation and a domestic amending formula during the first phase of discussions with the provinces, the White Paper proposed that these matters also be examined at a later date. The second phase of constitutional negotiations was to be completed by 1 July 1981, the fiftieth anniversary of the Statute of Westminster. Another deadline.

Bill C-60

Bill C-60 was the legislative manifestation of only the first phase of the proposed renewal of the federation. It was framed as a constitutional document which redrafted entire sections of the British North America Act, leaving intact those sections which would be later reformed under Phase 2. Acting out of frustration and purportedly acting under Parliament's authority under section 91(1) of the BNA Act to amend the federal aspects of the Constitution, the federal government introduced Bill C-60, which contained several important provisions. Part 2 enunciated the general statement of aims for the Constitution which included fundamental rights, the principle of the rule of law, and a recognition of Canada's diversity of language and culture. The proposed Charter of Rights and Freedoms, set out in Part 3, included, among other rights, equality of the French and English languages in the courts of Canada, the federal Parliament, and the provincial legislatures.[18] Official bilingualism would be guaranteed for other federal institutions as would minority language education rights.[19] The proposed charter would apply only to Parliament, but provinces could opt in if they so chose. As an inducement for provincial acceptance of the charter, once a province opted in, the federal powers of disallowance and reservation could no longer be employed against that province.[20]

Part 4 proposed a radical reform of the Senate. It would abolish the Senate as presently constituted and substitute for it a new House of the Federation with 118 members. Half of the members would be selected by the federal Parliament and the remaining half by the provincial legislatures on the basis of proportional party representation. The new members (who came to be called "Fedoras") would be granted a limited power of veto over federal legislation affecting certain relations between the federal government and the provinces. The veto would also extend to those issues "of special linguistic significance," but on French and English language matters it would be effective only if a majority of the House's English-speaking members and a majority of the French-speaking members agreed—a "double majority" requirement. Part 4 also proposed that the office of the governor general be transformed: rather than being a representative exercising power at the sovereign's prerogative, the governor general would exercise the sovereign's power in his own right, except when the sovereign was in Canada.

Part 8 merely reproduced the current distribution of powers and clearly was intended to await the results of the second phase of discussions. Part 9 proposed a constitutional commitment to the reduction of regional disparities and the principle of equalization. A mandatory annual conference between the prime minister and the provincial premiers was suggested in Part 10. Under this provision, the provinces would have to be consulted, but their consent was not required before the federal government employed the declaratory power. Finally, under the terms of Part 11, the Supreme Court of Canada would have been entrenched and confirmed as court of final appeal in Canada. Its size would be increased from nine members to eleven, at least four of whom would come from the province of Quebec.

Although the overall theme of these new federal initiatives was to revamp the nation's central institutions, and thereby secure a greater role for the regions in the decision making in Ottawa, a radical departure was evident from the approach Ottawa had formerly advocated. The emphasis had shifted from simple patriation with an amending formula to a major revision of the Senate and the Supreme Court and the inclusion of a new charter of rights. The new House of the Federation, unlike the Trudeau proposals of 1976–77, which had only promised a greater number of senators for the regions, was a new idea designed to enhance significantly the role of a second chamber and the influence of the provinces. The recognition of the principle of duality was contained in the proposals for the new House of the Federation and the proposed expansion of the Supreme Court of Canada. Moreover, in an attempt to assuage Alberta's concerns with respect to the federal declaratory power, Ottawa suggested the requirement of consulting provinces before the power was exercised.

The Charter of Rights and Freedoms, despite its breadth and its potential for limiting the sovereignty of Parliament, was an attractive idea which might have garnered the political support of most Canadians, if not their provincial governments. In all, the federal government's proposals were a bold enterprise which endeavoured to address the growing regional discontent and the political issues surrounding unity. Laudable as they may have been, however, they stood in opposition to the demands of the provinces first formulated in Edmonton, which were directed toward a redefinition of constitutional authority to provincial advantage.

Opposition in the House of Commons

The opposition parties in the House of Commons also criticized the proposals. Based on the "Kingston communiqué"[21] of September 1977 and the official party position of April 1978,[22] the Progressive Conservatives argued that the federal government had grown insensitive to the demands of the provinces. The Kingston communiqué, was the product of an agreement between the federal leader of the Progressive Conservative party, Joe Clark, and his provincial counterparts. It proposed that certain of the divisions of powers be rewritten as soon as possible to accommodate provincial concerns. Specifically, it urged a constitutional limitation on the use of the federal spending power in areas of provincial jurisdiction; shared jurisdiction in the cultural field; constitutional recognition of provincial ownership and jurisdiction over offshore resources; and a strengthening of provincial jurisdiction over natural resources in general. The Progressive Conservatives also advocated a new upper chamber, called the House of the Provinces, which would be composed primarily of nominees of the provincial governments and whose main task would be to review federal and provincial agreements, various constitutional issues affecting provincial jurisdiction, and nominations to the Supreme Court of Canada. With respect to the Supreme Court appointments, the Progressive Conservatives urged that provincial governments be directly consulted by the federal government. The Conservatives also supported the concept of a mandatory annual first ministers' conference on the Constitution but, unlike the federal government's White Paper, also advocated that the federal government be obligated to report directly to the full House of Commons on the agenda and progress of those meetings.

According to Clark, the Progressive Conservatives had demonstrated that they were able to understand and negotiate with the provinces, unlike the Trudeau administration. Inherent in this strategy, however, was an assumption that Lévesque's Parti Québécois government was like any other provincial government in that its constitutional goals could be accommodated within the framework of cooperative federalism. The Liberals characterized the Progressive Conservatives as the "party of the provinces," unconcerned with the protection of the national interest and naive with regard to the true intentions of the Parti Québécois. They ridiculed the notion that the objectives of the Parti Québécois could be accommodated within the federal framework since the first objective of the PQ's manifesto, as repeatedly interpreted by Ottawa's spokesmen, was "to separate from Canada."

The position of the federal New Democratic Party differed from that of the Progressive Conservatives. Although it also objected to the provisions of Bill C-60, it did so not because it preferred revision of the distribution of powers, but because the specific proposal of the House of the Federation was unacceptable to it. The NDP claimed that the proposed House of the Federation would result eventually in an even more undemocratic institution than the present Senate since its potential power to frustrate the wishes of the democratically elected House of Commons would be greater. Rather than resuscitation of the Senate, the federal NDP proposed radical reformation of the House of Commons through the creation of an additional one hundred seats on a regional basis allocated by proportional representation.[23] In the opinion of the New Democratic Party, the democratic process would be thereby respected, the influence of the regions in Ottawa strengthened, and the integrity of a strong central government maintained. This approach differed from that of the Progressive Conservatives because the focal point was reform of the central institutions and not reform of the division of powers. In this sense, at an early stage in the constitutional debate, the federal New Democratic Party aligned itself with the Liberals in opposition to the Progressive Conservatives.

Outside of the House of Commons, the unexpected election of the Parti Québécois generated numerous unity movements, conferences, and task forces as concerned Canadians sought to defend the federation and to articulate alternatives to existing constitutional arrangements. In 1977 and in the early part of 1978 there were many such fora at which both the provincial governments and the citizens could articulate their positions on the Constitution and national unity. The Pepin–Robarts Task Force on Canadian Unity was the most important of these activities although the conferences Options Canada[24] in Toronto and Alternatives Canada[25] in Banff, to list but two, attracted important submissions from governments and individuals. Established by the federal government, the Pepin–Robarts Task Force on Canadian Unity travelled across the nation to hear briefs from individuals, organizations, and governments. The task force reported to the federal government in late January 1979 in a third volume, *A Future*

Together.[26] The Senate and the House of Commons were not to be outdone and a Special Joint Committee on the Constitution[27] (called the Lamontagne/MacGuigan Committee after its co-chairmen) took evidence from many factions of Canadian society and articulated their recommendations to the Senate and the House of Commons in late 1978. Public participation in the debate over the future of Canada was an unusual but welcomed development, heralding a temporary change in the venue of constitutional deliberations from closed rooms to public forums. However, the immediate responses were those of the provincial governments.

The Regina Premiers' Conference, 1978

When the nineteenth annual premiers' conference convened in Regina in August 1978, it had two main items on its agenda: the economy and the Constitution. The objective of the meeting was to discuss the federal strategy and to devise a common position for the forthcoming First Ministers' Conference. Before 1973 the premiers' conferences were designed to permit informal communications between the provincial governments for the purpose of mutual understanding of problems. Little was organized by officials in advance of these meetings; as a consequence, the meetings often lacked focus. All of that changed, however, after the emergence of the oil crisis, as both provincial and federal governments were beset with numerous seemingly intractable economic, constitutional, and political problems. Efforts were made by provincial ministers and officials to distill and to coordinate provincial responses to various federal economic actions during this period. The cosy clubbiness which had formerly permeated the atmosphere of this annual gathering was transformed; gradually it became a more formalized and focussed event. The personal friendships which developed, regardless of differences in political ideologies, remained an important feature in the proceedings as was the opportunity for informal discussion. However, the contentious and complex issues before the premiers now required a structured and purposeful organization. Lévesque's election had temporarily disrupted the relationship which had been established with Bourassa, but the beguiling charm of the new premier, combined with the unrelenting approach of the Trudeau government on constitutional and economic issues, restored collegiality and a sense of common purpose. Suspicions as to the tactics and motivations of the new Quebec government persisted. But Lévesque spoke forthrightly and colourfully, understood the political problems of his colleagues, and consistently assured the group of his government's intentions to "play by the rules of the game." Thus, when the premiers convened in Regina, it was fairly simple for them to endorse a consensus which reaffirmed the position developed in August and October 1976 and which advanced some new claims.

The new consensus included a demand that the federal powers of reservation and disallowance be abolished outright. Ottawa's treaty-making power should be curtailed so that it could not invade areas of provincial responsibility. Provincial jurisdictional claims over indirect taxation in natural resources were widened to include a general call for the confirmation and strengthening of provincial powers. The premiers agreed to seek concurrent jurisdiction with respect to fisheries and insisted that there be full and formal consultation with the provinces on all federal judicial appointments, particularly the Supreme Court of Canada. More fundamentally, the premiers repeated that patriation and an amending formula should be effected only after the other items of reform had been agreed upon, thereby rebuffing Trudeau's hope for a phased achievement of constitutional reform.[28]

The premiers also opposed Bill C-60 because they believed that some parts of it amounted to an attack on existing provincial authority. These were the sections dealing with mobility rights, language provisions, and the absence of a section continuing section 109 of the British North America Act. Both Saskatchewan and Prince Edward Island had enacted legislation[29] which restricted foreign and non-resident ownership of land within their boundaries on the basis that absentee ownership was detrimental to provincial society. The mobility rights section of Bill C-60, guaranteeing the constitutional right to all Canadians to reside and own property anywhere in Canada, was seen as interfering with these provincial objectives. Although all of the premiers professed their agreement to the general idea that there should be free movement of persons within Canada, the atmosphere of general opposition to the Trudeau proposals and the arguments of the provinces specifically affected combined to produce a strong consensus opposing the proposed mobility rights.

With respect to language guarantees, the premiers had agreed in Montreal in 1978, as a follow up to their 1977 annual meeting in New Brunswick, to enter into a series of bilateral provincial agreements for the provision of minority language education services "where numbers warrant." Their position was based on the proposition that education and language of instruction were provincial responsibilities, a position fiercely supported by the new Parti Québécois government. Moreover, the premiers now foresaw practical problems in the proposed constitutional requirements related to bilingual legislative, governmental, and court services, even though they had generally endorsed this position in Edmonton in 1976. The discussion revealed that the real basis of this position was the opposition of most of the premiers to the principle of an entrenched charter of rights in which the language guarantees were set out. These premiers favoured the retention of the traditional parliamentary process as the method to protect individual rights in the country.

Finally, there was the issue of section 109, a particular concern for the sensitive western provinces. In general terms, section 109[30] granted to the original provinces of confederation the ownership of all lands, mines, minerals, and royalties. In 1930 Alberta, Saskatchewan, and Manitoba were placed on the same constitutional footing as the original provinces with respect to this matter when the Parliament enacted the Natural Resources Transfers Agreement Act and the complementary amendments to the British North America Act[31] were made. In *A Time for Action* the federal government stated that reform of the division of powers would be dealt with in the second stage. When Bill C-60 was tabled without specific reference to, or continuation of, section 109 but incorporating all sections allocating legislative powers, the western provinces immediately objected. They felt that if the true intention of the federal government was to preserve the status quo until subsequent negotiations were concluded, division of powers and the respective rights and privileges of governments should be carried forth in their entirety in Bill C-60. In the words of the final communiqué from Regina, "all Premiers expressed grave concern that section 109 of the B.N.A. Act, concerning provincial ownership of natural resources, has not been carried forward into the proposed new constitution." This position reflected excessive suspicion since federal enactment of Bill C-60 would not clearly have affected the provinces' rights under section 109.

However, the feelings of the western provinces with respect to both the ownership and the jurisdiction over natural resources had reached dangerous proportions. The federal government and the producing provinces in the West had confronted each other on numerous occasions since he dramatic increase in the value of natural resources in 1973. The producing provinces sought to appropriate the bulk of the new resource wealth to their treasuries so that new economic and social programs could be implemented and the local economies strengthened. But the federal government had its motivations too. In the May 1974[32] federal budget, the then minister of finance, John Turner, proposed that payment of royalties to provincial governments by private resource corporations could no longer be deducted by those corporations in the computation of their federal income tax, even though such deductions would still be allowed if the royalties were paid to private corporations and individuals. The rationale for the new provision was that the federal government had to maintain its tax revenue and that "a provincial resource was also a national resource."[33] The enactment of the Petroleum Administration Act,[34] empowering Ottawa to fix prices for oil, and the imposition of an export tax[35] in oil further challenged the provincial governments' perceived authority to manage and tax the natural resources within their boundaries. The producing provinces viewed these federal initiatives as a direct attack by the federal government on their rights of ownership and regulation of natural resources. At the practical level, the federal government actions disrupted

to: All Staff

from: Audrey

date: October 1, 1984

our file:

your file:

subject: Change of Telephone for Craig & Gilsdorf

Professors Craig and Gilsdorf have been given a new telephone number.

Please change your directory listing to 2282.

My thanks.

AJBH/rk

the longstanding informal arrangements between the producing provinces, the industry, and the federal government with respect to taxation of natural resources.

The extreme sensitivity of the situation was brought into sharp focus with the decision of the Supreme Court of Canada in the case of *CIGOL v. Government of Saskatchewan*[36] in which a private oil company had successfully challenged the constitutionality of the province's royalty regime, the basis for its heritage funds,[37] on the ground that the taxation scheme was indirect and, therefore, *ultra vires* the province. In another case, *Central Canada Potash v. Government of Saskatchewan*,[38] in which the federal minister of justice was granted standing as a co-plaintiff, a rare legal occurrence, the constitutionality of the province's prorationing scheme and minimum floor price for potash was again successfully challenged; since the commodity was shipped beyond the borders of the province, the matter fell constitutionally within the federal government's exclusive trade and commerce power. Two months after the Regina Premiers' Conference, the Supreme Court's acceptance of the contention of the potash company and the federal minister of justice was viewed as further undermining provincial jurisdiction over natural resources. When seen in this context and in the light of the ongoing disputes over pricing, taxation, and revenue distribution, the provinces interpreted the omission of section 109 as part of a continuing and coordinated strategy of the federal government to assume a greater control over natural resources.

In the West the decision in the *CIGOL* case was seen as attacking the principle of provincial ownership and jurisdiction over natural resources. But, in the province of Quebec, the decision also carried important implications. Claude Ryan, a person of influence and later leader of the Quebec Liberal party, wrote the following in *Le Devoir* about the judgment:

> In all of this, what results from the Supreme Court decision opposing CIGOL and the government of Saskatchewan is what could be a considerable and dangerous constitutional impact. The Supreme Court has just proposed an interpretation of the federal powers of indirect taxation and regulation of interprovincial and international trade which opens almost limitless horizons for the expansion of the federal presence in these areas. On the other hand, this interpretation restricts provincial power to control their natural resources to such extent that there is a risk of their being reduced to almost nothing each time Ottawa wishes to gain the same dominance in this area as it has in others.[39]

The linkage of the regional–resource issue to the regional–ethnic issue was extremely important. It placed the demands of the western provinces on a footing equal to those of Quebec. Lévesque, endorsed by federalist spokesmen in Quebec such as Ryan, supported the western provinces on the issue of natural resources and, in exchange, the western provinces moved closer to most of Quebec's positions on language and culture. This was the dominant mood of the Regina conference.

The Regina conference also registered its strong objections to the proposed process of constitutional reform and alerted Canadians to the spectre of unilateral action in some areas. The premiers asserted that both orders of government had to agree not only to the substance of the reform but also the process used to attain it. They argued that provincial governments must be treated as constitutional equals. Thus, they rejected the arbitrary deadlines of the federal White Paper urging, instead, that a steady and thoughtful process was more important than speedy agreement under the threat of deadlines imposed by one level of government. Above all, the premiers insisted that their concerns, the reform of the division of powers, must be considered at the same time and on the same basis as the institutional concerns of the federal government.

A New Era of Negotiation Begins

In the period of constitutional negotiations between October 1974 and August 1978, the opposing objectives of the federal and provincial governments were identified. In effect they were an extension of various economic disagreements that had manifested themselves throughout much of the intergovernmental process in the 1970s. The federal government, believing that quick action was needed, sought simple patriation with a domestic amending formula patterned after the Victoria Charter. Ottawa argued that the chances of altering the division of powers with everyone's concurrence were exceedingly slim and, therefore, complete Canadian constitutional independence should not be held up as a consequence. Undoubtedly, it was also feared that implementation of the demands of the premiers would weaken to an unacceptable degree the capacity of the central government to manage effectively the difficult economic and social issues of the country. On the other hand, the provinces, realizing that opportunities for fundamental restructuring of the Constitution were rare, and motivated by regional economic and ethnic forces, were determined to air their grievances and to enhance their legislative authority. In the opinion of the provinces, Ottawa's proposed constitutional solutions, based on the assumption that Quebec's nationalism was the prime constitutional issue, were no longer acceptable; they did not respond to the economic and political turbulence of the period.

Because of these objections, as well as those raised in the House, in support of the provincial position, and in the Senate, in response to its proposed reform, the federal government was not able to push ahead with its plan. *A Time for Action* with its deadlines and two phases was effectively buried, and Bill C-60 was to die on the Commons order paper. Canadians had entered an era of constitutional negotiations in which provincial priorities would, for a time, predominate.

Notes

1. Letter of 31 March 1976 from Pierre Trudeau, prime minister, to A.E. Blakeney, premier of Saskatchewan, at 2.
2. Victoria was a culmination of nearly three years of negotiations which produced agreement among nine of the eleven governments on patriation, a limited charter, and an amending formula. To meet the Quebec question within confederation, the Victoria amending formula conceived Canada as a regionally divided country, and for the first time an amending formula singled out provinces for special status. Although not expressly naming Quebec or Ontario, the formula called for the approval of "any province having or having had 25 percent of the population of Canada." Both Ontario and Quebec fulfilled the requirement. The Victoria conference failed when Quebec rejected the proposed arrangements on the ground that the province did not receive sufficient legislative jurisdiction over social policy.
3. *Supra*, note 1, at 4.
4. Under the terms of the Victoria amending formula the most important parts of the Canadian Constitution would be amendable by resolutions of the Senate and House of Commons and by at least a majority of the provinces which included: each province with a population at least 25 percent of the population of Canada; at least two of the Atlantic provinces; at least two of the western provinces having together at least half the population of all the western provinces.
5. See *infra*, at 35 for a full discussion of the Supreme Court provisions of the Victoria Charter.
6. Art. 35 of the draft proclamation was permissive. It allowed a provincial legislature to declare by resolution that provisions for the use of English or French would apply to the legislative assembly of that province, or to the provincial courts and provincial departments and agencies in like manner to the federal provisions contained in Arts. 32, 33, and 34.
7. For almost two years prior to Trudeau's letter of March 1976 to the premiers, Gordon Robertson, clerk of the Privy Council, had travelled and met with the premiers to ascertain their views on constitutional issues. During his meeting with Robertson, and later with Trudeau, Bourassa urged that there be special constitutional guarantees for Quebec with respect to matters of language and culture.
8. *House of Commons Debates*, 30th Parliament, 2nd Session, 1:1 (12 October 1976).
9. Letter from Peter Lougheed, premier of Alberta and then chairman of the annual premiers' conference to Pierre Trudeau, prime minister, dated 14 October 1976, at 1.
10. In November 1976 British Columbia published its views on the Constitution in *What Is British Columbia's Position on the Constitution of Canada*. The province stated, "Subject matters of concern to Parliament and all the provincial Legislatures should be amendable by the affirmative votes of the House of

Commons, the Atlantic Region, Quebec, Ontario, the Prairie Region, and British Columbia," at 4. British Columbia rejected the amending formula contained in the Victoria Charter "as not properly reflecting those realities. Instead it [B.C.] proposes that B.C. be treated as a separate region," at 5. Two years later in a further position paper British Columbia again set out its position: "The forum for aggregating the five regional votes required for constitutional amendments should be the Senate, provided that it is reformed so that its primary purpose is the representation of regional interests at the national level and provided that all Senators are appointed by, and are directly responsible to provincial governments." See *British Columbia's Constitutional Proposals, Paper No. 9—The Amendment of the Constitution of Canada*, at 18.

11. In the government of Canada's policy statement *Attack on Inflation: A Program of National Action*, tabled in the House of Commons by Donald S. Macdonald, minister of finance, 14 October 1975, the government committed itself to stemming the severe and prolonged inflationary spiral. There were four elements to its program: (1) fiscal and monetary policies; (2) government expenditure policies; (3) structural policies; (4) prices and incomes policy. Throughout the federal program was an emphasis on a "concerted national effort. . . ." "The federal government is depending heavily on the provinces to make the program work nationally. . . asking each of the 10 provincial governments to bring provincial and municipal employees and services under the guidelines." See Brown, Goodlet, Scace, and Smith, eds., *Canadian Price and Income Controls* (Butterworth and Co. (Canada) Ltd.: Toronto, 1977), 128.

12. The Anti-Inflation Act was enacted under the anti-inflation program. See Anti-Inflation Act, an Act to provide for the restraint of profit margins, prices, dividends, and compensation in Canada, S.C. 1974–75–76, c. 75. The discussion paper *Agenda for Co-operation* was tabled in the House of Commons on 27 May 1977. See *House of Commons Debates*, 30th Parliament, 2nd Session, 6: 6014 (27 May 1977).

13. Quoted in D. Brown, *Federal Year in Review—1977–78*, (Kingston: Institute of Intergovernmental Relations, 1978) 19.

14. *Ibid.*

15. Letter from Pierre Trudeau, prime minister, to Peter Lougheed, premier of Alberta, dated 19 January 1977. Accompanying this letter was a revised draft proclamation. The prime minister's response to the position taken at the Edmonton Premiers' Conference was to state that provincial demands were either "too much or too little." They were "too much" because they widened the constitutional agenda to include the complex negotiations over division of powers. They were "too little" since they reflected only the concerns of the provincial governments and not the objectives of the federal government.

16. *House of Commons Debates*, 30th Parliament, 3rd Session, 121: 6278 (12 June 1978).

17. *Ibid.*, at 6573 (20 June 1978) and see Canada, *The Constitutional Amendment Bill Text and Explanatory Notes.* This was issued "to encourage public discus-

sion of proposed changes in the Canadian Constitution" following the introduction of Bill C-60 in the House of Commons in June 1978.

18. The British North America Act, s.133; the Manitoba Act, 1870, s.23; and the
Official Languages of New Brunswick Act, s.3 provided for official bilingualism
in some provinces. The Victoria Charter had sought to entrench official bilingualism at the federal level, and under Art. 16 of the charter provincial acceptance of the principle was permissive. Bill C-60, s.19(2) mandated that, where
sufficient numbers used a minority language in an area of a province, any
member of the public had the right to communicate in the minority language
with the provincial institutions.

19. Minority language education rights were proposed in s.21(1)–(11). In any
area of an anglophone province where there were sufficient numbers of francophones to warrant the provision of basic school instruction in French, resident
non-anglophone parents who were citizens of Canada would have the right to
have their children receive their schooling in French. The converse was true
for minority non-francophones in Quebec to have their children schooled in
English whenever numbers were sufficient to trigger the provision of public
school facilities in English. Limitations on this right were restricted to the
giving of notice (s.21(2)) and to reasonable provincial determination of
whether there were sufficient numbers to warrant implementation of the right.
Subsections 21(3) and (4) ensured maintenance of existing rights and non-
abrogation of rights of provincial residents to have their children schooled in
the majority language of the province. At the 18th annual premiers' conference,
St. Andrews, New Brunswick, 18–19 August 1977, the premiers said: "Recognizing that education is the foundation on which language and culture rest;
The Premiers agree that they will make their best efforts to provide instruction
in education in English and French wherever numbers warrant; The Premiers
direct the Council of Education Ministers to meet as soon as possible to review
the state of minority language education in each province. The Premiers ask
further that the Council of Education Ministers report to each Premier within
six months. Following this, each province would undertake to ensure such
provision of Canadian minority language education, and would then make a
declaration of the policy plan and programme to be adopted by the Government of that Province, in this respect" (C.I.C.S. Doc. 850-8/027).

20. Under s.13(3) of Bill C-60, whenever a province adopted the charter, the
federal government would no longer be able to disallow the statutes of that
province. Paragraph 13(3)(a) made it clear that the reservation of assent to
bills, the disallowance of Acts and the signification of pleasure on bills reserved
as matters following within provincial legislative authority would cease to
extend and be applicable to the legislature of a province and its legislation.
This provision is in keeping with the federal government's statement of principle contained in s.5 of Bill C-60, that certain rights should be incapable of
being alienated by ordinary legislative procedures.

21. The so called Kingston communiqué was a Progressive Conservative policy

paper entitled "Making Canada Work." It was a joint statement by national Progressive Conservative leader Joe Clark and Progressive Conservative Premiers Moores, Hatfield, Davis, and Lougheed dated 16 September 1977. See N. Nurgitz and H. Segal, *No Small Measure* (Ottawa: Deneau Press, 1983), 117.

22. *The Constitution and National Unity*, Progressive Conservative paper dated April 1978.

23. The reform of the House of Commons has always been a traditional policy of the federal NDP. As recently as 1983 the official representative of the party on the Special Joint Parliamentary Committee articulated once again this position.

24. *Options Canada*, Proceedings of the Conference on the Future of Canadian Confederation, University of Toronto, Toronto, 14–15 October 1977.

25. *Alternatives Canada*, sponsored by Canada West Foundation, Banff, March 1978.

26. *House of Commons Debates*, 30th Parliament, 4th Session, 3: 2552 (25 January 1979).

27. This joint committee, the second in the period of constitutional reform since 1972, was convened to consider the federal government's initiative for reform taken in Bill C-60. *Supra*, note 16, at 6781 (27 June, 1978).

28. See *Proposals on the Constitution — 1971–1978*, Collections by the Canadian Intergovernmental Conference Secretariat (Ottawa: December, 1978), 24–25.

29. Farm Security Act, R.S.S. 1978, c. F-9; Lands Protection Act, Prince Edward Island, S.P.E.I., 1982, c. 16, R.S.P.E.I. 1974, c. L-7.1

30. Section 109 of the British North America Act, 1867, 30 & 31 Vict., c.3 (U.K.), states: "All Lands, Mines, Minerals, and Royalties belonging to the several Provinces of Canada, Nova Scotia, and New Brunswick at the Union, and all Sums then due or payable for such Lands, Mines, Minerals, or Royalties, shall belong to the several provinces of Ontario, Quebec, Nova Scotia, and several Provinces of Quebec, Ontario, Nova Scotia, and New Brunswick in which the same are situate or arise, subject to any Trusts existing in respect thereof, and to any Interest, other than that of the Province in the same."

31. British North America Act, 1930, 20 & 21 Geo. 5, c. 26 (U.K.)

32. Budget address by John Turner, minister of finance, *House of Commons Debates*, 29th Parliament, 2nd Session, 2:2076 (6 May 1974).

33. *Ibid.,* at 2079–80.

34. Petroleum Administration Act, S.C. 1974–75–76, c. 47, Part I. Renamed by S.C. 1980–81–82, c.114, s.1, the Energy Administration Act.

35. *Ibid.,* Part II.

36. *Canadian Industrial Gas & Oil Ltd. v. Government of Saskatchewan et al.,* [1979] 1 S.C.R. 37, 80 D.L.R. (3d) 449.

37. Heritage Fund (Saskatchewan) Act, R.S.S. 1978, c. 22.

38. *Central Canada Potash Co. v. Attorney General of Saskatchewan,* [1979] 1 S.C.R. 42, 88 D.L.R. (3d) 609.

39. *Le Devoir*, 29 November 1977, at 4 (trans.).

Chapter 2
The Search for a Quick Solution

Learning To Talk Together

The First Ministers' Conference of 31 October and 1 November 1978, convened by Ottawa in the final year of the Thirty-First Parliament, saw the federal government change the constitutional strategy outlined just three months previously in *A Time for Action*. The prime minister proposed at the conference an "Agenda for Change,"[1] embracing fourteen specific agenda items, as the basis for an intensive, three months study by provincial and federal governments to find solutions to the constitutional issues. The agenda he described included both issues of institutional reform, favoured by Ottawa, and the rearrangement of the division of powers, urged by most of the provincial governments. That speech by the prime minister marked a significant moment in the history of constitutional reform: the federal government agreed to negotiate changes in the division of legislative powers to an extent far greater than during previous periods of constitutional negotiations and to contemplate some diminution of federal authority.

The vehicle chosen by the first ministers to pursue the agenda items was patterned after the one used in the period preceding the Victoria conference: a committee of federal and provincial ministers called the Continuing Committee of Ministers on the Constitution, or CCMC for short. The ministers met at the conclusion of the First Ministers' Conference and selected two co-chairmen. The provincial co-chairman was Roy Romanow, the attorney general of Saskatchewan, chosen because Saskatchewan was the chairing province of the 1978 premiers' conference. The federal co-chairman was Otto Lang, the minister of justice. Lang was shortly replaced by Marc Lalonde when Lang's Cabinet responsibilities were switched from justice to transport and Lalonde became the minister of justice.

The ministers discussed the agenda for the CCMC meetings and arranged three-week-long meetings to be held in Mont Ste. Marie in late November, Toronto in early December, and Vancouver in January 1979. The last meeting was to be held just days before the first ministers were to reconvene in Ottawa on 6 February 1979. Clearly the CCMC task was herculean: to identify the problems, develop possible solutions, and strive to obtain agreement on specific draft texts.

The composition of the CCMC varied from government to government. Some designated the minister of justice or attorney general as the head of the delegation, while others gave that responsibility to the minister of intergovernmental affairs; some designated both. The concept of a special ministry for intergovernmental affairs was an outgrowth of the many intergovernmental issues and conferences of this period. Trudeau's government, struggling with its multi-dimensional economic policy, Quebec, and the West, named Marc Lalonde as its first minister of federal–provincial relations.[2] Some provincial governments such as Alberta, Ontario, and Newfoundland already had ministers of intergovernmental affairs; others quickly followed suit. Thus, the federal government, as well as British Columbia, Alberta, Ontario, Quebec, Nova Scotia, and, for a time, Newfoundland, all had two ministers, one responsible for intergovernmental affairs and the other for legal matters heading their delegations. Each delegation was also comprised of several advisors. Seated around a conference table, in the order of their entry into confederation, with formal deskplates, translation facilities, and numerous assistants, the meetings had all the trappings of an international conference of nation states.

One of the impediments to the success of the CCMC was the initial tendency of each government to present its formal position with respect to each agenda item and to refuse to budge in the subsequent deliberations. A number of explanations can be offered for this. First, the mandate given to ministers varied from delegation to delegation; many did not possess the negotiating freedom that was required if a consensus was to be forged. Thus, many provincial delegations opted for the safer course of adhering faithfully to the specific position of their premier, where that position had been clearly articulated. Where it had not, equally awkward problems developed. All ministers were concerned to preserve a maximum amount of freedom for their premiers at the First Ministers' Conference. This resulted in a tendency not to volunteer too much about what one's own position might ultimately be. Moreover, many saw the mandate of CCMC confined to an identification of the problems and possible solutions for the various constitutional issues rather than an active search for compromise.

Finally, the role of the advisors, always important in most governmental matters, took on a new and larger dimension. The CCMC established a series of officials' committees to examine in further detail each item on the agenda following ministerial discussion and direction. Frequently these meetings occurred concurrently with the ministerial sessions and, of necessity, were of a technical nature. In order for the minister to be informed of developments within the officials' committees, numerous private briefing sessions were held, during which the activities of the officials were translated and incorporated into a political framework. This process of secondhand communication, laced with technical detail, meant that ministers relied heavily on their advisors for interpretations of issues and events. In many cases, the tendency was merely to accept the report of the advisors. The combined effect of secondhand political assessments and the lack of firsthand grappling with technical details by ministers was that free-wheeling discussions leading to movement and consensus were less frequent.

However, on several occasions during 1978-79, as well as during the 1980 CCMC exercise, the ministers attempted to break out of the mould of structured responses through a series of private ministerial meetings, which were akin to constitutional group therapy sessions. The objective was to encourage the ministers to exchange freely their own perceptions of the issues, to predict the likely responses of their premiers, and to amend or overrule, if necessary, the positions taken by officials in the technical sessions. Most of the ministers freely participated in these meetings but they tended to be dominated by a few: Claude Morin, Quebec's minister of intergovernmental affairs; federal ministers Otto Lang and Marc Lalonde; Tom Wells, Ontario's intergovernmental affairs minister and Roy McMurtry, that province's attorney general; Alberta's Lou Hyndman and later his successor in intergovernmental affairs, Dick Johnston; and co-chairman Roy Romanow. The influence of these men was not necessarily the result of any special constitutional expertise; indeed, their training and experience varied greatly. Rather, their special role reflected the nature of the issues that now dominated the political landscape: the regional-cultural problems associated with Quebec and the regional-economic conflicts between the East and the West over energy pricing, industrialization, and related economic matters. Out of these ministerial meetings, personal friendships and political alliances arose.

Allegiances were shaped, too, by government objectives. Saskatchewan, for example, concentrated on maintaining its links with Alberta and Ontario in the hope that a "middle ground" on resource jurisdiction could be found. Ontario's representatives met frequently with Saskatchewan's and Ottawa's in the hope of finding a different middle ground which would be less provincially oriented than the one sought by Saskatchewan and, more especially, Alberta. Quebec's alliances were aimed at Alberta and Manitoba, because of its strident opposition to the Trudeau initiatives, and at Saskatchewan, because of its important role as co-chairman. Every delegation had its own "hidden agenda" and sought to persuade the others, formally and informally, to its position. The whole process represented a rich ideological, personal, and constitutional tapestry. Gradually the formalities gave way to easy familiarity, the exchanges were freer, the options were identified, and the differences were narrowed. The desire to succeed became stronger and stronger. By the time the first ministers met in February 1979, the result was a so-called "best efforts" draft, which enjoyed the support of most governments, for almost all matters.

No formal transcript of proceedings was made, and no votes were formally conducted, but there were official minutes. What follows, in the same order as considered by the CCMC, is a brief discussion of the best efforts draft and the debate on each of the fourteen items of the agenda. The somewhat technical nature of the text mirrors the detailed nature of the discussions; this reflects the purpose of the CCMC, namely, to produce consensus on specific drafts.

Natural Resources

The importance of natural resources was underlined by the placement of this item first on the agenda. Oil was the most important natural resource of the period. Alberta and Saskatchewan, the two provinces that produced it, took the lead in advocating new constitutional provisions with respect to natural resources. Their positions, however, were not identical. Alberta submitted a comprehensive, if not exhaustive, list of principles as the basis of its claim for greater constitutional authority. These principles included the right of the provinces to determine whether or not resources should be developed and, if so, by whom, when, and how; processing and refining within the province; disposition of resources; and, finally, the price to be charged.[3] This wide-ranging list prompted Ottawa to assert that its acceptance would virtually remove the federal government from any meaningful role in the field.

Saskatchewan's concerns and objectives were more limited, reflecting the need to remedy the problems created by the *CIGOL*[4] and *Central Canada Potash*[5] decisions of the Supreme Court of Canada. These cases seemed to expand Ottawa's trade and commerce power and, correspondingly, curtail the provincial government's right to manage and tax resources. Saskatchewan argued that provinces should have concurrent jurisdiction over trade and commerce power, with federal paramountcy limited to matters of "compelling national interest." Saskatchewan also asked for constitutional authority to tax the production of the resources either directly or indirectly. Saskatchewan's proposal for concurrent jurisdiction over the management of resources was derived from the sense that in areas which were jurisdictionally complex, concurrency, as a matter of both law and sound policy, permitted the best opportunity for giving appropriate reign to both federal and provincial interests, while allowing continuous political adjustments. The "concurrency" solution to resources and trade and commerce became the focus of virtually all subsequent constitutional discussions.

The Alberta approach reflected a view of the aims of constitutional reform which was, in part, shared by all Western Canadians. If confederation was truly to work, there had to be not only a sharing of wealth but also a sharing of power. With the wealth of natural resources, the western provinces had come of age, and they were insisting on full partnership within a restructured federalism. Alberta's Premier Lougheed described this objective:

> The only way there can be a fair deal for the citizens of the outlying parts of Canada is for the elected provincial governments of these parts to be sufficiently strong to offset the political power in the House of Commons of the populated centres. That strength can only flow from the provinces' jurisdiction over the management of their own economic destinies and the development of the natural resources owned by the provinces.[6]

When he addressed the October 1978 First Ministers' Conference, Trudeau also acknowledged the need to clarify federal and provincial powers over the control and regulation of natural resources but cautioned that any re-definition should "ensure that both orders of government had acquitted themselves of their responsibilities effectively, and that a fair share of the benefits from natural resources accrue to the people of the province where they are found, without depriving other Canadians of a reasonable share of these benefits."[7]

In the course of the deliberations of the CCMC, a best efforts draft was prepared which dealt with four major issues. First, it purported to strengthen provincial jurisdiction over natural resources in the provinces. Second, it granted the provinces concurrent jurisdiction over trade and commerce in resources with a limitation upon the general rule of federal paramountcy which was similar to Saskatchewan's proposal. Third, it gave the provinces constitutional authority to levy indirect, as well as direct, taxes on natural resources. Finally, it attempted to provide a way to deal with the omission of section 109 of the British North America Act from Bill C-60, a problem which was solved when Ottawa finally abandoned that bill.

The best efforts draft would have granted provinces exclusive legislative jurisdiction over the exploration, development, exploitation, extraction, conservation, and management of non-renewable resources, forestry resources, and "sites and facilities" for the generation of electrical energy in the province. In addition, this grant of exclusive legislative jurisdiction would have expressly provided that provinces could enact laws in relation to the primary production from these natural resources, enabling them to introduce prorationing schemes limiting supply for other than conservation purposes.

As demonstrated by the two Supreme Court of Canada resource decisions, provincial efforts to regulate resource production, such as Saskatchewan potash, could be frustrated because regulation which was felt to impinge on interprovincial and international trade and commerce would be held to be unconstitutional. To remedy this, the best efforts draft permitted the provinces to legislate "in relation to the export from the province of the primary production . . ." from non-renewable resources, forestry resources, and electrical energy. This was not a grant of exclusive jurisdiction but the establishment of a field of concurrent jurisdiction. However, federal legislation, based on the trade and commerce power, could still override provincial legislation if it were rendered necessary by a "compelling national interest that is not merely the aggregate of local interests." If the provincial law related to international trade and commerce, as opposed to interprovincial trade and commerce, then concurrency was subject to unqualified federal paramountcy. The best efforts draft also placed certain restrictions on a province's exercise of its power to enact laws in relation to resource exports. First, such provincial laws could not be discriminatory in respect of pricing. Second, they could apply only to primary production of resources. The definition of primary production in the best efforts draft excluded manufactured products refined from oil and gas.

In response to the striking down of Saskatchewan's oil tax legislation in the *CIGOL* case, the best efforts draft empowered the provinces to raise revenues by any mode or system of taxation on non-renewable natural resources, forestry resources, and electrical energy and upon the primary production therefrom. Again there was a non-discrimination provision: the power to levy indirect taxes on resources was made subject to the constitutional limitation that the taxes could not differentiate as between production exported to another part of Canada and that not exported from the province.

Finally, the best efforts draft attempted to set out a way to incorporate section 109 of the British North America Act into Bill C-60. The western provinces had demanded that if Bill C-60 was to proceed, despite the objections of most provinces, their proprietary rights under section 109 had to be carried forward. The governments identified three possible options but were unable to agree on one. The first was to leave the existing provisions of the British North America Act and Bill C-60 as they were and consider them at a later stage in constitutional negotiations. The second was to incorporate the principles of section 109 into Bill C-60 in the form of a new section. The third was to clarify and remove the ambiguities created by Bill C-60. When it became clear that Ottawa no longer intended to enact the legislation and had referred key portions of it, relating to a new second chamber, to the Supreme Court of Canada for a ruling on its constitutionality, the importance of the matter faded.

Three major issues respecting the resources provisions could not be fully resolved: the definition of natural resources; the rules for federal paramountcy over trade and commerce; and the non-discrimination provisions.

The best efforts draft applied to non-renewable natural resources, forestry resources, and electric energy. British Columbia and Quebec argued that the amendment should apply to all resources, and the draft should refer simply to natural resources. Alberta supported this contention. Newfoundland wanted offshore resources to be specifically included in any constitutional text, but the others resisted this on the grounds that jurisdiction over offshore resources was to be dealt with separately. The other objection to this definition in the best efforts draft involved the generation of electrical energy. British Columbia wanted the text to refer to "water" and "water resources." Ottawa strongly opposed all such requests for an extension of the definition of resources. A related issue was the concept of primary production. Everyone recognized that primary production meant more than resource extraction. However, where was the line to be drawn between primary production and manufacturing? Eventually, the discussion led to the development of a series of definitions which became the so-called Sixth Schedule contained in the Constitution Act, 1982.[8]

The second unresolved issue in the resources draft concerned the rules for federal paramountcy in trade and commerce legislation. In general terms, everyone conceded that Ottawa should, under certain circumstances, possess the authority to override provincial legislation dealing with the export of resource production from the province. But, under what circumstances? Alberta strongly objected to the test of compelling national interest and urged a significantly more stringent one. In Alberta's opinion, compelling national interest would restrict federal action much less rigorously than the "peace-time emergency" criterion set out by the Supreme Court of Canada in the *Anti-Inflation Reference.*[9] Alberta contended that the proposed non-discrimination provisions in respect of pricing and supply allocation removed any fears that a province would act in a manner destructive of the Canadian economic union. Moreover, Alberta's resource prices would be set by the market and not by fiat. Therefore, there was no basis for Ottawa's intervention, for compelling national interests to set the price of exported resources. Alberta argued instead that Ottawa should only be empowered to override provincial legislation in a "national or international crisis," and only when that crisis caused a shortage in supply which was substantially injurious to the economic and social well-being of Canada. Furthermore, in an effort to reverse the effect of the decision of the *Anti-Inflation Reference*, as well as the effect of earlier national emergency cases, Alberta proposed that the onus of proving that an emergency existed be put on the government that alleged it.

Alberta's draft sought not only to secure jurisdiction over natural resources but also to immunize provincial resource laws from virtually all federal powers and laws except those enacted under an emergency conception of the federal trade and commerce power. Although Saskatchewan preferred a slightly differently worded draft, it was prepared to accept the best efforts draft because it seemed to represent an appropriate balance between federal and provincial interests. In an attempt to find some ground between Ottawa and Alberta, Saskatchewan suggested a procedural safeguard as an alternative to finding more stringent wording to describe Ottawa's jurisdiction: before Ottawa could enact its overriding compelling national interest legislation, it would have to receive the prior approval of seven provinces. A variation of this safeguard was that the federal legislation would have to contain a specific declaration of compelling national interest and be supported by two-thirds of the members of Parliament. Saskatchewan also suggested that the draft contain the requirement that the onus for proving the existence of a compelling national interest fall on the federal government. None of these proposals, however, received the approval of either Alberta or Ottawa.

Saskatchewan's concerns with the best efforts provisions dealing with federal paramountcy differed from those of Alberta. It wanted to extend the compelling national interest condition to laws respecting international, not just interprovincial, trade because most of the province's resources left the country. On the final day of the First Ministers' Conference in February 1979, federal officials suggested, apparently without the express approval of their ministers, that a wording might be found under which federal paramountcy in respect of international trade in resources could be qualified. It was, unfortunately, too late in the process and too tentatively put forward to prompt a further attempt to find a consensus.

With respect to non-discrimination, the best efforts draft attempted to protect the Canadian economic union by ensuring that there would be no discrimination in price or supply in Canada. The issue was whether the non-discrimination provisions should be extended to prohibit provincial rebate schemes which reduced the cost of resources within a particular province. Ontario strongly urged the inclusion of such a clause, while Alberta equally strongly opposed it.

Other constitutional provisions to protect and enhance provincial jurisdiction over natural resources were also considered. A limitation of the federal trade and commerce power to prevent compulsory production against a province's will was sought. In 1974 the Alberta minister of energy, Merv Leitch, had speculated on possible federal responses if his province cut back on oil production in defence of its resources policies.[10] It was clear that Alberta feared Ottawa would pursue several constitutional remedies to stop the province from limiting production, and the possibility motivated this proposal. There was little discussion, however, since most of the other provinces viewed it as too extreme a position, advanced in the context of an exacerbated energy debate.

Another area, however, the federal declaratory power, received much favourable attention in the context of resources discussions. The federal government, in recognition of the premiers' demands in 1976 and 1978, tabled a proposal under which Parliament's declaratory power would be limited to those specific aspects of a work or an undertaking which were to the general advantage of Canada. The draft also required bilateral consultations for the purpose of reaching an agreement on any use of the declaratory power. If these failed, the matter would be placed before a First Ministers' Conference. Only after both of these measures had been taken would Parliament be permitted to invoke the declaratory power. Even then, the declaration would be limited to a five year period. For natural resources the draft went further: it specifically declared that the power could be applied only with the consent of the province in which the natural resource was located. This represented a major concession to provincial demands. Ottawa also offered to review previous declarations, such as those in respect of uranium, with a view to returning some or all of the declared works to provincial jurisdiction.

Indirect Taxation

In his statement to the First Ministers' Conference in October 1978, Prime Minister Trudeau identified the issue of provincial access to indirect taxation in general as a priority, but he attached as a condition of the grant of such power that its operation could not impair interprovincial and international trade and commerce. The task before the CCMC was to frame a constitutional provision which permitted a province to tax indirectly but only within its borders.

At the first meeting of the CCMC, the topic of indirect taxation was divided: indirect taxation as it related to natural resources and indirect taxation in general. Once the distinction was made, the provinces focussed their attention on natural resources, and a consideration of the general power diminished in importance. The risks of seriously disrupting existing tax arrangements, some of which stood on flimsy constitutional ground, and the prospect of novel judicial interpretations as a result of changed constitutional texts outweighed any benefits in pursuing this question. Although Ontario had prepared a draft proposal on the general issue of indirect taxation, it received little attention from the ministers and, eventually, the First Ministers' Conference in February 1979 decided to delete the item from future consideration.

Communications

Given the growth of Quebec nationalism, from Bourassa's vision of "cultural sovereignty" to Lévesque's "sovereignty-assocation," the demand for greatly increased provincial authority over communications could be understood. The challenge was to develop a constitutional framework which would serve both to unify the nation and to mirror the specific regional and cultural differences of Quebec. This challenge was all the more difficult because other regions also sought greater authority. Moreover, these objectives were out of step with the technology of communications which had widened choices and made it easier for Canadians to exchange ideas, beliefs, and cultures with people all over the world.

Over the years, the Supreme Court of Canada had assigned exclusive constitutional authority over all aspects of communications to the federal government. In 1976 the provinces, meeting in Edmonton, agreed in principle to a constitutional proposal which would have divided that authority by assigning to them jurisdiction over "communications systems in the province." At the First Ministers' Conference in October 1978, Ottawa appeared willing to devolve some constitutional authority over communications to the provinces. Trudeau outlined his intentions:

> The present constitution, as interpreted by our highest courts, over the years, seems to assign almost the entire field to the Parliament of Canada. We believe, however, that today's reality and the future, as we can best foresee it, required a more varied approach.[11]

Two important judgments of the Supreme Court of Canada provided the background for the discussions.[12] In both *Capital Cities Commission* and *Dionne*, the Supreme Court rejected Quebec's provincial regulatory authority over cable television undertakings and confirmed the exclusive jurisdiction of the federal government. In both cases, the three Supreme Court justices from Quebec rendered minority judgments based on Quebec's right to determine questions pertaining to its own culture and language. The *Globe and Mail* commented editorially that:

> The majority of the Supreme Court are saying that because cable firms distribute broadcast TV signals they must be designated as carriers and everything they distribute must come under federal control. Nonsense. Let Ottawa control the broadcast signals as it now does at points of origin. Let it prohibit any changes cable distributors want to make in broadcast shows, if it must. But please don't argue that the right to control the broadcast signal should give Ottawa the right to control everything else cable distributors want to disseminate.[13]

The provinces acknowledged Ottawa's important role of protecting and promoting a national communications policy. The issue was, however, how much of that role could be transferred to the provinces, enabling development of regional cultural and communications links while not destroying the national communications network.

Both Saskatchewan and Nova Scotia submitted proposals which, though different in some respects, urged that cable distribution systems and provincial telecommunications systems be exclusively provincial. The other provinces endorsed these demands. In response, the federal government stressed nine fundamental principles which, it stated, should form the basis of any agreement on legislative jurisdiction over communications. In the words of the federal paper, "an orderly development of efficient telecommunications systems [w]as essential to Canada's security . . . and economic growth." The paper also argued that national broadcasting networks should remain under federal jurisdiction because they served to "safeguard, enrich and strengthen the cultural, political, social and economic fabric of Canada as a whole and of every province."[14] Canadian content and Canadian ownership of broadcasting were also among the nine principles.

By the time the CCMC convened in Vancouver for its final session, it was clear that the only possible area of devolution of jurisdiction in communications was in cable distribution. Ottawa had insisted that a national broadcasting system, Canadian programming content, and technical standards should all remain within its jurisdiction. With respect to cable, two important but opposing proposals emerged: the first had the support of a majority of provinces; the second was Ottawa's. The substance of each was to provide for concurrency in the field of cable distribution with provincial paramountcy in all but three areas. It was in respect of the three areas of federal paramountcy that the two versions differed. The provincial proposal was that federal paramountcy would only apply in the reception and conditions of carriage of broadcast signals, the technical standards relating to the reception and carriage of the broadcast signals, and the national origin of broadcast program content. The federal version, however, proposed that federal paramountcy would apply with respect to "Canadian content, Canadian broadcast programs and services, and technical standards." The provinces claimed that the federal wording was so wide as to permit federal intervention in such non-programming services as computer operations or data transmission services.

Similarly, the provinces believed that the words "Canadian broadcast programs and services" would allow federal regulation of all programs and services which would be carried over cable provided they originated from a broadcast signal. The provincial draft had sought to constrain these federal powers by referring to broadcast signals instead of broadcast programs. Finally, the federal proposal for "technical standards" was also extremely broad, for they would have permitted federal regulation of closed circuit cable services, such as pay TV and other non-programming services, an area the provinces claimed was exclusively theirs.

Ottawa argued, with some merit, that the existing cable systems failed to serve Canada's cultural purposes since they so largely imported American material. Extensive regulatory control over content was required by the federal government if Canada's cultural objectives were to be met. Cable could not be dealt with in isolation, however, at least until a study of the effect of the whole system on Canada's cultural needs had been completed. For the moment, Ottawa stated it was unable to alter its position on the scope of federal paramountcy.

The differences between the two positions on the range of federal paramountcy persisted throughout the negotiations. Ottawa was willing to grant the provinces modest regulatory jurisdiction over cable television hardware and franchising in exchange for an expansion of its role in closed-circuit cable services and programming. The basis of this proposal was the importance of communications in the promotion of national identity and national unity. It was also based on the realization that, because of technological developments, much conventional broadcasting, as well as non-programming functions, such as electronic banking, would likely be delivered through cable. The provinces, however, recognized that the federal draft would have the effect of shifting jurisdiction to the federal government level. In their view, most aspects of cable communications were essentially "local works and undertakings" which did not fall within the federal jurisdiction over broadcasting, and the federal proposals relating to paramountcy would capture some of these aspects. This was particularly worrisome to those provinces which had provincially owned telephone systems; these provinces wished to leave provincial jurisdiction over cable systems, outside the broadcasting context, as unimpaired as possible in order to protect revenues. The search for "a more varied approach" to communications proved to be more elusive than was originally thought. Partly this was the result of competition for regulatory authority and partly it was the result of disintegration of meetings into exchanges of technical detail and industry jargon incomprehensible to ministers and other "non-expert" officials.

The Senate

Henri Bourassa described the reform of the Canadian Senate as something which "comes periodically like other forms of epidemics and other fevers."[15] In 1978 the "epidemic" of Senate reform appeared to be widespread. Ottawa proposed a major revision of the Senate in Bill C-60 and British Columbia, a strong advocate of reform since at least 1976, proposed that the Canadian Senate be remodelled along the lines of the West German upper chamber.

With all the advisory groups and studies on constitutional reform, there was no shortage of proposals. Bill C-60 had advocated the establishment of a new body of 118 members to be called the House of the Federation. The representation in that House would be based on the four traditional Senate regions, but Atlantic representation would be increased by two and Western representation by twelve. An equal number of members would be selected by Ottawa and the provinces following federal and provincial general elections. The tenure of members would correspond to that of the government which appointed them. The House of the Federation would have the authority to approve legislation which affected federal and provincial relations or French and English language issues. As a result of provincial criticisms that Ottawa did not possess the constitutional authority to reform the Senate unilaterally, the federal government referred the issue to the Supreme Court of Canada, in the words of the prime minister, "to clarify Parliament's jurisdiction to make changes affecting the Senate or to legislate for its replacement by a different second Chamber."[16] Although the Supreme Court decision which supported the provincial contention led to the shelving of the proposal in Bill C-60, the issue of Senate reform had clearly not disappeared.

In September 1978 British Columbia published a series of nine papers detailing its constitutional reform proposals, one of which was devoted to reform of the Senate.[17] British Columbia believed that its representation in national institutions, such as the Senate, was inadequate. It catalogued a variety of reforms to central institutions designed to enhance provincial or regional participation in the national decision-making process. Unlike the federal government in Bill C-60, British Columbia proposed that representation in a new second chamber be based upon five regions of Canada with that province being one of the regions. Each region would have equal representation with appointments being made by the provincial governments. The senators from each province would vote, in a bloc, at the direction of the provincial government. The leading senator for each province would be a member of the provincial Cabinet. Ottawa would have no representation in the upper house. This new Senate would possess an absolute veto over federal government nominees to the Supreme Court of Canada and various administrative tribunals; it would be able to veto certain matters dealing with federal and provincial relations and it could veto the use of the federal spending power in areas of provincial jurisdiction. It would also have a suspensive veto with respect to all remaining matters.

The epidemic of Senate reform, largely resulting from British Columbia's enthusiasm, was very much on the minds of the CCMC in 1978–79. British Columbia's position that Senate reform, along the lines it suggested, was a crucial matter was underlined at the First Ministers' Conference in February 1979, when Premier Bennett declared the province would have great difficulty approving any "package" of constitutional reforms that did not include a reconstituted Senate.

Though the epidemic was widespread, the cure could not be found. Ottawa sympathized with the objective of Senate reform and agreed in principle with British Columbia's position. But it insisted that British Columbia's model be amended to include federal as well as provincial appointments. The other governments were less enthusiastic about restructuring the Senate. They were of the view that changes in the division of powers should take precedence over institutional reform and that changes to the Senate should be considered only after the jurisdictional issues had been resolved. This view was persistently advanced and eventually dominated the 1980 CCMC meetings.

Some of the provinces, including New Brunswick, opposed the provincial participation in the Senate; the present Senate, they argued, was a national institution which must continue to be appointed by the federal government. Manitoba favoured limited revisions, such as provincial appointments of senators, but insisted that the name Senate should be retained. Alberta, Quebec, and Newfoundland, in particular, urged that the thrust of constitutional reform should be a decentralization of legislative power rather than greater provincial participation in central institutions. Alberta expressed grave reservations about the idea that any body, other than an elected body such as a provincial government, could or should represent provincial interests. Saskatchewan urged total abolition of the Senate on the ground that no appointed body should possess substantial powers. If, however, such an institution were necessary, it supported, without a great deal of enthusiasm, the notion of a body which was, at least partially, provincially appointed. In fact, Premier Blakeney had been one of the very few who reacted positively to the House of the Federation proposal contained in Bill C-60. He saw it as having potential in reconstructing national parties, whose failure was, in his view, as crucial a factor as any other in the current constitutional difficulties.

Simply stated, although there was general agreement that the Senate was neither democratically based nor fulfilling its role of providing regional voices at the centre, the governments were unable to agree about its reform. Four principal questions remained unanswered. First, what matters would the new second chamber consider? There was no consensus whether it should review all federal legislation or only that which impinged on provincial jurisdiction. Second, how should the members be chosen? Some favoured appointment by the provinces only, while others argued that the federal government should have representation. Furthermore, there was no agreement on the question of voting on instruction, and if so, on what matters? Third, should the new second chamber have an absolute or a suspensive veto, and over which matters? Most provinces felt that the second chamber should have only a suspensive veto and only in specific areas. Some provinces felt strongly that the federal spending power and declaratory power should be limited through a new division of powers rather than letting the reformed second chamber exercise an absolute veto over their exercise. Finally, how would the seats be distributed among the provinces? Some suggested equality among provinces, although Quebec expressed reservations about placing its traditional provincial authority over language and cultural issues in the hands of a non-Quebec majority.

Others supported a distribution weighted according to population, a position rejected by the smaller provinces. British Columbia's proposal, of course, advocated an equal number of seats for five regions. This was rejected by those provinces who believed that all provinces should be treated equally.

As a result of these wide-ranging and unresolved differences, the CCMC was unable to prepare a best efforts draft on the Senate, although several attempts were made. With the exception of British Columbia and Ottawa, the overwhelming mood of the CCMC was to pursue reform of the division of powers first. Moreover, the *Senate Reference* was before the Supreme Court and its outcome had the potential to affect future discussions significantly; if the federal government's argument were to prevail, the provincial voice would be considerably weakened.

The Supreme Court

A supreme court, as the final arbiter of jurisdictional disputes between governments in a federal system has been the subject of many proposed reforms, including the 1956 Tremblay report in Quebec,[18] the 1971 Victoria Charter,[19] and the 1972 report of the Joint Parliamentary Committee.[20]

In the period immediately preceding the constitutional negotiations, demands for reform of the Supreme Court of Canada had gained momentum as a result of a number of decisions against provincial interests: *CIGOL* and *Central Canada Potash* in natural resources; *Dionne* and *Capital Cities Commission* in communications; and the *Anti-Inflation Reference* in relation to the general power. These cases brought the Supreme Court under intensive provincial scrutiny and produced strong criticism. So much so that during the Saskatchewan provincial election in October 1978, it was rumoured that the Court was contemplating citing Premier Blakeney with contempt for his election comments on the Court's performance. It was not surprising, therefore, that some provinces sought greater representation on the Court or, at least, more involvement in the selection of judges.

One proposal was based on the 1971 Victoria Charter. In addition to entrenching in the Constitution a nine judge court, three of whom would be qualified in the civil law of Quebec, the Victoria Charter would have granted provincial governments a specific role in the selection of the judges. Although the federal minister of justice would retain responsibility for appointments, he would be required to consult with the attorney general of the province from which the prospective nominee came. The Victoria Charter also stipulated that, if no agreement was forthcoming, a nominating council would be convened and would recommend the candidate for appointment. This was a major gain for the provinces, which previously were consulted informally only if the minister of justice chose to do so.

In 1972 the Special Joint Committee on the Constitution of Canada reviewed the matter of the selection process. While it agreed with the methods of consultation proposed in the Victoria Charter on appointments, it wished to see a more expanded role for the provinces, permitting them to make nominations to the nominating councils which would be set up if the attorney general of Canada and the attorney general of a province failed to agree on an appointment to the Court.[21] The committee's report also recommended a new limitation on the Court's jurisdiction. It suggested that the provinces be given the right to vest in their own highest courts the final decision on matters falling strictly within provincial jurisdiction, leaving to the Supreme Court federal law, constitutional law, and Bill of Rights questions.[22]

Although Bill C-60 retained the essential ingredients of the Victoria Charter, it proposed that appointments be affirmed by the House of the Federation. Bill C-60 also proposed that the number of judges be increased from nine to eleven, four of whom would come from Quebec. As was the case in the Victoria Charter proposals, the Supreme Court of Canada would remain the final court of appeal for all cases.

The CCMC in the course of its deliberations in 1978–79 produced a best efforts draft with respect to the Supreme Court. There was general agreement that the Supreme Court should be established by the Constitution rather than through a federal statute. The draft established the Court as a final court of appeal for all matters. There would be nine judges on the court, three from Quebec with practical experience in the civil law. Any civil law cases were to be heard by a panel with a majority of civil law judges. Ironically, the best efforts draft provided for less provincial influence in the selection of the Supreme Court than had the proposals in Bill C-60, the Victoria Charter, the Special Joint Committee, and the Pepin–Robarts Task Force.[23] Judges would be appointed by the federal government after consultation with the province from which the judge was to come. None of the provisions in the earlier documents, which would have granted a more direct regional involvement, were present in the best efforts draft. The draft also provided that the provinces would be consulted before the appointment of superior, district or county court judges, now appointed by the federal government under the power granted to it in section 96 of the British North America Act. Finally, provinces would be granted the power to appeal to the Supreme Court from decisions of provincial courts of appeal on reference cases initiated by the province.

Most provinces were now less favourably disposed to the notion of a formally "regionalized" court than they had been in 1976. Instead, they preferred something closer to the status quo. Consequently, the idea of a separate constitutional court, based on regionalized appointment, as advocated by Alberta in its paper *Harmony in Diversity*[24] gained little support. The suggestion that the Court be expanded to eleven members to accommodate regional interests was also rejected. The majority of provinces even objected to any reference to the appointment of judges from Quebec, arguing instead that the constitutional text simply require the appointment of three judges with a civil law background.

However, disagreements persisted and not all governments supported the best efforts draft. Quebec, in particular, was opposed. The PQ government contended that the Constitution should provide for a separate constitutional court, that the provinces should have a major role in selecting that court, and that Quebec should be specifically represented. The province also argued that the Quebec Court of Appeal should be the final court with respect to civil law cases. Finally, Quebec wanted section 96 judges to be appointed by the provinces. In this matter as in others, Quebec's reasoning was premised on the duality of Canada—Canada as the product of two founding nations which, in joining together, retained parity in some important respects. The theme of duality was advanced most forcefully in discussions over the reform of central institutions. Unfortunately, neither in respect of the Court nor in respect of any other institutional issue was duality afforded sufficient concern by the other participants to forestall a sense of isolation in the Quebec delegation.

British Columbia also objected to the best efforts draft because it wanted its five region concept to be applied to the appointment of judges. It favoured the increase in the number of judges from nine to eleven. The actual appointments, according to British Columbia, should be ratified by the reconstituted upper chamber. Other provinces which had serious reservations were Alberta and Saskatchewan. Alberta wanted a special constitutional court, appointed on an ad hoc basis from a pool of judges across the country. It did not, however, vigorously press its position. Saskatchewan, on the other hand, supported the Victoria Charter mechanism for appointments, but it also did not strenuously push its view in the face of the majority consensus.

It is difficult to explain why there was a shift away from the earlier concept of a regionalized court. Earlier even Ontario, in rejecting "regional ratios," had advocated that appointments be made by a national judicial nominating council comprised of all eleven attorneys general.[25] Now it accepted much less. Perhaps the provinces were so preoccupied with reform of the division of powers that they did not focus attention on reform of the central institutions of the Senate and Supreme Court. The better explanation, however, may be that the governments were seriously searching for consensus positions, for realistic and workable solutions to effect constitutional reform.

The appointment of section 96 judges was not on the agenda given the ministers in 1978–79, but it surfaced during consideration of the Supreme Court. Led by Ontario and Quebec, the provinces argued that, since the constitutional responsibility for the administration of justice was provincial, they should be granted the authority to appoint these judges. This demand was fanned by resentment among the provincial attorneys general over the federal government's tendency to ignore them when making judicial appointments. Although the situation improved in the years immediately before 1979, the resentment remained. Ottawa's position was that it alone could best meet the objective of ensuring uniform quality of judicial appointments throughout the nation. The best efforts draft incorporated the provincial concerns with respect to section 96 appointments, although the federal government was clearly not enthusiastic about the proposal.

A further issue stemmed from the authority of the federal government to refer, through Cabinet order, constitutional questions directly to the Supreme Court of Canada, while the provinces lack this power. Alberta, in particular, desired direct access to the Supreme Court on reference questions, but neither a majority of the provinces nor Ottawa agreed with Alberta's claim. The basis of opposition was that this would undermine the status of provincial courts of appeal. These conflicting positions were accommodated in the best efforts draft by requiring provincial constitutional references to be heard first by provincial courts of appeal but then allowing appeals as a matter of right to the Supreme Court of Canada.

Family Law

The concept of a unified family court had gained support across the country in the 1970s. The idea was that a unified family court would possess jurisdiction over all family law matters such as marriage, divorce, separation, adoption, and guardianship. (Some even advocated that this specialist court hear matters involving the criminal law and juvenile law where relevant to disputes within the family situation.) The provincial governments had jurisdiction over the provisions of social services for families and, in some areas such as maintenance and adoption, this jurisdiction included the handling of legal disputes. However, the major element of family law litigation, that arising on divorce, fell under federal jurisdiction. Hence, both orders of government had enacted legislation and had assumed responsibility for determining disputes. The most efficient way of obtaining a unified jurisdiction for all family law disputes would be to bring about a constitutional amendment assigning the entire jurisdiction to one level of government. With the exception of Manitoba and Newfoundland, all provinces endorsed the transfer to provinces of jurisdiction over family law. The most ardent proponents were Ontario and Quebec. The latter had first advocated such a transfer in 1950 and did so again in 1968. Because of Quebec's long-standing enthusiasm for this topic it became an even more important issue during the 1978–79 discussions.

The CCMC best efforts draft contained several important provisions.

First, all matters relating to marriage, including solemnization, validity, and annulment, would be transferred to the provinces. Second, jurisdiction with respect to the grounds for divorce was to be concurrent, and there was to be provincial paramountcy. The paramountcy provision deviated from the usual rules that prevailed in situations of legislative concurrency in that it provided that a provincial enactment concerning the granting of divorce would oust federal jurisdiction to legislate in that matter for the province even where such federal legislation neither conflicted with nor duplicated provincial legislation. Corollary relief, such as alimony, maintenance, and custody would also be transferred to provincial jurisdiction. Parliament would, however, retain jurisdiction to recognize out-of-province and foreign divorces and to prevent the advent of divorce havens in Canada by stipulating minimum conditions for the recognition of divorces outside the granting jurisdiction. By granting Ottawa the power to enact reasonable residence requirements for granting divorces, interprovincial movement in search of quick divorces was to be prevented.

The last important feature of the draft was an amendment to section 96 of the British North America Act to allow provincially appointed judges to assume jurisdiction in all matters of family law even though such jurisdiction had been performed largely by superior courts—those courts whose role was constitutionally protected by section 96. The section specified that the unified family court would deal with a list of matters "arising out of family relationships." Quebec felt, however, that the proposed wording on this special issue posed problems under civil law jurisprudence and suggested a more general wording. In principle, the other provinces had no difficulty in accepting Quebec's formulation, but the details of this proposal were not worked out in time for the First Ministers' Conference in February.

Fisheries

On 1 January 1977 the federal government had extended Canadian jurisdiction over coastal waters to the two hundred mile limit, thereby bringing within its jurisdiction control over almost all the banks on the continental shelf. The extension was designed to boost the ailing Atlantic fishing industry. Nova Scotia had estimated that by 1985 it would triple its catch, increase the value of fishing to $750 million a year and provide 7,000 new jobs associated with the industry. Suffering from chronically high levels of unemployment and an underdeveloped economy, the extension appeared to be a windfall opportunity for the Atlantic provinces to stimulate their economies.[26]

However, a dispute over the merits of federal policy in fishing pitted the federal government against most of the Atlantic provinces. The federal fisheries department was aggressively pursuing a centralizing policy, apparently designed to put more power in the hands of Ottawa. The policy emphasized support for the inshore fleet. Newfoundland, instead, wanted an immediate investment of capital, as much as $900 million, to modernize the offshore fleet and the plants. In 1978 federal and provincial negotiations attempted to reconcile the differences, and it appeared for a while as though a consensus had been reached. Speaking for the Atlantic premiers, Alex Campbell of Prince Edward Island presented to the first ministers in October a position which indicated agreement that Ottawa should assume the leadership in controlling fish stocks and research but with more provincial consultation. The consensus proved to be temporary because Nova Scotia and Newfoundland, stressing the economic and social importance of fishing to their provinces, were not prepared to leave leadership on fisheries with the federal government.

Accordingly, the central issue before the CCMC was whether the governments could agree upon a constitutional provision which acknowledged the aspirations of the Atlantic region. The prospects for success receded when it became clear that the Atlantic provinces themselves were unable to agree. Newfoundland and Nova Scotia presented a draft for discussion which proposed concurrent jurisdiction over fisheries with federal paramountcy over some matters and provincial paramountcy over others. Throughout the deliberations of the CCMC, these two provinces insisted upon such a constitutional provision. As with natural resources and family law, concurrency was resorted to, with imaginative provisions for paramountcy, in order to attempt to resolve deeply conflicting jurisdictional claims and to create a constitutional order that would be adaptable to changing conditions.

Prince Edward Island and New Brunswick, as distinct from Newfoundland and Nova Scotia, were prepared to accept an administrative arrangement with Ottawa which would give them greater day-to-day authority without altering the distribution of constitutional power. In January 1979 the four Atlantic provinces met in Halifax in order to come to a common position. Two general principles were agreed upon: recognition of the provincial role and responsibilities in fisheries and constitutional amendment incorporating concurrent jurisdiction and the principle of joint management. The four provinces were, however, unable to agree upon an actual text since two of them demanded detailed constitutional provisions, while the other two wanted only recognition of the idea of joint administrative arrangements.

British Columbia's position was that the Constitution should entrench joint consultation on fisheries management. It proposed that tidal fisheries should be under exclusive provincial jurisdiction, while migratory species, such as salmon, would remain under exclusive federal jurisdiction.

All provinces expressed general support for concurrent jurisdiction over inland fisheries. Saskatchewan submitted a draft text which would have placed fisheries on the same constitutional footing as agriculture and immigration. Only Quebec adopted the position that inland waters and offshore waters up to the former twelve mile limit should be transferred to the exclusive jurisdiction of the provinces. Quebec also proposed a regime of concurrent jurisdiction with provincial paramountcy over fisheries for the rest of the two hundred mile limit.

Although the federal government was agreeable to transferring inland fisheries to the provinces, it nevertheless rejected any transfer of the tidal fishery on the grounds that Canada, as a whole, would be impaired in its ability to fulfil its international obligations by such a transfer. Instead, it preferred administrative arrangement to constitutional amendment. Throughout the CCMC discussions, the dispute over the fisheries remained unresolved. In Ottawa's view, some of the Atlantic provinces were not prepared to acknowledge the positive results of the two hundred mile extension and were merely determined to acquire more power. The constitutional demands of Nova Scotia and Newfoundland were described by the federal minister of fisheries:

> Easterners [the Atlantic region] . . . wanted this country to have control over the fisheries, to rebuild the stocks, and protect them from future overfishing. Many of those same people say, "now that we have the fishery under our management, let's start fragmenting it again, let's start breaking it up as if the fish understand the lines we draw on the map."[27]

Offshore Resources

The coastal provinces, particularly Newfoundland, were interested in acquiring ownership and jurisdiction over offshore resources, but in 1978–79, the issue was overshadowed by the immediate concerns of oil and natural gas in the West. The other Atlantic provinces had entered into a memorandum of understanding with Ottawa in 1977 which established a non-constitutional regime of administrative arrangements and revenue sharing with respect to offshore resources. Accordingly, they pursued less vigorously than Newfoundland a transfer of ownership and jurisdiction.

Newfoundland based its legal position on its status as a dominion before its entry into confederation and its political case on the ground of equal treatment with provinces which had ownership and jurisdiction over offshore resources. Its strategy was to press for consideration of offshore resources each time the CCMC deliberated on the issue of natural resources.

The federal government initially opposed Newfoundland's position, arguing that the 1977 memorandum of understanding fulfilled many of the province's objectives. Furthermore, Ottawa argued that it was undesirable in the face of complex environmental and international considerations to divide jurisdiction over the offshore resources. It also introduced one other consideration: that offshore resources should be treated as a "common property resource." However, during the final session of the CCMC in Vancouver, the federal government relented and tabled a discussion paper which partly accommodated Newfoundland's demands. This discussion paper contemplated the grant to provinces of concurrent jurisdiction over offshore resources with unqualified federal paramountcy in cases such as international treaty obligations and limited federal paramountcy in cases of compelling national interest. Significantly, however, no specific draft text was ever submitted. In the period immediately following this tentative proposal, Newfoundland entered into formal, bilateral negotiations with Ottawa, and the issue faded from the deliberations of the CCMC.

Equalization and Regional Development

Proposals respecting equalization and the reduction of regional disparities had been included in the Victoria Charter and Bill C-60. Under both documents, the governments of Canada would commit themselves to promoting equality of opportunity; to creating economic well-being for Canadians, regardless of place of residence; to providing essential public services to all Canadians; and to equalization payments to achieve these objectives. These ideas had become firmly fixed in Canada. In the words of Nova Scotia's submission to the CCMC:

> The necessity of transfer payments in Canada to all or some of the provinces has been a fact of life since 1867 and it is probable that the necessity for transfer payments will continue to exist although the provinces in need of assistance may change from time to time.[28]

Nova Scotia proposed to the CCMC that an equalization council be formed which would determine and report on the fiscal capacity of governments every three years. The ministers modified the suggestion to make the council an ongoing body which would report annually. However, as the CCMC further scrutinized the proposal, it was apparent that a majority of governments feared that the council might simply become yet another bureaucratic body which would hinder the realization of the objective.

The CCMC then prepared a best efforts draft which met the approval of all governments except British Columbia. The draft contained a general statement that federal and provincial governments were committed to promoting equal opportunities for the well-being of Canadians, furthering economic development to reduce disparities, and providing essential public services of reasonable quality to Canadians. But the statement of principles did not impose any legislative obligation upon any government. The draft also committed Ottawa to the principle of making equalization payments or the equivalent. The addition of "the equivalent" was a concession to British Columbia, which consistently resisted making equalization payments a constitutional matter. Finally, the draft obligated the governments to review the entire question of equalization and regional development at least once every five years.

British Columbia's objection to constitutional specification of the precise method for attaining equalization stemmed from its fear of a constitutional obligation to preserve the present equalization payment system even if, in the future, more suitable methods were devised. On the other hand, the Atlantic provinces were adamant that the text refer specifically to "equalization payments." Amendments to the draft failed to gain British Columbia's approval. It turned out that British Columbia's reluctance (revealed during the subsequent February's First Ministers' Conference) had little to do with specifying the method of equalization and everything to do with getting the Atlantic provinces to accept British Columbia's second chamber proposals. It is, of course, not surprising that bargaining of this sort was part of constitutional negotiations. It was, however, surprising that bargaining strategy threatened accord on the one established principle of Canadian federalism: the promotion of equal economic opportunity.

The Charter of Rights

The centrepiece of constitutional renewal for the Trudeau government was the entrenchment of a charter of rights with language guarantees.

The discussions with respect to a charter proceeded on the basis of seven categories of rights: fundamental freedoms, such as the freedom of religion, expression, and assembly; democratic rights, such as the right to vote and seek office; legal rights, such as the right not to be deprived of life, liberty, and security of person; non-discrimination rights, such as equality before the law; mobility rights; property rights; and language rights.

As to language, it was proposed by the federal government that both French and English be the official languages of Canada. Both could be used in Parliament and the legislatures. In Ontario, Quebec, and New Brunswick, the constitutional right would extend to the publication of legislative proceedings and to the conduct of judicial proceedings. The proposed minority language education provisions stated that parents could choose either official language for the schooling of their children in those areas where the provision of schooling in both languages was reasonable.

New Brunswick and Prince Edward Island accepted the proposed minority language education provisions. New Brunswick requested that its language rights be incorporated in the Constitution, while Prince Edward Island urged that they be entrenched only at the federal level. Manitoba simply opposed any entrenchment on the ground that the principle of parliamentary sovereignty would be undermined. Newfoundland indicated it was prepared to support the entrenchment of "some rights" (fundamental freedoms and democratic rights) and that it would consider the entrenchment of some of the legal rights and minority language education rights. Its position with respect to language rights, shared by British Columbia and Nova Scotia, was, however, that they be defined at the provincial level only by the province concerned. This view was patterned on the position taken at the 1977 annual premiers' conference at St. Andrews-by-the-Sea.

Although, like Manitoba, Quebec did not favour entrenchment, it was prepared to accept the entrenchment of fundamental freedoms and democratic rights if the others agreed. It remained adamantly opposed to entrenchment of the other rights, particularly language rights. Saskatchewan also opposed the principle of entrenchment but argued that language rights, a key part of the "confederation bargain," should be entrenched at the federal level and minority language education rights guaranteed. Alberta's initial opposition to any form of entrenchment gradually gave way to agreement regarding fundamental freedoms, democratic rights, and a limited set of legal rights. Alberta also endorsed the entrenchment of French and English language rights at the federal level but insisted that minority language education rights could only be defined by the province concerned. Most of the provincial governments opposed entrenchment of property rights, fearing judicial review not only of the procedural fairness of legislation affecting property rights but also of the substantive policy behind it. If review by the courts could be limited to procedural matters, most of the provinces were prepared to accept the entrenchment of property rights. Finally, Ontario, while an advocate of an entrenched charter of rights, expressed a number of serious concerns with the proposed wording of the sections setting out the legal rights. It was most worried, however, by the possible application of section 133 of the British North America Act, 1867.

Section 133,[29] the only constitutional provision dealing specifically with language rights, imposes certain obligations upon the federal government and the government of Quebec with respect to the provision of French and English languages. Quebec sought to delete what it described as the "discriminatory" provisions of section 133, pointing out that it did not apply to other provinces, especially Ontario, where there was substantial French-speaking minorities. The PQ government was committed to demonstrating that confederation was a "one-sided affair," and argued forcefully that it should not be constitutionally compelled to recognize English if the other provinces refused to give French equal status in their legislation and before their courts. The PQ solution was to permit each province to determine for itself the appropriate language provisions. Instead of agreeing to Quebec's proposal, however, Ottawa wanted the application of section 133 to be extended to both Ontario and New Brunswick, although in the case of the latter province it indicated its willingness to be so bound.

The report of the Pepin–Robarts Task Force, released during the third CCMC session in Vancouver in January 1979, recommended that the principle of jurisdictional sovereignty apply to language. The equality of the two languages should be entrenched federally, but linguistic rights for provincial purposes, including education, should be determined by provincial legislatures. Ottawa was philosophically opposed to such reasoning because it feared the provinces would only enact policies which reinforced the dominant language within their boundaries, with the eventual result that Canada would be firmly divided into two separate linguistic camps. The federal government negotiators made various attempts during the CCMC negotiations to persuade Ontario to adopt section 133 but were unsuccessful. Ontario did not reject the federal requests outright, but stressed that it had achieved considerable progress in advancing both languages through pragmatic action and without a constitutional commitment. Politically, Ontario did not want to be painted as a villain by Lévesque in the upcoming referendum debate, but neither did it want full entrenchment of section 133.

The 1978–79 CCMC meetings generated considerable movement towards a consensus for constitutional entrenchment of at least a limited charter of rights with some language guarantees. Many of the provinces were prepared to accept the entrenchment of fundamental freedoms and democratic rights as well as official language rights applied exclusively to areas of federal jurisdiction. A significant number were prepared to accept minority language education rights along the lines of the 1977 premiers' communiqué from St. Andrews. The largest continuing obstacle to full agreement remained the fundamental difference between those who favoured the principle of entrenchment and those who supported the status quo. The idea of a legislative "notwithstanding clause," capable of overriding the charter, was introduced to the debate by Saskatchewan as a possible compromise. But the gulf between the participants on the fundamental question of entrenchment was too wide and grew wider with each attempt to expand the scope of the charter.

Federal Spending Power

The elaborate network of fiscal sharing arrangements developed over the years in Canada has been a source of pride for many Canadians but an irritant for some provincial governments. Transfer payments from Ottawa have enabled all governments, particularly those suffering from financial hardship, to provide equal services and programs to their residents. Some provinces, however, have felt an increasing use by Ottawa of its spending power to impose its own priorities on areas of provincial jurisdiction. Quebec, in particular, objected to federal funding in that province and insisted that the Constitution be amended to prohibit Ottawa's spending power from encroaching on areas of provincial jurisdiction. The clash over spending priorities was especially pointed since Ottawa and Quebec City were engaged in preliminary skirmishes over the impending referendum, and Ottawa wanted to demonstrate the tangible benefits of confederation to the citizens of Quebec through federally funded public programs. Quebec claimed that this was an invasion of its jurisdiction.

The other governments rejected Quebec's extreme position on this issue, preferring to tailor the federal spending power to conform with provincial priorities. At the first meeting of the CCMC, the federal government proposed to restrict its use of the spending power with respect to conditional grants and shared cost programs, the two areas of prime concern for the other provinces. The essence of the proposal was that provincial approval for federal spending in these areas must be obtained through the new second chamber. However, because Quebec persisted in its position that, as a matter of principle, Ottawa should not possess any constitutional authority in this field whatsoever, the CCMC directed its efforts to making an alternative draft.

The best efforts draft, produced by the CCMC, would have continued the federal government's authority to spend in areas of provincial jurisdiction but with significant limitations. Where the federal expenditures involved direct payments to the provinces, use of the federal spending power had to be authorized by a majority of the provinces containing 50 percent of the population of Canada. Furthermore, in those instances where programs were so authorized, a non-participating province would receive financial compensation equivalent to the amount it would have received had it participated. Finally, if the federal spending power involved payments directly to individuals, as opposed to governments, Ottawa would be required to consult provincial governments before introducing the program. If a province objected to the implementation of the program, it would be suspended for three months and a federal–provincial meeting convened to discuss it.

The CCMC could not agree on the proposal to require provincial authorization for federal expenditure made directly to provinces. Some governments, such as British Columbia and Ottawa, insisted the approval take place in a new second chamber. Of course, Quebec rejected both the best efforts formulation and the proposal that a second chamber decide the issue. Also unresolved was how a non-participating province would be paid. Ottawa urged that it make the compensation payments directly to the residents of the province and not to the governments. Predictably, most of the provinces and especially Quebec, objected to that suggestion. Some provinces shared Ottawa's concern that compensation payments to a non-participating provincial government would be an incentive to "opt out," resulting in a patchwork of programs across Canada. In order to prevent this, the CCMC considered a proposal limiting compensation to the non-participating province to either 80 or 90 percent of the total value of the program. Some of the provinces were inclined to accept this as a compromise. Quebec, however, completely rejected it.

Declaratory Power

The federal declaratory power which arises from section 92(10)(c) of the British North America Act, permits Parliament to declare "works" to be for the general advantage of Canada or of two or more provinces. The effect of a declaration is to bring the "works" and their related undertakings within the exclusive legislative jurisdiction of Parliament. There are few fetters on this power. In the past it has been used in respect of railways, grain elevators, and atomic energy, including uranium mines and mills, bringing all vital parts of the "works" under federal legislative authority.

The Canadian federal declaratory power is unique. It does not exist in any other federal system. Although its use in the past was justified as being in the national interest, most provinces saw it as a distortion of federalism since it granted one order of government the power to add unilaterally to its legislative jurisdiction at the expense of the other order. The western provincial governments, embroiled with Ottawa in disputes over natural resources, were particularly anxious to have it reformed. In response to these pressures, the federal government introduced a proposal which would have curtailed but not eliminated the use of the declaratory power. It proposed consultation with the provincial government to be affected by a declaration and, failing agreement, the convening of a first ministers' conference. While such a conference would not have the power to stop the declaration from taking effect, the mechanism would ensure, so it was argued, that the declaratory power was not used capriciously. Also, any declaration would be effective for only five years, after which time the entire process would need to be repeated. Most provinces still were not satisfied.

After considerable opposition to the federal proposal by the provinces, which sought the elimination of the power, a best efforts draft was created in which it was proposed that the power be restricted to specific purposes. As under the original draft, Ottawa would have to consult with the affected province, but, unlike the original, the declaration could not be repeated after five years. Moreover, Parliament was empowered to revoke or limit the declaration before the full five years. Finally, no declaration could be made without the concurrence of the affected province if the work concerned the primary production or initial processing of non-renewable or forestry resources or the generation of electrical energy. The federal government, somewhat surprisingly in light of its previous position, agreed with this formulation, as did most of the provinces. However, Quebec wanted the power abolished, pure and simple.

Amending Formula and Patriation

Two issues were at the centre of the CCMC deliberations with respect to an amending formula and patriation: the need to develop an amending formula acceptable to all and the timing of patriation. At the end of the CCMC discussions, there was no agreement with respect to either of these problems. However, two alternative amending formulas emerged.

During the second meeting of the CCMC in December, the ministers met privately, without officials, to discuss the amending formula. Quebec's Claude Morin, although present, did not participate in the discussions because he maintained that patriation and an amending formula could be considered only after the satisfactory completion of the review of the division of powers. Moreover, Quebec would not discuss this issue until after the outcome of its pending referendum. Ontario's Tom Wells, on the other hand, stressed the importance of immediate patriation, without an amending formula if necessary, in order to terminate Canada's colonial link to Westminster. Various past formulas, such as the one contained in the Victoria Charter of 1971 and the Fulton–Favreau formula of 1965, were also examined. The result, however, was a new amending formula which came to be known as the Toronto consensus.

The Toronto consensus proposed two categories of amendments. Matters relating to provincial ownership and jurisdiction over natural resources and concerning the amending formula would require unanimous approval. All other issues would be subject to a general formula which would require the approval of Parliament and seven provinces comprising 85 percent of the population of Canada. This population requirement would have the effect of giving a veto to Ontario and Quebec. Although no minister formally approved of this formula, the positive tone of the discussion gave rise to the hope that the Toronto consensus could be adopted eventually by all of the governments except, of course, Quebec.

However, the consensus that seemed apparent in Toronto disintegrated when the officials from the governments met in Ottawa on 11 and 12 January 1979 to review the proposal in detail. At that meeting, several provinces objected to being included in such a consensus. Ottawa feared that the part of the proposed formula requiring unanimity was too rigid. Other objections arose regarding the veto granted to Ontario and Quebec through the 85 percent population requirement; some provinces wished to have a lower percentage to ensure that no province would have a veto. Others wished to eliminate any specific reference to numbers of provinces and to replace this feature with a simple ratio, such as two-thirds, because it could accommodate any future increases in the number of provinces. Moreover, the principle of equality of provinces, advocated by Alberta, was gaining favour.

When the CCMC assembled in Vancouver, Ottawa introduced a new draft amending formula which, surprisingly, retained a list of matters requiring unanimity but, in respect of the matters not requiring unanimity, changed the requirement for provincial approval from seven provinces to two-thirds of the provinces having 85 percent of the population. Evidently Ottawa had abandoned its objections to unanimity. The main problem with this draft, however, as with the Toronto consensus, was that it still retained a veto for Ontario and Quebec by its reference to a required percentage of population. British Columbia, basing its entire constitutional position on the recognition of the five region concept in Canada, advocated an amending formula which would have placed it on the same footing as Ontario and Quebec. Furthermore, in British Columbia's view, a reconstituted second chamber based on the five region concept should exercise a major role in amendments. Alberta opposed any formula which granted a veto to some provinces but not others. There were other provinces which objected. New Brunswick feared that both the federal draft and the Toronto consensus would permit constitutional amendments without the consent of a majority of the Atlantic provinces. Therefore, it favoured a formula based on the regional concept, such as the one in the Victoria Charter. Manitoba considered the Toronto consensus to be too rigid. Finally, British Columbia, in addition to its other objections, criticized the Toronto consensus because it did not include language and culture in the list of matters which required unanimous consent.

At this point, Alberta introduced a new proposal which it had earlier raised in general terms and which was derived from a resolution of its legislative assembly.[30] It provided for a general amendment to the Constitution on the approval of Parliament and two-thirds of the provinces with 50 percent of the population. If, however, the amendment was one "affecting" the powers, rights, assets, and privileges of any province or the natural resources of the province, a province so affected could opt out of its provisions. The idea for the opting-out provision first appeared at the 1936 federal–provincial conference on the Constitution. At that time, the proposal before the governments entailed a general amending provision which stipulated that six provinces with 55 percent of the population had to concur in constitutional amendment.

In 1936 it was proposed that property and civil rights and matters of a local and private nature, both of which were areas of provincial jurisdiction under the British North America Act, be transferred from a list of items requiring unanimous approval for amendment to the list of matters which could be amended by the general formula. Clearly, the federal government wanted the constitutional authority to implement a series of new programs to combat the depression without their being struck down by the Privy Council as trenching upon provincial jurisdiction. These two provincial heads were the chief bases on which the Privy Council had enhanced provincial authority in earlier decisions. In exchange for the removal of these heads of power from the unanimity list, the provinces insisted upon the limited right to opt out of any proposed amendments which fell within these two fields. In 1936, no fiscal compensation was attached to the opting-out proposal.

Alberta's proposal for an amending formula, like that of the federal government, attracted only modest support from the other governments. Ottawa was fearful that the opting-out provisions might lead to a patchwork of constitutional arrangements in Canada. Saskatchewan favoured either the Toronto consensus or the Victoria Charter amending formula because of their uniform application throughout Canada and their greater flexibility than opting out. Of course, British Columbia rejected any proposal which failed to recognize the province as a distinct fifth region. What had clearly emerged from the discussions, however, was that the veto proposals for Quebec and Ontario, as set out in the Victoria Charter, were no longer acceptable to an overwhelming majority of the governments, a reversal of the 1971 position. The balance of the CCMC discussions repeatedly returned to a consideration of the conflicting proposals but with less and less consensus.

Monarchy

The role of the monarchy and how it should be stated in the Constitution provoked an open debate both within the CCMC and across the country. In 1972 the Special Joint Parliamentary Committee had observed that the role of the governor general as head of state had been gradually enhanced and concluded that, if this trend continued, "[e]ventually, the question of retaining or abolishing the Monarchy will have to be decided by way of clear consultation with the Canadian people."[31] The provisions of Bill C-60, which expanded on the theme of the 1972 report, were interpreted by the premiers at their 1978 conference in Regina as substituting the governor general for the monarch as the ultimate constitutional authority in Canada. The federal government insisted that the proposed amendments merely reflected the evolutionary development of the role of the monarchy. The prime minister, in a letter to Saskatchewan's Premier Blakeney in September 1978, wrote:

> ... [T]he purpose of the federal government is to make clear that the Queen remains the "sovereign head" of Canada and to have that position embedded formally in our Constitution. All that the proposals do with respect to the Monarch and Governor General is to state the present reality as it is, taking into account the developments in our constitutional

practice since 1867. It is the view of the federal government that, in any revised Constitution, such a statement of the present constitution reality is desirable.[32]

Several redrafts of the Bill C-60 provisions were presented to the CCMC in an attempt to assuage provincial concerns, but they did not succeed in doing so. Manitoba was particularly hostile to the federal attempts to clarify this matter. It submitted its own draft which clearly stated that the governor general was appointed by the monarch and could exercise only such powers as were delegated by the monarch. The point of provincial amendments to Bill C-60 was that any powers conferred upon the governor general must be seen as flowing directly from the monarch and not from some new constitutional measure. Buffetted by increasing public opposition to the provisions of Bill C-60 on the monarchy, Ottawa finally conceded during the CCMC meetings that the existing constitutional position would be neither modified or codified in the Constitution. As a result, provincial concerns were met and this item disappeared from future discussions.

The First Ministers' Conference, February 1979

The first ministers convened in Ottawa on 5 and 6 February 1979 to consider the report of their ministers. The opening statements of the first ministers reflected the same positions adopted by their ministers and officials during the CCMC meetings. For the western provinces, the best efforts draft fell short of expectations with respect to natural resources. In the case of Saskatchewan, the draft did not extend the limitation on federal paramountcy to international trade and commerce, while for Alberta the "compelling national interest" limitation was too vague and ignored the pervasive federal general power of "peace, order, and good government."

British Columbia clung to its demand that it be recognized as a fifth region in Canada and that the Supreme Court and a new second chamber reflect that fact. Manitoba was adamantly opposed to the concept of an entrenched charter of rights. Most other provinces sought to confine the scope of the charter. Differences abounded with respect to the guarantees for French and English languages and, particularly, with respect to educational language rights. With varying degrees of intensity, the Atlantic provinces desired greater authority over fisheries and offshore resources, in addition to constitutional recognition of equalization and a commitment to reducing regional disparities. Two competing amending formulas emerged, each attracting only lukewarm support. Finally, Ontario suggested immediate patriation, with or without reform of the division of powers or agreement on a new amending formula, while the other provinces, especially Quebec, vehemently objected.

The timing of patriation was raised during the conference. Ontario's

Premier Bill Davis advocated it occur immediately, thereby breaking away from the position of the other provinces. Davis, supported by Trudeau, stated his preference that an agreement regarding an amending formula precede patriation but acknowledged that such an agreement was not essential. Lougheed and Bennett declared that immediate patriation should be accompanied by a statement that amendments affecting provincial rights and powers would be made only with the unanimous consent of all governments. Nova Scotia's John Buchanan urged that patriation be accompanied by a new amending formula. Blakeney endorsed this position and added that patriation should occur only in conjunction with changes in the division of powers. Finally, Quebec categorically rejected patriation before a comprehensive realignment of the division of powers had been completed. Thus, although the constitutional negotiations had produced a significant level of agreement on a number of important areas, the premiers focussed on the differences; it was clear that there was neither the capacity nor the will to overcome the remaining obstacles. In particular, differences over the amending formula and the timing of patriation, the two issues over which so many preceding constitutional conferences had floundered, were given full play at the February conference.

The federal government introduced a "Second List of Items for Study in the Continuing Constitutional Review" at the conference. The eleven items to be reviewed at some future date included a consideration of the powers in the economic field to fight inflation, unemployment, and regional disparities; to control non-tariff barriers to interprovincial and international trade and commerce, and to the movement of goods and services; to regulate competition and securities; and to deal with marketing boards. Accompanying explanations described the federal government's concern that it did not possess sufficient constitutional authority to manage the overall economic interests of Canada.[33]

Assessing the Exercise

Notwithstanding the profusion of conflicting positions, it would be incorrect to conclude that the 1978–79 exercise was a total failure. The record of proceedings reveals that on each item of the constitutional agenda, with the exception of the amending formula and patriation, a significant number of the governments subscribed to a best efforts draft. For example, in the case of jurisdiction over natural resources, only Quebec and Alberta firmly rejected the best efforts draft of the CCMC. Furthermore, two of the items, family law and equalization, had obtained the support of all but one government. The problem, however, was that there emerged no coalition of governments agreeing upon a set of proposed solutions and capable of persuading the minority to its position.

When the CCMC was re-established in October 1978, its mandate was

to seek agreement through discussion and negotiation of the items identified by the first ministers. It succeeded in identifying and clarifying the
positions of the various governments. The best efforts texts also represented a high degree of consensus and accommodation, a considerable
accomplishment in the face of strongly held views. The substance of these
drafts is also significant. The direction of the negotiations was towards a
devolution of federal government authority; it was the assumption upon
which all governments formulated their positions. The proposed jurisdictional changes in the fields of natural resources, communications, family
law, institutional reform, the federal spending power, and the declaratory
power, all would have enhanced the constitutional power of the provinces.
When compared with the subsequent position of the federal government
in 1980 and the final outcome of the constitutional exercise in November
1981, the devolutionary thrust of this period held the potential for a major
redirection of Canadian federalism, which would have surpassed the impact of the Privy Council decisions in augmenting provincial powers at the
expense of the federal authority.

There are many explanations for this development, ranging from the
perilous position of the federal government in the winter of 1978–79 to
the urgency of the challenge posed by the Parti Québécois. However, at
the core was the general acknowledgment that the circumstances forced a
less centralized approach in the nation's constitutional organization. At
the close of the proceedings in February 1979, the prime minister despaired that ". . . we've almost given up the shop to you people . . . ," referring to the degree of decentralization his government had agreed upon.
Later, the Trudeau government would argue that decentralization only
generates demands for more decentralization and, therefore, the direction
of constitutional reform should be reversed. The second list clearly hinted
that Ottawa would attempt sooner or later to tilt the balance of federal and
provincial power back towards the central government. The vagaries of
political events gave the Trudeau administration an opportunity to pursue
a portion of the second list earlier than expected, but in February 1979 it
was of secondary importance to the overall thrust of the reform, represented by the best efforts drafts.

Why, then, was agreement not reached in February 1979? Why did
some provinces not accept the best efforts drafts? There are no simple
explanations or answers. However, from a practical perspective, the Parti
Québécois was not about to agree to any constitutional reform in advance
of its referendum on sovereignty-association; it could not negotiate the
constitutional issues until its electorate had answered the fundamental
question about its relationship to the rest of Canada. Moreover, since
unanimity was the implicitly understood prerequisite for constitutional
amendment, Quebec's rejection of the key proposals doomed the exercise.

Although many of the provincial governments feared that failure would enhance the success of the Parti Québécois in the referendum, such anxiety was insufficient to overcome their differences and persuade them to accept further compromises and accommodations. The situation in Quebec was serious but, in the minds of the participants, so too were the problems of western alienation and Atlantic regional disparity. Furthermore, intergovernmental antagonisms had grown and festered to the point where, in some instances, they could not be controlled. Finally, although the governments generally endeavoured to submerge their political and ideological differences while engaged in federal–provincial discussions at the CCMC level, by February 1979, with the general federal election only weeks away and the defeat of the Tudeau government looming as an increasingly important political event, the policy of non-partisanship evaporated.

The Clark Government

In May 1979 Joe Clark was elected as prime minister of Canada to head a minority Progressive Conservative government. Most provincial governments had few details about the new government's specific positions with respect to the outstanding constitutional issues. In opposition the Progressive Conservatives had criticized the "centralist approach" of the Trudeau government and proclaimed their constitutional goal to be a "strong government in Ottawa with strong governments in the provinces." Shortly after the Kingston communiqué had been issued, Clark confidently predicted, "I am sure that we will follow through on this agreement in less than six months after we are elected."[34] Once elected to office, however, the new Clark administration exhibited a disturbing tendency to avoid any elaboration of exactly what their pre-election policy meant in practice. Moreover, it proceeded to discuss constitutional reform on a bilateral basis in contrast to the established pattern of multilateralism. The formal intergovernmental structure of the CCMC, which was so vital to defining and understanding the issues, was downplayed, much to the concern of many provincial governments.

Clark's problems were further complicated by confusion and uncertainty with respect to the fate of senior federal officials who had advised the Trudeau administration on the Constitution. The two most senior advisors in the Privy Council office, Gordon Robertson and Michael Pitfield, had departed from their influential positions. While Pitfield had been forced out, Robertson, a long-time career civil servant, retired in 1979. It was clear, too, that most of the other officials did not enjoy the full confidence of new ministers. Thus, the new minister of federal–provincial relations, Bill Jarvis, preferred to conduct meetings with his provincial counterparts without the presence of his departmental advisors, stressing the need for political will, as opposed to technical advice from civil servants, to overcome constitutional impasses. But, lacking the continuity and experience of Robertson and Pitfield and the advice of the officers within the department, ministerial policy discussions tended to become highly generalized and to lack an appropriate follow-up by the civil service. Jarvis himself was able and well liked by his provincial colleagues, but the perception grew that the Clark government was unable or unwilling to come to grips with key issues: to resolve the growing Alberta–Ontario split over energy and the Newfoundland–Ontario split over offshore resources, or to thwart the well-organized and articulate PQ machine which was in high gear for the forthcoming referendum. The trend to bilateral discussions was seen by some governments as confirmation of the new administration's incapacities in this field since bilateralism led to separate, and occasionally contradictory, political positions struck with different provinces.

On one matter the Progressive Conservative government of Joe Clark knew its mind and acted decisively. Following a series of bilateral meetings in August and early September of 1979, Prime Minister Clark and Newfoundland's premier, Brian Peckford, confirmed, in an exchange of letters,[35] an agreement on four principles with respect to jurisdiction and ownership of offshore resources. The first principle was that Newfoundland would own the resources on the continental margin off its coast and would also exercise legislative jurisdiction over them in the "same nature as if these resources were located within the boundaries of the Province." Second, ownership and jurisdiction over the offshore resources would be consistent with, and subject to, the current division of powers under the Constitution. Third, federal jurisdiction in such areas as environmental protection, extra-provincial trade, and pipelines would continue. Finally, the principles would be confirmed by formal agreements, by legislation, and by constitutional change.

This agreement on the fundamental principles of offshore resources, however, raised several other important related issues such as the status of existing permits and leases; the special status of Petro-Canada, a federal Crown corporation; native claims; the impact of future provincial revenues on equalization; the provision of federal geological-hydrological and meteorological services; the lines of delimitation for the offshore areas, and the role of Newfoundland in future international discussions. It was agreed that further discussions would be held between Ottawa and Newfoundland to resolve these and other outstanding issues.

In his letter to Premier Peckford confirming the agreement, Prime Minister Clark stated that proposals for constitutional change would, in due course, need to be considered by all governments in the context of CCMC. But what could the CCMC do in the face of a finalized agreement? At least one premier, Allan Blakeney of Saskatchewan, expressed his concern at the practice of bilateral negotiation and raised the prospect that the entire process of constitutional reform might become fragmented. At the only full meeting of the CCMC held during the period of the Clark government, in October 1979 in Halifax, the issue of jurisdiction over offshore resources was on the agenda. At that meeting Ottawa was determined to limit the interventions of the other provinces on this issue as part of its strategy based on bilateral negotiations.

The short-lived Clark government quickly found itself caught in the middle of other basic disagreements over resources and energy policy. Petro-Canada and oil pricing created a dilemma for the Progressive Conservatives and the nation. As for Petro-Canada, the Clark government had been elected, in part, on a promise that governmental activity would be reduced. The government wanted the "privatization" of part of Petro-Canada so that the corporation would conduct its affairs "on the basis of commercial viability." The scheme entailed assumption of the debts of Petro-Canada by the government and distribution of the assets of the corporation amongst all Canadians, who would then be free to dispose of the shares as they saw fit. In mid-October 1979 a public disagreement emerged between Clark and the Ontario premier, William Davis, on this issue. Davis declared that the country needed Petro-Canada and that the federal government should retain ownership of Petro-Canada. Ontario fully understood that Petro-Canada was perceived by the Ontario public as a powerful instrument in the federal government's plan to secure oil supplies and maintain reasonable pricing. These were of crucial importance to Ontario, a province that was undergoing difficult economic times because of the oil price explosion. The Clark government's privatization scheme suddenly lost its political allure.

The other energy issue was oil pricing. Here the prime minister, an Albertan, found himself in the middle, between Premier Davis of Ontario and Premier Lougheed of Alberta. Lougheed demanded that the price of oil reach world levels as quickly as possible and that the majority of the proceeds accrue to the provincial treasury, while Davis sought economic protection for the industrial consumers of his province. At the time of the defeat of the Trudeau government, the oil-pricing agreement provided for increases on 1 July 1979 and 1 January 1980. Since the price for domestic oil was falling behind world prices, Alberta sought to renegotiate the agreement to reflect the upward changing world conditions. As negotiations over pricing progressed, the Ontario government's anxiety grew. Ontario politicians uniformly expressed concern about the detrimental effect of further oil price increases on Ontario.

The budget of the Clark government, introduced in December 1979, contained price increases for oil as a consequence of its negotiations with Alberta. Although the government attempted to justify these increases in terms of conservation and self-sufficiency, both the Liberals and the New Democratic Party condemned the increases and united in the Commons to defeat the government. In the ensuing federal general election the Liberal party was returned to office with wide support from Ontario, Quebec, and the Maritimes. Only two members, both from Manitoba, were elected to represent the Liberal party west of Ontario. The nation was sharply divided over energy policy on a "hinterland–heartland" basis, a division which crossed party lines. It was hardly a propitious political arrangement in which to carry on the search for constitutional renewal. yet the Quebec referendum was looming and, regardless of its outcome, the constitutional discussions could not be avoided.

Notes

1. *An Agenda for Change: Notes for Comments by the Prime Minister of Canada*, Ottawa, 31 October 1978, C.I.C.S. Doc. 800-8/051.
2. In the federal Cabinet shuffle of 24 November 1978, Marc Lalonde became the minister of justice and John Reid replaced him as minister of federal-provincial relations.
3. *Alberta Discussion Paper—Natural Resources*, submitted to CCMC, Mont. Ste. Marie, 25–27 November 1978, C.I.C.S. Doc. 830-65/012.
4. *Canadian Industrial Gas & Oil Ltd. v. Government of Saskatchewan et al.*, [1979] 1 S.C.R. 37, 80 D.L.R. (3d) 449.
5. *Central Canada Potash Co. v. Attorney General of Saskatchewan*, [1979] 1 S.C.R. 42, 88 D.L.R. (3d) 609.
6. Opening remarks by Peter Lougheed, Federal-Provincial Conference on the Constitution, Ottawa, 30 October–1 November 1978.
7. *Supra*, note 1, at 6.
8. For a critique of this schedule, see Moull, "Section 92A and the Constitution Act, 1867" (1983), 61 *Canadian Bar Review* 715.
9. *Reference Re Anti-Inflation Act*, [1976] 2 S.C.R. 373, 68 D.L.R. (3d) 452.
10. Notes for an address given to the Canadian Council of Resource and Environment Ministers by Merv Leitch, 21 November 1974.
11. *Supra*, note 1, at 7–8.
12. *Capital Cities Communications v. C.R.T.C.*, [1978] 2 S.C.R. 141, 81 D.L.R. (3d) 609; *Dionne v. Public Service Board (Quebec)*, [1978] 2 S.C.R. 191, 83 D.L.R. (3d) 178.
13. "The Centralist Urge," *Globe and Mail* (Toronto), 5 December 1977, at 6. Reproduced with permission of the *Globe and Mail*, Toronto.
14. *Discussion Draft, Communications—Federal*, Toronto, 14–16 December, 1978, C.I.C.S. Doc. 830-67/012.
15. Quoted in *British Columbia's Constitutional Proposals, Paper No. 3—Reform of the Canadian Senate*, at 42.
16. Letter from Pierre Trudeau, prime minister, to A.E. Blakeney, premier of Saskatchewan, dated 13 September 1978.
17. *Supra*, note 15. These nine papers were consolidated in *British Columbia's Constitutional Proposal* (Victoria, 1978).

18. *Report of the Royal Commission of Inquiry on Constitutional Problems* (Tremblay report), (Quebec, 1956).
19. Victoria Charter, Part IV, Arts. 22–42.
20. *Final Report to the Joint Committee of the Senate and of the House of Commons on the Constitution of Canada* (1972), Recommendations 44–46.
21. *Ibid.*, Recommendation 45.
22. *Ibid.*, Recommendation 46.
23. Task Force on Canadian Unity, *A Future Together* (1979), at 129–30, and Recommendations 58–64.
24. Alberta, in *Harmony in Diversity: A New Federalism for Canada* (1978) proposed in Recommendation 15 "[t]hat a representative constitutional court be established to resolve constitutional issues" at 24.
25. Ontario, in addressing the Constitutional Conference of First Ministers, Ottawa, 31 October–1 November 1978, stated, ". . . [t]he body which interprets disputes between governments should be appointed through a process of active collaboration among the elected representatives of the eleven governments," C.I.C.S. Doc. 800-8/056.
26. See, generally, D. Brown, *Federal Year in Review, 1977–78* (Kingston: Institute of Intergovernmental Relations, 1978), 95–96.
27. *Seattle Post–Intelligencer*, 23 January 1979, A4 col. 3.
28. *Submission by Nova Scotia on Equalization and Regional Development*, Mont. Ste. Marie, 24 November 1978, C.I.C.S. Doc. 830-65/022, at 2, para. 4.
29. Section 133 states: "Either the English or the French Language may be used by any Person in the Debates of the Houses of Parliament of Canada and of the Houses of the Legislature of Quebec; and both these Languages shall be used in the respective Records and Journals of those Houses; and either of those Languages may be used by any Person or in any Pleading or Process in or issuing from any Court of Canada established under this Act, and in or from all or any of the Courts of Quebec. The Acts of the Parliament of Canada and of the Legislature of Quebec shall be printed and published in both those Languages."
30. In the fall of 1976 a resolution was adopted by the Legislative Assembly of Alberta. It stated: "Be it resolved that the Legislative Assembly of Alberta, while supporting the objective of patriation of the Canadian Constitution, reaffirm the fundamental principle of Confederation that all provinces have equal rights within Confederation and hence direct the government that it should not agree to any revised amending formula for the Constitution which could allow any existing rights, proprietary interest or jurisdiction to be taken away from any province without the specific concurrence of that province and that it should refuse to give its support to any patriation prior to obtaining the unanimous consent of all provinces for a proper amending formula."
31. *Supra*, note 20, Recommendation 34.
32. *Supra*, note 16.

33. The items on the second list (from personal notes in possession of the authors) were: (1) powers in the economic field to fight inflation, unemployment, and regional disparities, and to protect the dollar; (2) the question of non-tariff barriers to interprovincial and international trade and investment; (3) the question of interprovincial and international movement of goods and services, including the right of passage of electricity and oil, gas, and other minerals; (4) the question of barriers to the movement of persons for employment; (5) regulation of competition; (6) regulation of the Canadian securities market; (7) the question of marketing boards; (8) the problem of jurisdiction over minimum wages; (9) foreign relations and the role of provinces; (10) the question of the appointment of superior court judges and the setting up of federal courts for the administration of federal laws; and (11) Canada's native peoples and the Constitution.
34. *House of Commons Debates*, 30th Parliament, 4th Session, 1: 24 (12 October 1978).
35. The exchange of correspondence was released by the office of Joe Clark, prime minister, on 3 October 1979.

Chapter 3
A New Bravado

A New Liberal Government

To those, like re-elected Prime Minister Trudeau, who despaired over the effect on the nation of the Clark government's sympathy with western and eastern aspirations, the resurrection of the Liberal government brought new hope. It was not that Trudeau himself refrained from flirting with devolution, but it had proven politically thankless. Furthermore, the Quebec referendum had been announced in December 1979; it was time to convey to Canadians, including residents of Quebec, a sense of Canada as a whole and to give a national, rather than a provincial or regional, focus to public life. Part of the national view which Trudeau and his ministers sought to present in Quebec during the early spring was that Canadians had the political resolve and goodwill to remake the Constitution and to meet the needs of French Canadians, generally, within confederation. Constitutional reform was the promise of the federalist campaign. But what kind of reform? In Trudeau's view certainly not reform which would fracture Canada. The reformed Canada was one in which Quebec could be a vital, integral, and equal part of the whole.

The federalist campaign succeeded. The referendum results demonstrated the limits of nationalist strength in Quebec. They directed the Parti Québécois to abandon its goals of sovereignty-association and to pursue a new arrangement for Quebec within the federal context. They also made clear to governments that promises to renew Canadian federalism had to yield results. On whose terms would renewal be based: Trudeau's view of a strong but flexible national entity or the premiers' views of new provincial autonomy, unquestioned control of resources, and narrowed federal powers? The promise of renewal was enthusiastically made and embraced by the prime minister and by most of the premiers; in retrospect, however, the enthusiasm was not accompanied by a shared conception of what was to be done.

On the day following the referendum, Trudeau addressed the House of Commons, in what was described by Opposition Leader Clark as a "climate of . . . near celebration." He announced that the government would immediately pursue the task of patriation and reform of the Constitution. Declaring that, in the referendum, "Quebeckers expressed a massive support for change within the federal framework." Trudeau set out his pre-conditions for constitutional change:

> First, that Canada continue to be a real federation, a state whose constitution establishes a federal Parliament with real powers applying to the country as a whole and provincial legislatures with powers just as real applying to the territory of each province. Second, that a charter of fundamental rights and freedoms be entrenched in the new constitution and that it extend to the collective aspect of these rights, such as language rights.[1]

As for all the other outstanding issues, Trudeau promised that ". . . we consider everything else to be negotiable."

Trudeau's statement dwelt on the promises that were made during the referendum and what the possible reaction of the government of Quebec to the renewed constitutional negotiations would be. He noted the commitments of those who campaigned against sovereignty-association and stated that Canadians ". . . cannot venture to ignore this will to change [in Quebec] which reflects that of all other areas of the country and to fall short of the expectations of Canadians. That is why, on May 14, I solemnly undertook to launch the constitutional renewal and never stop working at it until Canada finally has a new constitution." As for the possible response of the government of Quebec, the prime minister recalled a statement made by Premier Lévesque during the referendum debate that he would attend future constitutional conferences in order to pick up "the crumbs." Trudeau warned that constitutional reform might be obstructed by the Quebec government and, if that proved to be the case, the task would have to be completed "without the cooperation of the Quebec government." Near the conclusion of his speech, Trudeau said, "Quebeckers will not be satisfied with crumbs because they want a brand new constitution. . . ."

Seizing on the prime minister's allusion to the will to change that existed outside Quebec, both the leader of the opposition, Joe Clark, and the leader of the New Democratic Party, Ed Broadbent, emphasized that discussions should embrace the concerns of all regions of Canada. Clark acknowledged the seriousness of the situation in Quebec but also stressed that the constitutional agenda, "must be truly a Canadian agenda, not simply an Ottawa agenda, a Quebec agenda, an Alberta agenda or a Newfoundland agenda. Other provinces and other regions have specific proposals for change to which they are equally committed as Quebeckers are, and which they have a right to expect will be debated openly and honestly by all involved in the process." Underlining the difference in their visions of Canada, Clark described Trudeau as perceiving local and regional loyalties "draining strength from the larger community" while he himself saw those loyalties as "a source of strength."[2]

Relief and celebration dominated Canada on 21 May 1980. They produced optimism and hope for successful constitutional reform. And, indeed, the national will did seem strong enough to overwhelm the differences which had plagued previous attempts. Armed with the goodwill and gratitude of the Canadian people and the House of Commons, Jean Chrétien, the federal minister of justice, began a tour of the provincial capitals, except Quebec City, to build upon the promise of the referendum.

Chrétien Visits the Provinces

In his meeting with Saskatchewan Premier Allan Blakeney, Chrétien elaborated upon Trudeau's statement to the House. He outlined the federal government's objectives: patriation and constitutional reform. According to Chrétien, an agreement on patriation and reform had to be achieved quickly in order to capitalize on the positive mood within the nation. The urgency was heightened by the nagging uncertainty surrounding Quebec's attitude to the renewed negotiations. No one could be certain that Lévesque would act in good faith. In fact, Ottawa was apprehensive that the Parti Québécois would attempt to frustrate the process in a rearguard action to salvage its objectives and to revive its sagging provincial support. Furthermore, it was critical to follow the referendum results with a provincial election victory in Quebec, and early agreement on constitutional principles was essential to the campaign of the leader of the Liberal party, Claude Ryan. Chrétien also argued, convincingly, that the major issues had already been extensively studied by various parliamentary committees, the Pepin–Roberts Task Force and the CCMC in 1978–79. Further detailed studies were unnecessary, might encumber the process with bureaucracy, and cause loss of momentum and, eventually, another stalemate. For all these reasons, Ottawa wanted an early agreement.

Chrétien listed the reform proposals of the federal government. There was to be a new "made in Canada" Constitution with a preamble outlining certain principles and a short list of specific constitutional reforms in areas, such as equalization and family law, where there was a large degree of consensus. The agreement would include a commitment to a federal system with two orders of government; a recognition of French and English as the official languages of Canada, including a provision for minority language education rights; an entrenchment of individual rights in a charter; and a confirmation of the concept of equalization. Chrétien suggested that the provincial premiers could readily agree to this limited set of reforms when they met with Trudeau on 9 June 1980. Thereafter, Parliament would be requested to approve a joint resolution and dispatch it to Westminster for speedy passage. The remaining issues surrounding the division of powers would be dealt with at a later date in a forum similar to the 1978–79 CCMC.

Chrétien was more tentative with respect to the amending formula. He sought Blakeney's ideas. Should the principles of the Victoria Charter be adopted or was there an alternative amending formula that was acceptable to the governments? Chrétien was, however, clear on one issue: the unanimous consent of the provinces was not a legal precondition of the patriation plan and was likely unattainable because of the Parti Québécois.

Blakeney responded that the premiers would probably endorse a quick solution to many constitutional matters but not the proposed severance of issues into two stages, which hearkened back to *A Time for Action*. Ever since 1978 the premiers had unanimously insisted that the process of constitutional negotiations should examine all of the issues equally in order to arrive at an acceptable final package. In the case of Saskatchewan and Alberta, for example, legislative jurisdiction over natural resources was the most important priority. In a letter to Trudeau, written four days before the referendum in Quebec, Blakeney had cautioned that the unresolved federal and provincial debate over resources aggravated western alienation and reminded the prime minister that western nationalist groups had been increasingly active during the previous decade. If the constitutional discussions were to prove successful, Blakeney argued, they had to settle not only Quebec's role within confederation but western regional concerns as well.[3]

Another source of disagreement at the meeting with Chrétien was the question of the degree of support required to patriate the Constitution. If Quebec could be isolated and patriation occur without its approval, Blakeney reasoned that the other provinces could be placed in the same legal and political position with respect to contentious issues. This would force the provinces, especially the smaller ones, to develop a common front to prevent such a unilateral exercise of federal authority. Blakeney preferred to negotiate all of the issues with the objective of obtaining unanimous agreement. Finally, Blakeney urged that the negotiations in 1980 should begin where the 1979 discussions ended so as to build on the agreements and near-agreements of that period. These views were echoed in other provincial capitals.

24 Sussex Drive, 9 June 1980

On 9 June 1980, the first ministers gathered at 24 Sussex Drive to review the recent constitutional developments and to consider resumption of discussions. Although the Quebec referendum was undoubtedly the most important development since the First Ministers' Conference in February 1979, each premier had his own province's concerns and priorities in mind when he arrived. Newfoundland continued to seek ownership and constitutional authority over offshore resources, notwithstanding Trudeau's repudiation of the agreement between Clark and Peckford reached in the fall of 1979. Nova Scotia, New Brunswick, and Prince Edward Island again stressed the importance of equalization and regional development. Quebec was determined to test the proposition that the referendum meant long-standing, but unsatisfied, demands for fundamental change were now "achievable." Ontario fretted about provisions granting the provinces additional legislative jurisdiction over natural resources, while both Saskatchewan and Alberta restated their objective to acquire such authority. British Columbia maintained its position that a new upper chamber should be established, based on a recognition of five distinct regions in Canada. All of the provinces generally believed that the outstanding issues should be examined by a revived CCMC and, with the exception of Ontario, all felt that patriation should occur only after all governments had agreed upon the issues.

Significantly, Ottawa requested that two new matters, a constitutional preamble and a commitment to the maintenance of economic union, be placed on the agenda of the CCMC. Three days before the 9 June meeting, Trudeau had forwarded to the premiers a proposed statement of principles to "underline the values we share together and the goals we would like to pursue in devising a new constitution."[4] The proposed statement of principles, strong in natal imagery, acknowledged that Canada was "born of a meeting of the English and French presence" and continued:

> Faithful to our history, and united by a common desire to give new life and strength to our federation, we are resolved to create together a new constitution which:
>> shall be conceived and adopted in Canada,
>> shall reaffirm the official status of the French and English languages in Canada, and the diversity of cultures within Canadian society,
>> shall enshrine our fundamental freedoms, our basic civil, human and language rights, including the right to be educated in one's language, French or English, where numbers warrant, and the rights of our native peoples, and
>> shall define the authority of Parliament and of the legislative assemblies of our several provinces.[5]

It was an attempt to create a national view of the country. As to the economic union, the Pepin–Robarts report had recommended that the Constitution contain a provision that would maintain and enhance the economic union in Canada,[6] but there had been no discussion of the issue during the previous round of negotiations. At the 1979 First Ministers' Conference, Trudeau had declared Ottawa's intention to consider this issue at some future date. Now Trudeau wanted to place the whole matter before the governments. The details of what Ottawa contemplated would be revealed to the ministers when they began their meetings.

In these circumstances, it was obvious that immediate agreement on a general statement of principles and a short list of other issues as initially urged by Chrétien in his meetings with the premiers would not be forthcoming. Nevertheless, Ottawa still attempted to rank the items on the agenda of the forthcoming CCMC meetings. Trudeau argued that patriation with an amending formula, a preamble, an entrenched charter of rights with language provisions, and equalization and regional development were, by their very nature, of fundamental concern to all the people of Canada, whereas the other issues related more to the legislative power of governments. He claimed that the "peoples' issues" transcended the priorities of politicians and governments and were more readily understood and accepted by the public. Therefore they should be agreed upon by the governments as soon as possible. Since the remainder of the items on the agenda concerned only the sharing of government powers and were extremely contentious, Trudeau proposed they should be studied in detail after the "people's items" had been incorporated in a request for patriation.

The majority of premiers strongly objected and, as Blakeney had predicted, insisted that all of the issues be considered equally and simultaneously. The position of the premiers prevailed. The prime minister and premiers agreed to an agenda embracing all items, an intergovernmental mechanism for proceeding through it, and a timetable for the work of the ministers. What remained uncertain was the extent to which disagreements over the process and the timetable which had continually crept into the discussion had really been resolved. A majority of the provinces left 24 Sussex Drive harbouring the suspicion that the federal government had not abandoned its two-tier strategy.

CCMC

Getting Established

The Meeting of 17 June 1980. On 17 June 1980, at an organizational meeting, the CCMC decided to schedule its week-long sessions, once again, in three locations across Canada. The first would take place in Montreal, beginning on 8 July 1980 and would be followed by consecutive meetings in Toronto and Vancouver. After the completion of the first three weeks of discussions, the delegations were to adjourn for three weeks to assess progress. Thereafter, the fourth and final week of deliberations would take place in Ottawa immediately preceding the First Ministers' Conference set for 8 September 1980.

A minor skirmish occurred over setting the agenda. Ottawa wanted to rearrange the order of the agenda but the majority of the provinces insisted the agenda be set out and followed in the same manner as during the 1978–79 deliberations. Again the provinces prevailed. Although this dispute by itself was not of major importance, it symbolized the tug of war between Ottawa and most of the provinces over the dichotomy between "people issues" and "government issues," and the predominance each should assume at the summer's meetings.

Debate flared over the relative importance of the proposed September First Ministers' Conference in the overall timetable. For Ottawa the September conference was a deadline by which an agreement must be reached. Although Ottawa expressed its intention to proceed to patriate the Constitution alone, if necessary, most provinces believed that this could not be accomplished, either legally or politically. According to provincial analysis, Ottawa accepted that it could not proceed unilaterally and was merely using the threat as a rhetorical device to stress the urgency of the task. The provinces continued to object to Ottawa's imposition of its timetable on them in negotiations.

The constitutional demands of the aboriginal people had as yet received comparatively little attention. The leadership of the aboriginal groups, encouraged by their meetings with former Prime Minister Clark in 1979,[7] had insisted upon the right to participate fully on an ongoing basis concerning all of the issues before the CCMC. Trudeau had merely promised the native organizations the opportunity to meet with the governments on those items which directly affected them. Obviously, the federal government was apprehensive that consideration of the complex and emotional issues surrounding native rights would seriously complicate the chances of overall agreement. Also, the provinces were wary of the potential impact of aboriginal rights upon them. Hence, the CCMC decided to arrange a preliminary meeting with the native organizations late in August,[8] to receive their submissions, and to arrange a timetable for subsequent consideration of them.

Phases and Deadlines. When the first meeting of the CCMC convened in Montreal, Chrétien's opening statement set out the position of the federal government on the entire question of constitutional renewal. First, the importance of entrenchment of a charter of rights was underlined when Chrétien advised the committee that Ottawa would not bargain this issue against any other item on the agenda. Returning to the theme of "people issues," Chrétien declared:

> Our job as politicians responsible to the people is to ensure that we protect the fundamental rights of Canadians and promote the well-being of our *citizens*, and not merely re-arrange the powers of our *governments*. We would be failing in our responsibilities to the people we represent if

we get involved in a process where rights of citizens are traded off against powers of governments. Fundamental freedoms and the integrity of the constitution as a Canadian document expressing the aspirations of Canadian citizens must not be bartered against jurisdiction over fisheries or communications or anything else.[9]

This same message had been delivered earlier by Trudeau on 4 July 1980, speaking to the National Liberal Association in Winnipeg, when he had said:

> . . . we [the federal government] have drawn a distinction between the issues which are negotiable—that is, the powers, the politician's quarrels over who will exercise that power and what authority. We have drawn a distinction between these things and the other constitutional reforms which we consider essential for Canadians. The latter are the fundamental rights, including language rights. . . .[10]

Although the premiers and the prime minister had agreed on 9 June that there would be no such distinction with respect to the items on the agenda, it was clear that the demarcation between the "people" concerns and government powers was at the core of Ottawa's policy on constitutional reform and strategy for the CCMC sessions.

Chrétien's opening statement also declared that Ottawa would not be bound by its previous positions in February 1979 with respect to the "best efforts" draft on resource ownership and jurisdiction over interprovincial trade. He justified this shift on the ground that the drafts did not obtain the support of the energy-producing provinces. Furthermore, Ottawa now entertained serious reservations about the proposals. Although the power to levy indirect taxation on resources, in a non-discriminatory manner to other Canadians, would still be considered favourably by Ottawa, the other provisions were no longer acceptable.

Chrétien also stated that the federal government would not negotiate the principle of entrenchment of a charter of rights, a matter of concern to all Canadians. Finally, he observed that resources, offshore resources, and fisheries were economic matters which directly related to the new item on the agenda: Powers over the Economy. Ottawa would insist that consideration of matters related to resources, offshore resources, and fisheries occur in conjunction with consideration of the new agenda item dealing with the economic union in Canada. The reason was to "reestablish a proper balance between the two levels of government." Claiming that the free movement of labour, capital, services, and goods had been impaired by the actions of all governments, Chrétien stated, "we believe that Canadians would be better served if the federal government expanded some of its powers in the area of economic management. . . ." He reinforced the interdependence of this issue with questions of resources, fisheries, and offshore resources by concluding, "Without going into detail at this time, I think it is clear that progress on [Powers over the Economy] will facilitate progress on resources itself."[11]

Ottawa's three conditions—non-negotiability of entrenchment of a charter, withdrawal from the 1979 best efforts draft on resources, and linkage of resources, offshore resources, and fisheries with the new issue of the economic union—stunned and upset most provincial delegations. These conditions represented a major reversal in the direction of the CCMC from its previous 1978–79 activities, in which the thrust of the deliberations was towards the devolution of central government authority. Not only was this direction abruptly discontinued, but the phrasing of the economic union issue pointed to a significant enhancement of legislative authority for Parliament. Throughout the ensuing weeks, Ottawa resolutely refused to reconsider its position as enunciated in Montreal on the first day of the negotiations. The dominant debate, therefore, was on the maintenance of the economic union, a new matter, never previously considered in detail by governments in constitutional discussions.

Powers over the Economy

A Framework for Discussion. In a document entitled *A Framework for Discussion*, tabled at the Montreal CCMC meeting, Ottawa identified five "general functions of economic management" which were encompassed by the issue of "powers over the economy":

1. maintenance of an economic union in Canada;
2. redistribution of incomes among persons and regions;
3. promotion and influencing of economic development;
4. stabilization of the economy as a whole; and
5. conduct of international economic relations.

A Framework for Discussion analyzed each of the categories in terms of the economic objectives of the nation, reviewed the provisions of the Constitution which address those goals, and concluded that additional constitutional authority for the federal government was necessary to strengthen the economic union and promote economic stability and development. Although the perceived incongruities and deficiencies of the economic union would obligate all governments to address the five "functions" in the course of future discussions, Ottawa proposed that the attention of the CCMC be focussed on only the first, maintenance of the economic union in Canada. However, Ottawa's overall position was that "any agreement on all the other economic items on the negotiating list should be compatible with the protection and strengthening of the five basic principles. . . ."[12]

A second federal document, *Securing the Canadian Economic Union in the Constitution*, specifically dealt with the economic union. This paper described the trading arrangements of the General Agreement on Tariffs and Trade and the European Economic Community; cited key passages of the constitutions of other federations, such as the United States, Australia, the Federal Republic of Germany, Switzerland, and India; analyzed the meaning of section 121 of the British North America Act, 1867; and concluded with specific proposals which would strengthen Ottawa's legislative authority to manage the economy.

The provisions of the General Agreement on Tariffs and Trade and the Treaty of Rome were cited to illustrate the underlying goal of "reduction of tariffs and other barriers to trade and the elimination of discriminatory treatment in international commerce."[13] The constitutional features of other federations were identified to buttress the contention that Canada's Constitution did not contain adequate protection for the economic union. For example, it was pointed out that section 121[14] was the only provision in the British North America Act which specifically addressed the free flow of goods between provinces, but even here

> court interpretation has made it clear that section 121 prohibits the imposition of customs duties on the movement of goods between provinces, but had not been used to preclude non-fiscal impediments to the movement of goods, nor would it seem to prohibit the imposition of other kinds of taxes which might impede the free flow of goods.[15]

Citing the decision in *Murphy v. C.P.R. and Attorney General of Canada*,[16] Ottawa declared that "the only certitude is that this section prohibits customs duties affecting interprovincial trade in provincial products." This meant that section 121 was directed "to the formation of a customs union, not a common market." In fact, the "common market" was being constrained because of court decisions which limited federal authority under the trade and commerce power. In the words of the federal document, the decisions of the Judicial Committee of the Privy Council,

> compartmentalizing federal and provincial trade powers and its interpretation that Parliament's authority does not encompass the regulation of "the contracts of a particular business or trade within a province," together with the broad scope of provincial legislative jurisdiction pursuant to a number of headings but most importantly with respect to property and civil rights (s. 92(13)) has meant that there is a great capacity for provincial legislation to create barriers to trade.[17]

Provincial authority over securities, "near banks" and financial institutions other than banks also gave the provinces considerable potential to erect financial and economic barriers.[18] As a result, "there exist today numerous restrictions to economic mobility within Canada, originating in both federal and provincial domains . . . given the deficiencies and uncertainties of our constitutional framework."[19]

In another segment of the paper, a comparative analysis of the constitutional capacity of the federal government and the provinces to enact discriminatory legislation concluded that Parliament's power was constrained because it "emanates from a national constituency whose support any federal government must preserve in order to remain in office."[20] If Parliament enacted discriminatory legislation, the approval of a majority in the House of Commons would validate it in the national interest. Provinces were not similarly constrained; they did not possess the broad national constituency which would justify such legislation. Since provincial legislatures were only accountable to the people of their provinces, national constraints and national interest played no role in the decisions, and thus there was little to deter provincial governments from acting solely on self-interest.

On 16 July during the second week of the ministerial meetings, in Toronto, Ottawa submitted three detailed constitutional texts with respect to the economic union. First, the proposed charter of rights contained a special section which would entrench the mobility rights of citizens by guaranteeing the right of every citizen in Canada to reside and move to any province or territory, to acquire and hold property, and to pursue a livelihood in any province or territory. Second, a revised section 121 would prohibit all governments from enacting laws or practices which, "directly or indirectly, unduly impede" the free movement of persons, goods, services, and capital. A subsection would permit the federal government to derogate from the general prohibition where public safety, public order, public health, and public morals dictated or where Parliament enacted laws in pursuance of the principles of equalization and regional development, international obligations, or overriding national interest. The power of the provinces to derogate from section 121, however, was restricted to "the special needs of various areas and communities within a province." Third, the federal trade and commerce power would be broadened to apply specifically to the movement of services and capital and to regulate product standards and competition throughout Canada.[21]

Provincial Response. During the ministerial discussions, no government expressed opposition to the general principle of maintaining the economic union, but objections to Ottawa's analysis and its proposed constitutional solutions were voiced. Provinces objected to Ottawa's assumption that provincial governments based their economic and financial decisions solely on local interest without regard to national concerns. That assumption ignored the fact that most of the "discriminatory" provincial policies were motivated by a desire to reduce wide economic disparities in a country whose heartland enjoyed a significantly greater proportion of the nation's prosperity than its hinterland. The argument that Parliament was the best forum to act in the national interest was belied by the political and economic domination of Canada by the heartland. The federal government's own discussion paper admitted that Ottawa exercised virtually unlimited jurisdiction over international and interprovincial trade and commerce, taxation, banking, and monetary power; still, the problem of regional disparities persisted. In the opinion of most of the provinces, the primary reason for this was not the inability of Parliament to act but its unwillingness to do so, since programs which improved the economic situation of the regions would be implemented at the expense of the centre.

Furthermore, even if Ottawa had correctly assessed the state of the economic union, the proposed constitutional remedies were far worse than the disease. The balance between the two orders of government would be drastically tilted at the expense of the provinces. Quebec stated the case for a significant economic role for the provinces in these terms:

> Behind Quebec's traditional concerns regarding culture and social development of its people, underneath all of this, so that Quebec will mean something more than a collection of museum pieces, there have to be solid economic infrastructures in which Quebeckers can have enough decision-making power to see to their own interests.[22]

This argument was echoed by the other provinces which, for example, feared that absolute mobility would simply exaggerate regional disparities in the absence of offsetting provincial programs.

Not only would the federal proposals augment Parliament's role in a major way; they would also expand the role of the courts. The proposed constitutional provisions[23] would empower courts to adjudicate on complex economic matters and to strike down or alter accommodations between the rights of individuals and the responsibilities of governments. For example, under the proposed wording of section 121, the courts would be called upon to determine if provincial legislation "unduly impedes" the operation of the economic union. The words "unduly impedes," it was argued, introduced a standard of unmanageable indeterminacy. The dissenting provinces maintained that the judiciary was less well suited to the task of striking the appropriate balance between these competing goals than were legislatures. Because of the uncertainty of language and its unpredictable effect on legislative authority, provincial governments would be dissuaded from confronting social and economic problems. The word "discriminate" was similarly vague and might be interpreted to mean that any law or practice which simply classified goods, services, capital, or persons according to province was discriminatory per se. It might, however, apply only to laws whose intent, purpose, or effect was to interfere with the extraprovincial movement of those goods, services, capital, and persons.

It was unclear whether legislated economic preferences *within* a province would be allowed. As a matter of responsible economic planning, almost all provinces had enacted legislation which benefited certain regions within the borders of the province. For example, in Saskatchewan a program of employment preference for residents of northern Saskatchewan had been instituted in order to alleviate a situation of chronically high unemployment. Regina and Toronto workers were treated equally under the terms of the provincial program, but the residents of northern Saskatchewan enjoyed an advantage over everyone else. It seemed that this kind of program was precluded by the proposed federal amendments. The words "directly or indirectly" in the proposed new section 121 further enhanced the judiciary's direction to defeat any legislative program, regardless of its purpose.

The dissenting provinces also strenuously objected to the derogations granted to Parliament under section 121, especially when compared with the derogations granted to provinces. Provincial derogations were based on standards of public safety, order, health, and morality. These are vague notions, which would likely result in the substitution of the court's opinions for those of provincial legislatures. On the other hand, derogations based on equalization, international obligation, and "overriding national interest" which, under the draft provision, only the federal government enjoyed, left little room for judicial second guessing. The result would be a major transfer of legislative authority to the federal government, because the two provisions, when read together, could be seen as granting significantly more authority to Parliament than to the provincial legislatures. The provinces feared that eventually their responsibility over economic matters would flow to Ottawa.

The proposed amendments to section 91(2), of the British North America Act, the federal trade and commerce power, were also viewed as an invitation to the courts to confer full authority over a wide range of regulations affecting interprovincial economic activity upon Ottawa.

The Saskatchewan Compromise. Several changes to the federal drafts were proposed by the provinces. They were designed to limit the scope of the proposals by the use of more precise wording and by limiting the range of permissible federal derogations in section 121. Ottawa undertook to examine them, but the proposals were overshadowed by the deep differences between the federal government and a majority of the provinces over analysis of the problem and Ottawa's insistence on incorporating judicially enforceable provisions into the Constitution. In the third week of the ministerial meetings in Vancouver, Saskatchewan proposed[24] an alternative designed to bridge the gap between the federal demand for

entrenchment and provincial objection to enforcement of economic policies by the courts. Saskatchewan proposed to entrench in the Constitution
a commitment of all governments to the principles of the economic union
and a mechanism for the continuing review of economic policies by all
governments. Such a provision, patterned after the proposed provision on
equalization, would afford no opportunity for judicial interpretation or
enforcement.

In an accompanying discussion paper, Saskatchewan criticized the
federal proposals as showing a "lack of faith in the Canadian political
system and in the suggestion that political leaders should relinquish to the
judicial system their responsibilities for maintaining the economic
union."[25] Moreover, the majority of the barriers identified by Ottawa were
created deliberately by both orders of government "in the pursuit of other
social and economic objectives that are seen by political leaders to have a
higher priority" than simple economic efficiency. Saskatchewan also argued
that levels of taxation, tariffs, and transportation policies—uncontrolled
under the federal proposals—had a far greater impact on prices, rates of
return, and location of capital and labour than had preferential purchasing
and employment policies; accordingly, the richest provinces would still
possess the means of attracting business away from other weaker provinces. Observing that the problems of the economic union had never been
discussed in detail by federal and provincial governments before this time,
Saskatchwan's discussion paper compared the development of the issue to
"a child growing to full adulthood in weeks rather than years."[26] In view of
all the uncertainties and reservations expressed by the provinces, Saskatchewan argued that its suggestion was the best possible compromise. All of
the other provinces, with the exception of Ontario, endorsed Saskatchewan's alternative. Ontario, while introducing its own specific proposals
for the economic union, consistently supported the federal government
and the link between economic union and resources, offshore resources,
and fisheries. The first signs of polarization were becoming increasingly
evident.

Resources: Best Efforts Rejected

Resources. Consideration of legislative jurisdiction over resources, offshore resources, and fisheries produced the same cleavages amongst governments as did the debate on the economic union. In withdrawing its
support for a key portion of the 1979 best efforts draft on resources,
Ottawa rejected the provision which would have granted provinces concurrent powers over export of resources from the province of primary
production. With concurrency gone, there was no need to consider the
question of limitations upon the federal government's paramountcy, which
had been the subject of the compelling national interest debate in 1979.

The 1979 draft on the federal declaratory power, which stipulated that the approval of the province in which a resource was situated was required, before a federal declaration was effective in that province was also withdrawn. Ottawa continued to support only those sections which confirmed provincial jurisdiction over resources and permitted a province the right to levy both direct and indirect taxes on resource production.

Most provinces stuck to the 1979 best efforts draft, although Ontario and Prince Edward Island advocated incorporation of constitutional assurances to prohibit discriminatory pricing among Canadians and to guarantee security of supply. Both Quebec and Alberta presented new discussion drafts. Quebec's proposal considerably extended the provisions of the 1979 consensus and restricted Ottawa's ability to use the emergency power, an issue which had also been of concern to Alberta. Alberta's draft, which was submitted in the third week of negotiations, would have excluded Ottawa from any authority over "natural resources and the primary production therefrom." Both of these proposals received little attention from the other governments, who still favoured the 1979 draft. At the end of the third week, officials were once again requesting ministerial direction on the entire question of jurisdiction over resources. Stymied by the debate on the economic union, the ministers themselves were as far apart as their officials.

Offshore Resources. The same situation prevailed in relation to jurisdiction over offshore resources. During the conference in February 1979, Ottawa had unveiled a draft discussion paper which would have granted the provinces concurrent jurisdiction over offshore resources, leaving the question of ownership to be resolved at a later date. But in 1980 the federal government withdrew its 1979 proposal, simply claiming that concurrent jurisdiction "would give rise to many kinds of different difficulties for all governments."[27] Instead, it offered administrative arrangements to the coastal provinces, based on previous agreements with the three Maritime provinces. During the 1980 deliberations, Newfoundland presented a proposal which would have extended section 109 of the British North America Act to establish provincial ownership of offshore resources. By another amendment to section 92, the coastal provinces would have been granted a legislative scheme identical to that of the onshore provinces. Newfoundland claimed that it exercised its own jurisdiction over its territorial waters, as a self-governing dominion before entry into confederation in 1949, and that the Terms of Union reiterated the pre-confederation position.[28] It also alleged that the different constitutional regimes for resources relegated it to an unacceptable second-class category within confederation. Newfoundland insisted that the revenue from offshore resources and regulation of its development was crucial to its future economy. All provinces supported Newfoundland's contention that offshore resources should be treated in the same manner as onshore resources. Ottawa did not. It offered administrative arrangements.

Given these intractable differences, little could be done except identifying the options. The first option was a recognition of ownership and legislative jurisdiction by amendments to sections 92 and 109 of the British North America Act, as proposed by Newfoundland, or, alternatively, an extension of provincial boundaries seaward by appropriate federal and provincial action, as proposed by British Columbia. The committee of ministers preferred these approaches. The second option was modelled after the 1979 federal paper which would have given concurrent constitutional jurisdiction to the coastal provinces. Since Ottawa had already rejected this option and Newfoundland demanded ownership, this solution received no support. The third option involved administrative arrangements, as proposed by Ottawa, which would have established a joint federal and provincial management board and directed revenue from the resources to the coastal provinces until such time as the provinces became "have" provinces according to formulas used in the equalization program. The fundamental issue remained unresolved: should coastal provinces receive the same constitutional treatment as non-coastal provinces?

Fisheries. Consideration of jurisdiction over fisheries had been placed on the constitutional agenda in 1978 at the request of the Maritime provinces but no best effort draft had been developed. Ottawa had consistently argued that the issue of seacoast fisheries was so complicated by questions of fisheries management, allocation of resources, environmental protection, varying local circumstances, and international law that it would be impractical and undesirable to transfer jurisdiction to the provinces. In 1980 Chrétien observed ". . . the fish stocks are both migratory and widely distributed, and this fact is compounded by the mobility of fishermen as well."[29] Instead, Ottawa proposed administrative and consultative mechanisms, similar in its proposal for offshore resources. Although the federal government saw no need for a formal transfer of jurisdiction over inland fisheries to the provinces, it was prepared to entrench the longstanding arrangements on inland fisheries, whereby the federal government had delegated its authority to the provinces, on the condition that a satisfactory federal presence would be guaranteed for matters involving Indian rights, pollution issues, and transboundary habitat. However, it noted, any effective transfer of constitutional authority over inland fisheries to the provinces would bring about an end to federal funding for fisheries research and other related expenditures.

In Vancouver, the provinces produced their own best efforts draft which would have repealed the federal government's exclusive authority under section 91 and granted concurrent jurisdiction over seacoast fisheries to the provinces. This consensus, based on a proposal by Newfoundland, acknowledged the paramountcy of the federal government in the areas of establishing standards for, and identifying areas of, scientific research; setting limits to the total allowable catch of stocks; and allocating quotas to foreign countries. There would be provincial paramountcy over fixing quotas within federally set guidelines, issuing quotas and licences to individual domestic fishing vessels, and any other matter not specifically subject to federal paramountcy. British Columbia had suggested, as an alternative, that all aspects of fisheries be transferred to the exclusive jurisdiction of the provinces. Ottawa rejected the provincial consensus on the ground that such a transfer would leave it with the more difficult and expensive tasks of fisheries management, research, surveillance, enforcement, and fish inspections. The result of the CCMC deliberations was that fisheries joined offshore resources as an area in which fundamental and seemingly irreconcilable differences persisted.

The Charter of Rights

In Montreal the federal government clearly stated that entrenchment of a charter of rights with language provisions was a prerequisite to constitutional reform. While it was prepared to negotiate the wording of such a charter, the principle of entrenchment was not negotiable. As it had with the issue of the economic union, Ottawa unveiled a detailed draft charter, notes explaining the proposed sections, and a document advocating the merits of entrenchment.[30]

The proposed charter of rights, tabled by Chrétien on 8 July 1980, was significantly different from the one that had been considered by governments during 1978–79. The earlier draft had proposed that legal rights and non-discrimination rights would apply to the provinces only after they opted in; the new text applied to all legislatures and Parliament. Mobility rights were introduced, under which governments could not enact discriminatory legislation except where certain overriding economic and social conditions existed. The provinces of Manitoba, Ontario, and New Brunswick would be bound constitutionally by the provisions of section 133 of the British North America Act regarding official language rights.

Throughout the summer the majority of the provinces opposed the principle of entrenchment as vigorously as the federal government supported it. In order to permit a consideration of the federal draft, the debate over the principle of entrenchment was put aside so that officials could discuss, without prejudice, what a charter might contain. In the surrealistic atmosphere where each side denied the validity of the other's underlying position, officials and ministers tried to review the federal draft. Manitoba, however, refused to go along. It insisted that there was no agreement to discuss the specific language of the charter other than to review its effect on the constitutional powers of the provinces.

A number of concerns ranging from minor drafting problems to major questions of policy were identified by the committee during the first three weeks. Entrenchment of democratic rights and fundamental freedoms were the only issues on which there was no general conflict. Even here, however, there was concern with the wording of the fundamental freedoms section as it related to freedom of the press, religion, tax exemptions for religious institutions, and regulation of advertising. Other sections of the charter also attracted criticism and opposition. Most provincial governments argued that the proposed measures respecting legal rights would radically alter existing laws and practices to the detriment of the criminal justice system. The standard of "reasonableness" as it applied to search, seizure, and privacy was thought to grant too much latitude to the judiciary. Similar objections were raised with respect to the non-discrimination section.

Another major source of opposition was the "due process" clause, contained in the legal rights section. It was feared that it might lead to the importation of American jurisprudence to Canada. The response to mobility rights was part of the overall attack by a majority of provinces on the issue of the economic union. The entrenchment of property rights was opposed by a majority of provinces because it might allow courts to question the reasonableness of the expropriation rather than merely to adjudicate upon compensation and procedural fairness. The provinces complained that the specific derogations to the charter, such as legislation enacted in the interest of national security, health, and public order, were available to the federal government more than to the provinces. They viewed this as providing Ottawa with a way to escape the effects of the charter. Ontario and Manitoba wished to avoid being designated as officially bilingual provinces. The entrenchment of minority language education rights was vigorously opposed by Quebec, which saw it as a direct assault on provincial jurisdiction over education. Other governments expressed doubts about their ability to provide minority language education rights. Provinces feared that the section protecting "undeclared rights" would lead the courts to define new, unexpected rights. For example, since aboriginal rights were not mentioned, perhaps courts would recognize them as undeclared rights, and provincial authority would be affected in unforeseen ways. And so the discussion went.

Some provinces suggested that the governments consider an expansion of the existing provisions of the Canadian Bill of Rights as an alternative to the federal approach. Ottawa was not interested. The Bill of Rights was merely a statute which applied only at the federal level and, furthermore, it did not contain language rights. Entrenchment was the immovable objective of the federal government.

Another provincial suggestion was to insert a general *non obstante* clause which would permit legislatures and Parliament to override the sections of the charter by specific legislative enactment. The federal government rejected this on the ground that it would defeat the very purpose of entrenchment, namely, a guarantee of rights from abuse by governments, and this suggestion was abandoned as a possible answer to the dispute. The major issue, entrenchment of a charter, remained unresolved.

Communications

At the conclusion of the 1978–79 discussions, two drafts had been prepared on the issue of jurisdiction over communications. In 1980 Ottawa's position was that it was still prepared to implement its 1979 offer in respect of cable systems, which had been rejected by a majority of provinces at the time. It would also examine other aspects of communications, such as broadcasting, spectrum management, and telecommunications carriers. On the latter issue, Ottawa offered to transfer to the provinces of Newfoundland, Quebec, Ontario, and British Columbia the intraprovincial aspects of telecommunications but only if federal jurisdiction over all interprovincial and international telecommunications, unexercised in some parts of the country, were explicitly confirmed.

Quebec was the only government to submit a new discussion draft. It argued that:

> Quebec, the heartland of French Canada, feels justified in reasserting with insistence and conviction its will to assume the development and control over all communications in its territory. Communications are all the means or resources through which specific values of a community are transmitted, such as its language and culture, its attitudes and way of life; it seems meaningless to us to entrust to another majority the task of developing a communications policy for Quebeckers.[31]

This position was a traditional one with Quebec governments reaching back to the 1976 premiers' conference in Edmonton. The specific proposal provided for concurrency of jurisdiction with provincial paramountcy over "communications and communication systems within the province" with certain exceptions for the CBC, defence and emergency communications, and frequency spectrum, where the federal government would have paramountcy. Most of the governments, while wishing more authority over communications, felt this proposal left too little scope for the federal government.

After three weeks of ministerial meetings, nine provinces again endorsed the 1979 provincial draft on cable television, while Ottawa maintained its previous position. In late August, at the last meeting of the ministers, Ottawa tabled a new draft on communications based on concurrent jurisdiction with federal paramountcy over frequency spectrum, broadcasting, national cable undertakings, interprovincial carriers, and space and satellite carriers, including earth stations. This draft would have left the provinces with jurisdiction for telecommunication carriers within a province, the licensing of cable television and closed circuit systems, and programming of cable and closed circuit within a province. Although this was an important gain for the provinces, they were still unprepared to accept it, arguing that the technical aspects of the proposal enabled Ottawa to undo provincial policies with respect to cable and closed circuit programs. They also wanted to protect provincial telecommunications carriers from being subject to federal legislation for a national purpose. An important issue which continued to divide the governments was whether the provinces would be allowed a significant role in controlling programming on cable television. Provinces remained committed to their 1979 proposal.

The provinces feared that exclusive federal regulation of interprovincial and international communications would undermine revenues generated by provincially operated or regulated telephone systems. Tensions were increased by the federal government's resistance to any transfer of jurisdiction over broadcasting and programming.

Senate Reform

The issue of Senate reform resurrected the debate about the general approach to constitutional reform and reflected the larger conflict between Trudeau's view of the nation state and the earlier conception of a divided organic society. Should regional aspirations be accommodated by reform of the central institutions or by revisions to the legislative authority of the two orders of government? From the time of Bill C-60, Ottawa emphasized the argument that regional discontent and aspiration should be channelled through the reform of central institutions. Acceptance of this general approach would lessen the demand to rewrite the division of powers between the two orders of government; regional interests could be accommodated at the centre. The majority of provinces, however, did not share this view, and, from the 1978 premiers' conference in Regina, they had insisted that institutional reform be considered only in conjunction with a revision of legislative authority. These provinces knew that no new upper chamber, however structured, would acquire sufficient power over federal actions to satisfy provincial interests in the absence of change in the division of powers.

On the question whether reform of the Senate should await the completion of discussions on the division of powers, Quebec demonstrated a dilemma:

> For Quebec . . . how is it possible to determine the composition and powers of a new upper house, the function of which would be to provide provincial participation in the exercise of federal jurisdiction, if federal and provincial powers have not been redefined? The broader these

powers are, notably through Ottawa's great general powers, the more the presence and the weight of the provinces should make itself felt. And, vice versa. So, it is illogical to approach this matter backward. This is one of the major reasons why Quebec has always insisted, in the past and still at the present time, that priority should be given to the distribution of jurisdiction, before a study is made of the central institutions.[32]

Notwithstanding widespread provincial support for this position, British Columbia again pressured the participants to consider Senate reform. Numerous private sessions of ministers produced a document prepared by Ottawa and Saskatchewan, *Points of a Senate Consensus*, which suggested that a new upper chamber should be composed exclusively of provincial appointees whose role would be to ratify the actions of the federal government in such areas as the declaratory power and the spending power. But, "the consensus" fell apart on the question of composition. A majority of the delegations agreed to equal representation for all provinces, but British Columbia insisted on its traditional position that representation should be based on a weighted, five region division of the country. Subsequent meetings of ministers and officials resulted in four different models with different combinations of representation and powers. As well, the extent to which Canada's French–English duality should be reflected in the upper chamber proved to be an issue on which resolution could not be reached.

In the last week of the ministerial meetings, a proposal was developed which provided a temporary answer and seemed acceptable to most governments unable to answer the vexatious issue of Senate reform. Under it a new institution, to be known as the Council of the Provinces, would be established. The council would ratify exercises of the federal powers relating to the declaratory power, the spending power, and the emergency power. It would also ratify federal laws that were to be administered by the provinces and, as well, federal government appointments to certain boards, commissions, and agencies. Thirty members, appointed on an equal basis, would serve at the pleasure of the appointing governments. Each province would have only one vote, but the Quebec delegation would have to approve any measure with respect to language and culture before it was effective. In effect, the Council of the Provinces was a new intergovernmental body which would neither supplant the Senate nor review federal legislation. It might provide a compromise until reform of the division of powers was completed sometime in the future. But, in truth, the novel idea laboured under the same objections that had been attached to the main issue of Senate reform.

The Supreme Court
The discussion surrounding the Supreme Court also produced a convergence of views which appeared to satisfy the conflicting positions. All

governments agreed that the Supreme Court should be entrenched in the Constitution. Although Quebec urged the establishment of a special "constitutional bench . . . composed half of judges from Quebec and half of the judges from other parts of Canada,"[33] the other governments felt that the Supreme Court should be the final court of appeal for all cases, constitutional or otherwise. This was the best way to ensure clarity and uniformity in the law in Canada.

All governments felt that appointments to the Court should involve provincial agreement, not mere consultation, as was proposed during the 1978-79 phase of negotiations. If the federal minister of justice and provincial attorney general from whose province the appointment was to be made disagreed, each would select a person to join a selection committee. If these nominees could not agree on a third person to become the chairperson of the committee, the chief justice of Canada would be called on to select a chairperson, and the committee would then proceed to select the person to be appointed to the Court.

There was a great deal of discussion but no agreement on how to reflect dualism in the composition of the Court.[34] Although most delegations accepted the appropriateness of a dualistic aspect, they objected to Quebec's idea of an equally weighted constitutional court. Manitoba suggested that the size of the Supreme Court be expanded to eleven members, five of whom would be from the province of Quebec. However, as the summer talks progressed, the initial support that Manitoba's proposal received from the provinces waned. The federal government, which in 1980 had originally stated its support for a nine judge court as set out in the 1979 consensus, switched its position to favour the Manitoba principle, a position it had supported in 1978. The ministers were unable to reach an agreement on this issue.

There was, however, a large measure of support for a constitutional provision which would entrench the practice of alternating the post of chief justice between civil law and common law appointees. As well, most governments were favourable to a proposal to limit the term for the chief justice to seven years. Finally, most governments agreed that both provincial and federal governments should be allowed to refer constitutional cases directly to the Supreme Court for resolution.

There was no consensus, however, on the issue of granting to the provinces constitutional authority to create agencies which performed the functions of district and superior courts in the provinces. The provinces claimed that this change was consistent with provincial responsibility for the administration of justice as well as provincial jurisdiction over matters assigned to provinces in the Constitution. The federal government, on the other hand, maintained that the integrity of the bench could be preserved only through a uniform set of standards for judicial appointments throughout the country and a uniform scope of court jurisdiction. The provinces accepted entrenchment of the power of judicial review of provincial agencies, and Ottawa acknowledged diminishment of provincial power to establish administrative tribunals by court decisions based on sections 96 and 101 of the British North America Act; the federal government, however, refused to transfer any constitutional authority to the provinces in this matter.

Family Law

Consideration of jurisdiction over family law was carried out against the backdrop of growing opposition by women's rights organizations to the 1978–79 best efforts draft. The draft had provided that legislative jurisdiction in relation to grounds for divorce be concurrent and that corollary relief in such matters as custody and maintenance be transferred to provincial jurisdiction. Women's rights groups in Canada feared that the effect of these proposals would be to aggravate the unsatisfactory state of enforcement of maintenance and custody orders in Canada. Rather than less federal authority, they urged more federal power to guarantee effective enforcement of orders throughout the country. Some groups also felt that the proposed transfer of divorce jurisdiction to the provinces would result in divorce havens in some provinces, while other groups feared that conservative forces would apply pressure on provinces to institute rules which were archaic and against divorce. Both groups considered that the loss of a national standard for obtaining divorces would lead to confusion and to the exploitation of the partner in the marriage with fewer resources— usually the wife.

Manitoba had consistently opposed the main features of the 1978–79 best efforts draft. Bolstered by the reaction of citizen groups in the period following the First Ministers' Conference in February 1979, Manitoba renewed its opposition during the 1980 meetings, claiming that the increased mobility of Canadians buttressed its argument for a uniform divorce law and uniform corollary relief. Manitoba not only strongly urged the federal government to retain its present jurisdiction in relation to the grounds for divorce, and the ancillary relief related to it, but to expand its jurisdiction to include the monitoring and enforcement of all maintenance and custody orders, even those made outside the context of a divorce.

The purpose of transferring the legislative authority for corollary relief to the provinces was to end the conflict that existed between federal and provincial legislation. Ontario and Quebec particularly defended the principles of the 1978–79 best efforts draft. Quebec placed a high priority on a transfer of jurisdiction to it because the family was the basic unit of society and was "very much a local institution, which therefore requires legal protections suited to its specific needs."[35] In fact, most provinces have enacted a considerable body of legislation in relation to child protection, child welfare, adoption, paternity, maintenance, and custody. Quebec maintained that the transfer of jurisdiction to the provinces would produce a body of family law that was both consistent and responsive to local needs.

Partly in response to Quebec's participation and partly in support of Quebec's and Ontario's argument, the majority of provinces supported the best efforts draft. Jean Chrétien acknowledged that there was opposition from women's rights groups, but committed the federal government to accepting the proposal on the basis that private law should reflect the regional diversity of Canada.

During the summer negotiations, the governments explored possible solutions to two problems which, if answered, might provide the basis for agreement by all governments. The first was the problem of havens, both for obtaining divorces and for avoiding the application of corollary relief orders. The second was the problem of enforcing provincial maintenance and custody orders on an intraprovincial basis in a manner more effective than under the present reciprocal enforcement schemes. The committee produced a new draft which modified the best efforts draft by creating exclusive federal legislative competence to establish rules under which provinces would acquire divorce jurisdiction and recognize divorce decrees. In this way, the provinces would not be in a position to make rules which would create divorce havens or barriers to recognition across Canada of all divorce decrees. A compromise was proposed under which the Constitution would provide that all maintenance and custody orders made in Canada would have legal effect throughout Canada and, further, that all such orders could be registered as an enforceable order of each province's courts. These changes did not, however, dilute Manitoba's opposition; it resolutely opposed the principle of the amendment.

Equalization and Regional Development

The proposed amendment on equalization and regional development committed all governments to the principle of promoting equal opportunities for the well being of Canadians, furthering economic development to reduce disparities among the regions, and providing essential public services of reasonable quality to all Canadians. Notwithstanding the high degree of consensus on this subject, differences over how to word the provisions arose. In the first week in Montreal, Quebec presented a draft text which would have ensured that the equalization payments were made directly to provincial governments and not to individuals, organizations, or groups within the province. Quebec did not want the new provision on equalization and regional development to be taken as

> an invitation to the federal government to extend in any way a spending power which has led to abuses. Quebec does not believe that direct

payments to economic agencies or individuals over the provinces' heads, as was done in Quebec in the case of the dispute over the sales tax, is an acceptable form of federal intervention.[36]

Another version of an equalization amendment was advanced by Manitoba and Saskatchewan. This proposal was based on Quebec's argument but urged that the text state that revenues and not services were being equalized. The standard for equalization would be a "reasonably comparable level of public services." The provinces wanted to guarantee that the commitment to provision of essential public services would not be interpreted to mean the provision of a minimum level of services. A third draft, tabled by British Columbia, substantially deviated from the general views on language. In contrast to the other proposals, and in keeping with its traditional view, British Columbia suggested that only the objectives of equalization be entrenched without reference to method of payment. British Columbia was alone in this view, and its position was untenable in the face of strong opposition from all of the other governments.

Preamble

In his opening statement in Montreal, Chrétien declared, "I would like to be absolutely clear about what it is we, in the federal delegation, now see as the task in this regard. It is to draft, together, a Preamble of a New Constitution."[37] To request a committee of ministers from eleven governments with their officials, to "draft, together" a preamble was to be excessively optimistic. However, all of the delegations accepted the federal minister's invitation that they enter into discussions about what, if anything, should be contained in a preamble to the Constitution. Some twenty-seven differing themes and suggestions emerged from one meeting of officials. When their report was presented to the ministerial body, few of the themes received the support of a majority of the ministers. Disagreements ranged from differences over words, and their meaning, to fundamental concepts. Some governments argued that the preamble should be inspirational in tone and not a restatement of specific constitutional proposals. Others feared that any preamble would provide the judiciary with yet another avenue to impose their interpretations on the Constitution. Accordingly, it should be simple, concise, and brief.

Two issues, duality and self-determination, dominated the debate. How could the concept of duality be stated to the satisfaction of both Quebec and Ottawa? Should the right to self-determination be recognized? The difficulties of selecting correct words and with a mutually agreed meaning were demonstrated by a public debate in Quebec over the initial federal draft of 9 June 1980. The draft opened with the words, "We, the people of Canada. . . ." Quebec's premier publicly criticized the use of the word "people" on the ground that it implied a "nation," thereby denying the existence of the "Quebec nation" as one of the founding partners to confederation. Furthermore, if a founding "nation" could decide to join confederation, it could presumably also decide to withdraw from it. Even the leader of the Liberal party in Quebec, Claude Ryan, criticized the proposed federal draft and urged that it be totally rewritten. The apparent widespread support given these interpretations motivated Trudeau to write "an open letter to Quebeckers" on this subject. The prime minister argued that the term "the people of Canada" was used collectively to designate all the citizens of Canada regardless of their ethnic or sociological background. He described Canada as a single political entity and interpreted "people" in this sense to encompass "people composed of several nations (in the sociological sense)." It did not mean there was a sovereign state attached to each sociological nation. Criticizing the "semantic trap" laid by the Parti Québécois government, Trudeau denied the so-called two nations theory:

> We are no longer living in the world of Upper and Lower Canada. There are regional realities in this country with deep roots in history and geography, a fact which will have to be realized in Quebec one of these days if we are to stop simplifying Canadian reality to suit our various theories. The Anglo-Saxon conquerors—as some people in Quebec like to picture them—have in fact been a minority for some time now throughout the country. . . . To think of Canada outside of Quebec as a vast land of Anglo-Saxons is to make a very bad mistake.[38]

Trudeau also addressed the issue of self-determination. In response to Quebec's theory that confederation was voluntarily created by Quebec in partnership with English Canada and, therefore, could be voluntarily discontinued, Trudeau described Quebec's demand that the specific right to self-determination be spelled out in the preamble as "the right to divorce spelled out at the beginning of the marriage contract." He claimed that the results of the Quebec referendum had removed this option and to include it in the Constitution would confound the choice of the people of Quebec to join in "the Canadian dream in all its richness and originality."[39]

The debate continued throughout the ministerial meetings. In the last meeting of the CCMC in August, the federal government introduced a new preamble with two objectives. The first was to modernize the language of the preamble to the British North America Act, changing, for example, references to the "Crown of the United Kingdom" to the "Crown of Canada" and replacing reference to "the Interests of the British Empire" with reference to Canadian well being. The second was to include in the statement of fundamental ideals a commitment "to the distinct French-speaking society centred in though not confined to Quebec." The federal draft also set out "that the provinces are freely united in the federation."[40]

The CCMC did not accept the new federal draft and was unable to recommend any draft which did not feature several competing options of phrases and words which had been advocated by the various delegations. Although Quebec saw the term "freely united" as, at least, an indirect recognition of the right of the province to self-determination, it preferred an opening statement which emphasized that "the Provinces of Canada chose *to remain* freely united in a federation. . . ." In contrast to Ottawa's view that the French-speaking society was "centred in but not confined to Quebec," Quebec also proposed that the preamble recognize the "distinctive character of Quebec society with its French-speaking majority" without any reference to other regions of Canada. Central to the differences between the federal government and Quebec was the right way to recognize duality.

Patriation and Amending Formula

Timing of Patriation. While every government professed the desire that Canada terminate the last vestige of its links to Great Britain, the timing of patriation and the nature of an amending formula persisted as major stumbling blocks. The federal government was determined that patriation would take place "as soon as possible." Telegraphing the federal government's patriation strategy, Chrétien said, "neither the Parliament of the United Kingdom nor the people of Canada are blocking the way to complete the constitutional emancipation for this country. It is we, Canada's political leaders, who have not shown the necessary political determination to resolve this issue. . . ."[41] The federal minister committed his government to examine any of the formulas, past or present, to find a satisfactory answer to this problem. In private sessions with the ministers, Chrétien emphasized the urgency to patriate and warned that Ottawa intended to patriate the Constitution soon, unilaterally if it had to.

During the 1978–79 phase of constitutional discussions, Quebec consistently refused to participate in the discussions surrounding an amending formula on the ground that the matter could only be dealt with after reform of the division of powers. Although the outcome of the referendum might have been expected to attenuate this view, Quebec reiterated its position at the outset of the 1980 talks in Montreal. In its paper to the conference, Quebec enumerated five "serious misgivings" about the "premature patriation of the Constitution." Quebec likened the Constitution to a contract which contained a number of clauses requiring renegotiation. The twelve agenda items under review by the ministers would deal with some of the clauses of that contract, but Quebec cautioned that many more would have to be considered in future discussions. Quebec said:

> Patriating the constitution now or in the immediate future amounts to asking Quebeckers to accept as a valid basis of discussion the very docu-

ment which they have been wanting for years to replace with a new, more modern one. Such an approach takes for granted that Quebeckers will be satisfied with minor alterations to federalism as it now exists, when what most of them want is a new federalism.[42]

The Quebec government also expressed concern that once patriation was achieved, there would no longer exist a determination in the rest of Canada to renegotiate the other items important to Quebec. Quebec also made the somewhat circular argument that the entire public debate about patriation was misleading since "it does not appear to Quebec to be particularly appropriate to begin constitutional renewal by making a priority of patriating an ancient document which everyone agrees is politically and institutionally outdated: if it were not, there would be no point to the current negotiations."[43] Thus, Quebec did not intend to participate to any great extent in discussion of a new amending formula. In fact, it was an active participant. On the matter of specific terms of a future amending formula, Quebec stated its preference for the principles of the Victoria Charter or some other formula which granted the province a veto in recognition of its special place in Canada.

The Alberta Model Reexamined. In the last week of the CCMC deliberations, the ministers were finally able to present a proposed amending formula which was based on one submitted by Alberta in February 1979 and became known during the summer of 1980 as the Vancouver amending formula. This formula provided that a general amendment could be accomplished with the assent of the federal Parliament and seven of the provinces with at least 50 percent of the population. However, a province could opt out of the effects of an amendment if it was one which "affected" the powers of the legislature to make laws; the rights and privileges of the legislature or the government as set out in the Constitution; the assets or property of a province; or the natural resources of a province. No veto would be granted to any province; provincial interests would be protected by a provision that no amendment directly affecting a province's interests could be imposed against its will. Quebec still indicated its preference for the Victoria Charter formula but stated that it would be prepared to consider Alberta's proposal subject to developments on the other agenda items. Quebec also raised the question of financial compensation to a province that opted out of a general amendment. Because opting out could lead to different constitutional regimes in different parts of the country, a situation might develop where the federal government levied taxes everywhere in Canada, although its responsibilities did not extend to the opted-out province. A province which decided to opt out would be penalized in financial terms. Quebec wished fiscal compensation to be a part of the opting-out feature of the Vancouver model if it were adopted.

The federal government saw two major problems with this formula. First, constitutional changes would not be binding upon all the provinces although all provinces would participate in making the decision. Because the proposal would apply to those provincial powers that were "affected," virtually no amendments would escape a potential provincial opt out. This might lead to different constitutional regimes in different provinces, which would only be aggravated over time. Moreover, if provinces were compensated financially, a strong incentive would be created for additional opt outs. In Ottawa's judgment, the unity of the country would be further weakened. The second problem concerned amendments to matters such as the Supreme Court, the Senate, and the monarchy; while such amendments might affect the rights of provinces, they could not, because of their central importance, be subject to provincial opting out. What rule would govern?

Delegation of Legislative Authority. In 1979, all governments had been in general agreement with the principle that one order of government should be able to delegate to the other order the power to enact laws that came within the scope of the delegating authority. In this way, flexibility would be introduced into the Constitution since governments could voluntarily enter into relationships without the necessity of passing a constitutional amendment. Some governments in 1980, however, felt that the 1979 draft required additional clarification, although the general intent was clear. A technical problem was found in the wording: delegation could occur by two methods, on a statute-by-statute basis or in relation to a complete legislative subject matter.

A more fundamental concern was raised by Quebec: the scope of the proposed delegation power would enable certain transfers of jurisdiction unavailable through the general amending formula. In effect, delegation would compete with the amending formula and undermine its certainty. Quebec refused to endorse the delegation draft until this problem was clarified. British Columbia saw another difficulty with the proposal. It argued that the draft should state that, if Parliament were to delegate authority to one province, it could not refuse to delegate the same authority to another province. Ottawa argued that acceptance of British Columbia's suggestion would offend parliamentary sovereignty; it was unwilling to accept a proposal under which Parliament could bind future parliaments. Because of these differences, the matter of delegation was not resolved by the ministerial meetings before the First Ministers' Conference.

Getting Ready for September

The Quebec National Assembly's Special Committee
After three full weeks of deliberations not much had been settled. Major disagreements on the economic union, resources, offshore resources, and fisheries were in evidence. At the completion of the first three ministerial

meetings, all governments took stock of the progress of the negotiations. Two events were of particular importance. In Quebec, the National Assembly's Committee on the Presidency and the Constitution was convened to debate the activities of the ministerial group. In Winnipeg, the ten provincial premiers, in their annual meeting, also considered the situation. In Quebec, the government was in search of as much unity as possible for its general position. The strongest disagreement with the Quebec Liberal party focussed on the entrenchment of a charter of rights with minority language education provisions. The Parti Québécois rejected any provision which would impose these rights on the province; the Liberals supported the concept but opposed the actual wording of the federal draft. The Liberals urged deletion of the phrase "where numbers warrant," and the inclusion of a principle guaranteeing the provision of health and social services. There were no other areas of major disagreement between the two parties.

The most important development was the unanimous endorsement of the Parti Québécois stance with respect to patriation and the amending formula. Furthermore, the committee agreed that any future amending formula must guarantee a veto for Quebec. It also rejected unanimously any suggestion that the September First Ministers' Conference was a deadline for patriation and reform of the Constitution. Finally, it was agreed that the drafting of a preamble should only follow successful resolution of issues related to the division of powers.

Although the Liberal party disagreed with some of the Parti Québécois' specific positions, the result of the committee's hearings was that the Quebec Liberal party was at odds with its federal counterpart on the crucial tactical issue of reform. This was a major boost for the Lévesque government because it refuted the accusation that the government was not in tune with Quebec's people. The government was no longer isolated within Quebec as it had been since the results of the referendum. The Quebec government would, therefore, return to the fourth and final week of ministerial negotiations as firm in its positions as it had been at the outset.

The Premiers' Conference in Winnipeg
The ten provincial premiers met in Winnipeg on 20 August for their annual conference and received reports on the constitutional negotiations and the bilateral talks between Edmonton and Ottawa on oil pricing. The debates within the CCMC and the increasingly frequent pronouncements that September was a deadline gave credence to the apprehension of premiers that Ottawa was "getting tough" with the provinces. Moreover, the energy negotiations appeared to be stalled after a meeting between Premier Lougheed and Prime Minister Trudeau failed to produce any results. Shortly after that meeting, Alberta unilaterally imposed an increase in the price of its oil. Ottawa's national advertising campaign, stressing to

"the people" the importance of patriation and entrenchment of a charter of rights, was an obvious attempt to bypass provincial governments and to appeal directly to the electorate; it was correctly perceived by some premiers as a prelude to more drastic strategies. Both energy and constitutional issues appeared to have deeply divided the governments without prospect of an agreement.

Unlike previous premiers' conferences, however, there was not the same degree of solidarity in Winnipeg, since both Ontario and New Brunswick had favoured many of the federal positions during the CCMC negotiations. The premiers were unwilling, if not unable, to renew their earlier accords. In any event, it would be politically unwise for them to articulate their common position in the midst of the CCMC deliberations. Still, the tendency of this body was to find common ground, and the final communiqué, reverting to a familiar theme, urged that constitutional reform must embrace a "package of changes" which would take into account the interests of all regions of the country. The premiers rejected the suggestion that September was a deadline for an agreement. "If," in the words of the communiqué, "despite determined efforts, final agreement cannot be reached next month, the Premiers are committed to continue the negotiations, to pursue constitutional negotiations to a successful conclusion."[44] Finally, the premiers warned of the dangers to the unity of the country if Ottawa proceeded on its own with patriation and a set of constitutional amendments.

While the premiers could not agree on what they wanted in constitutional reform, they agreed to delay the process until such time as a consensus on the issues emerged. For the federal government, the premiers' conference must have been a confirmation of its suspicion that agreement was not possible within a reasonable time. The best that could be achieved would be agreement with some of the provinces on some of the issues. The strategy of unilateral action, or action with limited provincial support, was one step closer to implementation.

The Leaked Pitfield Memorandum

During the premiers' conference a newspaper article in the Ottawa *Citizen* reported that the federal government had already prepared a joint parliamentary resolution to patriate the Constitution unilaterally "before Christmas." According to the report, Michael Pitfield, clerk of the Privy Council, in a secret memorandum to Trudeau, had recommended that it would be necessary to wait a few weeks (after the First Ministers' Conference in September) to table the resolution in order to avoid providing substance to the inevitable provincial allegations that the government wanted the September talks to fail in order to proceed unilaterally. Pitfield also referred to the stalled energy negotiations and predicted that the federal government would have to act on its own over energy pricing in this area as well. Some premiers, at least, were stunned by the blatancy of the federal planning, and the news of the memorandum went to the heart of the matters being discussed in Winnipeg. Nevertheless, the premiers refused to be drawn into public discussion of what was simply an internal policy recommendation of an official to his minister. In any event they hardly wished to act as if their own agenda could be discarded in favour of the themes that seemed to preoccupy the clerk of the Privy Council.

The next week, when the fourth week's meeting of the CCMC commenced in Ottawa, the provincial ministers were not as studiously cool. The meeting began with an acrimonious debate as provincial ministers angrily accused Chrétien of negotiating in bad faith. They claimed that Ottawa had intended the summer-long process to be only an exercise in public relations, designed to demonsrate that the provinces were either unable or unwilling to reach an agreement. Chrétien's only defence was that the memorandum outlined a contingency plan for Ottawa in the event of failure to reach agreement; negotiated settlement remained the government's objective. As for the threat of unilateral action, Chrétien restated the federal government's determination to patriate as quickly as possible. In his previous statements, however, Chrétien had alluded to a twelve month period as a "deadline" for an agreement. Now, the Pitfield memorandum specifically targeted patriation "before Christmas," which seemed to confirm that the forthcoming First Ministers' Conference was indeed a final attempt to reach agreement. Chrétien's explanation only partially mollified the ministers. Mistrust and suspicion were rampant.

Provincial Ministers Attempt Another Consensus

Most of the provincial ministers had now concluded that Ottawa was determined to proceed to Westminster with or without their consent. The only way to forestall this was to develop a united provincial position on the agenda items to illustrate that the provinces were able to compromise their differences. In this way, they reasoned, the federal government might be deterred from proceeding to Westminster with a package that most strongly opposed. The enthusiasm for such a strategy varied from province to province with Ontario and New Brunswick both reticent. Nevertheless, the provincial ministers embarked on a series of informal meetings to devise such an agreement.

There was only a partial success. A handwritten document was produced which was described as a "Consensus reached by governments . . . as part of a total package." Only three of the twelve items—communications, offshore resources, and fisheries—received the unanimous approval of the governments; the remainder attracted reservations or caveats from one, or more, provinces. The major stumbling block again proved to be the issues of patriation and amending formula. At one end of the spectrum, Quebec maintained that patriation could be accomplished only after major reform of the division of powers. Ontario, at the other end, argued that immediate patriation was necessary and desirable. Notwithstanding this major difference, all the ministers agreed in principle to the Vancouver amending formula, with Quebec repeating its earlier request that the opt-out feature of the formula include fiscal compensation. An attempt to compromise the two extreme positions on patriation involved a proposal, similar to the one suggested by Ottawa in 1976, under which there would be a "suspensive" patriation, namely, return of the British North America Act to Canada with formal proclamation postponed to a later date agreed upon by all eleven governments. This idea floundered for the same reasons that it had in 1976

New Proposals from Ottawa

In this tense atmosphere in Ottawa in the last week of the CCMC, the federal government introduced a set of new positions on most of the major issues under review, designed to meet, in part, the objections of the provinces as stated in the previous three weeks of negotiations. With respect to "powers over the economy," the most important of three changes dealt with proposed section 121. First, the "unduly impedes" test was deleted; judicial review would be limited to the narrower test of discrimination on the basis of provincial residence. The second change was deletion of the words "directly or indirectly" in the proposed sub-section (1) of section 121. The third proposed change clarified the right of the provinces to discriminate on a sub-provincial basis, provided that the action did not discriminate against non-residents, goods, services, and capital to a degree greater than those resident within a province. An important change to proposed section 91(2) was that the provinces should retain their jurisdiction to enact laws affecting "competition" and "product standards" unless such provincial laws collided with a specific federal law, in which case the federal law was paramount. This amendment reduced, but did not eliminate, the perceived threat to provincially created monopolies, provincially regulated industries and professions, and consumer legislation.

Although Ottawa rejected Saskatchewan's draft on the maintenance of the economic union, it indicated a willingness to consider the draft as an alternative to its proposals if an enforcement mechanism, political, judicial or both, were incorporated in it. This prompted a renewed examination of the role of a new second chamber. At the end of the last week of meetings, the ministers agreed upon a solution involving both the judiciary and a new upper chamber: it was proposed that where a law or practice was found by the courts to be in violation of the general provisions of section

121, such a ruling would be valid and operative unless, within six months of the judgment, the new proposed upper chamber ratified the law or practice as being desirable public policy notwithstanding its inconsistency with the general prohibition. As well, derogations to the general provisions of section 121 would have to be ratified by the new upper chamber when the federal government exercised them. However, since the ministers were unable to agree on the composition and role of a new upper chamber, this proposal was obviously deficient. Therefore, the CCMC concluded its work with four different drafts dealing with section 121. These divided into one of two opposing positions; three of the proposals were premised on an enforceable mechanism, while Saskatchewan's alternative was based on entrenchment of only a commitment to the economic union.

Polarization had also set in with respect to the other major issues. During this final week, the federal government partially restored the provision from the 1979 best efforts draft on natural resources, which granted concurrent legislative jurisdiction on interprovincial trade with unqualified federal paramountcy; But Ottawa would not, however, agree to include international trade and commerce in the proposal. Saskatchewan objected and urged a return to the "compelling national interest" test of 1979. Alberta, locked in negotiations with Ottawa over energy pricing, also expressed its serious reservations about the new offer. As for the declaratory power, Ottawa stated a willingness to make its use subject to the consent of a new upper chamber.

Ottawa tabled a new proposal establishing a joint federal–provincial administrative arrangement and offered the provinces "100% of the offshore resources revenue" until such time as they became "have" provinces under the equalization formula. The proposal was unanimously rejected, and the question of equal treatment for coastal provinces with respect to natural resources remained unanswered after four weeks of negotiations. A general consensus that jurisdiction over inland fisheries be transferred to the provinces was reached, but questions were posed as to the meaning of certain words. On the issue of seacoast fisheries, Ottawa's proposal to entrench a "mandatory consultative mechanism," similar to that advocated with respect to offshore resources, was countered by the provinces, which again urged constitutional entrenchment of concurrent jurisdiction. It was obvious that the differences between the federal government and the majority of the provinces with respect to resources, offshore resources, and fisheries were extremely deep; even if they could be resolved, there was still the complex problem of finding a satisfactory solution on "powers over the economy." The prospects for these sorts of major accommodations were dim, in light of the provincial fears of unilateralism, anger with federal advertising, and conflicting positions of the governments.

The first concern of the federal government, a charter of rights with language provisions, was entangled in the debate over entrenchment.

Although major changes were introduced by Ottawa in the last week, limiting the scope of sections involving legal rights and non-discrimination, deleting the entrenchment of property rights, and adding a new general derogation clause applicable to the whole charter, the majority of provinces remained adamantly opposed to the proposed charter both in principle and in application. On 28 August the provinces unveiled their own charter, deleting many of the legal rights and qualifying the remaining ones to allow Parliament and legislatures to define the extent of the protection they would provide. Only fundamental freedoms and democratic rights were included in undiluted form in the provincial proposal. The thorny problem of language rights was sidestepped, because the provinces could not agree amongst themselves.

Even in those areas where substantial progress had been achieved, such as a Council of the Provinces (as a halfway house for reform of the upper chamber), the Supreme Court, family law, equalization, and regional development, most governments had some reservations or objections to the specific proposals. Moreover, the governments of Quebec and Canada sharply and frequently clashed over fundamental differences about entrenchment of language rights, duality, the right to self-determination, and, of course, the timing for patriation. A number of irritants to the process, such as the Pitfield memorandum, the continuing designation of matters as either "people" or "government power" concerns, and the retreat by the federal government from several of its 1979 best efforts positions served to sharpen the difference between the two groups with their opposing visions of Canada's federalism. In retrospect, the 1980 CCMC was successful in one regard: it identified the differences among the governments on all of the issues assigned to it. To this extent, it fulfilled its mandate. It failed, however, to bridge the wide gulfs between governments on contentious issues; in fact, the summer-long process only exaggerated the differences.

The September 1980 First Ministers' Conference

The Kirby Memorandum

On Sunday evening, 7 September, the governor general hosted a dinner attended by the premiers and their ministers. Later that evening the Quebec delegation circulated to the other provinces a copy of a memorandum,[45] written by Michael Kirby, secretary for federal-provincial relations to the Cabinet and responsible for organizing the federal government's position. The memorandum assessed the progress of the negotiations on an item-by-item basis and discussed federal strategy. Kirby identified three objectives for Ottawa. First, since the federal government had decided to patriate the Constitution, alone if necessary, this should be clearly communicated to the premiers to promote compromise, motivated by a desire to avoid imposition of a patriation package. Second, the distinction between "people" items and "government powers" should be maintained—implicit confirmation that the federal government was interested only in its own limited set of reforms. Third, the link between economic union and resources should be confirmed, thus undermining the constitutional demands of the resource-rich western provinces, forcing them to choose, in the words of the memorandum ". . . between the *status quo* of resources, which they know is good for the federal government and agreeing to make a concession to the federal government on economic union."[46]

The tenor of the memorandum clearly suggested that the federal government could live with a failed First Ministers' Conference because it could then proceed to patriate the Constitution. But the federal government had to be careful. According to Kirby, it had to demonstrate flexibility during the First Ministers' Conference. In Kirby's words, "the challenge now lies with the federal government . . . to show that disagreement leading to unilateral action is the result of . . . the intransigence of the provincial governments and not the fault of the federal government."[47] When the premiers read the Kirby memorandum, most of them privately conceded that their worst suspicions had been proven and that the First Ministers' Conference would inevitably end badly. The conference was a failure before it started.

The Conference

The opening statements of the first ministers revealed that there had been virtually no change in their positions since the ministerial meetings. Essentially the prime minister offered the premiers the same concessions that Chrétien had offered in the course of the meetings. A new draft of a charter of rights which modified the previous federal draft of 22 August, tabled at the Ottawa ministerial meeting, was unveiled. To accommodate the argument that entrenchment would undermine parliamentary sovereignty, the federal government widened the general derogation provision of the charter and replaced the due process clause, with its American connotations of broad judicial review, with what was claimed to be the more limited "principles of fundamental justice" clause. There were also refinements to the legal rights and the mobility rights sections designed to give broader scope to legislative and governmental choices.

The angry and uncompromising mood of the participants was carried to the private sessions on the fifth floor of the Conference Centre. Here, four main issues dominated. First, the proposed statement of principles became of far greater concern to the first ministers, especially Trudeau and Lévesque, than it had ever been during the ministerial sessions. The main protagonists each insisted on a preamble which would express their own concept of Canada. The debate was a repetition of the one in which both Lévesque and Trudeau had engaged during the summer, with Trudeau demanding a clear reference to Canada as a union of the people and Lévesque equally adamant that Canada was a union of the provinces. Trudeau claimed that Canada was an indissoluble federation while Lévesque insisted the preamble recognize the right to self-determination for the provinces. Second, the same two protagonists duelled over the entrenchment of language rights, with the prime minister interpreting the outcome of the referendum as a mandate to entrench these rights while the Quebec premier argued that language rights represented a fundamental attack on Quebec's educational and cultural sovereignty.

The "two scorpions in a bottle" relationship between Trudeau and Lévesque, although part of the context of constitutional renewal for nearly four years, dominated the September 1980 conference to an extent which was both unexpected and destructive of attempts to improve the mood of the conference. Perhaps it was because neither Trudeau nor Lévesque particularly desired the conference to conclude in an agreement which embraced both of their views that they were free to indulge in acrimony.

The third issue over which there was a major altercation was the extent to which the provinces should be granted additional constitutional authority over natural resources and offshore resources. Alberta and Saskatchewan had not agreed upon a specific constitutional text on resources; the main disagreement involved the extent of limitations that should be placed on exercises of federal authority over trade and commerce. Both provinces, however, agreed that the offer to give the provinces concurrent jurisdiction over interprovincial trade and commerce, with unqualified federal paramountcy, and to give them the power to impose indirect taxes was insufficient. On the other hand, Ottawa's demands with respect to the economic union were too much for them. In the case of Newfoundland, having reached an agreement in principle with the former Clark administration, it could not accept anything less than full constitutional recognition of its ownership and jurisdictional right over offshore resources. Fourth, the impasse in the negotiations over oil pricing and the prospect of a new export tax on natural gas militated against any compromise on the jurisdictional issues. The energy dispute was not addressed directly in the private sessions, but the governments involved, recognizing the gravity of the negotiating situation, refused to budge on their positions on the jurisdictional issues.

The Chateau Consensus

Armed with the Kirby report and convinced that the conference was structured to fail, the provincial governments once again adopted the tactic of formulating their own agreement in principle on the issues. The basis of the provincial agreement was the document the provincial ministers had produced in the last week of the CCMC. Quebec undertook to refine this position for the premiers. After numerous private and informal meetings among provincial ministers and officials, the premiers met in the Chateau Laurier to consider Quebec's discussion draft. On each of the specific items under consideration, Quebec proposed adoption of the position which carried the highest number of endorsements by the other provincial governments. However, there were a number of new wrinkles. For example, Quebec proposed that entrenchment of fundamental freedoms and democratic rights be implemented in a charter of rights but with a provision which safeguarded existing laws. Also a *non obstante* provision would be attached to the legal rights and non-discrimination clauses. Multilateral reciprocity agreements, entered into by provincial governments, would be the manner of guaranteeing minority language education rights, in those provinces which concurred.

As for the amending formula, Quebec stated it could accept the Vancouver opting-out provisions, provided fiscal compensation was incorporated; moreover, for those matters in which a province did not have the right to opt out, the formula would have to embrace a veto for Quebec. In order to meet the objectives of the provinces which favoured immediate patriation, the discussion draft set out a delayed or suspensive device under which the patriating legislation would be enacted immediately, but implementation would be delayed until all governments agreed to it. Quebec also inserted a list for a second phase of constitutional negotiations, which contained the federal spending power, declaratory power and emergency power, culture and social affairs, urban and regional affairs, international relations, and the administration of justice. Quebec's draft patriation would not occur until these and the twelve issues under review in 1980 were resolved.

Quebec's presentation was rejected by some of the premiers who noted that Ottawa had already turned down most of the positions set out in it. Furthermore, some of the suggestions were unacceptable to some provinces because they exceeded the degree to which they felt Ottawa's power should be devolved. Some provinces stated that Trudeau would portray the "consensus" as a grab for power by greedy provinces. The counter argument was that the Chateau consensus would at least permit the provinces to demonstrate that they had achieved some agreement and were committed to further discussions. It would blunt any federal strategy based on a claim that the provinces could not agree amongst themselves. It was finally decided that the consensus would be presented to the prime minister when the premiers met privately with him on Friday morning. What happened when it was presented to Trudeau was reported by him at a press conference some months later:

> . . . and that is what happened last September when we met on the Friday morning at my house. They had their shopping list, and I said, "Well, you

know, we cannot do it all. We are not about to give everything the provinces are asking now—fisheries to one, the offshore to the other, cultural
sovereignty to the next, the right to separate or what was self-determination that the other wanted, and so on. We are not about to give that." So, a
couple of them, who will remain nameless, unless they want to name
themselves, got up and said, "Okay, well, let's forget the shopping list and
make a deal." And, two of them, who shall not remain nameless, Bennett
and Peckford, stood up and shook their fists and said, "Hey, we just had
breakfast this morning and we vowed that we would never split the
common front, and what are you guys saying—that you are going to make
a deal on patriation?" So, the others just gently bowed their heads and
said, "Yes, we did vow at breakfast this morning never to break the common front." So, the thing failed—and you heard it fail in public that
Saturday morning on television.[48]

The two who were unwilling to see the long process end in this
climate of hostility and unrealism, and who made the one further attempt
to avoid sending the country into a period of intense confrontation were
Premiers Blakeney and Davis. Realization of the complete futility of their
offer to continue bargaining must have hit them as soon as they made it.
Yet, after the other eight premiers left 24 Sussex Drive, the two stayed on
with Trudeau. Their purpose was not to engage in a postmortem examination but, rather, to suggest that there might be, if only the real source of
the conflict could be found, some offer or concession which could gener-
ate the sense of optimism needed to bring the premiers back to the table.
If that was too much to hope for, perhaps, they thought, they could bring
about a slight change in Trudeau's attitude which would lessen the bitter-
ness of the seemingly inevitable fight between Ottawa and the provinces.
They did not remain long.

What Went Wrong?
Launched in June 1980, in an atmosphere of near celebration, the constitutional negotiations collapsed in September in an atmosphere of open
confrontation and recriminations. The nation was poised to enter upon
one of the most critical phases of its history in its search for renewal. What
went wrong?

Undoubtedly, one of the most important factors in the failure was the
reversal by the federal government of its 1980 policy towards constitutional
reform from the 1978–79 period. In response to the pressures of western
Canada and the challenge of the new separatist government in Quebec,
the 1978–79 CCMC discussions were characterized by a number of specific
constitutional proposals, the so-called best efforts drafts, which, taken
together, represented a considerable accretion in the constitutional authority of the provincial governments. Instead of resuming the 1980 dis-

cussions at the point where they were adjourned in 1979, Ottawa wiped the slate clean and proceeded in an entirely different direction. Support by Ottawa for any new measures on resources, offshore resources, and fisheries was made conditional upon agreement by the provinces to new provisions dealing with the maintenance and enhancement of the economic union. A successful resolution of this latter issue would have meant significant enhancement, rather than curtailment, of Ottawa's legislative authority. The retreat from the best effort drafts on the most controversial matters and the insertion of the new issue of the economic union, taken together, constituted a major redirection in the thrust of discussions: the devolution of central authority to the provinces had given way to the enlargement of the federal government's constitutional powers. Psychologically and politically, the majority of the provinces could not accept this position.

Unlike the other items on the agenda, the powers over the economy had not been studied in detail by the governments before 1980. All of the other concerns had been debated extensively amongst governments in one way or another since 1976 and earlier. As a consequence, there had been a significant reduction of the areas of conflict and an identification of possible areas of agreement on most matters. The dynamics of interpersonal relationships and an increasing understanding of each government's position gently nudged the negotiators in 1978–79 towards a spirit of compromise and accommodation.

There was no such history pertaining to the economic union. All governments acknowledged the importance of maintaining and enhancing the economic union in Canada, but most of the provinces argued that entrenchment would upset the balance of power between the provinces and the federal government. They urged alternative provisions which would prevent such a development. At the heart of the matter was the desire by the provincial governments to gain additional time to understand the legal and political consequences of the proposed new amendments to section 91(2), section 121, and the charter of rights. The majority of the provinces wanted the subject set aside to a future time when ramifications could have been studied or, alternatively, subscribed to Saskatchewan's idea of simply entrenching the principle of the economic union. The linkage of powers over the economy to the matters of resources, offshore resources, and fisheries was, as the leaked Kirby memorandum correctly observed, a "no win" situation for those provinces which began the 1980 discussions on the erroneous assumption that the objective of the negotiations was the devolution of federal authority.

Other developments in federal and provincial relationships indicated that constitutional negotiations were not the only area in which a new approach was being taken by the federal government to federalism. The stalled negotiations on energy pricing provided additional evidence that irreconcilable positions had emerged. Failure to obtain a quick agreement on energy was not new to Canadians since previous successful negotiations had often been preceded by protracted and acrimonious bargaining. However, the impasse in the energy negotiations between Edmonton and Ottawa which existed in the summer of 1980 resulted from an important new factor. The former Clark administration had been defeated in the House of Commons in December 1979 on a non-confidence vote on that government's first budget. One of the key aspects of that budget which spurred the opposition of Liberal and New Democratic parties was an energy pricing arrangement between Alberta and Ottawa which contained a major increase in the price of oil. The ensuing general election saw the re-election of the Liberal party, led by Pierre Trudeau, largely on that party's promise to implement a new "made in Canada" energy policy, with the clear implication that future oil prices would be lower than proposed in the December 1979 budget.

The agreement which had been negotiated with the former Clark administration was the least that the Lougheed government could accept when the unfinished business of fixing the new oil prices resumed in 1980. That was, however, too much for the newly re-elected Trudeau administration. The prime minister declared in his speech to the national Liberal party in July 1980 that his government did not believe that Canadian consumers should necessarily be obligated to pay the world price for oil and natural gas. In order to circumvent a reactive position whenever world factors forced the price for oil and natural gas upwards, his administration would introduce a new national energy policy based on the assumption that Canadian interests were first and foremost. This comprehensive energy policy would include conservation and development of "hard to get oil," which would be funded, in part, from increased revenues to the federal treasury from a greater share of the new negotiated oil price. Therefore, both governments were held hostage to these political events of late 1979 and early 1980, a factor which had not been present during the previous negotiations. The federal government had also decided upon a new interventionist energy policy, a position particularly troublesome to the Alberta government. Ottawa's retreat from the 1979 best efforts draft on resources, even though it had never been accepted by Alberta, increased the apprehension of the producing provinces that federal actions on the Constitution and energy policy would result in a significant reduction of provincial constitutional authority.

Another important factor in the ultimate failure of the 1980 constitutional exercise was the federal government's division of the agenda items into concerns of the "people" and "government powers." To provincial governments this distinction seemed superficial. In the words of Premier Blakeney, resources was "very much of a concern of the people."[49] As in 1978 the distinction implied two levels of importance in the issues. The tension produced by the creation of two lists was compounded by the federal government's unilateral determination of which items belonged in which category. The clear message for the provincial governments was that they were inferior to the federal government in the process of arranging the bargaining. Most important, however, provinces feared that, if the distinction were adopted, momentum to reform the division of powers and resolve provincial concerns would fade once the "people" items were resolved.

In an attempt to strengthen their bargaining position, the provinces tried to form common positions on all the items under review, even though some of those issues had little direct relevance to some provinces. The result was a wide-sweeping series of provincial proposals which amounted, even in the eyes of many of the premiers, to an unacceptable degree of devolution of federal authority.

The Chateau consensus, arrived at in the dying hours of the First Ministers' Conference, buttressed Ottawa's position. Although it was intended to be a defensive document in the face of impending federal action, the Chateau consensus accumulated the genuine positions of the various provinces. Together, the proposals amounted to a far greater devolution of federal authority than was ever contemplated in 1979. And, even if Ottawa had agreed to the specific proposals of the "consensus," Quebec insisted that no patriation could take place until a second, even more inclusive list of issues, was considered. However, too much emphasis should not be placed on the Chateau document as proof of the wisdom of Ottawa's overall strategy since that "consensus" was reached after most provinces realized that no agreement was possible and that a common front, any common front, might help impede the federal government in acting unilaterally.

What degree of devolution would have produced an agreement? It was apparent that Ottawa had decided that any set of proposals which significantly weakened the authority of the federal government would not lead to a settlement. Accordingly, it was necessary to return to the general strategy of 1978 under which a small list of constitutional concerns, perceived to be popular with the people, would be separated from the more complex, and more demanding, concerns of the provincial governments. In this way, the agenda would be more manageable and more acceptable to the electorate should unilateral action be undertaken. The federal government vigorously pursued this approach throughout the entire summer of 1980 even though the prime minister had indicated in June that it would not do so. Just as doggedly, the provinces sought to link all the items of the agenda with the view of settling finally on an "acceptable package."

Although the Quebec referendum on sovereignty-association had been completed, it had an ongoing impact on the constitutional process. Before the election of the Parti Québécois, federal and provincial negotiations on the Constitution and other issues were conducted exclusively in formal intergovernmental settings. The arrival of the Parti Québécois government raised doubts that traditional intergovernmental forums were the best way in which to achieve an acceptable agreement on constitutional issues. How could intergovernmental negotiations proceed when one government was dedicated to a radical and fundamental rearrangement of confederation while the other governments, although seeking a general strengthening of provincial power, were still pursuing refinement of the existing federal structure? Furthermore, Ottawa was concerned that the other provinces would support Quebec simply to strengthen their overall bargaining position.

In any event, the referendum itself had switched the focus of debate on the Constitution from the confines of the closed intergovernmental negotiating rooms to the public halls and meeting rooms of Quebec. For the first time since confederation, political leaders publicly outlined their visions of Canada and actively sought the support of the people in Quebec for their particular points of view. Thus, a new forum was created for the resolution of constitutional issues and the referendum debate only enhanced the importance of this forum. If the most nationalistic region of Canada voted to reject the position of its government, the federal government reasoned that other regions of the country would similarly oppose other radical solutions, even if proposed by their own provincial governments. Since the federal government was able to challenge and defeat the Quebec government on its own turf, perhaps it might also find out whether the people of western Canada truly wanted a constitutional provision over natural resources, as their governments alleged, which would weaken the ability of the federal government to determine price and supply in the interest of both consumer and producer? The lesson of the Quebec referendum was that the demands of provincial governments did not necessarily correspond to the wishes of the people and that Ottawa could appeal directly to the electorate to support its position. The traditional intergovernmental process, while still having an impact, lost much of its former authority. Under this analysis it was logical to separate the objectives of the provincial governments from the objectives of the people, as demonstrated by the designation of "people" issues and "government power" issues.

Finally, since the meaning of the Quebec referendum could not be agreed upon by Ottawa and Quebec City, there remained, in respect of most issues, two fundamentally opposed positions. For the Parti Québécois government, the result of the referendum meant that the federal government had promised a substantial revision to most of the present provisions of the British North America Act. For Ottawa, notwithstanding the prime minister's assessment on 21 May in the House of Commons, the result of the referendum was a mandate for patriation of the Constitution with an amending formula and entrenched charter of rights with language provisions. To the prime minister, the people of Quebec had endorsed a strong, united Canada and rejected any approach which would weaken the federal government. Disagreement over interpretation infected consideration of

all of the items on the agenda, particularly language rights and the preamble. Anything offered by Ottawa was too little for Quebec, and anything
requested by Quebec was too much for Ottawa. In effect, the government
of Quebec dared Ottawa to adjust the federal system to the degree required, while the federal government, led by a man who also claimed to
know the aspirations of that province, challenged the Parti Québécois to
abandon its political objectives and endorse the principle of a united
Canada. Notwithstanding the referendum, the battle for the hearts and
minds of residents of the province of Quebec had not yet been settled.

Faced with all of these factors, the majority of provinces gravitated to
a common front which included Quebec even though many harboured
deep reservations about its motives. A determined federal government,
displaying a new bravado, relentlessly pursued its timetable, its agenda,
and its priorities. There was no real basis on which to seek common
ground between these extremes. There was no mediator or arbitrator. Each
side was confident that ultimately its position would succeed. In less than
four months, Canadians had travelled from near celebration to open confrontation.

Notes

1. *House of Commons Debates*, 32nd Parliament, 1st Session, 2: 1261–68 (21 May
   1980).
2. *Ibid.*, at 1265.
3. Letter from A.E. Blakeney, premier of Saskatchewan, to Pierre Trudeau, 16 May
   1980, at 1.
4. Telex from Michael Kirby, secretary to the Cabinet for federal–provincial relations, to Howard Leeson, deputy minister of intergovernmental affairs of Saskatchewan, 6 June 1980.
5. *House of Commons Debates*, 32nd Parliament, 1st Session, 11: 1977 (10 June
   1980).
6. Task Force on Canadian Unity, *A Future Together*, Recommendation 20.
7. This meeting was held in Ottawa on 28 September 1979 between Joe Clark,
   prime minister, and the leadership of the National Indian Brotherhood, the
   Inuit Committee on National Issues, and the Native Council of Canada.
8. The meeting took place in Ottawa on 26 August 1980 between a Subcommittee
   of the CCMC—comprised of J. Chrétien (Canada), R. Romanow (Saskatchewan), G. Mercier (Manitoba), and R. Johnston (Alberta)—and native leaders
   Del Riley, president of the Nation Indian Brotherhood, Charlie Watt and John
   Amagoalik, co-chairpersons of the Inuit Committee on National Issues, and
   Harry Daniels, president of the Native Council of Canada.
9. *Opening Statement by Jean Chrétien*, Montreal, 8 July 1980, C.I.C.S. Doc. 830-
   81/005, at 1.
10. Speech by Pierre Trudeau, prime minister, to the National Convention of the
    Liberal Party of Canada, Winnipeg, 4 July 1980, at 7.
11. *Supra*, note 9, at 2–4.

12. *Supra*, note 9, at 3.
13. Canada, *Powers Over the Economy: Securing the Canadian Economic Union in the Constitution*, Montreal, 9 July 1980, C.I.C.S. Doc. 830-81/036, at 6.
14. Section 121 states, "All Articles of the Growth, Produce, or Manufacture of any one of the Provinces shall, from and after the Union, be admitted free into each of the other Provinces."
15. *Supra*, note 13, at 16.
16. *Murphy v. C.P.R. and Attorney General of Canada*, [1958] 1 S.C.R. 626, 15 D.L.R. (2d) 145.
17. *Supra*, note 13, at 17.
18. *Ibid.*, at 18.
19. *Ibid.*, at 19.
20. *Ibid.*, at 21.
21. In *Labatt Breweries of Canada Ltd. v. Attorney General of Canada*, [1980] 1 S.C.R. 914, 110 D.L.R. (3d) 594, the Supreme Court of Canada found ss. 6 and 25(1)(c) of the Food and Drugs Act, R.S.C. 1970, c. F-27, to be unconstitutional. The majority judgment found no federal jurisdiction in this case under the British North America Act head "The Regulations of Trade and Commerce." The third proposal would have the effect of overcoming that decision.
22. Quebec, *Notes for a Speech on Powers Affecting the Economy*, Montreal, 9 July 1980, C.I.C.S. 830-81/021, at 2.
23. The government of Canada submitted a draft text, *Options Submitted for Consideration by the Government of Canada to Safeguard the Canadian Economic Union in the Constitution*, Toronto, 15 July 1980, C.I.C.S. Doc. 830-82/007.
24. Saskatchewan, *Draft Text on the Canadian Economic Union*, Vancouver, 23 July 1980, C.I.C.S. Doc. 830-83/004.
25. Saskatchewan, *Discussion Paper on Securing the Canadian Economic Union*, Vancouver, 22–25 July 1980, C.I.C.S. Doc. 830-83/003, at 3.
26. *Ibid.*
27. *Statement by Jean Chrétien, Minister of Justice, on Offshore Resources*, Montreal, 9 July 1980, C.I.C.S. Doc. 830-81/023.
28. This argument was outlined in a Newfoundland position paper, *Towards the Twenty-First Century—Together* by Brian Peckford, premier and minister for intergovernmental affairs, 18 August 1980, at 20 and 21. The government of Newfoundland later referred the question of offshore ownership to the Newfoundland court of appeal on 12 February 1982. See *Reference Re Mineral and Other Natural Resources of the Continental Shelf* (1983), 145 D.L.R. (3d) 9 (Nfld. C.A.)
29. *Statement by Jean Chrétien, Minister of Finance, on Fisheries*, Montreal, 8 July 1980, C.I.C.S. Doc. 830-81/015.
30. Canada, *Proposed Text of the Canadian Charter of Rights and Freedoms and Background Notes*, Montreal, 8 July 1980, C.I.C.S. Doc. 830-81/027.
31. Quebec, *Notes for a Statement on Communications*, Montreal, 8–11 July 1980, C.I.C.S. Doc. 830-81/011, at 1–2.

32. Quebec, *Notes for a Statement on the Senate*, Montreal, 8 July 1980, C.I.C.S. Doc. 830-81/016.

33. Quebec, *Notes for a Statement on the Supreme Court of Canada*, Montreal, 8 July 1980, C.I.C.S. Doc. 830-81/032, at 2.

34. The Task Force on Canadian Unity, in *A Future Together*, recommended at 101 that duality be reflected on the Supreme Court but, unlike the position of the Quebec government, which stressed the difference between the common law and civil law systems as its rationale for duality, the task force, in part, based its recommendations on the distinctive cultural aspects of Quebec society.

35. Quebec, *Notes for a Statement on Family Law*, Montreal, 8 July 1980, C.I.C.S. Doc. 830-81/017.

36. Quebec, *Notes for a Statement on Equalization and Regional Disparities*, Montreal, 8 July 1980, C.I.C.S. Doc. 830-81/020, at 4.

37. *Statement by Jean Chrétien, Minister of Justice, on the Statement of Principles*, Montreal, 9 July 1980, C.I.C.S. Doc. 830-81/031. The proposed text of the statement was the same as that tabled in the House of Commons on 10 June 1980. See *supra*, note 5.

38. Letter by Pierre Trudeau, prime minister, 11 July 1980, at 2. This letter was submitted to the newspapers of Quebec. In it Trudeau defended the first words of his government's proposed statement of principles. In his covering letter to the editors, Trudeau declared that the debate was more than a semantic one since "what is at stake is the very conception of the country which we want to build together." The letter was widely published throughout Quebec.

39. *Ibid.*, at 3.

40. Canada, *Proposals for a Preamble to the Constitution*, Ottawa, 26 August 1980, C.I.C.S. Doc. 830-84/015, at 1–2.

41. *Statement by Jean Chrétien, Minister of Justice, on the Patriation of the Constitution*, Montreal, 9 July 1980, C.I.C.S. Doc. 830-81/029, at 1.

42. Quebec, *Position on Patriation and the Amending Formula*, Montreal, 8–11 July 1980, C.I.C.S. Doc. 830-82/004, at 2.

43. *Ibid.*

44. Final communiqué of the Twenty-First Annual Premiers' Conference, Winnipeg, 24 August 1980.

45. Federal–Provincial Relation's Office, *Report to Cabinet on Constitutional Discussions, Summer 1980, and the Outlook for the First Ministers' Conference and Beyond* (30 August 1980). The paper was prepared by officials involved in the constitutional negotiations, under the direction of the FPRO and the Department of Justice.

46. *Ibid.*, at 34.

47. *Ibid.*, at 3.

48. Transcript of the prime minister's news conference held in the National Press Theatre, Ottawa, 30 January 1981, at 5–6.

49. A. E. Blakeney, premier of Saskatchewan, *Notes for an Opening Statement to the First Ministers' Conference*, 8–12 September 1980, at 4.

Chapter 4
The Year of Confrontation

After the failure of the September First Ministers' Conference, most provincial governments expected some form of unilateral action. Both the
leaked Pitfield and Kirby memoranda had referred to this option in the
event of failure in September. The precise nature of that action was unclear
before 2 October 1980. In general, however, the provinces believed that
unilateral action would involve an amending formula based on the Victoria
Charter and an entrenched charter of rights applying only to the federal
government with an opt-in provision for provinces. Provincial reaction
would undoubtedly have been negative but would not have provoked the
degree of protest inevitable in a federal attempt to bind the provinces to a
charter or impose substantive provisions.

Unilateralism, 2 October 1980

On 2 October 1980 the federal government unveiled its proposed joint
resolution for patriation and reform of the Constitution. The key features
of the resolution were an amending formula, a charter of rights which
applied to both orders of government, and a commitment to the principles
of equalization and the reduction of regional disparities. The most dramatic change from September was the introduction of a referendum
mechanism as an alternative device by which future constitutional amendments could be approved. The idea and the details of a referendum as a
way to amend the Constitution had never been debated by the CCMC or
the first ministers before its appearance in the resolution. The proposed
referendum could be initiated by resolutions of both Houses of Parliament.
In order to succeed, it would need the approval of a majority of voters in
the same combination of provinces whose consent was required by the
amending formula under the Victoria Charter. The other amendment
procedure set out in the resolution was based on obtaining approvals of
Parliament and provincial legislatures in the number and distribution as
set out under the Victoria Charter.

Since under the proposal the federal government alone possessed the power to frame the referendum question and set rules for the subsequent campaign, there seemed little doubt of the referendum's potential to alter the balance of federalism to lessen the role of provincial governments.

The Progressive Conservatives React

The federal Progressive Conservatives were in an unenviable position. Structurally, as the official opposition, they were compelled to oppose the resolution and the process of unilateralism. As well, Joe Clark desperately needed a high-profile political issue to resurrect his hopes of continuing to head a party now totally demoralized by the results of the February election and at odds with itself. Finally, the majority of Progressive Conservative provincial governments and parties were opposed to the proposed joint resolution, making the decision for federal Conservatives easier. This was especially so in light of the western base of the federal caucus. The major problem, however, lay in the position taken by the Progressive Conservative government of Ontario, which supported the federal government's actions on both constitutional patriation and on the energy issues.

The position of Ontario was crucial to the federal government since it allowed Trudeau to argue convincingly that he, more than Lévesque, represented Quebec; he could further argue, as he did, that the provinces with a majority of the population in the country were behind him. As a bonus, both provinces were represented by the two major political parties. A favourable response by Davis was, therefore, vital to Ottawa's interests.

Davis's position was based on Ontario's interests and the major economic issues. Only one aspect of the constitutional question, official bilingualism, posed any political problem for his government. The extension of section 133 to Ontario would have been politically unacceptable. However, once that danger was settled, the Conservatives in Ontario could adopt a stance on the Constitution consonant with their position in confederation. Ottawa and Queen's Park were on the same side with respect to the economic issues. They understood the need to combat the potentially disruptive force of new regional wealth through emphasis on constitutional provisions which "perfected" the economic union and emphasized "national" symbols that would further reinforce the preeminent position of central Canada. There was little to decide; given the looming debates on the national energy program,[1] Ontario was firmly in support of the federal proposal.

This caused trouble for Joe Clark. He had attempted to reconcile the economic and constitutional interests of Conservative Ontario and Conservative Alberta during his short time as prime minister. His government had floundered on that attempt; it had failed to reconcile Ontario's interests with the regionalist demands with respect to oil pricing, offshore resources, and resource management. In all three cases, Clark chose to champion the interests of the hinterlands, eventually sealing his electoral fate in Ontario.

The Provinces React

For Alberta, British Columbia, and Newfoundland the battle on the federal resolution represented a clear fight between the new wealth of the hinterland and the old wealth of the centre. Quebec also opposed it for obvious reasons. The position of Nova Scotia was unclear for several months, but it eventually joined the opposition when negotiations between itself and the federal government on the revenue and administration of offshore energy resources broke down.

New Brunswick and Manitoba were in similar positions: both had long been considered "tails" of the Ontario economy, more intimately bound to central Canada than to the outlying resource provinces. In addition, there were other powerful social and cultural reasons for both to support the federal initiative. New Brunswick, after some brief hesitation, announced its support for the resolution.

Manitoba's response was negative, reflecting its ambiguous position within confederation. On the one hand, Manitoba had always had strong links to Ontario and to central Canada; on the other, it was obviously a "western" province. For a variety of personal and political reasons, including Premier Sterling Lyon's reaction to "that man" Trudeau, Manitoba chose to oppose the resolution.

Prince Edward Island also decided to oppose the federal action, though it was obvious that the government's heart was not in the decision. Caught between sizable transfer payments from Ottawa, and Conservative party ties, the political economy of the island dictated no clear position. Reluctantly, the government chose to emphasize its fraternal connections with the federal Conservative party and the opposing provinces. The decision taken by New Brunswick and Nova Scotia not to oppose Trudeau made that choice a difficult one for Prince Edward Island.

The Split in the New Democratic Party

In understanding the differences which developed between the federal New Democratic Party and the New Democratic government of Saskatchewan, two important traditions in the NDP need to be examined: its commitment to centralism, and its commitment to socialism. The party has had a long history of belief in the wisdom of positive intervention by the state into the economic life of the nation. The Regina Manifesto of 1933 is filled with references to such matters as "national" planning agencies, "national" interest, "national" investment boards, and "national" labour codes. While recognizing the rights of linguistic and cultural minorities, its stance was to call for a centralized state, with broad powers to intervene in national economic life. Throughout its history the CCF, and its successor the NDP, maintained in varying degrees the commitment to centralized planning. One of the important by-products of that emphasis, however, was that the orientation of the party became anglophone. Unable to comprehend the nuances of Quebec politics, and unwilling to alter its centralist concept of Canadian federalism to accommodate that province's demand for legislative authority, the party remained a minor actor in Quebec, with little direct influence from Quebec citizens, and, as a necessary consequence, a third party in Canada.

The party's orientation had undergone some changes in the 1970s, as it became more successful at the provincial level, but seemed further and further away from power in Ottawa. Young New Democrats were attracted into provincial governments elected in Manitoba, Saskatchewan, and British Columbia, as opportunities to put their ideas into practice arose. This produced a change of focus in the party. Furthermore, the importance of provincial legislative jurisdiction, especially to western Canada, where resource revenues and management were major issues, became increasingly evident, until there was a substantial body of opinion in the provincial party favouring a more decentralized form of planning for Canada. Decentralist New Democrats embraced a "many roads to socialism" view. By 1980, therefore, there was not likely to be a homogeneous body of opinion in the party on an issue such as the unilateral patriation and amendment of the British North America Act.

The second characteristic relevant to the NDP's response was the party's commitment to democratic socialism. There was clearly a body of opinion opposed to creating the liberal individualist society through entrenchment of a charter of rights; however, most NDP members, committed to human rights and to equality, held the contrary point of view. Having never been in office, and having witnessed the unfettered power of the state from the vantage point of a third party, the majority of the party firmly supported the entrenchment of a charter of rights. The perceived enhancement of native's and women's rights provided further support for the entrenchment of a charter.

The competing commitments to regionalism and nationalism, liberalism and socialism were further complicated by the personalities of those directly involved. The two chief actors were Ed Broadbent, federal leader of the NDP, and Allan Blakeney, premier of Saskatchewan. Ed Broadbent's approach to the Constitution was fairly straightforward: he believed in the need for central economic planning, abhorred Lougheed-style regionalism, was committed to a charter of rights, and saw nothing wrong with unilateral action on the Constitution if an agreement were unattainable. He recognized that the process might be distasteful to a number of provincial governments but thought that the end certainly justified the means in this case. Broadbent knew that supporting Trudeau would not be popular in the West, and he knew that westerners would require concessions in any unilateral patriation, particularly on the question of resources. Still, in the light of his ideas of Canada, he would recoil from the sort of decentralization of powers proposed by some of the premiers and welcome Trudeau's plan to patriate without making those sorts of concessions.

In many ways Allan Blakeney presented a marked contrast to Broadbent: he was a curious mixture of socialism and red toryism. Blakeney's political style was to combine a mastery of facts and arguments, highly principled analyses of issues, and political bravery. These attributes were evident in his position on entrenchment. He was obviously out of step with a majority of the federal party and opposed an entrenched charter on carefully reasoned grounds. Entrenchment would transfer political power to the courts, which were generally conservative and would oppose redistribution of power and wealth in society. No democratic socialist, he argued, should voluntarily hand power from the political forum, where the policies of the majority find expression, to the judicial forum. Unarticulated, but no less real, were his loyalties to the British parliamentary system, based on the supremacy of Parliament. These factors made Blakeney a resolute foe of an entrenched charter of rights, and therefore, surprisingly, an ally of Sterling Lyon.

More importantly, without abandoning his notions of "balanced federalism" in Canada, Blakeney had become a convinced advocate of provincial economic initiative, as witnessed by Saskatchewan's establishment of provincial crown resource corporations and enactment of legislation pertaining to resource management and taxation. He was not a fervent decentralist but a pragmatic provincialist—one who understood that New Democrats had to use the governments that they controlled now. This made more sense than adding powers to the federal level, in the hope that the New Democratic Party would someday form the government of Canada. Furthermore, Blakeney was a federalist who believed that the interests of the people were served through regional governments, elected by people with a common regional perspective. In that sense, Blakeney was an ally of the western region's economic and social elite. However, in Saskatchewan, such people played only a minor role; while they supported him on this issue, they did not form part of the political support for the NDP in Saskatchewan. In sum, Blakeney was a moderate regionalist in his approach to constitutional reform, someone who displayed an astute understanding of Canada as a whole, of its dual linguistic heritage and of its regional strengths and differences.

While Blakeney believed that Ottawa could legally proceed to patriate the Constitution unilaterally, he believed that it should not, and certainly not without a Supreme Court ruling. At the centre of his calculations, therefore, was a fear that, once launched, there was little hope of completely blocking the federal initiative. One either prevented the federal government from proceeding, or one bargained the contents of such an action on the assumption that it could be delayed, but not stopped. He was, as most knew him, someone who would bargain tenaciously for whatever small portion could be secured in negotiation, settling for half a loaf without a qualm, and a quarter-loaf if need be. It was this last calculation which left Saskatchewan "fighting for change," long after most others had chosen a side.

It was part of the problem for the NDP, as it was for the Progressive Conservatives, that neither the federal nor provincial parties were homogeneous in opinion. Within the federal party itself there were both members of Parliament and advisors who differed from Broadbent's position. In particular, Lorne Nystrom, the party's critic for federal–provincial relations, was strongly against aligning the NDP with Trudeau on the question of unilateral action. He, and three other Saskatchewan members publicly opposed the position of their caucus. Grant Notley, leader of the opposition in Alberta, also vigorously opposed any support for the proposed federal resolution. By contrast, Dave Barrett, former premier of British Columbia, had little time for the issue, and wanted to keep it "east of the mountains." When that proved impossible, he adopted a strategy of support for the position of the federal caucus, partly because it put him in opposition to Bennett, and partly because he thought that it would more quickly remove the issue from the stage. Howard Pawley, then leader of the opposition in Manitoba, adroitly chose not to become identified with the issue, leaving Sterling Lyon to use opposition to the federal action as a platform.

The varying positions adopted within the NDP reflected growing ideological discord: the "liberals" in the party were at odds with the old-line socialists; those who adhered to dreams of national power collided with those who had governed at the provincial level. As if mirroring Canada itself, the NDP broke into factions, suffering the same internal anguish as did the country as a whole.

Thus, all three of Canada's major political parties were split internally over the issue of the Constitution. The Quebec Liberal party differed dramatically from the federal Liberals on unilateral action, causing considerable ill feeling in the period prior to the provincial election. The party system, as well as the federal system, was placed under severe strain by Ottawa's action.

The Premiers Meet and Divide

When the premiers assembled in Toronto on 14 October 1980 to assess their situation in light of the federal government's unilateral action, it was already obvious that no common position could be found; most had conceded this likelihood before journeying to Toronto. The meeting was symbolic of what had transpired in Canada during the previous decade. Increasingly, the regions and Quebec had come into confrontation with the centre, Ontario and the federal government. The issues had varied, but attitudes had hardened by October. At the end of their session, three separate press conferences identified the three distinct positions of the group and mirrored the growing polarization within the nation. Ontario announced its support for the resolution while the others, with the exception of New Brunswick, Nova Scotia, and Saskatchewan, declared their opposition. Nova Scotia, under considerable pressure to join the six dissenting provinces, refused to declare publicly its position. Saskatchewan's position was characterized by the phrase "fighting for change." New Brunswick announced its support for the federal action only one day after the 14 October meeting.

Confrontation in the Commons

Although the federal government's initiative created much less public controversy than some politicians had expected, the House of Commons, nevertheless, was the scene of a highly polarized, frequently bitter debate over the proposed resolution. The federal government's objective of forwarding the resolution to Westminster by January 1981, coupled with its plans to implement the new national energy program and alterations to established financing arrangements, dictated the necessity for a carefully controlled strategy with strict deadlines for the House of Commons. The Conservative caucus, although divided on the substance of the proposed resolution, sought to counter this strategy by mounting a determined and protracted debate against the unilateral process employed by the government. The federal NDP had decided to support the package in principle if the government agreed to incorporate a section into the resolution which enhanced provincial legislative jurisdiction over natural resources. Since the government of Saskatchewan and the federal government had embarked upon secret, bilateral negotiations with respect to the elements of such a provision, the caucus' position was somewhat muted but still favoured the position of the government.

One of the most important aspects of the federal government's strategy was to obtain the approval of the House of Commons for the resolution as quickly as possible and refer it to a joint parliamentary committee for detailed study. This strategy would shift the political limelight from the glare of intensive debate in the Commons to the more tranquil circumstances of committee consideration. This could only be accomplished through the invocation of closure which came three weeks after the resolution was introduced.[2] It was also proposed that the committee report back to the Commons by 9 December 1980. If this goal were to be reached, there could be no public hearings. This decision and timetable fuelled the official opposition with additional arguments for blocking quick passage of the resolution. Ultimately the opposition forced the government to permit both public hearings and the televising of the proceedings. Public response to the committee hearings coupled with persistent pressure from both opposition parties forced the government to extend the committee's mandate[3] with the result that the government's January objective for final passage of the resolution was not met.

A significant feature of the work of the Joint Parliamentary Committee is that, of a total of twenty-two amendments proposed by the members of the Progressive Conservative caucus, seven were accepted by the government members and were reflected in the final report, while only two of forty-three moved by the NDP members were accepted. The chronicle of the constitutional debate is replete with ironies and contradictions of which one is that the party which so adamantly and forcefully opposed the resolution played such an important part in shaping its formation.

When the committee reported to the full House on 13 February 1981, the federal government was still determined to complete the process in Canada as quickly as possible. But this time the original six dissenting provinces had initiated references on the constitutionality of the proposed federal resolution to the courts of appeal of Manitoba, Quebec, and New-foundland. It was obvious that an appeal to the Supreme Court of Canada was inevitable. The January deadline elapsed but the federal government's resolve to pass the resolution quickly, especially in light of the growing opposition of the provinces, did not. The new issue arose in the House: should Parliament deal with the proposed resolution before the Supreme Court of Canada rendered its judgment? The Conservatives, emboldened by the success of their strategy to date, and supported by the dissenting provinces, relentlessly argued for the postponement of consideration of the resolution until the decision and, in effect, stopped the proceedings of the House.

Frustrated by the filibustering of the official opposition and appre-hensive that patriation would be greatly delayed, life in the Commons became even more than usually exasperating for the government. The original dissenting provinces were joined first by Nova Scotia and then by Saskatchewan, adding their voices in protest to the resolution. The eight provinces then demanded an early meeting to discuss the "Provincial Patriation Plan." Trudeau summed up the government's frustration: "First it was delay because of the substance, then it was delay because of the process, then it was delay because of the courts, and now it is delay because of the premiers."[4]

On 31 March 1981, the Newfoundland court of appeal delivered its judgment on the constitutional legality of the proposed federal action.[5] In a unanimous judgment the court ruled the federal proposal illegal, putting an end to federal government plans to proceed before the Supreme Court had heard the appeals, and unwittingly provided the instrument which would resolve the parliamentary impasse. All parties agreed to postpone further consideration of the resolution until after the appeal to the Supreme Court had been decided. The House would vote on the resolution within forty-eight hours after its reintroduction. However, if any changes were introduced, there would be no time limit for the debate, an important feature which would reduce the options available to the government.

The National Energy Program

In addition to the confrontation in Parliament over the resolution, the federal government introduced its comprehensive new energy program on 28 October 1980, which had a considerable impact on the constitutional debate. The oil-pricing agreement between the producing provinces and Ottawa had expired on 30 June 1980. A month earlier Alberta had enacted a new law which placed extraordinary power in the hands of its Executive Council to regulate the production of the province's oil. When no progress had been made in the negotiations on a new price, Alberta unilaterally raised the price of its crude oil. The prospect of a new federal export tax on natural gas encouraged British Columbia, an important producer of the commodity, to support Alberta in its general position.

The national energy program set out three objectives. The first was security of supply, to make Canada self-sufficient in oil by 1990. The second was to provide Canadians with an opportunity to participate in the energy industry and to share in the benefits of the expected expansion of the industry through a "Canadianization" of the industry. The third was to attain a better petroleum-pricing and revenue-sharing regime for the government of Canada. The national energy program proposed increases in the wellhead price for conventional oil until it reached parity with "the reference price." The costs of subsidizing oil imports for eastern Canada would be gradually shifted from the federal treasury to the consumer. In the absence of an agreement with the producing provinces, the program imposed a new pricing and revenue-sharing regime upon the producing provinces under the terms of the Petroleum Administration Act[6]; such a regime had never been imposed since the Act was presented in 1974. A related feature of the budget, which never materialized, was a $4 billion Western Canadian Economic fund, intended to finance a series of economic development programs in the four western provinces.

Several new energy measures were also unveiled. The most important of these was a new natural gas and gas liquids tax which was levied on all natural gas sales in Canada, including those destined to the export market. A new petroleum and gas revenue tax was announced. Ottawa's share of the export tax on oil, however, was reduced to 50 percent of the revenues.

The objective of Canadianization was to increase the percentage of Canadian ownership of oil and gas production in Canada to 50 percent by 1990. To aid the process, special exploration and development incentives were announced for companies in the "Canada lands" of the North and for Canadian companies in the South.

Ottawa's treasury was a major beneficiary of the program since it would collect 24 percent of all the revenues from oil and gas production over the period 1980-83 as compared with 17 percent under the ill-fated Clark proposals. In real dollars, it was projected that the federal treasury would receive $24 billion during this period. Under the Clark proposal, the revenues of the producing provinces were assured through yearly wellhead price increases. Under the national energy program, however, a large portion of provincial revenues would be dependent upon the uncertain foreign market which, as subsequent events unfolded, again proved to be extremely unpredictable. Furthermore, Trudeau's proposals included a gradual reduction in oil exports, resulting in a further loss of income for the producing provinces.

Alberta's reaction was outlined by Lougheed in a television and radio address to the province on 30 October 1980. Effective 1 February 1981 the Alberta government would decrease oil production by 60,000 barrels per day, followed by further cutbacks of 60,000 barrels per day on 1 May and 1 August 1981. The order to cutback would be rescinded only if negotiations on oil pricing resumed or if a serious shortage of oil supplies occurred in Canada. Alberta would take other steps such as a court challenge to the constitutionality of the proposed federal tax on natural gas sales on the basis that section 125 of the British North America Act prevented one level of government from taxing another. It would postpone the Cold Lake and Alsands oil projects and launch a national advertising campaign to explain its case to all Canadians. Alberta's hostility was reflected in the premier's description of the program as "an outright attempt to take over the resources of this province, owned by each of you, as Albertans." Lougheed identified the province's policies in natural resources as the reason for its economic success:

> At the same time—when we look at motives—we have the constitution proposals that are before this country. I am concerned—as I have expressed on other occasions—that those constitutional proposals through an amending formula make Albertans and provinces, other than Ontario and Quebec, into second class citizens by permitting amendments to the constitution that could complete the takeover of our resources which are now being engineered on a pricing and taxation basis.[7]

Lougheed defiantly declared that his government would not be deterred in its objectives since ". . . what is involved is a matter of principle, a matter of federal government trying to change the rules that we have abided by in the Confederation for so long. They are trying to change the rules because we are winning for a short period of time, so to speak."[8] British Columbia joined Alberta in its opposition to the program and, like Alberta, withheld payment of the new taxes.

Saskatchewan generally supported Alberta's position but decided that, since its production of oil was small by comparison, it would be impractical to cut production. The province decided instead to monitor Alberta's constitutional challenge of section 125 of the British North America Act, 1867[9] and to explore its own legal options. In the meantime, the Saskatchewan government stressed that the fixing of the oil prices rendered the proposed constitutional amendments over natural resources, agreed to by Broadbent and Trudeau, meaningless.

The energy dispute added vigour and new dimensions to the constitutional conflict. The two disputes were inextricably linked, and everyone understood that the resolution of one depended on the other. Negotiation on the Constitution, therefore, was doubly difficult for provinces, such as Saskatchewan which were intimately involved in the energy pricing negotiations.

Ottawa Negotiates with the NDP and with Saskatchewan

Trudeau had sounded out Broadbent about his unilateral action on the Constitution in the spring of 1980, but the NDP leader had been ambivalent, insisting that there must be a genuine effort to achieve an agreement with the provinces. By late September, after the acrimonious collapse of the First Ministers' Conference, he was more amenable to suggestions that the federal government act without provincial approval.

Trudeau and Broadbent met on 1 October 1980, at which time the elements of the proposed resolution, to be tabled the next day, were explained to the NDP leader. He was requested to endorse the resolution publicly. Broadbent, while generally satisfied with the contents, especially the charter, insisted that his support was conditional upon the federal government's agreeing to a section which would confirm and enhance provincial legislative jurisdiction over natural resources. Since most of the federal NDP caucus was elected from western Canada, it was highly important to the party's position that this provision be added. Trudeau's acceptance of a natural resources section would permit the federal NDP to avoid being caught on only one side of the constitutional debate. The party could both support the charter, which was expected to be popular in Ontario, and engineer a constitutional confirmation of provincial jurisdiction over natural resources, which would be popular in the West. It was an imaginative attempt at making the contents attractive enough to outweigh the risk of a backlash to federal unilateral action.

The provincial leaders of the NDP were then contacted by Broadbent who explained, in general terms, the provisions of the proposed resolution as they were explained to him by the prime minister. Most of the provincial leaders concurred with Broadbent's strategy. However, the approval of Blakeney, the only NDP leader in power, whose government depended on a satisfactory resolution of the resources question, was pivotal to the success of the strategy.

Blakeney's reaction to the proposed solution, with a natural resources section incorporated, was ambivalent. First, he did not like to have someone else negotiating for the province, particularly when the legal issues were so highly complex and of central importance to Saskatchewan. Second, it bothered him that the federal government seemed to have so little interest in negotiating directly with the provincial government. Third, he was uncertain how to react to a unilateral federal initiative, believing that such action was wrong according to constitutional convention but possibly correct according to law. The legal ambiguity confirmed his preference for concentrating on the substance of the package, especially as it related to resources and the referendum in the amending formula. Considering the substance of the resolution, with the proposed addition on resources, he concluded that, for the time being, he was compelled to reserve his decision.

This position was reinforced by his own conviction, which was not substantially shaken until late November, that Trudeau was using the unilateral action to force a "centre group" of premiers to coalesce around a moderate compromise. His "fighting for change" posture seemed to him, therefore, to provide maximum opportunity to participate in such a moderate group.

The precise shape of the future amendments Ottawa would be willing to make to the resolution, especially with respect to the referendum and resources, was initially defined during a telephone conversation between Trudeau and Blakeney on 7 October 1980. Blakeney began by strongly urging that the equalization section be strengthened and that the amending formula be changed to enhance Prince Edward Island's role by removing the 50 percent population requirement of the formula. He also wanted provincial concurrency on international trade and commerce with respect to resources and a removal of the referendum provisions. Although Trudeau indicated a willingness to accept some changes to equalization and the amending formula, his government apparently was wedded to the principle of the referendum and, furthermore, was opposed to granting the provinces any access to the device. Moreover, the proposed natural resources section would not likely be amended to restrict the unqualified federal paramountcy over interprovincial trade and commerce and grant concurrent admission to the international side of the trade power. The two men agreed to have their ministers meet on these matters. That week

Romanow and a team of officials were dispatched to Ottawa to negotiate with the federal government.

A series of meetings was held in Ottawa in October in which Saskatchewan's representatives went through a list of changes, including amendments to the charter of rights. Chrétien and the federal officials listened patiently, although Chrétien regarded many of the changes to be no more than technical and of no political significance. He instructed his officials to meet with Saskatchewan officials to come to an agreement. Since his assumption about the political insignificance of some of Saskatchewan's proposals was wrong, agreements between the officials with respect to the charter were never reached.

On the issues of the referendum and resources, discussions were lengthy and detailed, but Ottawa made virtually no concessions at these early meetings. In respect of jurisdiction over resources, the two sides reviewed the proposed Trudeau–Broadbent agreement. It was essentially the same as the one presented by the federal government to the premiers during the First Ministers' Conference in September. The proposal was for a separate section numbered 92A and headed "Non-Renewable Natural Resources, Forestry Resources and Electrical Energy" to be inserted into the British North America Act. The section would contain the following terms: Under the first subsection the provinces would be granted exclusive jurisdiction over the exploration, development, conservation, and management of non-renewable natural resources, forests, and generation of electricity. The next subsection would admit the provinces to the field of interprovincial trade in resources, with a non-discrimination clause that was virtually identical to that which appeared before the first ministers and was debated by the CCMC. The third subsection established unqualified federal paramountcy in the event of conflicting interprovincial trade laws. As such, it too, was identical to the provision of the First Ministers' Conference. The fourth provision permitted the provinces to levy both direct and indirect taxes on resource production, subject to a non-discrimination provision. The fifth and sixth subsections and the schedule of resources to be covered by the amendment were identical to the provisions submitted during the First Ministers' Conference except that the reference to "uranium and thorium" had been deleted from the schedule.

The Saskatchewan representatives proposed two major amendments to this proposal. The first one was the addition of the "tag end" words to the first subsection to ensure that provincial regulation of a resource sold outside the province would not be invalid merely because it affected interprovincial or international trade. The tag end words suggested were: ". . . and such legislation shall not be invalid merely because part or all of the product may enter interprovincial or international trade." The federal government negotiators rejected Saskatchewan's demands on this issue, arguing that the clause would have the effect of granting provinces jurisdiction over trade and commerce albeit unintentionally and would exclude the federal government from that area. Since the section in question did not relate to trade and commerce but to "exploration, development, conservation and management" in the province, this would not likely have been the interpretation of the tag end. The sole purpose of the tag end was to prevent the courts from concluding that incidental and consequential trade effects of provincial legislation transformed development legislation to trade legislation.

The second Saskatchewan amendment would have admitted the provinces to concurrent jurisdiction in international, as well as interprovincial, trade and commerce by deleting the words ". . . to another part of Canada" in the second subsection of the proposed amendment. Instead of granting the provinces concurrent access to international trade and commerce, the federal government suggested either a legislative amendment or an administrative arrangement to satisfy Saskatchewan's concerns. Although Saskatchewan was not completely disinterested in the possibility of a delegation of regulation-making authority from Parliament over international trade, this proposal was not explored.

The talks made it clear that the federal government was not interested in altering the Trudeau–Broadbent agreement by limiting federal paramountcy in the area of interprovincial trade; it was not interested in accepting the compelling national interest test from the 1978–79 round of talks, nor the requirement for a parliamentary declaration as a prerequisite to the exercise of federal paramountcy claims.

The federal government was just as adamant on its unwillingness to change the referendum provision of the amending formula. Not only was Chrétien unwilling to consider substantial changes; he indicated that even minor changes were unlikely to be accepted. The Saskatchewan delegation was upset by the apparent unwillingness of the federal government to consider any changes to the resolution. At this time the federal government still had considerable momentum, and was extremely confident. It seemed interested in playing at negotiation to increase the internal disunity of the NDP. These early negotiations came to nothing.

On 30 October 1980 Prime Minister Trudeau, while in Regina for other purposes, met Premier Blakeney to discuss a variety of matters pertaining to the Constitution. During this meeting, the prime minister told the premier that he would not accept the "tag end" to the first subsection nor the inclusion of "uranium or thorium" to the Schedule. Again administrative arrangements with regard to international trade were proposed, but this time the prime minister introduced a new wrinkle: perhaps these should not be considered until the second phase of constitutional negotiations.

The referendum proposal afforded little common ground, and Premier Blakeney had been quick to set out his objections to it. In a speech at

Dalhousie on 27 October 1980, he characterized the referendum in the following manner:

> The process could be used to by-pass totally the provincial legislatures. . . .
> The process permits a referendum where *provincial* legislatures fail to agree but does not provide for a referendum where *Parliament* fails to agree to a proposal for constitutional amendment passed by all the provincial legislatures. It is a way to temper provincial intransigence, but not federal intransigence.[10]

What the Saskatchewan government did not fully appreciate was that the referendum procedure had become, somewhat belatedly, an inviolable section of the resolution. This point became clear when Ottawa rejected a request for change to the referendum from Premier Davis, who urged that provinces be allowed to be a part of the referendum process. In a letter to Trudeau, Davis stated:

> At the present, Parliament alone would have the right to determine that the referendum procedures should be used. In my view, it would be a significant improvement to ensure that provinces are part of the process of authorizing a referendum.
>
> To that effect, the following approach is suggested: Allow the use of the referendum to be authorized by the resolution of Parliament and the legislative assemblies of at least four provinces. By requiring both Parliament and a minimum number of provinces to be in agreement, the notion of consensus and dead-lock breaking are brought into better balance.[11]

Trudeau rejected that request:

> You suggest that the referendum mechanism be used only when at least four provinces agree to its use. While I find the suggestion somewhat attractive, I do think it undercuts the purpose of establishing the referendum mechanism as a means of breaking intergovernmental, that is federal-provincial deadlock. I think it is more in keeping with the principle embodied in such a mechanism that its use not require provincial assent.[12]

In the course of negotiations with Ottawa, Saskatchewan achieved two small successes in reforming the terms of the referendum proposal. First, before a referendum could be initiated, there would be an obligation to seek the necessary provincial governmental support in accordance with the principles of the amending formula under the Victoria Charter, as set out in the resolution. If no such agreement was forthcoming after one year, Ottawa could initiate the referendum. This linkage of the referendum provision set out in section 42 of the resolution to the process of amendment through obtaining governmental consents, set out in section 41 of the resolution, made the referendum purely a deadlock-breaking mechanism in the event of a constitutional impasse.* Second, a Referendum Rules Committee, headed by the chief electoral officer of Canada, would supervise the conduct of the actual referendum. As important as these changes were, they failed to address the fundamental issue, namely, the propriety of giving access to the referendum mechanism to only one order of government. Without this major change to the provisions, Saskatchewan would not be able to agree to the resolution. The process of bilateral negotiations between the two governments ground to a halt.

Losing Momentum

The activities of the Joint Parliamentary Committee became highly significant in the evolution of the strategies of both the federal government and its provincial opponents. Because the committee gave non-governmental people and organizations their first opportunity to participate directly in the formation of the new Constitution, it acquired an importance, and a power, that no one had predicted for it. From the perspective of the confrontation between Ottawa and the provinces, the committee's growing role and extended timetable became crucial factors. Had the original timetable been met, the resolution would likely have reached Westminster in January, before substantial domestic opposition could have been mobilized. Keeping the debate in Canada permitted the six opposing provinces time to refer the question to courts of appeal, beginning, in December, with Manitoba's reference.

On the other hand, the committee's work also helped the federal government strategy. The presentations and concerns of a large number of special interest groups supporting the charter created a large reservoir of support for the resolution. Both the parliamentary committee and the federal government responded positively to many of the submissions.

... To the Aboriginal Groups

Not all of the activities of the committee, however, ended in success. The national Indian, Métis and Inuit organizations in Canada had energetically pressured the Joint Parliamentary Committee to amend the proposed resolution to entrench aboriginal and treaty rights. In a dramatic reversal of

---

One could argue that this first "small success" did not truly emerge from the negotiations with Saskatchewan. In his telegram of November 5, 1980, Prime Minister Trudeau also assured Premier Davis that the federal government would bring forward an amendment to the resolution at the committee stage requiring that a year elapse after the initiation of an amendment before resort could be had to a referendum.

policy, the federal government agreed in late January to a number of important changes which, at least partially, met the requests of the native organizations. Section 25 of the proposed resolution, dealing with "undeclared rights," was amended to state that the provisions of the charter could not violate the rights of aboriginal peoples. Section 34 of the resolution was amended to entrench aboriginal and treaty rights. Finally, section 37 obligated the federal and provincial governments to future constitutional meetings with aboriginal leaders on all of the other outstanding issues. The Joint Parliamentary Committee unanimously approved the amendments on 30 January.

The dramatic turnabout by the federal government in accepting the changes was matched by the enthusiastic endorsement of the amendments by the native leadership. The National Indian Brotherhood had earlier advocated wide-sweeping and important amendments, such as Indian government. Denied a place at the CCMC negotiating table in 1980, the position of the brotherhood was that patriation should not occur at that time. The Métis supported this position. Prior to the decision of the Joint Parliamentary Committee, the "undeclared rights" section preserved rights not specifically identified in the charter, "including those that may pertain to native peoples," and this was clearly inadequate for all of the native organizations. The result was that the National Indian Brotherhood launched a campaign in Great Britain against the failure in the proposed federal resolution to meet its demands.

The support of aboriginal groups quickly disintegrated, however, when Chrétien advised that the new section 35 fell within the ambit of the proposed amending process. For these groups, this arrangement meant that future governments could undo by constitutional amendment what they insisted was absolutely inviolate. Support began to crumble when some constituent groups of the National Indian Brotherhood, echoing the differences displayed months before at its general assembly meeting on the Constitution in Calgary, attacked the federal deal. Shortly after, the executive repudiated its shortlived acceptance of the changes and reverted to its position of opposition. The gulf between the Indians and Ottawa, which appeared to have been bridged, was reopened and even widened as Indian organizations once again took up their political and legal action in London and in Canada.

. . . To the Provinces

The dissenting provinces saw the delays and growing opposition caused by the committee's hearings as helpful to their cause. They placed their hope on securing a legal decision which would prevent Parliament from transmitting the resolution to Westminster or, failing that, would convince Westminster that it was its moral duty to delay or defeat the measure. Anything which delayed transmission to London was beneficial.

Momentum was crucial to both sides. The federal government obviously had the momentum in October, November, and early December. It had introduced the resolution, secured important allies, including the governments of Ontario and New Brunswick, moved the resolution quickly into committee, and marshalled a coalition of support amongst the general public. Its policies in other areas, notably energy pricing and federal–provincial financing, further escalated the opposition by provinces but also kept them off balance. The federal government not only secured the support of two provinces, but skilfully managed to keep two provinces, Saskatchewan and Nova Scotia, in a neutral position. Having just six provinces opposed to the resolution was a serious but manageable problem.

On the provincial side, Quebec alone seemed to understand the importance of creating as many fronts as possible and broadening the coalition. The province worked hard to muster opposition in London, which later became crucial; it promoted early court challenges. Most importantly, Quebec provided the glue which kept the opposing provinces together. Although the Quebec government was not in a strong political position, judged by its numerous by-election losses, it displayed a cunningness towards federal–provincial relations, which created the maximum level of uncertainty and, in fact, began to place the federal government on the defensive in both Canada and London.

By January of 1981 the opponents had shifted the momentum. The joint committee's work would not be completed until, at least, the end of the month. There would be a final rancorous debate in the House after that. The federal Conservatives, though understanding the inconsistency of their position, continued to press for changes in the charter, while opposing the resolution in principle. In general, the fight over the Constitution had rejuvenated the party. In London there were rumours that the Thatcher government might not be able to meet Ottawa's timetable, and that the Kershaw committee (the Select Committee on Foreign Affairs) might report unfavourably on the federal initiative. As well, the decision of the Manitoba court of appeal in the challenge to the patriation resolution was awaited. Whatever its outcome, it would most certainly be appealed to the Supreme Court. Increasingly, it became obvious that the appeal would be heard before the resolution had passed through the House of Commons and the Senate and, if this were the case, Britain would not be willing to act while the matter was before Canada's highest court. The provincial opposition was slowly gaining ground.

Last Ditch Negotiations

The Saskatchewan government faced a hard choice in November of 1980. It could accept what small changes to the resolution it could extract from the federal government and support the initiative or it could oppose it. If it chose to oppose, Saskatchewan would align itself with a number of governments which were neither its ideological allies nor on common ground in political style. Neither choice was attractive. One of the problems was that the issues presented by the resolution could not be analyzed according to the normal ideological categories. It presented issues about the right relationship between the regions and the centre and not class issues. These were issues of power sharing within the establishment, not between the powerless and the powerful.

In a lengthy appearance before the Joint Parliamentary Committee, on 17 December,[13] Blakeney outlined Saskatchewan's position and indicated that the government would make its decision on the resolution when it emerged, in its final form, from committee. In the absence of significant changes, however, Saskatchewan would oppose it. His testimony to the committee was vintage Blakeney. It was the kind of forum, and the sort of subject, which allowed him to demonstrate his ability to analyze the problem and to articulate a vision of Canada considerably different from either of the opposing camps. In many ways, it was his finest contribution to the constitutional debate.

On 19 January 1981 the federal Cabinet decided, in the light of mounting opposition, to "try one more time," to deal with Saskatchewan. Apparently Prime Minister Trudeau only agreed reluctantly. The next day the minister of energy, Marc Lalonde, acting for an exhausted and hospitalized Chrétien, contacted Romanow to arrange a series of meetings in Toronto to pursue negotiations once more. At the first meeting of officials, the federal side outlined a new offer. With respect to jurisdiction over resources, the federal government moved from its position of October 1980. It now offered to include a provision which would allow provincial governments to legislate in respect of international trade and commerce but only insofar as the rate of production was concerned and only to the extent that the economy of the particular resource industry was threatened. The proposal was designed to allow the provinces to set production levels where such regulation was demonstrably necessary to ensure the economic health of the industry. The proposal was clearly aimed at the kind of situation exemplified by the prorationing legislation in Saskatchewan, which was struck down by the Supreme Court in the *Central Canada Potash*[14] case in 1978. Federal paramountcy would be unqualified. The federal government planned to introduce legislation under which it would be allowed to exercise its authority over international trade in resources by order in council, where, in the opinion of Ottawa, circumstances demanded. Hence, the new provincial power would be subject to federal executive paramountcy.

The federal government was still willing to insert a provision limiting use of the referendum to instances in which constitutional amendment was unsuccessfully sought through obtaining governmental consents. Ottawa remained reluctant to grant provinces the right to use the referendum procedure in instances where Parliament refused to accept constitutional amendments adopted by the provinces. Alternatives such as a mechanism by which provinces could block Parliament's decision to initiate a referendum did not appear to be acceptable to the federal government. In exchange for its limited concessions, Ottawa wanted some things from Saskatchewan: if an agreement were reached, there would have to be a public declaration of support for the resolution from Saskatchewan, and letters of agreement would have to be exchanged between Trudeau and Blakeney. The federal government also informed Saskatchewan that there could be no guarantee against the use of closure in the debate on the resolution in the House of Commons.

Finally, federal officials informed Saskatchewan officials that in order to placate an incipient revolt by senators, who strongly objected to the provisions of the resolution, which removed the senate's veto over constitutional amendments, there would be further changes to the resolution. Saskatchewan officials understood that these changes would not be consequential and that the Senate would have only a suspensive veto over constitutional amendments. Even the need to make minor concessions to senators struck the officials as incongruously premised on the unlikely situation that Trudeau could not control the Liberal Senate. In any event, no federal text was available at the meeting; indeed, it is unlikely that at the time there had not been a final agreement on concessions with the senators. The issue was described by officials on both sides as "doing something for the senators."

Saskatchewan officials considered the federal gesture, if not the substance of the offer, to be significant. A reporting memorandum was prepared for Romanow, stating:

> First it indicates that the federal government now considers it important to gain our support. Previously it did not. I believe this results from the perception that they have lost momentum on the issue. Second, they have accepted the idea that some form of international text is acceptable. However, and notwithstanding their protest that they are not negotiating, they obviously are testing the water to see if *resources* is really our only bottom line.

Romanow called Blakeney, who was vacationing in Hawaii. On receiving the report, Blakeney suggested that an attempt be made to negotiate a provision which would bind the federal government to obtain the consent of the provinces, or some appropriate combination of them, before initiating a referendum. In this way, although the provinces would not possess the same right to deploy a referendum as the federal government (a concession which seemed beyond obtaining), at least the provinces would be able to stop a referendum if they acted in concert. It was a compromise between the proposed unlimited authority of Ottawa to launch a referendum and the provincial request to be granted access to it. Blakeney told Romanow that he was worried about the deepening crisis in Canada over the Constitution and expressed his desire to ease the impasse. If an acceptable compromise could be reached, he would be willing to support the resolution.

One other issue had unexpectedly arisen. In its eagerness to attract as many adherents to the charter and the entire proposed resolution, Ottawa had, the evening before its officials met with Saskatchewan, indicated to the Joint Parliamentary Committee its support for an amendment which would entrench property rights. This did not represent a great shift for the federal government since it had initially proposed such a provision, as early as 1978 in Bill C-60; the proposal had, however, been withdrawn during the summer negotiations of 1980 in an attempt to mollify the provinces, all of whom opposed it. For Saskatchewan, it was important that the federal government reverse its acceptance of property rights and quickly made such a withdrawal a precondition to any possible bilateral agreement with the federal government.

The day after the initial officials' meeting, Romanow and Lalonde met to pursue negotiations. An agreement was made with respect to the wording of the proposed additions to the section on natural resources. However, the principle of a federally initiated referendum caused problems. A vigorous discussion of the function and effect in a federal state of such a referendum provision did not weaken federal resolve. However, a compromise was eventually proposed. Lalonde said Ottawa could agree to allowing seven provinces with at least 50 percent of the population of Canada to prevent a referendum from being held. This was a version of the suggestion that Blakeney had made from Hawaii. Lalonde agreed that Ottawa would withdraw its support for the entrenchment of property rights so long as Saskatchewan indicated that it had accepted the bilateral agreement before the next session of the Joint Parliamentary Committee, which was scheduled to resume the following Monday evening, seventy-two hours later.

Finally, it was agreed that there would be "no surprises"; that is, that there would be no further amendments to the resolution not agreed to by the two governments. The next day was spent finalizing the precise texts which would amend the natural resources section and the referendum provision, and obtaining the prime minister's signature to the material. It was decided that Romanow and his deputy minister, Howard Leeson, would fly to Hawaii to present the deal to Blakeney and obtain his agreement. The federal government appointed Fred Gibson to go to Hawaii to answer any questions from Blakeney.

In Hawaii Blakeney examined the draft amendments and letters of agreement. In the draft letter of his acceptance to the prime minister, Blakeney inserted three qualifications. First, if the courts eventually ruled the action of the federal government to be unconstitutional, Saskatchewan's support would be withdrawn. Second, in the light of October's closure in the Commons, the federal government should permit a "full and fair" debate on the resolution when the committee reported. Finally, Blakeney wished the federal government to forward to him a copy of any draft amendments to the Constitution that it was prepared to endorse before the committee. The federal government, beset by numerous demands to amend the resolution, was simultaneously conducting negotiations with several different groups, such as the Senate and native organizations. This raised the prospect of subsequent amendments objectionable to the government of Saskatchewan, and Blakeney wanted to see for himself what the amendments might be.

A telephone conversation between Blakeney and Trudeau was to confirm the proposed agreement; at the time planned for the call, however, Gibson advised Blakeney that Trudeau would not be able to place the call because his car was stranded between Montreal and Ottawa with a flat tire. In the interim, Blakeney again questioned both Romanow and Leeson regarding possible amendments, including those agreed upon in Toronto with respect to the role of the Senate in making future constitutional amendments. In particular, he wanted to be assured that the proposed limitation upon the Senate's veto would remain in the resolution. He had not been one of the most active proponents of Senate reform, but had always been opposed in principle to any Senate veto. The key question then was: did "doing something for the senators" actually mean doing something for the Senate?

Leeson's recollection of his conversations with federal officials in Toronto was that any amendment made by the government concerning the Senate would protect the status quo of the present senators. He had been given no text of the amendments, although they were referred to in Pierre Trudeau's letter to Premier Blakeney. Prompted by Blakeney's questions, they decided to secure a more complete understanding of the proposed changes. Kirby was immediately contacted. He indicated that, according to his recollection, he had informed the Saskatchewan officials that the Senate's veto would likely be restored. Any uncertainty he showed in Toronto was a result of the fact that discussions with the Senators were still proceeding. It was apparent at this point that there had been a serious misunderstanding between the two senior officials on this issue during the intensive and hurried negotiations in Toronto, which had focussed on the referendum proposal and resources.

The reform of the Senate had been a major recommendation of every committee, task force, or organization that had studied the constitutional question in recent years. The NDP had consistently urged its total abolition. If the Senate veto were restored, the likelihood of any Senate reform in the near future was extremely slight. Blakeney would not agree to such a provision. When Gibson produced the text of proposed amendments to the resolution the next day, Blakeney's worst fears were confirmed. The veto over constitutional amendments was clearly granted to the Senate. He now had to weigh this development against the potential benefits of the significant improvements to the resolution that had been negotiated. In addition, after further questioning Gibson and speaking with Saskatchewan lawyers in Ottawa, Blakeney discovered a kaleidoscope of amendments being considered. To agree to something today was not to preclude change tomorrow. While he could try to bind the federal government to securing his approval for each change, the practical administration of such an agreement made it unworkable. It would mean little if the federal government decided it had to secure a change in order to obtain the support of some other party.

To Blakeney the process of the past several months seemed to have been conducted on shifting sands. In October the federal government agreed to include a resources section negotiated by Ed Broadbent, as NDP spokesman, but the resolution included unacceptable provisions in the amending formula and failed to include an international section in the resource provisions. Then, in January, an international section on resources was added, but still no change on the referendum was conceded. Finally, an offer on both resources and the referendum was put forward, but a new problem arose: the Senate veto was added. Now there was a prospect of more changes. At each stage where one problem seemed resolved, another previously uncontemplated problem seemed to arise. When added to the undoubted political risks of agreeing with the Trudeau government, both the substance and the process of bilateral negotiation became unacceptable.

Later that morning, in the telephone conversation that was to have taken place the day before, Blakeney explained his position to Trudeau with respect to the Senate and the uncertainty generated by the federal government's frantic negotiations with several other groups. Trudeau offered "to fight the Senate together" but Blakeney declined, not certain that Trudeau would or could.

Saskatchewan Joins the Opposing Provinces

The Hawaii episode marked the last set of serious negotiations between the federal government and any of the dissenting provinces. Each side's intransigence was reinforced by its perception that it could, and would, ultimately win the struggle.

Quebec, in particular, had a massive stake in prolonging the battle. Its opinion polls showed that the government's electoral position was slowly turning to its advantage after a string of by-election defeats. Quebec's strategy of dogged opposition and pursuit of a united front was working. The judgment of the Manitoba court of appeal in the *Patriation Reference*[15] supported the argument of the federal government in a 3:2 decision. But obtaining two strong dissenting votes represented a moral victory for the

Gang of Six. The report of the Kershaw committee at Westminster supported the provincial argument that the federal government's plan of unilateral patriation broke with constitutional conventions. The Manitoba court decision, the Kershaw report, the collapse of negotiations with Saskatchewan, and embarassing questions about the federal government's tactics in London, all lent credence to Quebec's perception that the federal effort was in "heavy water."

Saskatchewan announced in early February 1981 that it would oppose the resolution. However, it was not possible for the province to join the six dissenting provinces immediately. There were several fundamental differences of opinion. The six were arguing before the courts that unanimous consent of the provinces was required for a resolution to Westminster, a position to which Saskatchewan did not subscribe. Alberta was embroiled in a major confrontation over the national energy program, and its constitutional position was a chip in a hard-headed energy poker game with the federal government. Quebec was intent on focussing the confrontation to the point where it provided a good election issue. Manitoba was adamantly opposed to entrenchment of a charter of rights. Only British Columbia and Nova Scotia appeared willing to consider alternatives to these positions, but they seemed to be overwhelmed by the group. Finally, there was the problem of abandoning NDP friends, in favour of a group of Conservative and separatist allies. Saskatchewan, while opposing the resolution, was not ready to join the Gang of Six.

Accordingly, Saskatchewan attempted to chart an independent course of opposition, which involved three major elements. The first was to force the federal government back to the federal–provincial negotiating table by convincing the federal NDP caucus to withdraw its support for the resolution. Second, the activities in London would be accelerated to create more "heavy water" for the federal government and, thus, pressure it to return to the negotiating table. Finally, there would be an ongoing attempt to assemble a "middle group" of provinces, more willing to negotiate on the issue. By mid-March, all of these tactics had failed to produce results. Going it alone was simply not achieving the objectives set by Premier Blakeney in charting his constitutional strategy. There seemed to be no prospect of getting changes made to the resolution that would widen government support for it. Nor was his attempt to open a door for both sides to reenter the negotiation room producing results. Accordingly, Saskatchewan became the eighth province to join the defensive provincial alliance.

The Provincial Patriation Plan, April 1981
The strategy of the opposing provinces was beginning to succeed in the spring of 1981. Filibuster in Parliament, unrest at Westminster, and court challenges at the provincial level had combined to attract support for the

opposing provinces and stiffen the resolve of Conservatives in the House of Commons. Most of dissenting provinces pinned their hopes on the defeat of the resolution at Westminster or a successful result in the Supreme Court of Canada.

An important element of the dissenting provinces' strategy, however, was missing: a positive alternative to the resolution in Parliament. This deficiency portrayed the Gang of Eight as essentially negativist, intent only on delay and destruction, with nothing positive to contribute. During the winter of 1981 various attempts were made to develop a positive alternative patriation plan. The differing positions of this disparate group were highlighted by these efforts. First, Quebec was generally opposed to producing any alternate plan, believing that simple opposition would eventually succeed. A second group led by Alberta and Manitoba, and including Newfoundland, thought it was tactically advantageous to present a plan. Alberta, in particular, urged a provincial patriation plan which included its preferred opting-out amending formula; Manitoba argued for an alternative that did not have a charter of rights. Later, a third group including Saskatchewan and British Columbia, and sometimes Prince Edward Island and Nova Scotia, argued for an alternative to accommodate the two conflicting positions. Those provinces felt that a proposal with a different amending formula than Alberta's and some form of a limited charter was justified.

Several meetings of ministers and officials of the dissenting eight provinces were held in March, but the principal meeting was in Winnipeg on 24 March 1981. At that meeting ministers agreed to a variation of the Alberta opting-out formula which included a provision for full fiscal compensation to any province which opted-out of a constitutional amendment. Saskatchewan and British Columbia both argued that the provision in the formula which permitted provinces to opt out from those amendments "affecting" provincial rights was too broad. The discussions produced a variation of this feature by limiting the opt out to only those amendments which derogated from provincial rights. As well, Saskatchewan and British Columbia convinced the others to insert a provision that opting out required a two-thirds vote of the legislature. Several of the provinces, including Newfoundland, Manitoba, and Alberta, hesitated at the two-thirds majority provision, but all, including Quebec, finally agreed. (Quebec was represented only by an official since the government was in the midst of a general provincial election.) These arrangements were confirmed in a conference telephone call amongst the premiers on 30 March 1981.

On 15 April 1981, after scoring a massive victory over Claude Ryan and the Quebec Liberals, Lévesque met in Ottawa with the premiers of the other provinces which had dissented from the federal initiatives. He was particularly apprehensive about signing the Provincial Patriation Plan. The plan, containing patriation, the opt-out amending formula with fiscal compensation and a provision for the delegation of legislative authority, meant the abandonment of Quebec's traditional position that it had a veto over constitutional amendment. The two-thirds provision only compounded the situation since it made opting out all the more difficult. He insisted that this provision be deleted. Although his demand was resisted by some premiers, it was inevitable that his wishes on this would prevail since the premiers simply could not leave Ottawa without agreement. The media had been informed of the dissenting provinces' intention to sign publicly an alternative proposal for patriation. It was too late to withdraw. When the premiers' meeting finally adjourned at 3:00 a.m., after a night of acrimonious debate, the two-thirds provision, considered extremely important by Saskatchewan and British Columbia, was gone. Hours later, the formal signing of the Provincial Patriation Plan by the premiers took place. Almost immediately the federal government strongly condemned the provincial plan, particularly the proposal to allow opting out of amendments with fiscal compensation. Chrétien described it as "sovereignty-association by installment."

The uneasiness generated by Quebec's change in position on 15 April persisted as a problem for the dissenting provinces. It was reinforced for some at a later meeting of ministers in Winnipeg when Claude Morin seemed to emphasize that the Quebec government was more interested in settling scores with the federal Liberal party than in finding an acceptable constitutional compromise. This should not have surprised the provinces. The unexpected electoral victory of the PQ had breathed new life into the separatist movement, giving it a new mandate to fight the federal government. However, the attitude of Lévesque on 15 April and Morin in Winnipeg confirmed, in the minds of some ministers, that Quebec would never agree to any compromise.

Conclusion

In the year of confrontation, two important provincial elections widened the cleavages within Canada. Ontario, contrary to its history of championing provincial rights, had wed itself to Ottawa and Prime Minister Pierre Trudeau. It had thereby relinquished its traditional role as conciliator in federal–provincial controversies. Davis was re-elected with a majority in Ontario. Ottawa's hand had been strengthened. However, the general provincial election results in Quebec had the opposite effect. The Parti Québécois vigorously campaigned against the constitutional proposals and won. Its victory was all the more remarkable because it was unexpected after the Parti Québécois's repudiation in the referendum and several by-elections. When the dust had settled, the people of Quebec and Ontario, two of the original partners to Confederation, had mandated their respective governments to pursue opposing visions of Canada.

Saskatchewan was the eighth and last province to declare formally its opposition to the federal constitutional resolution after its attempts to modify the impact of the resolution collapsed. Unable to change the federal position, Saskatchewan joined the seven other provinces to form a defensive alliance to block Ottawa. It was an affiliation of disparate personalities and widely divergent positions. Opposition to Ottawa was the unifying factor which kept this shaky and mistrustful group together. Forced by the relentless pressure of Ottawa's determination to proceed, even in the face of widespread controversy, members of the opposing alliance submerged their differences, which ranged from the pursuit of separatism to the maintenance of the status quo, in order to stop unilateral federal action. In April 1981 it did more: in a document containing only the bare bones of patriation and an amending formula, the alliance presented a patriation alternative for Canada. The April document was a major development, in that Quebec, for the first time since Confederation, had formally agreed to fundamental constitutional reform. Even more significantly, Lévesque had abandoned Quebec's traditional claim to a veto over future constitutional change. Born of necessity, the gang's provincial patriation plan became a major statement on one of the issues which would ultimately dominate the final constitutional agreement.

Few nations survive internal turmoil without political scars. In particular, no country can question its most basic assumption — its continued existence as a discrete entity — without severe strain and eventual political rearrangement. It should have been obvious to provincial governments that national politicians, freshly victorious in the most serious challenge to Canada's existence, would object to a return to the state of affairs which appeared to have precipitated the clash. To do so would have been to betray the cause. The year of confrontation was, therefore, inevitable. The victor was determined to press for the spoils of victory, the vanquished was just as determined to reduce the inevitable losses, and the others were forced to adjust to an obviously altered balance of power. Although the battles focussed on the Constitution, oil pricing, and revenue sharing, the actual confrontation was about the future of Canada, a future which was now to be determined, not by confrontations in Parliament or at Westminster, but by compromises in courts and conferences.

Notes

1. Canada, *The National Energy Program, 1980* (Ottawa, 1980).
2. See *House of Commons Debates*, 32nd Parliament, 1st Session, 4:3978-79 (23 October 1980).
3. See *House of Commons Debates*, 32nd Parliament, 1st Session, 5:5243 (2 December 1980).
4. *House of Commons Debates*, 32nd Parliament, 1st Session, 8:8980 (6 April 1981).

5. *Reference Re Amendment of the Constitution of Canada (No. 2)*, (1980), 29 Nfld & P.E.I.R. 503, 118 D.L.R. (3d) 1 (Nfld. C.A.).
6. Petroleum Administration Act, S.C. 1974–75–76, c. 47. Renamed by 1980–81–82, c. 114, s. 1, the Energy Administration Act.
7. Address by Peter Lougheed to the province of Alberta in reaction to the federal budget, Edmonton, Thursday, 30 October 1980.
8. *Ibid.*
9. See *Reference Re Proposed Federal Tax on Exported Natural Gas* (1982), 136 D.L.R. (3d) 385 (S.C.C.).
10. Speech by A.E. Blakeney delivered at the Faculty of Law, Dalhousie University, Halifax, 27 October 1980.
11. Telex from William Davis, premier of Ontario, to Pierre Trudeau, prime minister, 27 October 1980.
12. Telex from Pierre Trudeau to William Davis, 5 November 1980.
13. See *Minutes of Proceedings and Evidence of the Special Joint Committee of the Senate and of the House of Commons on the Constitution of Canada*, Issue No. 30 (19 December 1980).
14. *Central Canada Potash Co. v. Attorney General of Saskatchewan*, [1979] 1 S.C.R. 42, 88 D.L.R. (3d) 609.
15. *Reference Re Amendment of the Constitution of Canada (No. 1)* (1981), 7 Man. R. (2d) 269, 117 D.L.R. (3d) 1 (C.A.).

Chapter 5
The Battle of Britain

Only three institutions had the authority to stop the federal government's plan to have the Constitution patriated through a unilateral request to the British Parliament: the Supreme Court of Canada, the Parliament of Canada, and the Parliament of the United Kingdom. In the opinion of the federal government, the first couldn't, the second wouldn't, and the last shouldn't.

The government reasoned that the Supreme Court was prevented from acting for several reasons, the most important being a lack of *legal* impediment to implementation of the plan. Furthermore, even if there were a constitutional convention against the unilateral request, the Court could not act to stop it because conventions do not create legal rules. As for the Parliament of Canada, although it had a legitimate role in deciding whether to transmit the resolution to Westminster, the Liberal majorities in the House of Commons and the Senate would ensure that neither of these institutions would frustrate the government's strategy. Westminster posed the greatest threat: there was no question that it had the legal right to thwart the federal government's plans. The United Kingdom's constitutional position was that its Parliament had the authority to enact, or refuse to enact, any provision which was put before it. That it would actually use this power to refuse to enact a Canadian request for amendment to the British North America Act was, until the winter of 1980–81, virtually unthinkable. Then, during 1981, the unthinkable gradually became a possibility; this change in thinking about what, in the circumstances, would constitute an appropriate response by Westminster to the Canadian request is one of the most interesting aspects of the story of constitutional patriation.

In the long search for Canada's constitutional independence, one feature remained constant: few, if any, including Pierre Trudeau and Richard Hatfield, who mumbled aloud about the possibility of a unilateral declaration of independence, ever expected constitutional independence to be achieved otherwise than through Westminster. A Canadian declaration of independence, severing all ties with the United Kingdom, in light of Canada's undoubted status as a sovereign nation, would certainly not have caused concern among the nations of the world; but it was never advanced as a serious option for achieving constitutional patriation. When it comes to matters of constitutional order, Canada is a conservative society, dominated by legal positivism. A grant of the Westminster Parliament was an unavoidable step in formalizing our independence as a nation. The seemingly contradictory quality of this view was largely ignored.

There can be no doubt that, from the British perspective, the Canadian request was a petty annoyance—an annoyance because it would take up scarce parliamentary time and because it would call upon the British Parliament to perform an anomolous, imperialistic task. Furthermore, as it soon became apparent, its most annoying feature was that the political wrangle from which it sprang in Canada would be brought to London, and then, transferred to both of the major British parties. Among the members of the Conservative and Labour caucuses, there were some who were willing to turn the question of implementing the Canadian request into a political free-for-all.

Notwithstanding these serious problems for the British political order, the issue was, at first, a minor one in a nation which was deeply engaged in a fight over sharply defined ideologies. It is true that the major national papers each assigned a writer to cover the Canadian request and that the parade of Canadians to London was considered newsworthy. It is also true that the question of political morality raised by the request was the sort of issue much loved by English journalists and, as a result, long, thoughtful articles about the problems of amending the Canadian Constitution appeared in the *Times*, the *Guardian*, the *Financial Times*, and the *Economist*. Finally, the realization, at the end of this episode in October 1981, that implementation of the Canadian request could lead to serious political embarassment for Prime Minister Thatcher sparked widespread interest in Great Britain.

The Role of the British Parliament

The United Kingdom's role was determined both by the manner in which amendments had been made to the British North America Act since 1930 and, in particular, by Westminster's position under section 7(1) of the Statute of Westminster, enacted by London in 1931.[1] The period before 1931 was of only limited interest in determining Westminster's responsibilities in constitutional amendment, since Canada did not become an independent nation until some time between the commencement of the First World War and 1931. From 1867 until, arguably, 1926 Canada was, in varying degrees, not a legally separate national entity from Great Britain.[2] Even after 1931 the fact that the British North America Act, Canada's constitutional document, was an ordinary Act of the British Parliament, sustained a view of Canada as a peculiarly dependent nation. The federal government adhered to this view according to its 1981 background paper, *The Role of the United Kingdom in the Amending of the Canadian Constitution*:

> Because of these colonial origins, the basic documents of the Constitution of Canada are British statutes, which cannot at present be amended in certain important respects without the co-operation of the Parliament of the United Kingdom.[3]

In practice, after considerable early experimentation, amendments to the British North America Act took place according to two conventions. An amendment would be made at Westminster only upon a request by the Dominion involved, and, after 1871, such a request was conveyed to Westminster by joint resolution of the House of Commons and the Senate.

Prior to 1931 there was no firm convention of consulting provincial legislatures when amendments were made which affected them, although consultation was undertaken on several occasions.[4] For example, the issue of the provincial role in making a proper request arose in 1907 when an amendment was requested establishing a new scale of financial subsidies to provinces in lieu of those set forth in section 118 of the British North America Act. There had been substantial discussion and agreement at a dominion–provincial conference, but one province, British Columbia, continued to object and voiced those objections directly to Westminster. They were noted by Westminster, resulting in a change to the original request. However, the change was explained in the following manner in a letter from the colonial office to the premier of British Columbia:

> I am directed by the Earl of Elgin [Secretary of State for the Colonies] to inform you that His Lordship has given the most careful consideration to the documents which you presented to him and to the views advanced against the proposed amendment of the British North America Act fixing the scale of payments to be made by the Dominion of Canada to the several Provinces.
>
> 2. Lord Elgin fully appreciates the force of the opinion expressed that the British North America Act was the result of *terms of union agreed upon by the contracting Provinces and that its terms cannot be altered merely at the wish of the Dominion Government.*
>
> 3. But, in this case, besides the unanimous approval of the Dominion Parliament in which British Columbia is of course represented to the proposed amendment of section 118 of the British North America Act, His Lordship is bound to take into account the fact that at the Conference of 1906 the representatives of all the other Provinces of Canada have concurred. . . .
>
> 4. His Lordship feels therefore that *in view of the unanimity of the Dominion Parliament and of all the Provincial Governments save that of British Columbia*, he would not in the interests of Canada be justified in any effort to override the decision of the Dominion Parliament.[5]

The under-secretary for the colonies, Mr. Churchill, went even further in a statement to the British House of Commons:

> On the other hand, he would be very sorry if it were thought that the action which His Majesty's Government had decided to take meant that they had decided to establish as a precedent that whenever there was a difference on a constitutional question between the Federal Government and one of the provinces, the Imperial Government would always be prepared to accept the Federal point of view as against the provincial. In deference to the representations of British Columbia the words "final and unalterable" applying to the revised scale had been omitted from the Bill.[6]

Although the passing of the Statute of Westminster in 1931 did nothing to change the legal status of Westminster, at least with respect to the British North America Act, both British and Canadian conventions relating to constitutional amendment began to become clearer between 1931 and 1964. In 1965 the federal government, in *The Amendment of the Constitution of Canada*, a document published by Guy Favreau, the minister of justice, summarized the principles for proper constitutional amendment:

> The first general principle that emerges in the foregoing resumé is that although an enactment of the United Kingdom is necessary to amend the British North America Act, such action is taken only upon formal request from Canada. No Act of the United Kingdom parliament affecting Canada is therefore passed unless it is requested and consented to by Canada.

> The second general principle is that the sanction of Parliament is required for a request to the British Parliament for an amendment to the British North America Act. This principle was established early in the history of Canada's constitutional amendments, and has not been violated since 1895. The procedure invariably is to seek amendments by a Joint Address of the Canadian House of Commons and Senate to the Crown.

> The third general principle is that no amendment to Canada's Constitution will be made by the British Parliament merely upon the request of a Canadian province. A number of attempts to secure such amendments have been made, but none has been successful. The first such attempt was made as early as 1868, by a province which was at the time dissatisfied with the terms of Confederation. This was followed by other attempts in 1869, 1974 and 1887. The British Government refused in all cases to act on provincial government representations on the grounds that it should not intervene in the affairs of Canada except at the request of the federal government representing all of Canada.

> The fourth general principle is that the Canadian Parliament will not request an amendment directly affecting federal–provincial relationships without prior consultation and agreement with the provinces. This principle did not emerge as early as the others but since 1907, and particularly

since 1930, has gained increasing recognition and acceptance. The nature and degree of provincial participation in the amending process, however, have not lent themselves to easy definition.[7]

The first three conventions were well established. But the first principle did not resolve an important question: was Westminster required to pass, unchanged, whatever request emerged by joint address from the Parliament of Canada? The answer in law was obviously "no." The answer from convention was ambiguous. Before October 1980 there would have been virtually unanimous agreement that Westminster should not involve itself substantively in Canadian affairs, either by rejecting or amending a request. But this consensus was based on the existence of a "proper" request, that is, one which met the test of the fourth part of the Favreau paper. In 1980–81 such was not the case.

Thinking about the Unilateral Request

During the summer of 1980 it became evident that the federal government was considering a unilateral request to Westminster, based on its conviction that Westminster should not "look behind" any request from the federal Parliament.

Constitutional experts in Canada expressed differing views on the question of how Britian should respond to a unilateral request. Some, such as W.R. Lederman and former Supreme Court Justice Ivan Rand, maintained that Westminster could, and should, look behind any request.[8] Others, such as Peter Hogg, felt that Westminster retained no guardianship role and that any request, properly transferred, should be enacted.[9]

In this context of unclear precedents and divided legal opinion, Prime Minister Trudeau spoke to Prime Minister Thatcher in June 1980. After their meeting, when questioned about the possibility of unilateral action, Trudeau responded that such a possibility was only a hypothesis and that he did not ask her to consider it. In truth, the possibility of provincial opposition was raised at the meeting and Trudeau later acknowledged that he had misled the press and public on this matter—"lack of candour," he later called it.[10]

In preparation for a unilateral request, Trudeau sought allies for his plan prior to his meeting with the premiers on 9 June. On 4 June 1980 Trudeau discussed constitutional reform and his target date of 1 July 1981 with Ed Broadbent. Broadbent later reported to the press on his discussion, detailing the six conditions that he had outlined for NDP support. When questioned about unilateral action, Broadbent hedged, saying that he was confident that there would be a federal–provincial agreement. In fact, the issue was raised by Trudeau, who posed two questions to the NDP leader. First, if the governments failed to reach agreement by 1 July 1981, would the NDP support a joint address to Westminster, including a charter of rights, language rights, and perhaps some other changes? And, second, would the NDP support *immediate* patriation with a bill of rights and language rights? Broadbent's response is not known, but it seems unlikely that the NDP leader would have supported immediate unilateral action.

Trudeau was not alone in exploring Britain's response to a request from Parliament. By the time of the meeting of first ministers in Ottawa on 9 June, some provincial governments had begun to consider reception in London of unilateral federal action. Provinces began to outline strategies. In late May 1980 Saskatchewan officials began to assess the likely results of a London-based struggle over patriation. They reported to Premier Blakeney that it would likely be possible to convince some U.K. members of Parliament that any unilateral resolution from the Canadian government was in conflict with basic constitutional principles and should not be acted on. On the other hand, they recognized that the U.K. government would no doubt feel itself bound to accept the joint resolution of the Canadian Parliament; the Callaghan government was on record as being willing to act on a resolution that did not have provincial support, and it was not likely that the Thatcher government would be more sympathetic to the provinces. They also felt that the British government would deal with this situation as if it were a problem of international relations and, according to those norms, would consider the only appropriate spokesperson for Canada to be the federal government.

Perhaps the most striking feature of the period just before the October introduction of the resolution is the casualness with which Ottawa viewed the role of the U.K. Parliament. In private discussions, federal officials treated Westminster's role as pro forma, and any suggestion that there might be trouble was not considered credible. The role of London was only peripherally referred to in the Kirby memorandum,[11] usually in conjunction with the possibility of legal challenges. All references were to "speedy passage" in London. According to the memorandum, there was only one case which could present a problem:

> . . . proceed with patriation action through both Parliaments, but make a commitment that a reference will be made to the Supreme Court and that the patriation measure, *enacted in the meantime*, will not be brought into effect until after the Supreme Court decision; this has the advantage of avoiding delay in patriation and would strengthen our position before the Court if the U.K. had already acted. It could however, make the British reluctant to act.[12]

Nowhere else was a reluctance to act discussed, and British warnings in June that Ottawa should beware of transporting domestic conflict across the Atlantic apparently made little impression on the federal government.

In October 1980 enactment by Westminster was considered a foregone conclusion by the federal government and, in fact, by most provinces.

Public musings by a few backbenchers in London that Westminster should not simply pass whatever was sent to it were first used by Trudeau to whip up the Liberal party faithful in Winnipeg in July 1980, and then forgotten in the tumult of the summer's events. Even the first stirrings of opposition at Westminster, headed chiefly by Labour M.P. Bruce George in October, after introduction of the resolution in the Canadian House of Commons, were viewed as mere annoyances.

Linking events in London and public opinion in Canada, Trudeau was willing to use London as a nationalist whipping boy, showing little appreciation of how British controversy could erode favourable public opinion in Canada. This was a serious miscalculation. The federal government no doubt correctly perceived that Canadians would be outraged by delay or deferral after the resolution had reached Westminster, forcing Thatcher to push through the amendments. What it did not anticipate was the impact of British comment in Canada on the process and substance of the resolution while it was still before the Canadian House of Commons. It did not predict that news of minor political controversy in London would, upon reaching Canada, be interpreted as grave British misgivings about the whole federal plan.

Ironically, the principal actor was not, initially, the federal government, nor Ontario, nor any other anglophone government: the loudest advocate of intervention by the British Parliament was the separatist government of Quebec. Perhaps, this too should have been anticipated. Nationalist forces plead their causes in international arenas in preference to conferring legitimacy on the nation in which they are trapped by waging their battles at home. Furthermore, international centres are more likely to be sympathetic to nationalist claims than the home nation, whose integrity is being challenged.

During the early period, October 1980 to February 1981, the strongest support of Trudeau's plan came not from the governing Conservative party, which was publicly committed to introduction and passage of the resolution when it arrived, but rather from the opposition Labour party. Labour took its position from former Prime Minister Callaghan, a staunch supporter of the federal NDP. In the fall of 1980 Labour members who gave any thought to the Canadian question were inclined to favour the federal initiative.

The Battle Begins: Kershaw Provides
the Battlefield

A great deal of credit for organizing resistance in London has been accorded to the government of Quebec and, in particular, to its agent general, Gilles Loiselle. In *The National Deal*, Valpy and Sheppard say:

> Of the many hands which helped carry the constitution conflict across the

Atlantic to Britain, none were more skilled than those of Gilles Loiselle, Quebec's Agent-General in London.[13]

He began his work even before Trudeau formally announced his intention to proceed to London without provincial consent. The *Financial Times* in London reported on 16 September, that "the more militant among the Canadian provinces . . . are already cautiously lobbying for support at Westminster."[14] In a confidential letter to his government on 10 September 1980, the agent general for Saskatchewan, Merv Johnson, reported that Loiselle had already been "very active" in connection with unilateral action and Westminster's response. Loiselle had invited Johnson to lunch in early September to discuss possible responses. At that meeting Loiselle revealed that he had already explored the procedures for petitioning Westminster and had begun to assemble an "inventory" of people likely to have a special interest in this problem. At that point Johnson was not optimistic about launching an effective lobby, noting that the only reliable support would be from the Scottish and Welsh devolutionists. His pessimistic view was not shared by Loiselle, who from early days believed that a program explaining the anti-federal nature of Trudeau's plans could have a significant impact.

Quebec was most effective, however, not in lobbying or petitioning or making inventories, but in encouraging the United Kingdom House of Commons Foreign Affairs Committee, under the chairmanship of Sir Anthony Kershaw, to investigate and report on Britain's obligations under the British North America Act. Whether or not Loiselle was directly responsible for the decision to hold hearings on the subject, there is little doubt that Quebec's early lobbying made the issue more visible and attractive to British politicians.

In the weeks following the announcement by Prime Minister Trudeau that a unilateral federal request would be made to the United Kingdom Parliament, six provinces—Alberta, British Columbia, Manitoba, Newfoundland, Prince Edward Island, and Quebec—decided to oppose the plan. They agreed to coordinate their activities directed at British parliamentarians. Initially, only Quebec and Newfoundland were enthusiastic about a London strategy. The others hesitated. There were unpredictable political consequences to consider, especially if Trudeau turned their opposition in London into apparent anti-Canadianism.

Ontario immediately announced its support for Trudeau, followed shortly by New Brunswick, and, at first, they played only a minor role in London. Saskatchewan and Nova Scotia adopted negotiating positions and, consequently, stayed away from involvement. The reluctance of the opposing provinces to be active in London eased somewhat with the announcement on 5 November 1980 that the Foreign Affairs Committee would hold hearings on the impending resolution. What might have been perceived as un-Canadian and unnecessary meddling in British politics now became legitimate. The British parliamentary committee requested submissions from interested participants, and it was only reasonable to aid the British in their inquiry. In a single stroke, it had become a matter of courtesy for the provinces to participate at Westminster.

In all, the Kershaw committee met ten times. The majority of those meetings were private sittings to debate the content of the report. Some oral presentations were heard. The most prominent was that of the Hon. Nicholas Ridley, minister of state for the Foreign and Commonwealth Office. The federal government of Canada did not make a presentation. Doubtlessly, it perceived the enquiry by the parliamentary committee as misguidedly imperialistic. The governments of Alberta, British Columbia, Newfoundland, Prince Edward Island, and Quebec submitted written memoranda.[15] The government of Manitoba did not make a submission and, of course, neither did Saskatchewan nor Nova Scotia.

The fundamental question before the committee was whether Britain had any residual guardianship role in the enactment of amendments to the British North America Act; if it had such a role, the committee was to determine its nature and how it could be discharged by the United Kingdom Parliament. What the committee had before it on one side was the provinces' view that Parliament had the duty to preserve the principle of federalism, which Great Britain had adopted in 1867 and which had been nurtured through the succeeding one hundred years. On the other side, was an equally strongly held view, advanced by legal advisors for the British government, that Canada was independent and any British guardianship role that might once have existed had long since vanished. The Canadian people, and only the Canadian people, should preserve what had been built.

After reviewing the submissions made to it and considering the advice of its own legal advisor, the Kershaw committee concluded that the British Parliament was not bound, in the conventional sense, to act automatically on the federal request. (Clearly, under the British constitutional doctrine of the sovereignty of Parliament, Parliament could not be bound in the legal sense.)

The report stated:

> There can be no doubt that if a request by the Canadian Government and Parliament is a proper request, it is the responsibility of the U.K. Government and Parliament to secure the enactment of the request with all the urgency or priority which the Canadian government may reasonably desire. That, indeed, is the practice of the U.K. Parliament and it should be adhered to. But it is one thing to treat all proper requests as matters of priority, and quite another to consider oneself bound to regard all requests as proper.[16]

The report, reviewing the practice of implementing Canadian requests for amendment since 1931 said:

We know of nothing in constitutional practice in Canada since the Statute of Westminster that provides any solid support for the view that a rule of automatic action by the U.K. Parliament has developed since 1931. As the 1965 White Paper says, the whole tendency of Canadian constitutional thinking since 1930 has been towards the more explicit recognition of a right of the provinces to be consulted about certain sorts of proposed amendment, and of a duty not to forward to the U.K. Parliament a request for any amendment of those sorts without provincial assent, perhaps even unanimous provincial assent.[17]

The report acknowledged that, in many circumstances, a request from the Canadian Parliament could be taken to convey the wish of Canada as a whole for the amendment; however, when the request was for an amendment which directly affected the federal structure of Canada and when that request was opposed by the provinces, the United Kingdom Parliament had the responsibility to ensure the integrity of Canada's federal structure. It could not perform the function, according to the Kershaw report, if it were automatically to enact all Canadian requests:

If the U.K. Parliament were to proceed on the basis that it ought to accede to such requests automatically (subject only to the requirements of correct legislative form), it would be treating itself as for all relevant purposes the agent of the Canadian Government and Parliament. It would thus be treating the Canadian Government and Parliament as having, in constitutional reality, a substantially unilateral power of amending or abolishing Canada's federal system. For any one Government and Parliament to have such a unilateral power is inconsistent with the federal character of that system; nor is it in accord with the "rules and principles relating to amendment procedures" which have emerged from the practices and procedures employed in securing various amendments to the British North America Act since 1867.[18]

The guardianship role of the United Kingdom related only to maintaining the integrity of Canada's federal structure, and not to any other facet of Canadian institutional or political life.

Despite the claims by some federal officials that Kershaw was caught in a time warp tending to the welfare of the colonies, the committee certainly did not glory in the implications of its conclusion. To assume responsibility to enact only amendments which maintained Canada as a federally structured whole was to take on "an unpalatable and thankless" role which was fraught with "embarassing potentialities."[19]

The Kershaw committee, having advocated a limited legislative role for the British Parliament, was faced with the task of setting out the conditions under which the "federally structured whole" would not be undermined. A proposed amendment not significantly affecting provincial powers was an instance when the problem would not arise. For example, in the committee's view, if the federal request contained only a request for patriation with an amending formula like the one in the proposed resolution, Canada's federal structure would not be threatened. But in cases in which the request contained terms, as this one did, affecting the federal structure, the committee felt that a criterion was available to assess the request:

> We think that it would not be inappropriate for the U.K. Parliament to expect that a request for patriation by an enactment significantly affecting the federal structure of Canada should be conveyed to it with *at least that degree of Provincial concurrence* (expressed by governments, legislatures or referendum majorities) *which would be required for a post-patriation amendment* affecting the federal structure in a similar way. For example a federal request that had the support of the two largest Provinces and Provinces containing 50 percent of the Western and 50 percent of the Atlantic populations would be one that could be said to correspond to the wishes of the Canadian people on a whole. This criterion has roots in the historic structure of Canadian federalism as reflected in the Divisions of Canada for the purposes of the Provincial representation in the Senate of Canada; . . .[20]

The federal government quickly issued its paper on the *Role of the United Kingdom in Constitutional Amendments* in rebuttal of the Kershaw Report. It is not clear who the intended audience was. The preface is careful to state that the book was prepared to help Canadians understand the issues, but there was a British edition which contained, on the first page, a notice stating that additional copies could be obtained from the Canadian High Commission in Grosvenor Square. The federal position was that Canada was autonomous and not subordinate to Britain in any aspect of domestic or external affairs, and that this had been the case since the Balfour Declaration in 1926. The paradox created by enjoying autonomy while at the same time being required to amend the Constitution through this last legal link could, according to the federal view, be resolved only if Britain exercised its power conventionally in accordance with the wishes of the "Canadian authorities." Since the provinces had no standing to submit requests to Britain, "Canadian authorities" meant the federal order of government only.[21]

Apart from the question of accuracy in the interpretation of the British convention, the argument displayed a chameleon-like ability to adopt an attitude toward conventions and their importance befitting a particular purpose. In Canada, where the federal government claimed that Parliament had the legal authority to pass and transmit the resolution to London without consulting the provinces, but should refrain from doing so under the convention, federal authorities stressed the legal right. They argued forcefully that the convention was either not present or could be broken for a higher purpose; they stressed the need to look behind and beyond the convention in order properly to discharge Parliament's guardianship role over all of Canada. When the federal level held the legal power, it was legality that mattered. When the federal government lacked the legal power to stop British legislative debate, it strenuously argued that the convention should be adhered to; that the United Kingdom Parliament should exercise its legal power only in accordance with federal request; and that any interference in the domestic affairs of Canada, or in the pursuit of national purposes of Canada, was totally unacceptable.

The federal paper also attacked the factual premise of the Kershaw report. It said that the concern in the Kershaw report over amendments "significantly affecting the federal structure of Canada" was misplaced because, "as has been explained earlier, [the] proposals, when implemented, will not affect the "federal structure" of Canada in any way that would be detrimental to the provinces."[22] The federal government persisted in believing that the creation of a charter of rights, which imposed substantial limits on both provincial and federal powers, was not detrimental to the constitutional status of provinces. The government's obtuseness on this point could not have inspired confidence in those whom they were trying to convince.

The federal government's paper and the Foreign Affairs Committee's supplementary report,[23] which was written in order to meet the criticisms levelled against the earlier report, traded blows on the historical evidence available to support their respective views on the British convention. The exchange was doomed to irresolution since there had been neither a prior British denial of a request nor a unilateral request which so frontally diminished the legislative powers of provinces. History, obviously, would provide no crisp answers.

The effect of the Kershaw report in Canada was electric. It was interpreted as inflicting a body blow to the federal patriation plan. Not only did it confirm the underlying claim of illegitimacy, which the provinces were making, the conclusions of the report also brought home the realization that implementation at Westminster would require pressuring that Parliament to act against its traditions. Any disappointment felt by the Gang of Six provinces over the report's conclusion that British convention did not require unanimous provincial consent was more than compensated by the elation occasioned by embarassment to the federal plan.

As an actual impediment to the legislative process in the United Kingdom the report was not, in fact, highly significant. Parliamentary committees in the U.K. do not normally assume tasks on the request of Parliament or the government. They exist to give government backbenchers and opposition members a chance to focus their parliamentary interests. Committee reports do not normally influence government policy and not all committees enjoy political credibility. The Foreign Affairs Committee undertook its inquiry simply because it felt that British parliamentarians might find its conclusions interesting. The committee did not have a directive from Parliament to examine this issue, and it was certainly not encouraged by the British government. Likewise the report did not have the slightest impact on the stated intentions of the Thatcher government nor did it cause an immediate growth in the support for the provincial position. In fact, the Supreme Court of Canada's decision,[24] issued eight months after the publication of the report stiffened parliamentary opposition in Britain far more effectively. There is no doubt, however, that the Kershaw pronouncement that British parliamentary responsibility exists to protect Canadian constitutional values created the climate in which the Supreme Court's conclusion that unilateralism violated a constitutional convention had an impact on British thinking.

The relative unimportance of the Kershaw report, in the context of British parliamentary procedure, may not have been completely understood by provinces. Certainly the level of provincial optimism over the possibility of actually stopping the constitutional amendments at Westminster was raised by the report. That optimism produced an enormous wave of Canadian lobbyists.

Lobbying British Parliamentarians

Quebec continued to be the best organized and most prominent province in lobbying parliamentarians. (The "Quebec lunch" grew notorious.) Quebec consistently maintained, publicly and privately, that the federal proposal would be defeated in London. Other governments were less convinced. Whatever the truth might have been, an extraordinary amount of effort was dedicated to the London lobby by Quebec. Beyond urging the creation of the Kershaw committee, Quebec appears to have been influential in establishing an all-party select committee of British M.P.s who met weekly to discuss the "Canada matter" and to hear speakers. Quebec also made progress with the 1922 committee, the Conservative party's House of Commons caucus of backbenchers. Recognizing the need to conduct lobbying evenly between the two major parties, Quebec assigned officials to lobby both the Labour party and the Conservative party.

Whatever the early successes, they were not such that, in February 1981, passage of the resolution could have been prevented. The other provincial governments were in various states of unpreparedness. Nova Scotia's agent general did not seem to relish cooperating with Quebec on this matter, and, since his government was not yet officially in opposition to the federal government, he tended not to participate. The British Columbia agent general, relatively new in London, lacked specific instructions as to how to proceed, although he was enthusiastic about doing something. Alberta's agent general was the most active, apart from Quebec's, in "informing," as he put it, but not lobbying. His major contacts were with the business community and, hence, the Conservative party. Because of its negotiations with Ottawa, Saskatchewan did not become active in London until after those negotiations had broken down in mid-February.

These various provincial efforts were at first uncoordinated and often not complementary. Part of the tendency to work at cross purposes was the result of mistrust of Quebec and its objectives. Although Gilles Loiselle was affable and smooth, few doubted that Quebec's agenda was fundamentally different from that of the other provinces and, consequently, did not share ideas or information.

The provincial governments showed ingenuity in proposing what to do, if not in coordinating it. Always foremost was the constant contact and lobbying with individual M.P.s. No one ever abandoned the objective of trying to assemble a sufficient coalition either to defeat the resolution or to cause anticipation of a delay of such magnitude that Prime Minister Thatcher would be dissuaded from introducing it. Everyone understood that Westminster differed from Ottawa in this regard; British M.P.s were less likely than those in Ottawa to respond to party discipline on constitutional matters.

Transatlantic party ties were important in the lobby effort. Conservative party contacts, both federal and provincial, were made during this time, albeit with only mixed success. The Thatcher government was in an awkward position, having to support a Liberal government initiative in Ottawa. The ties, tenuous as they were, could only be strained by the exercise. Although the government could count on the "payroll vote," of ministers and parliamentary secretaries, numbering about 150 members, the other M.P.s and lords were not predictable. It was, in all, an uncomfortable position for the Tories.

The Labour party also proved to be a complex organism, reflecting a curious mixture of positions. It was a potentially fertile ground for lobbying, and yet its leadership was extremely difficult to crack. The difficulty arose from two main sources. First, Harold Wilson, Jim Callaghan, and Dennis Healey had a fixed position on the issue, arising mainly from their days in power and their contacts with Canadian leaders. They all believed that whatever resolution was sent to Westminster should be passed without change and without delay. They obviously had a powerful influence in the Labour party, especially since Healey was the frontbench spokesman on the issue. Second, the Labour party had close international ties with other socialist parties, including the New Democratic Party of Canada. At a conference of the Socialist International in Madrid in late 1980, Ed Broadbent had effectively sought, and received, assurances from Michael Foot, Labour leader at that time, that Labour would not impede the passage of the resolution. On the surface, the Labour party was not fertile ground for the provinces. This was especially true before February 1981, since most of the provinces had no ideological or party ties with Labour. And yet, an opposition party could always be tempted to use any issue to try and thwart the government's program. As well, Labour was not a homogeneous party. There were Labour party agencies and committees outside the control of the frontbenchers, which Quebec had earlier exploited to its advantage.

In February 1981 Saskatchewan sent Howard Leeson, deputy minister for intergovernmental affairs, on a fact-finding mission to London. He reported that Quebec believed that, if a vote were held at that time, the resolution would not pass. Saskatchewan officials were skeptical of that assessment. He also noted that, in Sir Anthony Kershaw's view, fewer than one hundred M.P.s would be opposed to the measure, and some of those would not bother to vote. Finally, Leeson reported that Alberta officials were of the opinion that, barring some change in Labour's attitude, the matter could go through the House of Commons in forty-eight hours, leaving little opportunity for mustering support during the course of debate.

The most significant conclusion from the trip was that, despite federal NDP lobbying, and the positions of important frontbench M.P.s in favour of speedy passage, the position of the Labour party was still in flux. Many M.P.s, including Denzil Davies, a young Labour frontbencher, and Joan Lester, a Canadian-born M.P., had not yet made up their minds. They both reported that the Canadian High Commission had been clumsy and high handed with Labour, and that the federal NDP in Canada had not adequately made its case. The report changed Saskatchewan's mind about the usefulness of lobbying in London. After February 1981 Saskatchewan became, along with Quebec and Alberta, one of the active provinces in London. It particularly cultivated contacts with Labour party M.P.s. That, of course, exacerbated problems within the NDP in Canada.

At this point, the provinces reconsidered their options. Simple lobbying of members was obviously not sufficient. Most provinces, Quebec excepted, believed that Westminster would pass the matter without lengthy delay. But delay anywhere would give opponents to the federal plan more time to cause a shift in opinion in Canada, and would also give time for one of the provincial courts of appeal to find in favour of the provincial position. Consideration was given, therefore, to those mechanisms which would produce maximum delay. In order to explore these possibilities, solicitors and parliamentary agents were retained by some provinces.

British political awareness about the Canadian issue was enhanced by trips to London by premiers. Peckford visited in November 1980, Hatfield in January, and Lyon in February 1981. By February a prominent M.P., John Peyton, reportedly said that it was growing increasingly unlikely that the British Parliament would be willing to do for the Canadian Parliament what it could not legally do for itself. The British government was under increasing pressure, especially when it appeared that the federal government was not willing to wait for a definitive word from the Canadian courts before sending the matter to Westminster.

It was felt that further trips by Canadian politicians could be helpful, and so Roy Romanow and Bob Weese from Saskatchewan travelled to London in March 1981. They asked to meet Nicholas Ridley, minister of state for the Foreign and Commonwealth Office. Ridley, who was obviously trying to slow down provincial efforts in London, joined with the Department of External Affairs in Canada to try to prevent a meeting between himself and Romanow. Although Romanow was primarily interested in meeting Labour frontbenchers, the politics of the trip dictated a meeting with a senior government minister as well. When the request for a meeting with Ridley was made, it was referred to the Canadian High Commission in London by the British Foreign Office. The matter was referred to Ottawa, where the meeting was initially vetoed. At the last minute, it was decided that Romanow should meet Ridley, and that Ridley should convey to all of the provinces, through Romanow, the British government's extreme displeasure at the activities of the provinces in London.

Romanow began the meeting by describing the provincial position, but Ridley almost immediately asked why the provinces insisted on coming to London and putting the British government in an awkward position. Romanow's response was that it was Trudeau who was responsible for the position in which the British government found itself. The remainder of the meeting was blunt, with Ridley restating the position that the British government did not want the provinces to lobby London and Romanow restating the provincial position that the provinces had a legitimate claim to make, especially in light of the conclusions of the Kershaw report and the provisions of section 7(1) of the Statute of Westminster. When questioned about the British government's position on waiting for a decision by the Supreme Court of Canada, Ridley demurred. His attitude, however, indicated that the British preferred to wait. The meeting concluded with Ridley's emphasizing the damage to Anglo–Canadian relations should the provinces continue to lobby in London and should they be successful.

Although Romanow was surprised by the fierceness of Ridley's attack, the provinces were pleased with the meeting. Ridley was obviously deeply worried about a bitter fight between British parliamentarians, and this was an indication that the British government did not at all have control of the situation. However, despite the positive aspects of the meeting with Ridley and the optimism generated by Romanow's other meetings with interested parliamentarians, Saskatchewan remained convinced that the provinces could not win in London. The emphasis on causing delays in the legislative process continued.

The English lawyers suggested four separate delaying activities: a formal letter to the British government and to the Houses of Parliament from the eight opposing governments; a formal petition to Parliament signed by the premiers of all opposing provincial governments; introduction by friendly M.P.s, of a variety of amendments which would delay implementation, or reduce the scope of the resolution, or make its implementation conditional on greater provincial support of the proposal; and the commencement of legal action in London.

The last plan was not enthusiastically pursued, and none of the other three were expected to stop the enactment of the requested amendments. However, they would create a perception of "trouble" for the federal request at Westminster and this, it was felt, might persuade Thatcher to try to persuade Trudeau not to put her government in this difficult position.

A further strategy which was considered was a visit to London by all of the eight dissenting premiers. This, of course, would be appropriate only after it was clear that the federal resolution would be placed before the U.K. Parliament. No final decision was ever made on whether such a visit would be effective in generating parliamentary opposition to enacting the Canadian request.

When Newfoundland's court of appeal issued its decision against the constitutionality of the unilateral request[25] and when the legal test was set down for hearing in the Supreme Court for late April, more time was created for the development of delaying strategies. Since it was predicted that the Supreme Court decision might not be definitive on the question of the legitimacy of the request, preparation for a legislative fight in London continued.

After the PQ decisively won the Quebec election in April 1981, cracks began to appear in the provincial alliance. The other provinces were fearful that Quebec's objectives were not identical to theirs. Furthermore, Quebec tended not to trust the other provinces, was jealous of its success at Westminster, and often treated the other provinces as slightly incompetent latecomers. The Quebec agent general did not always keep his counterparts informed of his office's activities. Quebec officials resented comments about the "over-exposure" of Quebec, or of the need to moderate its activities. When Saskatchewan joined the other provinces in London, it tended to monopolize contacts with the Labour party. Quebec resisted this concentrated approach, despite Saskatchewan's obviously close connections with segments of the Labour party. Quebec, always conscious of maintaining as broad an opposition as possible, feared that the Conservative provinces would resent focussing the effort to build British opposition on the Labour party. It also did not want the Canadian amendments to become a Labour issue and thereby risk losing the support of Conservative backbenchers.

Saskatchewan's campaign with the Labour party led to further escalation of the struggle within the NDP in Canada. The federal NDP had earlier secured the support of the key frontbenchers in labour, with the exception of Michael Foot, the leader of the opposition. By contrast, Saskatchewan was more successful in convincing younger Labour M.P.s, their researchers, and some important Labour lords that the federal NDP was wrong in the matter. This was achieved in the face of the strong tendency of Labour to turn to the federal NDP for guidance on the issue.

Despite provincial efforts, the struggle in London was not, on balance, going well because of difficulty in coordinating the various provincial activities. Saskatchewan officials reported in late May that the opposing provinces could lose the fight in London badly.

Growing Success at Westminster

When the Supreme Court did not render a decision before the end of the spring term in June 1981, it seemed likely that there would be no decision until the fall. Given this extra time, the provinces decided they should make an attempt to improve coordination of their efforts in London. A deputy minister from each province was sent in September to establish a chain of command and a plan of action. This, however, caused eruption of the already growing conflict between London agents general and provincial officials. The agents general, removed from the political masters, by both distance and the troublesome time differences, were not kept abreast of events in Canada. They were, however, charged with the responsibility for organizing a coherent British campaign. Their offices were subject to abnormal burdens and they were saddled with extra staff, who were often not responsible to them directly but to people in the provincial capital. The result was considerable resentment.

The Supreme Court's decision in September put the provinces back on the offensive. They knew that Westminster would understand the significance of a decision based on constitutional convention. Although the Canadian High Commission was first off the mark with a pro-federal interpretation of the decision, delivered to the hotel rooms of the delegates to the Conservative party's annual meeting in Brighton, the provinces realized that they had good fighting ground.

Ministers from the eight dissenting provinces meeting in Ottawa on the afternoon of 28 September, the day of the Supreme Court's judgment, decided to dispatch a legal team to London. The lawyers were to explain the significance of the court's majority opinion on convention, in favour of the provincial view, to British parliamentarians and the press. Former Supreme Court Justice Yves Pratte; counsel for British Columbia in the Patriation Reference, Michael Goldie; and Saskatchewan's constitutional advisor, John Whyte, arrived in London the week after the decision was issued. They met significant numbers of lords and members of Parliament, as well as journalists, whose interest in the provincial case was suddenly renewed. That same week Alberta's Premier Lougheed arrived in London on his way home from a meeting of the Olympics committee in Germany and he began to visit important Conservative members of Parliament.

During that week it was learned that the chairman of the Conservative party's 1922 committee, Edward DuCann, had indicated to Margaret Thatcher his own pro-provincial sympathies and that of fully one-third of the caucus. The provincial strategy was no longer simply to delay and embarrass: victory seemed possible. Optimism bubbled about the provinces and efforts were intensified. The annual conventions of both the Conservative party and Labour party were lobbied by the provinces. Plans were made to have constitutional scholars speak to the select committee as well as at a conference dealing with the patriation issue which Quebec, with the concurrence of some of the provinces, was organizing. A brochure outlining the provincial case, with extensive quotes from the Supreme Court judgment, was prepared.

By October the long drawn-out quibbling over the wording of the petitions to be presented to the Houses of Parliament had come to an end. A text which was acceptable to all eight provinces was settled on under pressure from the British parliamentary agents, who pointed out that the parliamentary rules required petitions to be hand inscribed and that this would take time. The signatures of the premiers were collected at a meeting in Montreal in mid-October. The petitions were then complete and were held in London waiting to be presented to Westminster as soon as the federal resolution came before the British Parliament. Amendments to the constitutional amendment bill were being planned and M.P.s and lords who would introduce them in the Commons and House of Lords were lined up. And, always, the lobbying and list-making of sympathetic parliamentarians continued.

But on 5 November 1981 the constitutional accord was signed in Ottawa and in a very few days the London lobby began to vanish. Agents general went back to the more leisurely pursuits of the past and the London air-lift, as it had been called, went into reverse, taking everyone home, except the Quebec officials.

Assessment

It is difficult to assess accurately the impact of the various activities in London, although some conclusions are unavoidable. The federal government misunderstood both the potential for trouble at Westminster and how to react to it. Federal politicians in Canada and federal officials in London lost the initiative to provincial advocates early, and never regained control of events. This seems to have been true in large part because the events were unexpected, but also because of inadequate planning and poor execution. It may also have been the result of the awkward position Canada found itself in during the lobbying effort. Canada's case was based on the blunt claim that Westminster should not inquire into the merits of, or process behind, the request. To the extent that Canada tried to justify the content of its proposed resolution, as opposed simply to reminding

Britain of its duty not to review the Canadian request, it was caught in a contradiction. Provinces experienced no such restraint: they argued that Westminster should examine the federal resolution and the method of its approval. They were willing to provide the information needed to make that examination.

Had the resolution arrived in London after another stalemate in Ottawa it is impossible to guess the result. Federal officials claimed that the number of British parliamentarians who would have voted against the resolution was very low. They stressed the fact that matters were hypothetical before the resolution arrived and that M.P.s, especially Conservatives, who might have dallied with the idea of voting against it, would have understood the hard political realities of damaging Anglo–Canadian relations. They would have "held their noses" and voted for the measure. The same, they argued, would have been largely true of members of the Labour party. Federal officials also hinted that provincial lobbying would have paled by comparison to the kind of effort that the federal government would have mounted, including, if necessary, a prime ministerial speech to the British Parliament.

By contrast, the Quebec government had consistently maintained that a majority would have voted against the measure. They presented convincing arguments to support their case, including the British understanding of the importance of convention, the independence of M.P.s in comparison to Canadian M.P.s, the impact that the Kershaw reports, and their own lists of M.P.s prepared to vote against the measure. The Quebec assessment was not clearly wrong.

In the final analysis, however, without knowing the actual conditions under which the resolution would have been transmitted in the absence of an agreement in Canada, it is impossible to know whether it would have been defeated at Westminster. One does know, however, that there were sizeable numbers of M.P.s who were prepared to oppose the measure under the conditions which might have existed in October 1981, and the battle in both the Commons and the House of Lords would have been serious. Although the winner of a fight in London will never be known, it is perfectly clear who the losers would have been: both Britain and Canada.

Notes

1. Section 7(1) of the Statute of Westminster, 1931, 22 & 23 Geo. 5, c.4 (U.K.) states: Nothing in this Act shall be deemed to apply to the repeal, amendment or alteration of the British North America Acts, 1867 to 1930, or to any order, rule or regulation made thereunder.
2. At the imperial conference of 1926, it was decided that the dominions should no longer have a status subordinate to Great Britain but, rather, that they

should enjoy self-governing status equal to that of the United Kingdom. Judicial independence came later when Canadian appeals to the Privy Council were abolished in 1949. See *Attorney General of Ontario v. Attorney General of Canada*, [1947] A.C. 127, [1947] 1 D.L.R. 801 (P.C.).

3. Canada (J. Chrétien) *The Role of the United Kingdom in the Amendment of the Canadian Constitution* (Ottawa: Publications Canada, 1981), at 1.

4. House of Commons (U.K.), *British North America Acts: The Role of Parliament*, first report from the Foreign Affairs Committee (London: Her Majesty's Stationery Office, 1981) [hereinafter referred to as the Kershaw report], reproduced with permission of the controller of Her Britannic Majesty's Stationery Office. See Part IV: "Is there a Requirement of Automatic Action?, paragraphs 56–66, at xxxii–xxxvii.

5. Kershaw report, para. 39, at xxiii, xxiv.

6. *Ibid.*, para. 38, at xxiii.

7. G. Favreau, *The Amendment of the Constitution of Canada* (Ottawa: Queen's Printer, 1965), 15. Reproduced by permission of the minister of supply and services, Canada.

8. W.R. Lederman, "Constitutional Amendment and Canadian Unity," in *Continuing Canadian Constitutional Dilemmas* (Toronto: Butterworth and Co. (Canada) Ltd., 1981), 91 at 95. See I. Rand, "Some Aspects of Canadian Constitutionalism" (1960), 38 *Canadian Bar Review* 135.

9. See, for example, P. Hogg, *Constitutional Law of Canada* (Toronto: Carswell, 1977), 7–11 and 18–21.

10. R. Sheppard and M. Valpy, *The National Deal: The Fight for a Canadian Constitution* (Toronto: Fleet Books, 1982), 201–202.

11. Federal–Provincial Relation's Office, *Report to Cabinet on Constitutional Discussions, Summer 1980, and the Outlook for the First Ministers' Conference and Beyond*, (30 August 1980).

12. *Ibid.*, at 54.

13. *Supra*, note 10, at 215.

14. *Financial Times* (London), 16 September 1980, at 16.

15. These submissions are contained in volume 2 of the Kershaw report.

16. Kershaw report, para. 57, at xxxii.

17. *Ibid.*, para. 67, at xxxvii.

18. *Ibid.*, para. 83, at xlv.

19. *Ibid.*, para. 112, at lvi.

20. *Ibid.*, para. 114, at lvi.

21. *Supra*, note 3, at 5–6.

22. *Ibid.*, at 31–32.

23. *Ibid.*

24. *Reference Re Amendment of the Constitution of Canada (Nos. 1, 2, and 3)*, [1981] 1 S.C.R. 753, 125 D.L.R. (3d) 1.

25. *Reference Re Amendment of the Constitution of Canada (No. 2)* (1981), 118 D.L.R. (3d) 1 (Nfld. C.A.). The decision was issued on 31 March 1981.

Chapter 6
The Battle Goes to Court

The announcement by Prime Minister Trudeau on 2 October 1980 that Ottawa would attempt to produce a new Constitution without further participation by the provinces was not unexpected. The guarded optimism present during the meeting held in Ottawa on 16 June 1980 to plan the summer's constitutional talks soon dissipated in the face of intimations from Ottawa that failure to reach a settlement during the summer's meeting would prompt its pursuit of an amendment unilaterally. To add to this, the acerbic character of the first CCMC meeting in Montreal in July 1980 made it apparent to the participants that Ottawa did not consider provincial agreement to be an essential precondition to the patriation of Canada's Constitution.

In response to growing fears of federal unilateralism, provincial officials were set to work considering how the provinces could best respond. Although waging a war against the federal request in London became, at a later date, a large part of the resisting provinces' strategy, the early provincial response was focused almost entirely on the legal propriety of a unilateral federal request.

Provincial government lawyers differed as to whether the federal government could proceed unilaterally. Some argued that there were no legal constraints whatsoever on the power of the British Parliament to amend the British North America Act, 1867, and that, although it was unthinkable that the British Parliament would proceed to repeal or amend the Act without a Canadian request, strict legal theory provided no impediment. The need for a Canadian request and the need for provincial participation in that request were based on convention; as such they would not provide a basis for challenging the validity of any amendment to the Constitution approved by Westminster, even if no province participated in the request. This analysis was reflected in the famous memorandum prepared by Michael Kirby.

Other provincial lawyers did not agree that constitutional convention could not form the basis of an enforceable constitutional rule. These analysts addressed the question whether an amendment enacted by the

United Kingdom Parliament would be valid regardless of whether there had been a Canadian initiative or not. They argued that no such rule existed as a matter of constitutional law. The reason for this view was that any court would be bound to find, as a legal reality, that Canada was independent and not subject to control from Westminster; that being the case, the court would be forced to discover a constitutional rule which matched the reality of Canada's independence. That rule could only be that the United Kingdom's role was merely formal and subsidiary. The dominant role was Canada's and, if this were the case, the domestic process would need to reflect federalism. These analysts took heart from Robert Stanfield's perceptive cross-examination of Professor Peter Hogg, a constitutional expert who appeared before the Special Joint Committee of the Senate and House of Commons on the Constitution considering Bill C-60 in September 1978.[1] Peter Hogg had testified that provincial participation in the making of requests to Westminster was merely a convention and Mr. Stanfield had asked whether some "mere conventions" would not have the force of law? He said:

> Supposing the Parliament of Westminster was just on its own to pass the statute which altered the distribution of powers between the federal government and the provinces, what would the Supreme Court of Canada do with that?

Professor Hogg replied:

> That is a very difficult question. The conventional view would be that the Supreme Court of Canada would have to acknowledge that the statute was law even though it has been enacted in violation of a convention. I think, however, it is possible that the Supreme Court of Canada would say that a convention that is so fundamental to the independence of the country is one that would simply have to be recognized now as having full legal status.

Mr. Stanfield then observed that there seemed to be some conventions which so accurately reflect the fundamental order and principles of the nation that they are, for all intents and purposes, law; Professor Hogg agreed with this description of how fundamental law might be formed.

Once it was conceded that a court might recognize the *legal* requirement for a Canadian initiative to amend the Constitution, it was not difficult to find authority for the need for provincial participation in the amending process. These provincial lawyers felt that the *Senate Reference* case[2] not only recognized the presence of a convention concerning provincial participation, but also treated such participation as a legal rule. In these early analyses of the legality of unilateral federal action, emphasis was placed on the meaning of the *Senate Reference*, but that emphasis was not sustained throughout the whole period of the legal battle. Why that case was thought to be determinative initially and irrelevant later to the litigation commenced in response to the federal resolution is worth closer analysis.

The Senate Reference

One of the proposals contained in the federal government's Bill C-60 was to amend the Senate of Canada and transform it into a House of the Federation. Bill C-60 immediately ran into opposition from the Senate, the Special Joint Committee of the Senate and House of Commons, and from the provincial premiers meeting in August 1978 in Regina. Part of the opposition was based on allegations that what the federal government was purporting to do by an ordinary act of Parliament was beyond Parliament's powers. The federal government chose to deal with this challenge by presenting a request to the Supreme Court of Canada to render an advisory opinion on the legality of their proposed legislation. The federal government argued that under Section 91(1) of the British North America Act, Parliament was given power to enact amendments to the Constitution of Canada subject to certain exceptions. The most important exception precluded Parliament from tampering with the federal nature of Canada. The federal government had argued that the Senate, as the upper chamber of the federal legislative process, had nothing to do with the federal structure of Canada and that the alteration of its composition and function did not, therefore, bear on federalism.

The Supreme Court of Canada did not accept this argument because it viewed the Senate as embodying a system of regional representation which is an essential aspect of the Canadian federal scheme. The Court noted that, under section 91(1), the power that Parliament enjoyed was merely to amend the Constitution of "Canada" and this referred not to a geographical or national unit but to "the juristic federal unit."[3] In other words, this power relates only to matters which are within the interest of the federal government alone. The Senate could not be said to fall within this narrow ambit since it was formed with the idea of affording protection "to the various sectional interests in Canada in relation to the enactment of federal legislation."[4] The Court went to the heart of the federal bargain in Canada and found the Senate to be an important part of it. Although the Senate is a component of Parliament, its constitutional significance goes well beyond Parliament's concern or authority.

Analyzed in this way, on the basis of the text of section 91(1), the Supreme Court judgment offers no guide as to whether the convention of provincial participation could be enforced as a rule of law. However, this account of the reasons for judgment is not complete. Before analyzing the scope of power conferred by section 91(1), the Court reviewed the history of amendments to the British North America Act. At the end of its review, it stated four general principles governing constitutional amendment which were taken from the federal government's 1965 White Paper, *The Amend-ment of the Constitution of Canada.*[5] The fourth of these principles was that the Canadian Parliament would not request an amendment directly affecting federal–provincial relationships without prior consultation and agreement among the provinces. Of course, the Court's mere identification and reproduction of the principles found in the White Paper did not transform those principles into legal rules. The Court did more, however. It stated that the enactment of section 91(1) in 1949, which was designed to give Parliament legislative authority over some amendments, was framed to comply with the principles of constitutional amendment developed by that time and formally articulated in 1965. The deliberate failure, in section 91(1), to give Parliament any amending authority over federal–provincial relations indicated that these sorts of amendments were beyond federal legislative competence. Only a process that recognized federalism would be appropriate for such amendments. In short, the amendment made to the British North America Act, 1949, gave constitutional recognition to the pattern of amendment articulated in the four principles. The principles which governed constitutional amendment had been followed in making the 1949 constitutional amendment and had, therefore, become part of our law.

A different reading of the *Senate Reference* case is that the Supreme Court, though mentioning the publication of the White Paper and the making of the 1949 amendment, did not intend to recognize rules pertaining to constitutional amendment beyond those strictly necessary for deciding the issue before it. What was before the Court was an examination of the limits of what could be done through parliamentary enactments, and not the question of the requirements for making a valid request to Westminster for amendments to the British North America Act. The difference between the federal strategy involved in the *Senate Reference* in 1978 and the federal strategy involved in a unilateral request to Westminster led lawyers for the provinces to realize, as they prepared for the latter case, that the *Senate Reference* was not adequate in itself to support the provincial side of the argument. More elaborate argumentation evolved in the course of preparing to take the issue of unilateralism to court. The *Senate Reference* diminished in importance.

Preparation for the Court Battle

Within days of the prime minister's announcement that the request for constitutional amendment would be made without provincial participation, the governments of British Columbia and Alberta announced that they had set up their own task forces to study the federal resolution, including the legality of the federal plan. Also within days, the provincial premiers agreed to meet in Toronto, immediately after the Thanksgiving weekend, in order to confer on the appropriate response to the prime minister's announcement. On 6 October 1980 officials from Premier Peckford's staff informed the provinces of Newfoundland's eagerness to start a legal test to the unilateral plan. Premier Peckford, it was reported, would be at the Toronto meeting and would raise the question of launching a court case.

When the premiers met in Toronto on the Tuesday following Thanksgiving Day 1980, it was evident that there would be no common provincial position. Consequently, there was no detailed discussion of a strategy of opposition. It was also evident, however, that there were six provinces who intended by legal means to fight against the implementation of the federal strategy. Lawyers travelling with the premiers of some of these provinces met to discuss potential legal arguments that could be mustered in opposition to unilateral patriation. Before the end of October, Manitoba invited legal representatives from the other five members of the Gang of Six to Winnipeg to discuss in detail a program of legal opposition. It was obviously felt that a coordinated legal attack was preferable to a series of legal actions and posturings involving disparate claims and pursuing a wide range of goals.

The clearest danger to any legal challenge to the federal government was that it would be portrayed by the prime minister as a desperate tactic of a desperate opposition, raising no coherent or commonly appreciated legal point. The course of events that would make that form of counter-attack most likely would occur if some provinces claimed legal invalidity under Canadian law, while some claimed only a violation of constitutional tradition, and still others claimed in the English court that the federal request could not be acted on by the British Parliament. Driven by the fear that the diversity of legal arguments and actions would be represented by the federal government as proof of no single compelling argument, the lawyers meeting in Winnipeg sought to design a common plan.

The issues which were before the lawyers were: first, the wisdom of urging a legal challenge on their respective Cabinets; second, the mode of bringing such a challenge to court; third, the provinces in which legal actions should be commenced; and fourth, if the preferred route were a reference by provincial Cabinets to provincial courts of appeal, the precise questions to be referred. An important factor was the strength of the legal claims which could be made on behalf of the provinces; it was not essential for the provinces' purposes that a legal challenge be a certain success. At a political level the resisting provinces had already attacked Prime Minister Trudeau on the basis that his plan entailed a constitutional breach. The provinces had not simply argued that the prime minister was acting imprudently or in a way destructive to the well being of Canada; they had said he was violating constitutional principle. Consequently, it was important for the provinces to lend credibility to their outrage by putting the issue of constitutionality before the courts as soon as possible. On the other hand, if the claims of the provinces did not raise at least troubling issues for the courts, the litigation would appear simply to be harrassment and the parallel political campaign waged by the premiers against the prime minister would be weakened.

The lawyers at that meeting determined that credible arguments could be mounted in a court challenge and decided that they could responsibly urge their respective governments to litigate. One of the reasons for this optimism was the realization that, even if there were no legal rule requiring provincial participation for requests to the United Kingdom, there was, they felt, a clear convention to that effect; if the courts were asked to pass on the existence of a convention, the federal government would be hard pressed to argue that no such constitutional convention had ever formed. In the first place, the 1965 White Paper seemed to recognize, in setting out the four principles of constitutional amendment, the presence of a convention requiring provincial participation. Beyond that, parliamentary debates repeatedly showed recognition by prime ministers and ministers that provincial concurrence is a conventional necessity for formal constitutional amendment. These statements covered the forty-year period from 1925 to 1965. An example is found in the comments of St. Laurent, then the minister of justice, in the House of Commons in 1943:

> I would readily concede to hon. members that if there were to be any suggested amendment to change the allocation of legislative or administrative jurisdiction as between the provinces, on the one hand, and the federal parliament, on the other, it could not properly be done without the consent of the organism that was set up by the constitution to have powers that would assumedly be taken from that organism.[6]

Recognition of the strength of the conventional argument determined the answer to the second question. Other options were considered and rejected. It would have been possible to wait until the British Parliament had enacted amendments to the Constitution and then challenge their legal validity. Such a strategy would put before the court the blunt question of whether there was a rule of law which made provincial participation an absolute precondition of validly enacted amendments to the British North America Act by Westminster. Likewise, the provinces could have initiated a legal action designed to forestall the federal government from proceeding with the unilateral request, such as an application for an order prohibiting the federal government from transmitting the parliamentary resolution to Westminster before provincial consents were obtained. The success of this action, also, would have depended on the provinces' ability to demonstrate a legal rule. At best, there was ambiguity about such a rule, whereas there was considerably less ambiguity, it was felt, about the presence of a convention. Since neither of the suits just described could be based on the claim that there was a constitutional convention, it was felt best to pursue litigation which would ensure that the question of the existence of a convention was brought before the courts.

The preference for seeking an advisory opinion from provincial courts of appeal was buttressed by another important factor. Each province has legislation confering on the provincial Cabinet the authority to put questions before the court of appeal. By starting the court process at the appellate level, the time until final resolution would not be intolerably long. The provinces, of course, were not particularly bothered by stalling the federal process in the courts: however, if a challenge would require years to resolve, it was felt that the federal government would have an easier task in securing political agreement to proceed in Parliament without waiting for a decision from the Supreme Court of Canada. On the other hand, if the Supreme Court's decision could be expected within a reasonably short period, the prime minister would appear to be acting in indecent haste, or out of fear of the outcome, if he chose not to wait.

Once it was decided that questions would be referred, it was necessary to decide which province or provinces would initiate the reference. Manitoba had called the meeting because it was the province most eager to proceed with a court challenge and it had done the most preparation; for this reason it wanted to place questions before its court of appeal. Quebec expressed the most resolute determination to stop the federal plan and wanted to be seen to be doing everything possible. Failure to refer questions to its court of appeal would, it felt, be viewed by the Quebec population as a failure to employ every weapon in its arsenal. It was, therefore, essential that the government of Quebec also refer questions to its appellate court. Newfoundland's objection to the federal plan varied from that of the other provinces in the Gang of Six in that it viewed unilateral patriation to be a violation of the Terms of Union under which Newfoundland entered into confederation in 1949. It wished to raise the unique issue of whether the prime minister's request to Westminster violated the 1949 agreement. For this reason, it insisted on presenting questions to its court of appeal. There were no special factors in the positions of Prince Edward Island, British Columbia, and Alberta; although it would not be entirely accurate to say they were all content with, or confident in, Manitoba's carriage of the challenge, they felt that their interests would be served so long as they had standing to argue their points of view in each of the reference cases.

The precise questions to be put to the courts of appeal in Manitoba, Quebec, and Newfoundland were, in part, easily determinable but, in part, presented the Gang of Six lawyers with a problem. Clearly the question of whether there was a constitutional convention requiring provincial agreement to any request had to be asked. Because the convention or the legal rule, if it were a legal rule, applied only to those amendments which altered the federal–provincial relationship, it was also essential that the provinces first establish that the changes proposed in the federal resolution did affect provincial powers. So each of the three provinces asked whether the federal resolution affected provincial powers. In the view of the dissenting provinces the answer was obvious: the proposed charter of rights would unquestionably limit the legislative capacity of provinces. The federal government, through the three courts of appeal hearings strenuously denied that the proposed amendments would affect provincial legislative powers. It argued that, since the proposed provisions affected both federal and provincial levels equally, the equilibrium in Canada's federal arrangement would not be upset and that was what was important in any convention, if one existed.

In the Supreme Court of Canada, however, John J. Robinette, arguing on behalf of the federal government, conceded at the outset that the provincial claims were correct—the constitutional amendments did affect provincial powers by limiting them.[7] As prudent as this concession seemed to be, Robinette's announcement was one of the dramatic moments in the Supreme Court hearing. In part this was because of the presence, in the Court, of Jean Chrétien, the minister of justice. He had come to the Court to hear Robinette open the federal argument. Within minutes of its commencement, he witnessed the admission of a fact which, inexplicably, federal lawyers and federal ministers, including Chrétien, had so long and so vehemently denied.

At Winnipeg there had been discussion about whether a question should be asked concerning the legality of the federal government's proposal. Alberta was willing to put to the court the blunt question of whether amendments to the Constitution enacted by the Parliament of the United Kingdom would be valid in Canada in the absence of prior provincial consent to them. The language finally chosen was capable of being read as asking that hard question:

> Is the agreement of the provinces of Canada constitutionally required for amendment to the Constitution of Canada where such amendment affects federal–provincial relationships . . . ?

It was equally capable of being read as just putting the question concerning the existence of a convention in other words. Alternatively, it could be interpreted as relating to the legality of the simple federal action of transmitting the resolution to Westminster without provincial concurrence. Having created this ambiguity, the provinces were free to argue the legality of the prime minister's proposal without ever addressing the consequence of illegality, if it were found.

Quebec chose to phrase its questions somewhat differently. It merged the questions of convention and law in the single enquiry whether the Constitution empowers by statute, convention, or otherwise amendment by the Senate and House of Commons acting alone. This placed a burden on the federal government to show the constitutional mandate for what it was doing, a burden not easily met in the absence of constitutional text or historical practice which clearly supported the federal plan. The federal government would need to argue that inherent in the constitutional arrangement was its power to cause amendments unilaterally. Of all the constitutional rules, both legal and conventional which are derivable from the Constitution and from history, the most obvious is not that the federal level can proceed to amend the Constitution on its own. Nevertheless, the Quebec court of appeal found no restraint on the power of the Senate and House of Commons to pass resolutions and no reason why the British Parliament's authority over the British North America Act had diminished.[8] The Supreme Court of Canada subsumed the Quebec questions under the Manitoba questions and offered no analysis of the former in their own terms. Thus, the challenge to the federal government to prove the constitutional legitimacy of unilateralism was first met and, then, avoided.

Court Argument

When the federal government and the provinces began to prepare their arguments, they both found that, in the absence of clear authority, they would have to found their cases on very basic conceptions of the Canadian federation. For instance, the provincial argument regarding convention depended, to a large extent, on discovering a coherent historical pattern of provincial involvement in past constitutional amendments. The pattern must be found to reflect other principles, characteristics, or values, accepted by the persons and institutions governed by the convention. Ultimately, then, arguments in favour of conventional requirements for amendments rested on conceptions of the Canadian federation.

Likewise, the question of legal requirements for amendment was not answerable without reference to the Canadian federation and the nature of the relationship between the government in Canada and the United Kingdom Parliament. The argument that the Canadian law of constitutional amendment mandates a role for provinces depended on establishing a particular view of Canadian sovereignty; first, that Canada was a legally sovereign nation and, second, that sovereignty was not confined to the federal legislative body, notwithstanding its unique responsibility for all of Canada. In short, the provincial arguments for a provincial role, either as a matter of convention or as a matter of legal requirement, were premised on particular ideas about the meaning of history and the meaning of constitutional structures and relationships.

The debate about the rules for constitutional amendment was a debate about the definition of the nation's sovereignty. Rules which govern reformation of the constitution are the most basic expression of the legal nature of the country. That Canada's rules were so unclear was historically anomalous in light of its self-perception as both independent and organized under an accepted legal order. The debate revealed that independence may have been illusory and that the roots of our legal existence were virtually untraceable.

The Question of Canadian Independence

The federal government's most straightforward argument was that amendments by Westminster to the British North America Act were binding on Canada, regardless of the process by which they came about. The British North America Act was a piece of Imperial legislation; once amended according to the requirements of the enacting legislative body, its terms would necessarily be altered. The counter argument was that, although Britain could do what it liked with its laws, what it did would not change Canadian law, including Canadian constitutional law, unless altered by a process recognized by Canadian law. That process had three parts: first, there had to be a request for amendment from Canada; second, that request had to be concurred in by the provinces; and, third, formal implementation by Westminster was required.

The first major point of difference between these positions was whether Canadian constitutional law was independent of Britain. The provinces did not maintain that the British Parliament could play no role but, rather, advocated that the British role be recognized, prescribed, and controlled as a matter of Canadian law. The other view, advanced by Ottawa, was that Canada was subject to Imperial law solely in the matter of constitutional amendment, a matter over which Britain enjoyed plenary legal sovereignty.

The provinces' argument against full British authority over the Constitution, besides relating to the question of the legal validity of amendments, was also relevant to the more limited provincial argument against the right of the House of Commons and Senate to request Britain to act. If the courts were required to recognize as valid any constitutional amendment which Westminster chose to enact, there might have been plausibility to the federal argument that a joint constitutional resolution of the House of Commons and the Senate was unchallengeable in the courts. If Westminster were in full legal command, perhaps the courts should not declare against the right of the House and the Senate to present Westminster with a request. But if Westminster's actions were legally void without an expression of consent from the proper Canadian authorities, a resolution by the House and Senate purporting to give the necessary consent might be seen as a serious and legally consequential step which the courts have the duty to review.

One substantial counter-argument to the provincial position opposing unlimited British sovereignty was section 7(1) of the Statute of Westminster: "Nothing in this Act shall be deemed to apply to the repeal, amendment or alteration of the British North America Acts, 1867 to 1930, or any order, rule or regulation made thereunder." If the right of Britain to amend the British North America Act were preserved in the 1930 constitutional instrument enacted by Great Britain at the request of the federal government, with the consent of the provinces, then the previous status quo—that the British North America Act is a British statute amendable by Britain—must be continued.

Counsel for Manitoba took a bold and straightforward approach in the Manitoba court of appeal. He argued that, even though no formal declaration had established Canadian political independence, the reality was that Canada had long been fully independent, and "the reality is the law." Since no declaration by Great Britain declaring the independence of a former colony can ever legally prevent a subsequent Parliament from reasserting legislative control, colonies can only become legally independent in the eyes of their own courts when those courts accept the fact that there has been a change in the fundamental legal order. In his factum, counsel for Manitoba wrote:

> The theory that the British Parliament cannot surrender its sovereignty is as false for Canada with its silent revolution as for the Americas with war. The municipal courts in England may not recognize the "revolution," but will the Courts of Canada say that Britain retains a decision making power as to provincial legislative powers, property rights and other privileges?[9]

But how to reconcile the fact of Canadian political independence with the section of the Statute of Westminster exempting the British North America Act from provisions proclaiming legislative autonomy for the former colonies? The solution Manitoba recommended was to view the retained British power as merely formal, as a technical step necessary to perfect constitutional reform, but not in itself as a sufficient step. Only if British action were prompted by initiatives from the proper Canadian authorities would its actions be valid. According to Manitoba, the Westminster Parliament was just formal machinery to be used by Canadians to amend their own Constitution; the proper Canadian authorities were to be determined by the ordinary division of legislative powers. Each province must, therefore, consent to constitutional amendments which directly affect their legislative powers. Manitoba suggested that these ideas could be understood by adopting a metaphor of Ivan Rand, a former judge of the Supreme Court of Canada: Great Britain was a "bare legislative trustee"; it carried out legal actions in respect of Canada's constitutional reform, not for its own benefit or under its own discretion, but for the benefit of, and under the direction of, the beneficiaries of the trust, the federal and provincial governments of Canada.[10]

The factums of some of the other provinces revealed a similar line of attack to that of Manitoba. Newfoundland contended that "while the United Kingdom Parliament has the formal power to legislate in respect to the British North America Act, they do not have the substantive power,"[11] and Quebec argued that "since the passage of the Statute of Westminster, which conferred full sovereignty on Canada, the U.K. Parliament has acted solely as an agent of Canada when amending the B.N.A. Act."[12] British Columbia referred to the trustee metaphor and contended that "it is only for the sake of form that 'patriation' is required as the U.K. Parliament has long ceased to have any substantive role in the amendment of the Constitution of Canada."[13]

The Chief Justice of Manitoba was sufficiently impressed by this argument to begin his judgment by saying that "Canada is a sovereign nation. It is so recognized throughout the world." But by the next sentence his conviction had dissipated: "But one vestige of colonialism still adheres to her national status, namely, that she is unable to amend her Constitution." He did not determine whether Britain can amend Canada's Constitution without any Canadian consent at all; he simply concluded that the unanimous consent of the provinces is not required by any convention, nor is it supported by a valid theory of provincial sovereignty.[14]

For Justices O'Sullivan and Huband, who upheld the provincial claim that there was a requirement of unanimous consent, the issue of Canadian political independence was of first importance. Mr. Justice O'Sullivan was categorical:

> In my opinion, under the Constitution of the Commonwealth, Canada is a free and sovereign and completely independent country. It is so by international law; it is so by Canadian law. To hold that the United Kingdom Parliament has still the legal power to alter the fundamental structure of our Confederation without the consent of its constituents would be to decline to give effect to constitutional principles and practices that are by now well settled.[15]

He noted that the queen acts only on the advice of ministers who are responsible to a legislature with jurisdiction over the subject matter at hand, and neither federal nor British ministers have any authority to advise the queen to assent to legislation affecting matters assigned to the provinces by the British North America Act. It followed that the courts should not recognize unilateral action by the United Kingdom, not just because it would be colonialist but also because it would be contrary to basic principles of representative democracy.

All five judges in the Quebec court of appeal stated that Britain's sovereignty over the Canadian Constitution remained unimpaired, and none of them seemed to view this conclusion as genuinely controversial.

The Newfoundland court of appeal, in its joint opinion, left no doubt where it stood on the issue of Westminster's omnipotence; the court adopted the trustee metaphor of Ivan Rand. For the Newfoundland court of appeal, the events leading to the passing of the Statute of Westminster and the statute's effect of freeing both the provinces and the federal government of Canada from the restrictions imposed upon them by any British legislation meant that by 1930 "to all intents and purposes, the Parliament of Great Britain renounced all external legislative sovereignty over the land and people of Canada." Accordingly, notice to Westminster of provincial protests precluded it from acting to restrict the "powers, rights and privileges" granted the provinces under the British North America Act.[16]

When the case got to the Supreme Court of Canada, the justices were disturbed by the claims of Canadian political independence. The majority, in the opinion on the legal question, referred to the need to resort to the British Parliament for constitutional reform as "the remaining badge of subservience" in Canada's independence. On the other hand, the Court at times seemed to suggest that the reason the federal government alone is entitled to request amendments to the British North America Act is the "foreign relations aspect" to such a request.[17]

In the end, however, the Supreme Court majority held that the "legal competence" of the Imperial Parliament "remains unimpaired."[18] The justification offered for this view was that no legal event specifically intervened to remove legal sovereignty from the United Kingdom Parliament. The "old machinery" remained in place. The majority never explained, however, why the old machinery was not simply an instrument which could only be validly operated by Canadian hands.

The Supreme Court has long been the final arbiter of the federal–provincial division of powers and so has come to be accepted as the ultimate arbiter of legal legitimacy in general. Had the Supreme Court of Canada determined that Great Britain's role in amending the Canadian Constitution was strictly formal, it would have, in effect, completed Canada's acquisition of political independence. The Court could have found support for such a move in the texts of Anglo–Canadian constitutional history, such as the Balfour Declaration and the Statute of Westminster, and in the evolving political reality of Anglo–Canadian relations. It is a minor pity that the Court did not take the opportunity to declare the completeness of Canadian sovereignty before it was "conferred" on us by another nation's Parliament in the spring of 1982.

It must be conceded, however, that Canadian constitutional history did not dictate a certain answer to the question of independence. A judge who was hostile to unilateral patriation because it was anti-federal to proceed without the provinces would have expressed that view through a refusal to accept the unimpaired power of Westminster. A judge who accepted the moral legitimacy of the federal House and Senate to speak for the Canadian people as a whole, and who regarded the requirement of provincial consent as an unnecessary impediment to constitutional reform, would have been more inclined to view Great Britain's continued power as an acceptable alternative to provincial obstructionism.

The Compact Theory

The compact theory of federalism is that the Canadian nation is the consequence of an agreement by autonomous colonies to delegate some of their power to a central government. According to the compact theory, the basic unit of Canadian federalism is not the individual citizen but the province. The rights of the provinces under the Constitution must be fully respected, and the Constitution cannot be amended to alter the bargain which induced a province to enter confederation in the first place.

It is easy to discount the compact theory as a statement of the legal nature of Canadian federalism. To begin with, none of the original parties to the agreement was independent; the British North America Act was a British statute which rearranged the affairs of three crown colonies. Furthermore, immediately before 1867, Quebec and Ontario did not exist as separate provinces; they were combined in 1840 to form the single Province of Canada.

Compact theorists refer to the Quebec Conference of 1864 and the London Conference of 1866, where delegates from Canada, Nova Scotia, and New Brunswick agreed upon principles that were ultimately embodied in the British North America Act. But the delegates to the Quebec or London conferences did not have mandates from their elected legislatures to conclude a binding agreement. Only the legislature of Canada approved, at a later time, the Quebec resolutions. They were rejected by the Prince Edward Island legislature; discussion was postponed in Newfoundland "to a more convenient season"; hostility in the Nova Scotia legislature to the confederation project caused Tupper to refrain from submitting them for approval; and a government supporting the resolutions was decisively defeated at a general election in New Brunswick. Furthermore, the legislatures never were authorized by the Imperial Parliament to enter into binding agreements concerning confederation. Under pressure from the Imperial Parliament, the Nova Scotia and New Brunswick legislatures, neither of which accepted the Quebec resolutions, both authorized delegates to arrange terms of union with the delegates from other provinces and the Imperial government.[19] And what of the provinces subsequently admitted? During the hearing in the Supreme Court of Canada Mr. Justice Estey asked counsel for Manitoba how the admission of Saskatchewan into the federation fit into the compact theory. Counsel understandably did not give a direct response. Prior to its admission, what is now Saskatchewan consisted of two districts of the Northwest Territories. The Territorial Council passed a resolution calling for the admission of the territories into confederation. There were negotiations between territorial leaders and officials of the federal government, but the discussions were not those of equal representatives of equal and mutually independent units. Parliament had legislative authority over the Northwest Territories and unfettered power under the British North America Act of 1876 to create new provinces in the territories as it saw fit. In 1905, contrary to the assembly's request, Parliament created not one but two new provinces, Alberta and Saskatchewan, and denied both of them ownership of their natural resources.[20]

If confederation cannot be explained as a legally binding bargain among equals, the compact theory may still provide an appealing account of the moral foundations of Canadian federalism. Several decisions of the Judicial Committee of the Privy Council, once Canada's highest constitutional court, seem to accept the compact theory as a guide to legal interpretation. In *Re the Regulation and Control of Aeronautics in Canada*, Lord Sankey said that "the process of interpretation . . . ought not to be allowed to dim or whittle down the provisions of the original contract upon which federation was founded. . . ."[21] Canadian politicians have often cited the need to respect the original bargain between the parties to confederation. For example, G. Howard Ferguson, the premier of Ontario, relied upon the compact theory to support his successful campaign to have the provinces consulted in the drafting and adoption of the Statute of Westminster. Prime Ministers Laurier, Borden, King, and Meighen, all opposed an amending process which failed to give due respect to the compact on which confederation was founded.[22]

Even on grounds of political morality, the compact theory may be objectionable. Since it views the basic unit of federalism as provinces, rather than people, it denies that the general will of the Canadian people can override the objections of one or a few dissenting provincial governments. The compact theory is based on an analogy between the morality of promises between political units and promises between persons. But the analogy is limited. The parties to promises normally retain their identities; political agreement, however, results in the elimination or alteration of some of the participants and the creation of new entities. The original three colonies united to form four federal units and a national government. As a result of confederation, a new political community was born. While the federal government was wrong to claim to speak for the new political community in all respects, supporters of the compact theory failed to acknowledge the existence of the new community, whose development should not be frustrated by the objections of a small number of participant units.

Discussion of the compact theory was initiated by counsel for Manitoba in the Manitoba reference.[23] The claim, however, was very modest. A convention requires a "reason," and Manitoba argued that one of the two reasons for the convention of provincial consent was respect for the original contract. Manitoba was forthright in admitting that the compact theory could not form the basis for a legal requirement of provincial consent. Despite the modesty of Manitoba's argument, it was doomed from the beginning. When the courts look for a "reason" behind a convention, they must find a reason accepted by the politicians who use the convention as the basis for their conduct. The politicians who created the convention of provincial participation in amendments were motivated by respect for the federal principle, but certainly not all of them accepted the compact theory.

Chief Justice Freedman of Manitoba held that there simply was not a constitutional convention of the sort alleged by the provinces to exist.[24] On this view there was no need to comment on the compact theory; nevertheless, the chief justice went to the extra effort of denouncing it as unsupported by history, usage, or practice. Among other things, he noted that the legislatures of New Brunswick and Nova Scotia never assented to the Quebec resolutions, and that the Constitution has been amended many times since Confederation without unanimous provincial consent. The chief justice's point is a sound one. Under the compact theory it is hard to distinguish the cases in which Parliament obtained unanimous provincial consent from the cases in which it did not. All amendments alter the parties' bargain, and all should be based on their consent. On the other hand, the argument for convention based on the "reason" of the federal principle accounts for the precedents far more successfully. If Prince Edward Island is seen as a party to the Canadian partnership, reductions in the representation allotted to it in the federal Parliament would seem to be just as fundamental a violation of its contractual rights as diminution in the power of its provincial legislatures. Yet this sort of amendment has been effected without provincial consent.[25]

Justices Matas, Hall, and Huband did not deal with the compact theory. Mr. Justice O'Sullivan, however, gave a compact theory considerable attention. In the first part of his judgment he inferred, from Canadian political independence and from provincial legislative and executive sovereignty over the subject matters enumerated in the British North America Act, that it would be "unconstitutional and illegal" for either the Canadian or British parliaments to interfere with a province within an area of exclusive jurisdiction.[26] Later he used a form of the compact theory to draw an even broader conclusion: no legislature can alter one of the "fundamental Terms of Union" without consent from all the provinces. Thus, Newfoundland could not now secede from Canada without the consent of the other provinces, because that would change an essential term of the union; and each province had entered the union on the understanding that fundamental terms would not be changed without its consent. But it is, in truth, only invented "fact" to suppose that British Columbia joined confederation in 1871 on the understanding that a province on the other side of the continent would not join, and then later leave, the union.

In its factum in the Quebec court of appeal, Manitoba avoided the word "compact" but did maintain its previous position that one of the reasons for the convention of unanimous provincial consent was the need to "maintain the integrity of the agreement by which the provinces joined the union."[27] Despite this careful wording by counsel, all of the judges addressed the compact issue. Chief Justice Crête and Justices Turgeon and Owen each rejected the theory.[28] Mr. Justice Belanger found that, while the British Parliament intended to give effect to the desire of the provinces to be united federally and the notion of a compact could be applied to understanding certain of the rights guaranteed in the Constitution, nothing suggested that every province had a veto over constitutional amendment. The British Parliament evidently retained its own power to amend the British North America Act.[29]

The judgment of Mr. Justice Bisson, by contrast, is based on compact theory reasoning. Examining the history of confederation in some detail, His Lordship determined that the British North America Act conferred legislative sanction upon the agreement at the Quebec and London conferences made by those who became parties to confederation. It was in the context of that agreement that the other provinces joined confederation. Concerning the federal plan to move unilaterally to request amendments affecting the provincial legislative powers, Mr. Justice Bisson said:

> It is conceivable that the provincial partners of 1867 granted such powers to Parliament, powers which *they* decided to create and which *without them* would not have existed?
>
> Unless one is willing to deny that the Quebec and London Resolutions have any constitutional or legal value . . . there is only one possible reply: the Parliament of Canada does not have the legal capacity to act as it is doing presently.
>
> An affirmative response would seem to me seriously to compromise, on a legal level, the concept of federation pursued by those who wanted to create Canada at the Quebec and London Conferences, a concept which was consecrated legislatively in 1867, by the B.N.A. Act and which was accepted by the six Provinces which subsequently joined the first four.[30]

One might have expected the compact theory to be of special interest in the case heard in the Newfoundland court of appeal, given that Newfoundland had negotiated its Terms of Union with the rest of Canada only thirty-two years previously. But counsel put no more weight on the pact idea than they had in Quebec, and the Newfoundland court essentially ignored the concept.

In the Supreme Court of Canada, counsel for Manitoba presented his old argument one last time, this time under the name of "modified compact theory." The majority in the Supreme Court did accept the existence of a convention, but found the basis of it to be "the federal principle" rather than the compact theory. Since the Court found the convention to require only substantial agreement, not unanimity, it could hardly have relied on a justification which viewed each province as a partner to a binding agreement.

On the legal question the majority of the Court dismissed the compact theory as operating in the "political" rather than the "legal" realm.

The Theory of Provincial Sovereignty

When Colin Irving, counsel for Quebec, presented that province's case to the Quebec court of appeal, his argument was austere. There was no talk of convention, no speculations on the compact theory. Supported by a few Privy Council precedents, the core of Irving's argument was simply this:

1. The provinces have been allotted certain areas of exclusive legislative jurisdiction under the British North America Act.
2. The courts have held that within these areas the provinces are supreme, and Parliament cannot interfere in these areas by legislation.
3. The British North America Act defines the nature of Canadian federalism.
4. It is inconsistent with the legal nature of Canadian federalism for the House of Commons and Senate to cause constitutional changes within areas of exclusive provincial legislative jurisdiction.

Courts should look at the real nature of the federal resolution requesting constitutional change, Irving argued. The resolution would have serious legal consequences. The House of Commons and Senate had no authority to attempt to cause constitutional change with respect to matters over which they had no legislative authority.

In the Manitoba reference, the provinces were not able to present the sovereignty argument with the precision and restraint that Colin Irving achieved in the subsequent cases. Both Manitoba and Quebec focussed their arguments pertaining to the legal question on the crystallized convention theory; but, from this point on, the arguments diverged. Manitoba persisted with the crystallized convention argument right up to the hearing before the Supreme Court of Canada. None of the twenty judges who heard the case in the four courts accepted its basic tenet, that the courts should infer a rule of law from the historical course of conduct surrounding constitutional amendments. The majority in the Supreme Court closed this chapter of the legal battle by observing, "What is desirable as a political limitation does not translate into a legal limitation, without expression in imperative constitutional text or statute."[31]

Quebec, on the other hand, quickly abandoned the attempt to found its argument upon the existence of a convention. The importance of the argument based on provincial sovereignty was demonstrated by Quebec's decision not to make any argument at all before the Supreme Court of Canada touching upon the constitutional convention.

Notwithstanding the subsidiary role of the provincial sovereignty argument before the Manitoba court of appeal, Chief Justice Freedman dealt with it, rejecting it on the basis that it bore "a direct relationship" to the compact theory which he had earlier rejected.[32] Furthermore, he did not accept that Parliament's inability to legislate directly with respect to provincial subject matters implied an inability to request Westminster to legislate with respect to provincial subject matters. He quoted this passage from the federal factum:

> It is claimed that to do so would be to do indirectly what cannot be done directly. This is a complete misapplication of a well-known maxim. The fact is that nothing is being done indirectly and nothing is proposed to be done indirectly. Should the Senate and House of Commons decide to send the proposed Joint Address to Westminster, they would be doing directly exactly what they have always done directly in such cases, and the United Kingdom Parliament, in acting upon the request, would be doing directly exactly what it has always done directly when given such a request.[33]

The passage is an exercise in semanticism rather than a response to the substance of the provincial argument. For all its assertiveness, the passage begs the question. The direct/indirect argument of the provinces was that, if Parliament cannot intrude upon provincial legislative jurisdiction by legislative means, it should not be able to do so by resolution. The point was not addressed by the chief justice.

Admittedly, there are problems in moving from the legislative divisions of power to the division of powers with respect to constitutional amendment. Just because an institution has exclusive power under an existing constitution does not imply, as a matter of inexorable logic, that it has exclusive power with respect to changing the constitution. In a state such as the United States or Australia, with an amending formula requiring something less than unanimity, the implication clearly does not hold. Indeed, the opinion of Mr. Justice Matas, with respect to the sovereignty issue, is based on the assertion that, while the provinces were sovereign with respect to the existing heads of power, they were not sovereign in the sense of having a veto over amendment to the British North America Act.[34]

The judgment of Mr. Justice O'Sullivan, in support of the provincial claim, did not rely solely on the division of powers under the Constitution. It also relied on the limited power of Great Britain over the Constitution and on the principle of responsible government.[35] His Lordship put great weight on the idea that ministers are responsible to a legislature with constitutional authority over a subject matter. The argument could have been elaborated further: provincial governments are democratically elected to deal with provincial subject matters. The House of Commons and Senate have no democratic mandate to speak for the people of Canada on provincial subject matters. The British North America Act, in many places, spells out that majoritarian democracy is an important feature of the Canadian Constitution.[36] A unilateral resolution would be an instance of purported representation by those who were not elected to deal with matters addressed in the resolution, matters which were, in part, within provincial jurisdiction.

The federal government justified its reply to the Kershaw report on the principle of responsible government: the House of Commons was responsible to the people of Canada for any measures taken in respect of the Constitution. Thus, the federal government and Mr. Justice O'Sullivan started from the same constitutional principle but took radically different positions on the legitimate role of Parliament, the federal government assuming a role for Parliament which went far beyond anything assigned in the Constitution.

In its written submission to the Quebec court of appeal, Quebec made no mention of the democratic objection to unilateral federal action. When Mr. Justice Turgeon suggested from the bench that the federal level of government spoke in London for all Canadians, Irving replied, however, that the federal level is not elected to deal with matters within provincial jurisdiction.

Quebec's provincial sovereignty did not fare well before its court of appeal. The judgment of Chief Justice Crête never seemed to confront it directly. "The principles of federalism" are mentioned in his judgment as one provincial argument, but he seems to have understood provincial sovereignty to be based on the compact theory, which he rejected. Justices Owen and Turgeon interpreted Quebec's argument as amounting to a claim of quasi-statehood in the international sense.

Mr. Justice Turgeon responded to this straw man by stating that the sovereign authority of the provincial legislatures within their field is merely internal, that there is an essential difference between the two types of government with respect to extra-territorial legislative authority, and that the provinces are not sovereign states.

Mr. Justice Belanger rejected the pivotal contention of the provincial sovereignty argument: that provincial rights with respect to the process of constitutional amendment can be inferred from provincial rights with respect to ordinary legislation.

> . . . I cannot agree to the statement that may be found in certain of the opinions already expressed in previous references that it is incompatible with the federal system established by the Federative Act that the Canadian

Parliament might cause some part of it to be amended without the consent of the provinces. In this regard, one might also wonder whether it is in the nature of this federal union to remain stagnant and incapable of evolution because of the opposition of a single Province in its own particular interests not necessarily compatible with those of the general population which the central power represents.[37]

The Newfoundland court of appeal accepted the provincial sovereignty argument. It concluded that the intention of the Statute of Westminster was to recognize the complete political independence of Canada and to leave the United Kingdom Parliament a strictly formal role in assenting to amendments to the Constitution under the direction of the proper Canadian authorities. The scheme of the British North America Act determined the identity of the proper authorities.

> Any amendment enacted by the Parliament of Great Britain affecting the legislative competence of either of the parties, without that party's consent, would not only be contrary to the intendment of the Statute of Westminster, 1931, but it could defeat the whole scheme of the Canadian federal Constitution.[38]

Thus, the court adopted the "legislative trustee" theory; Great Britain could only validly amend the Constitution of Canada with the consent of the Canadian political unit with legislative authority over the subject matter of the amendment.

At the end of April 1981, when first addressing the Supreme Court of Canada, Colin Irving again did not include the democratic objection to unilateral federal action. In his final reply, however, he argued that the federal government's proposed course of action was inconsistent with the principle of responsible government, because the federal government lacked any democratic mandate to speak for Canadians on provincial subject matters.

Perhaps the provinces made little use of the democratic argument because their own claim had something of an anti-democratic character. To argue a requirement of unanimous provincial consent was to argue that the political will of the overwhelming majority of the Canadian population could be blocked by the objection of one provincial government.[39]

On the legal question, the majority of the Supreme Court of Canada rejected the provincial sovereignty argument. Considerable emphasis was placed on the external relations aspect of a request to Westminster, and, in that light, the idea of internally divided sovereignty, a tenet of Quebec's argument, created an unmanageable concept. The majority judgment said: "What is put forward by the Provinces which oppose the forwarding of the address without provincial consent is that external relations with Great Britain in this respect must take account of the nature and character of

Canadian federalism."[40] The majority, however, is lamentably inconsistent in playing up the external relations character of the amending process, while at the same time characterizing the United Kingdom Parliament as the fully sovereign master of the Canadian Constitution.

The Supreme Court's majority reasoning for rejecting the provincial legislative supremacy argument seems to include the following points. First, as far as the Constitution is concerned, the British Parliament is the only supreme authority. Second, because there is a foreign relations aspect to Canadian requests for constitutional enactment by the British Parliament, only the federal government of Canada may properly make such a request. Third, there is no legal precedent or statutory authority requiring the federal government to obtain provincial consent before making a request.[41] The majority of the Supreme Court never explained its unwillingness to create a precedent by extrapolating a requirement of provincial consent to resolutions from the federalist nature of the division of legislative powers under the British North America Act. Nor is any attention paid to the democratic objection to unilateral federal action.

Federalism Theory
The constraint on unilateral patriation created by Canada's federal form of government was, in the court of appeal, incorporated into provincial arguments based on provincial sovereignty and compact theory. However, the marriage of federalism to sovereignty of the provinces is an uneasy one. Provinces are supreme within their area of legislative competence and, consequently, are beyond interference, in the exercise of their powers, from Parliament. The federal arrangement does not, however, dictate that *any* province's dissent to a constitutional alteration can block constitutional change under a process which recognized both levels of government and gave neither effective unilateral control. For instance, the report of the Kershaw committee to the British House of Commons concluded that Canada's "established constitutional position" precluded action on a request from Canada for constitutional amendment if "the request did not convey the clearly expressed wishes of Canada as a federally structured whole because it did not enjoy a sufficient level and distribution of Provincial concurrence."[42] This standard flows from federalism, but it is not provincial sovereignty. The difference is between saying that federalism requires that all holders of legislative power in the federal scheme must concur in adjustments of power, and recognizing that in an autonomous federally constituted country both levels of government must accede to alterations to the federal structure. Sovereign power means possession of powers which are not alterable without consent. Federalism means the absence of overriding powers, or political ambitions, of the other level of government. A theory of federalism may be inconclusive about what sorts

of processes may alter or reduce the powers enjoyed by provinces.

Federalism theory came of age when the reference cases reached the Supreme Court of Canada on 28 April. Because the theory provides an argument against unilateral parliamentary authority, rather than a specific amending formula, an appeal to the federal principle was thought by Saskatchewan to be a sufficient argument. Saskatchewan, alone of the provinces opposing the federal government, was not interested in establishing the principle that unanimous concurrence was required for constitutional change. It was interested, when it first became involved at the Supreme Court level, in showing only that the federal government alone could not effect the change.

Once it became apparent to Saskatchewan in the final days of January 1981 that it could not reach agreement with the federal government on how to amend the resolution to make it more acceptable both to itself and the other provinces, an all-out effort was made to stop the federal government from proceeding with unilateral patriation. With this in mind, Saskatchewan joined the court challenge, not to establish a particular conception of provincial rights, but to show that the federal government's plan was unconstitutional in both the conventional and legal sense.

The province's rejection of the requirement of unanimous consent for constitutional change had already been announced by Premier Blakeney. In the concluding moments of the failed First Ministers' Conference in September 1980, Premier Blakeney responded to the musings of the prime minister that the federal government would consider its options, including patriation without provincial consent. Blakeney's positive requirements for constitutional change were contained in his response to the prime minister:

> I do not believe that the national interest is represented by a consensus of all provincial governments. The federal government has a role to play. It is not a creature of the provinces. . . . Nor, however, do I believe that the national interest is to be ascertained by the majority will of Canadians. This is something more than a collection of citizens and, accordingly, the national interest cannot be stated by the majority view in the House of Commons. That is the view of a unitary state and under those circumstances one does not really need a constitution. One can deal with the national interest and identify it from time to time. The essence of Canada is that it is a federation. The essence of Canada is therefore that on major matters we need a double majority. We need the majority of citizens as expressed by the popular will in the House of Commons and we need the majority, however defined, of the regional will. That is the essence of a federal state.[43]

It will be noted that in rejecting the view that the national will, in relation to changing the Constitution, can be ascertained through a parliamentary vote, Premier Blakeney made the broader statement that national interest is not to be determined by the majority will of Canadians. His statement contained an ambiguity: it raised the suggestion that obtaining approval for constitutional amendments through a national referendum might also violate Canadian constitutional principles.

The problem with rejecting referendums stems from the view that in a democratic federal state the legislators at both levels of government re-present individual Canadians, all of whose interests span both section 91 concerns and section 92 concerns. Although representatives are given, through elections, a limited mandate—to represent persons with respect to section 91 matters or with respect to section 92 matters—the people themselves may, if the election or referendum is framed in the right terms, address the totality of interests, including their interests in constitutional structure.

However, simple referendums are problematic in a federal state; if the result is determined by majority vote, persons in provinces with special regional or minority interests would have no protection against national majorities. Consequently, a national referendum which honoured the concept of federalism would require a majority of voters nationally and from, for example, a majority of provinces. The latter requirement could of course be refined to require consent from a majority of voters in a majority of provinces in a majority of regions, or a majority of voters in two-thirds of the provinces, or a majority of voters in a majority of regions, or some other like formula. The precise requirement was, in the context of 1980–81, extremely hard to discover. It is enough to say that federalism required some level of provincial concurrence, whether represented through voters or elected governments.

Early versions of the Saskatchewan factum prepared for the Supreme Court of Canada hearing did contain these ideas. Saskatchewan considered presenting an argument for a set of requirements for amendment which were derived, first, from Canada's independence from Britain; second, from the respect for regional diversity based on the federal principle; and, third, from respect for the political will of Canadians, which is represented by neither federal or provincial powers. However, as the hearing date approached, it was feared that the approach was both too ambitious and too conceptual. In the end, Saskatchewan chose not to define either the level of governmental consent or the configuration of consent necessary to satisfy the requirements created by the fact of federalism. Instead, it argued that the federal principle created a constitutional requirement for agreement of the provinces and that adoption of the unanimity principle was not required in the context of the challenge to the federal plan of 2 October 1980. With only two provinces, Ontario and New Brunswick, agreeing to the federal proposal, however, the requirement of provincial concurrence was not met. It was unnecessary for the Court to state the exact level of provincial consent which would satisfy the principle of federalism in order to dispose of the case. The argument on this point took the following form in the factum:

> It is further submitted that it is unnecessary for this Court, on the present Reference, either to find that the measure of provincial agreement required is agreement of all the provinces (the unanimity principle) or to attempt to devise or approve any specific formula imposing a less demanding standard. With respect to the former, the questions referred to do not require or invite the Court to consider whether agreement of all ten provinces is necessary. With respect to the latter, it is submitted that it is sufficient for the Court to conclude that the question should be answered in the affirmative on the basis that:
>
> > First: there is a constitutional requirement for a measure of provincial agreement for constitutional amendments of the type described; and
> >
> > Second: the situation before the Court does not disclose a sufficient measure of provincial agreement.[44]

Technically Saskatchewan's submission did not preclude the possibility that the rule for amendment was unanimity; by stating that the Court need only decide that federalism required a measure of consent and that agreement of two provinces was not a sufficient measure, the issue of the level of provincial consent was left entirely open.

In this way the Saskatchewan argument, designed for the purpose of making the best possible case on the issues then before the Court, deviated from the standard of provincial measurement advanced by Premier Blakeney which, although imprecise, clearly did not include unanimity. Similarly, the Saskatchewan argument, although based on a line of reasoning similar to that adopted by the Kershaw committee, did not accord with that committee's conclusion that "a sufficient level and distribution of Provincial concurrence" could be tentatively defined in terms of the concurrence required "by the least demanding of the formulae for post-patriation amendment . . . which have been put forward by the Canadian authorities."[45]

In the Supreme Court of Canada, Saskatchewan's argument was given a great deal of attention by the judges. Undoubtedly this was because those judges who felt that federal unilateralism was contrary to the spirit of the Constitution were not willing to consign Canada's constitutional future to the requirement of unanimity. Only Saskatchewan offered a middle position. The yearning for a diplomatic solution was most clearly expressed by Mr. Justice Dickson, who on three occasions during the hearing asked counsel if they would not accept some middle position between unilateralism and unanimity.

Perhaps these hints led Ken Lysyk, counsel for Saskatchewan, on the sixth day of argument, to offer yet a further middle position. After considering the strategy all weekend, and discussing it with Premier Blakeney, Lysyk suggested that perhaps federal unilateralism could be tolerated in respect of the provisions of the resolution affecting patriation and creating an amending formula but not in respect of the substantive provisions, most notably the charter of rights. Again Mr. Justice Dickson appeared intrigued, and pleased, by the argument. But when the judgment was issued in September, the majority judgment on the legal question crisply recorded Lysyk's argument and rejected it with the observation that "the legal arguments pro and con do not engage the contents of the package and it is impossible to qualify the issue of legality by considerations of fairness or equity or political acceptability or even judicial desirability."[46] These are noble words, but they belie the undoubted political interest of the court in coming to some result which left the federal government neither entirely unhindered in pursuing its constitutional objectives nor captive to a provincial right of veto.

In the end the majority on the legal question did not accept Saskatchewan's argument. The majority on the convention question, however, found there was a convention for less than unanimous consent and stated that this conclusion was made in agreement with submissions advanced by Saskatchewan. In addressing the question of the convention, Saskatchewan had, in fact, paralleled its argument on the law question and in its factum had stated, "it does not follow that the agreement of *all* the provinces must be obtained." Saskatchewan was non-committal on the level of provincial consent beyond observing that the consent of two provinces was insufficient; as in the argument on the law question, the purpose behind the convention was said to be the need to maintain the integrity of the federal system.

Consequently, the federal principle, with its requirement that provinces be represented but not necessarily enjoy a veto power, positions developed most forcefully by Saskatchewan, prevailed in the Court's majority opinion on the convention.

The failure of the federal principle argument on the law question resulted from the majority's refusal to accept the validity of the legal claim of Canada's independence. Federalism is the central organizing principle of the Canadian nation. It is so central that the Court in the *Senate Reference* viewed it as a constraint on political action in Canada to amend the Constitution. The point was, however, that the current process of amending the Constitution was neither formally nor effectively being done in Canada. Federalism is the idea of Canada to which Canadians must be loyal. But it was not, according to the Supreme Court, the most basic idea relevant to constitutional amendment. The Supreme Court of Canada expressed the idea that informed its decision in these paragraphs of the majority judgment on the law question:

Whatever the [Statute of Westminster] may import as to intra-Canadian conventional procedures, there is nothing in it or in the proceedings leading up to it that casts any doubt in law as to the undiminished authority of the Parliament of the United Kingdom over the British North America Act, 1867.[47]

. . . [I]t is argued, [there] is no reason for conceding unilateral federal authority to accomplish, through invocation of legislation by the United Kingdom Parliament, the purposes of the Resolution. There is here, however, an unprecedented situation in which the one constant since the enactment of the British North America Act in 1867 has been the legal authority of the United Kingdom Parliament to amend it.[48]

This judgment comes perilously close to viewing Canada as a colony.

Convention
In no part of its argument was the federal government more dedicated than in showing why there was no convention requiring provincial consent in the constitutional amendment process. In its argument to the Manitoba court of appeal, it was faced with the challenge of presenting two lines of argument that were inconsistent with each other. First, the federal government strenuously argued that the question relating to the existence of a constitutional convention should not be answered by the court. It viewed the question to be inappropriate for judicial assessment because it was directed to standards of political conduct, not to a rule of law. In making this argument, the federal government focussed on the vague and indeterminate nature of conventions thereby involving the court in ambiguities of a sort not appropriate to its role. For example, the federal lawyers offered this comparison: in differentiating a convention from a political practice "it is impossible to determine the line between the two," whereas a law is "imposed" and "inflexible." In short, conventions, because of their imprecision and flexibility, were unsuitable for enforcement by the courts. This is an amazingly wrongheaded view of the nature of law and the legal process, and Chief Justice Freedman stated that the federal argument "overstates the case."[49] In his view, the question on the convention, notwithstanding its political significance, "possesses a constitutional feature" and calls for a reply. On the other hand, Mr. Justice Hall, who was also in the majority, held against the provinces on the question of a convention precisely on this ground. He employed a metaphor to describe why he would not deal with the argument for a convention: "it is not appropriate to the exercise of the judicial function to find a political orange and turn it into a judicial apple. . . . [B]oth are separate and precious fruits on the Canadian constitutional table."[50]

Federal lawyers, having made much of the indeterminate nature of constitutional conventions for the purpose of showing their inappropriateness for judicial attention, then proceeded to argue that there was no convention because the practices surrounding constitutional conventions had not achieved the degree of precision that characterizes a true constitutional convention. They advanced two different conceptions of convention which simply do not live easily together.

The federal factum demonstrated the convention's vague contours through a number of strategies. First, the history of amendments were presented as if there were no possible way to sort out or differentiate the twenty-one amendments made to the British North America Act by the British Parliament. The history of these amendments is extremely varied respecting the nature of the Canadian initiative and the participation of the provinces, yet the amendments achieve varied objectives and may be grouped to reveal a pattern.

The federal factum attempted to confound the grouping process by describing some thirteen constitutional amendments as affecting federal–provincial relations even though, for many of these amendments, the effect was trivial and did not bear on provincial powers. For example, the description of the amendment postponing redistribution of House of Commons representation is commenced with the same litany as the amendment transferring the ownership of western crown lands to the four western provinces or the amendment conferring authority over unemployment insurance on the federal governments, both of which were accompanied with provincial consent. This attempt to disguise any pattern to constitutional amendment was successful with Chief Justice Freedman and Mr. Justice Matas. The latter found it "odd that we are requested to declare that a state of affairs exists while at the same time we are asked to define what the state of affairs may be."[51]

The federal government enhanced the impression of uncertainty by raising other questions which bore little relevance to the single question the provinces had asked the courts: was there a constitutional convention requiring the agreement of the provinces? Much attention was directed to the question of whether British ministers considered there to be a constitutional convention requiring consent. This question is not related to the presence or absence of a *Canadian* constitutional convention. Because of Canadian independence, which all parties agreed had occurred *politically* at least by 1930, the impression of British politicians would neither determine nor illuminate the conventional constraints felt by Canadian politicians.

The federal government also attempted to enhance the impression of uncertainty by pointing to the absence of an understanding of when conventions could be breached and when the convention concerning consent came into existence. Moreover, the federal government pointed to the indeterminate nature of requirements of conventions. The questions of the precise content of a convention, when it arose, and when its effect may be terminated are appropriate to virtually every constitutional convention whose existence is not open to challenge. They are not evidence of the absence of a conventional standard.

The federal government persisted in this approach to the convention argument through the Quebec and Newfoundland courts of appeal and in the Supreme Court of Canada. It enjoyed success in the Quebec case with three of the four-judge majority explicitly deciding that there was no convention in respect of constitutional amendment. Chief Justice Crête stated there might be a convention, but it tends to favour the federal thesis rather than that of the provinces.[52] The federal thesis was that there was no convention except the convention that the British Parliament must implement a Canadian request for amendment.

In Newfoundland the three-judge appeal court found there was a constitutional convention of provincial consent. That court stated there were five amendments of "direct concern" to provinces, for which provincial consent was obtained. Later the court stated that, in respect of the first of these five instances, there was objection from one province, but it was not a genuine counter example since the amendment did not impair the rights of provinces. The choice of the remaining four amendments is neither exhaustive of instances in which provincial rights are directly affected or for which provincial consent was obtained. Clearly the Newfoundland court was determined to emerge from the morass of history and doubt created in the federal argument. It did not, however, present a convincingly classified view of Canada's amendment history.

In its factum for the Supreme Court of Canada, Saskatchewan decided to deal as directly as possible with the federal strategy of confounding any attempt to categorize past practice. It presented a complete history of amendments and offered this synopsis.

> The precedents relating to constitutional amendments that have changed legislative powers are consistent and uniform and may be readily summarized as follows: *in positive terms*, every amendment since Confederation changing provincial legislative powers has been agreed to by the province(s) whose legislative authority was affected; *in negative terms*, no amendment changing provincial legislative powers has been made since Confederation when agreement of a province whose legislative authority would have been changed was withheld. There are no exceptions.[53]

This statement is followed by a description of the manner of Chief Justice Freedman's confusion in the face of the federal argument.

The majority of the Supreme Court of Canada on the convention question accepted Saskatchewan's clarification of the history of amendment, even quoting, without attribution, most of the synopsis.[54]

Having found that there was an intelligible historical basis for a convention, the two other prerequisites for conventions were examined: have political actors felt bound by the convention and is the practice for a clearly articulated and accepted purpose? As for the views of Canadian politicians prior to the federal government in 1980, there are few matters in Canadian political history for which there is clearer documentary history than that federal politicians felt bound to obtain provincial consent to amendments to the Constitution.

The argument based on federalism which was the basis of Saskatchewan's unsuccessful legal argument proved useful in the context of convention. The federal nature of Canada, constitutionally established and judicially enforced with remarkable zeal for well over a century, was the clear purpose behind the historical pattern of conduct and permitted the practice to be regarded by the Supreme Court as convention.

The Decision

On 28 September 1981 most of the thirty-seven lawyers who had appeared before the court during the hearing in late April and early May returned to Ottawa to hear judgment delivered. In a break with tradition, Chief Justice Laskin allowed television cameras into the court so that the decision could be broadcast to the waiting Canadian public. The event did not prove to be as dramatic as expected. The television microphones failed to work so that the words of the chief justice in delivering the formal judgment were virtually inaudible to the television audience. Furthermore, the formal judgment was presented in such an abstract form it was difficult to get a sense of who had decided what. And, finally, the one thing that was clear was that nobody had won, and the euphoria of victory could be neither felt nor communicated to a waiting public. Varying majorities of the court had decided that the federal plan, if carried out, would breach constitutional convention but encounter no legal impediment.

Notwithstanding the ambiguous nature of the result, the minister of justice, Jean Chrétien, took the inevitable step of putting the federal government's position in its best light. He swept out of the justice building with an army of officials at his side, crossed the hundred metres of open square to the Supreme Court of Canada, and marched into the court lobby and into a battery of television cameras. Within minutes of the court's handing down a long multi-faceted decision, Chrétien appeared on national television declaring that the federal position had been clearly vindicated. The federal government, he said, had known all along that what it was doing was legal. In ranking the two aspects of the judgment, he declared the legal question to be far more significant than the finding of a breach of constitutional convention. He chose a disarming example to put convention in its rightful place. The Supreme Court, he said, had a convention against allowing television cameras in its courtrooms. That convention that day had been swept away to meet new conditions, and nobody claimed that this was wrong or harmful to the court. Likewise, national conditions were right for by-passing the judicially recognized convention of provincial consent. This, perhaps somewhat inappropriate, comparison between televising a court proceeding and overriding a federal principle indicated that the next struggle would be over the placement of the court's decision in a political perspective.

Much later that day, after lawyers and officials had spent frantic hours plowing through the hundreds of pages of typescripts and preparing statements for their political bosses, Colin Irving, counsel for Quebec, was checking out of his Ottawa hotel to return to Montreal. When he was asked how he felt about the Supreme Court's ignoring his argument on the legal question, he replied that it didn't matter. "We've won," he said, "now the federal government will never bring it off without the provinces."

We will never know whether the federal government could somehow have bulldozed the resolution through Parliament and, then, through Westminster. What we do know is that the Supreme Court's decision produced the conditions under which the governments of Canada were forced to continue once again their long search for constitutional agreement.

Notes

1. *Minutes and Proceedings of the Special Joint Committee of the Senate and of the House of Commons on the Constitution of Canada*, 30th Parliament, 3d Session, 15:19–20 (19 September 1978).

2. *Reference Re Legislative Authority of Parliament in Relation to the Upper House*, [1980] 1 S.C.R. 54, 102 D.L.R. (3d) 1.

3. *Ibid.*, at 70 (S.C.R.), 12 (D.L.R.).

4. *Ibid.*, at 67 (S.C.R.), 10 (D.L.R.).

5. *Ibid.*, at 60 (S.C.R.) 5 (D.L.R.), referring to G. Favreau, *The Amendment of the Constitution of Canada* (Ottawa: Queen's Printer, 1965).

6. *House of Commons Debates*, 19th Parliament, 4th Session, 5: 4366 (5 July 1943).

7. Indeed, counsel for the attorney general of Canada conceded that the federal resolution would affect federal as well as provincial powers. See *Reference Re Amendment of the Constitution of Canada, (Nos. 1, 2, and 3)*, [1981] 1 S.C.R. 753 at 772, 125 D.L.R. (3d) 1 at 20.

8. The judgment of the Quebec court of appeal, led by Chief Justice Crête (Owen, Turgeon, and Belanger, JJ.A. concurring, Bisson J.A. dissenting) answered in favour of Ottawa: *Reference Re Amendment of the Constitution of Canada (No. 3)* (1981), 120 D.L.R. (3d) 385. Crête, C.J. said at 407–408: "1. Whether or not one agrees with the form or the content of the resolution before the two federal Houses, this resolution is not subject to review by the Courts and neither do the Courts have the right to decide upon what legislative measures

the Parliament of the United Kingdom can or could adopt. 2. Whether or not one subscribes to the compact theory of confederation, it must be recognized that, on a judicial level, the British North America Act, 1867, is a statute which can only be amended or repealed by another statute emanating from the same legislative authority which adopted the initial statute, namely, the Parliament of the United Kingdom."

9. Factum of the attorney general for Manitoba on the Manitoba reference, at 47.

10. Ivan C. Rand, "Some Aspects of Canadian Constitutionalism" (1960), 38 *Canadian Bar Review* 135, at 145.

11. Factum of the attorney general for Newfoundland on the Manitoba reference, at 26.

12. Factum of le procureur general du Québec on the Manitoba reference, at 19.

13. Factum of the attorney general of British Columbia on the Manitoba reference, at 50.

14. *Reference Re Amendment of the Constitution of Canada* (No. 1) (1981), 7 Man.R. (2d) 269, 117 D.L.R. (3d) 1 (C.A.), at 7–8.

15. *Ibid.*, at 326 (Man.R.), 49–50 (D.L.R.).

16. *Reference Re Amendment of the Constitution of Canada (No. 2)* (1981), 118 D.L.R. (3d) 1 (Nfld. C.A.), at 16.

17. *Supra*, note 7, at 43–44 (D.L.R.).

18. *Ibid.*, at 41.

19. See N. McL. Rogers, "The Compact Theory of Confederation" (1931), 9 *Canadian Bar Review* 395, at 398–405; P. Gerin-Lajoie, *Constitutional Amendment in Canada* (Toronto: University of Toronto Press, 1950), 208–209.

20. The Alberta Act (1905), 4–5 Edw. 7, c. 3, 21 (Can.); The Saskatchewan Act (1905), 4–5 Edw. 7, c. 42, s. 21 (Can.).

21. [1932] A.C. 54 (P.C.), at 70.

22. *Supra*, note 19: Gerin-Lajoie at 207 and at 292–96 (Appendix C: "Some Statements of Leading Public Men").

23. Factum of the attorney general for Manitoba on the Manitoba reference, at 15 and 17–18.

24. *Supra*, note 14, at 22–23 (D.L.R.).

25. The British North America Act, 1946, which amended s. 51 of the 1867 Act, readjusting representation in the House of Commons, was effected without provincial consent, on the grounds that it concerned only the government of Canada. See *supra*, note 7, at 64 (D.L.R.).

26. *Supra*, note 14, at 52 (D.L.R.).

27. Factum of the attorney general of Manitoba on the Quebec reference at 38.

28. *Supra*, note 8, at 407–408, 436–37, and 417 respectively.

29. *Ibid.*, at 443–444.

30. *Ibid.*, at 464–465.

31. *Supra*, note 7, at 29 (D.L.R.).

32. *Supra*, note 14, at 24 (D.L.R.).

33. *Ibid.*, at 23.

34. *Ibid.*, at 43.

35. *Ibid.*, at 50–51, 54.

36. Section 91(1) of the Constitution Act, 1867, for example, provides that there must be parliamentary elections every five years. Section 51 provides for representation in the House of Commons. It has been amended several times, but has always provided for a system based essentially on representation by population.

37. *Supra*, note 8, at 443.

38. *Supra*, note 16, at 17.

39. Canadian constitutionalism involves a tension between respect for regional diversity (the basis of the federal principle) and respect for the domestic equality of each Canadian. The provincial sovereignty argument places a vast preference for the former over the latter. For an elaborated argument on how the tension between federalism and majoritarianism can be creatively used to provide an argument for a legal requirement of provincial consent which is less than unanimity, see Schwartz, "General National Agreement: The Legal Sanctions for Constitutional Reform in Canada" (1981), 6 *Queen's Law Journal.*

40. *Supra*, note 7, S.C.C. judgment, at 44 (D.L.R.).

41. *Ibid.*, at 43–47.

42. House of Commons (U.K.), *British North America Acts: The Role of Parliament*, first report from the Foreign Affairs Committee (Session 1980–81, 30 January 1981), para. 14(10), at xii.

43. *Federal-Provincial Conference of First Ministers on the Constitution, Verbatim Transcript*, Ottawa, 8–13 September 1980, C.I.C.S. Doc. 800-14/042, at 1087–88. Extract from an unverified and unofficial verbatim transcript.

44. Supreme Court of Canada factum of the attorney general of Saskatchewan, at 35–36.

45. *Supra*, note 42, at para. 14 (10).

46. *Supra*, note 7, at 32 (D.L.R.).

47. *Ibid.*, at 42.

48. *Ibid.*, at 47.

49. *Supra*, note 14, at 13 (D.L.R.).

50. *Ibid.*, at 30.

51. *Ibid.*, at 39.

52. *Supra*, note 8, at 406.

53. *Supra*, note 44.

54. *Supra*, note 7, at 94 (D.L.R.).

Chapter 7
The Week That Was

Aftermath of the Court Decision

On 28 September 1981 the Supreme Court's decision on the constitutionality of the federal resolution compelled all of the governments to meet again to seek compromise. The political impact of the Court's decision was immense. In Britain the *Guardian* reported that the Canada bill, even under the strenuous sponsorship of the Thatcher government, would have a tough time in the House of Commons.[1] Some members of the Trudeau government privately acknowledged that the resolution's fate in Westminster was unclear, even if it cleared the Canadian House of Commons. The opposing provinces, while buoyed by partial success in the Supreme Court, were divided on the situation in London. Quebec believed that the provinces' position had been greatly strengthened by the Court's judgment and that a majority of the members of the British Parliament would oppose the bill. Saskatchewan and Alberta, also active in London, did not share Quebec's conclusion. The opposing provinces were divided on the next step to take. Some argued that the judgment had taken the steam out of the federal patriation plan and predicted that the entire federal proposal would be shelved. Others argued that the federal government would continue to push ahead relentlessly on the basis of the legal aspect of the judgment and, accordingly, this necessitated a resumption of the federal–provincial negotiations. The prime minister, speaking from Seoul, Korea, on 28 September told Canadians that the Supreme Court had "ducked" the question of how many provinces were needed to agree to the resolution. Therefore, "we are . . . in the same situation . . . (as) before the matter went to the Supreme Court, and the position of the federal government should be the same. . . ."[2] However, it was not the same situation. The important new element was, of course, that the Supreme Court had stated the rule of unanimity under which past constitutional conferences laboured and ultimately failed was not a conventional requirement. As each side claimed victory, there was a growing public demand that another attempt to reach agreement be made, in light of the new ground rules.

The position of the federal leader of the New Democratic Party, Ed Broadbent, provided yet another important impetus for a resumption of the constitutional negotiations. The NDP had aligned itself with Ottawa on the constitutional issue, its western-based caucus lending political legitimacy to the federal resolution. Broadbent now, as a result of the Court's decision, urged the prime minister to convene a first ministers' conference in an attempt to obtain a broader consensus for a patriation package with an amending formula and a charter of rights. Broadbent warned that the NDP would vote against the present resolution if Ottawa attempted to act on it before holding another conference. This greatly weakened Ottawa's political position since it threatened to end the only significant support for the resolution from western Canada.

On 1 September 1981, the federal government and Alberta had agreed on a comprehensive energy program. The most contentious issues of the national energy program—pricing, taxation, revenue sharing, exploration incentives, and "Canadianization" of the petroleum industry—were largely resolved through negotiation. If as complicated a matter as energy could be so resolved, Canadians wondered why constitutional matters could not be resolved as well.

Three new developments had changed the political environment. First, the Supreme Court decision was a clear signal to the Trudeau government that it had violated the rules of the constitutional game; but the decision also told the provinces that the federal government had the legal authority to ignore these rules if it so chose. The unanswered question was whether both sides would heed the implicit meaning in the judgment. Second, the federal NDP had withdrawn its support for the federal resolution, which forced the government to reconsider its approach of proceeding to Westminster regardless of the consequences of the Court's decision. Finally, the energy agreements pressured governments to return to the bargaining table to duplicate their success on the Constitution.

In Quebec the government issued a strongly worded statement which criticized Ottawa's apparent refusal to acknowledge the impact of the Supreme Court's decision on the conventionality of the resolution. Following negotiations with the Liberal opposition, the government introduced a motion in the National Assembly which demanded "that the federal government renounce its unilateral course of action that could impair its rights and affects its powers without its consent. . . ." However, it too concluded with a request that new negotiations should take place "with full respect for the principles and conventions that must apply to any modification of the Canadian federal system."[3] In private meetings with its allies, Quebec predicted that the federal government would have either to withdraw the resolution or accept the April provincial patriation plan. Since Ottawa intensely disliked the plan, it would be forced to withdraw the resolution. Therefore, any meeting of the first ministers should stress the unity and commitment of the eight dissenting provinces to the provincial patriation plan.

British Columbia's premier, Bill Bennett, had assumed the chairmanship of the premiers' conference in August. It was generally understood by the premiers of the eight dissenting provinces that he would also serve as the chairman of their group. Obviously, the two positions conflicted since Ontario and New Brunswick both supported the initiatives of the federal government and were members of the premiers' conference. Bennett would have to walk a fine line between the interests of the eight dissenting provinces and the interests of all ten. Immediately after the decision of the Court, he declared his intention to travel to each provincial capital "to seek ways and means of, not only achieving a 'Made in Canada constitution,' but also resolving our economic difficulties."[4] Bennett's statement also emphasized that both he and Lougheed had just recently concluded new energy agreements with the prime minister demonstrating that "the constitutional discussion is not a question of energy versus rights or fish versus rights or resources versus rights. . . ."[5] In fact, he cited the energy agreements as proof that the goodwill of governments was the key ingredient to attaining federal and provincial cooperation on the Constitution. Finally, reflecting Canada's growing economic problems of high interest rates and inflation, Bennett's statement stressed the need to convene a conference on the economy, a request the prime minister had previously rejected.

In his visits Bennett told the premiers that, as a result of his private conversations with Trudeau, he was convinced that the prime minister was now prepared to strike a bargain on the Constitution. According to Bennett, the prime minister made an offer of sorts to him. The offer, only generally explained, was immediate patriation with the entrenchment of the provisions on language and mobility rights, equalization, resources, and fundamental and democratic rights. With respect to the amending formula, the unanimity rule would be entrenched for a two-year period, during which time the governments would pursue an agreement for a new formula. At the end of two years, a referendum would decide the nature of the amending formula if the governments failed to agree. These proposals, of course, tracked the proposals of the October 1980 federal resolution. According to Bennett, the prime minister also indicated that he might be prepared to abandon the referendum if there were an acceptable agreement. In a later meeting between Jean Chrétien and Roy Romanow, Chrétien disputed this version of the meeting.

This "offer" was hardly a new one, being based structurally and substantively on the proposed federal resolution. As well, many were skeptical that Trudeau was really prepared to compromise the basic federal plan to an extent satisfactory to the majority of the eight dissenting provinces. Nevertheless, after each provincial visit, Bennett expressed to the press his optimism that a solution was possible, and urged the governments to find a compromise. Quebec was increasingly apprehensive that Bennett had confused his role of chairman of the eight dissenting provinces with that of chairman of the entire ten. At two meetings of ministers of the eight dissenting provinces, on 21 October in Montreal and 27 October in Toronto, there was an attempt to assess the true motives of British Columbia. On each occasion the group was assured by British Columbia that it was still committed to the provincial patriation plan. However, there was mounting confusion as to precisely what Trudeau had offered and, as this confusion persisted, it was apparent that Bennett would soon incur the wrath of both the federal government and the eight dissenting provinces. Nevertheless, his unwavering stance that there was room for negotiation, even if not supported by clear evidence of change, nurtured the incipient mood for compromise and prevented an immediate recommitment to the original opposing positions. A more strident supporter of the inviolability of the position of the dissenting provinces might have greatly worsened the crisis.

Bennett's initiatives, however, were not the only ones. On the night of the Court's decision, the federal minister of justice, Jean Chrétien, Saskatchewan's attorney general, Roy Romanow, and Ontario's attorney general, Roy McMurtry, met in Chrétien's home to review the judgment informally and to assess its impact. McMurtry suggested that Ontario might consider giving up its traditional veto in the amending formula if this would appease the western provinces. However, both Chrétien and Romanow felt that, since Quebec would not agree to give up its veto, the western provinces would prefer their opting-out formula, which the federal government resolutely rejected. The meeting yielded no conclusions but resulted in a commitment that both Romanow and McMurtry would endeavour to determine the current thoughts of their provincial counterparts, in light of the Court's decision, at a meeting of provincial attorneys general in St. John's later in the week. This discreet lobbying produced no results. Romanow flew from St. John's to the meeting of the Gang of Eight in Montreal. Quebec's intergovernmental affairs minister, Claude Morin, pressed Romanow on whether media reports of a secret meeting in Chrétien's home were true. Romanow initially stressed the social and unplanned nature of the get-together, indicating that it was simply an occasion for a few lawyer–politicians to discuss the decision in the *Patriation Reference*. Bothered by his failure to disclose to his colleagues the full details of the discussion at Chrétien's home, Romanow, later the same day, asked for a meeting with all the provinces. When ministers and officials met in the hotel room of British Columbia's Garde Gardom, Romanow disclosed that during the visit with Chrétien and McMurtry the discussion about the *Patriation Reference* had, in fact, moved on to the matter of possible changes to the federal resolution. He also stressed Saskatchewan's commitment to looking for a compromise to the constitutional dispute and that his conversation in Ottawa reflected that view. In any event, the exercise by Ontario and Saskatchewan of canvassing the provinces for movement was discontinued.

Getting Ready to Meet Again

By late October, with the Bennett mission floundering, the likelihood of failure of the First Ministers' Conference loomed larger. All eleven of the governments had not met to discuss their positions since the September 1980 First Ministers' Conference. The prime minister, in convening the 2 November First Ministers' Conference, described the meeting as "one last time," while the opposing provinces portrayed it as another one in the ongoing struggle to resolve the constitutional issues. Moreover, each side blamed the other for the failure of Ottawa to introduce a new budget. The new circumstances, which initially appeared to be conducive to settlement, were being squandered. Consistent with his previous positions, Blakeney decided that yet another attempt would have to be made to seek a compromise before the conference. He telephoned Davis of Ontario, Bennett of British Columbia, and Buchanan of Nova Scotia and requested that they each delegate a minister to review the options for compromise with Romanow.[6] The tactic was designed to appeal to the "middle group" of provinces in the hope that serious negotiations over detailed proposals would produce an acceptable alternative to both the provincial patriation plan, already rejected by the federal government, and the federal resolution, rejected by the eight provinces. The premiers agreed to this approach. However, in Toronto the Nova Scotia minister, Harry How, excused himself from the meeting because his province was still committed to the provincial patriation plan. Garde Gardom of British Columbia, in keeping with his province's strategy of "keeping the situation fluid," advanced several general alternative solutions, some of which contradicted each other. The problem was the First Ministers' Conference was merely days away, there were still no acceptable alternatives, and the fluidity strategy was adding confusion to the process.

Ontario's minister of intergovernmental affairs, Tom Wells, confirmed McMurtry's earlier statement that Ontario would be prepared to adopt an amending formula which did not grant it a veto in exchange for acceptance of the charter. The province would even consider the amending formula contained in the provincial patriation plan if certain "refinements" were made to it. The most important refinement was an amendment of the opting-out provision, making it applicable only when a proposed constitutional amendment transferred legislative powers to the Parliament of Canada. This idea drew a distinction between the transfer of powers and the derogation of provincial powers, which was the provision in the provincial scheme. Romanow responded that the provinces were concerned with more than a mere transfer of power. For example, the general repeal of section 125 of the British North America Act, which prohibited the two orders of government from taxing each other, was a derogation of provincial powers, rights, and privileges but might not be seen as a transfer. Thus, if Ontario's suggestions were accepted, a province would not be permitted to opt out. To counter the concern that the formula would result in a "checkerboard Canada," Romanow argued that, since the opting-out provision applied only to those matters agreed upon and implemented after patriation, the prospect of checkerboarding was greatly reduced. After two days, however, it was clear that the discussions would not produce an acceptable middle ground. This sense of futility resulted in large measure from Nova Scotia's unwillingness to get involved and British Columbia's hesitancy to concentrate on one option; no proposal from the four provinces would be placed before the First Ministers' Conference the following week in Ottawa.

The November 1981 First Ministers' Conference

The First Ministers' Conference on 2 November 1981 was convened in a mixed mood of grudging necessity, persistent mistrust, and modest hope. On the Sunday evening before the formal opening of the conference, the premiers of the eight dissenting provinces met to confirm their defensive alliance and agreed to stress the unconventionality of the process employed by the federal government. Although it had already been publicly rejected by Ottawa, the group also decided once again to submit the provincial patriation plan as a solution to the impasse. Because of the tensions within the alliance, it was probably incapable of developing another fresh proposal. A final agreement was that before any member of the group advanced proposals other than the provincial patriation plan, or left the alliance, it would first notify the others of its intentions. This latter point proved to be of major consequence later in the week.

It is not possible to describe all the events that transpired during the week of the conference. The major portion of the deliberations took place in private sessions, and no official transcripts or records of decisions were made. The whirling events of the four-day conference took on the characteristics of the aurora borealis on a clear winter's night on the prairies, as positions shifted and danced through the conference room, each displaying a multitude of shades and hues. In this kind of an atmosphere, observations differ and conclusions are difficult. Nevertheless, an overview of the week's most important developments must be attempted in order to understand the compromises that were ultimately achieved.

Monday

At the opening public session on Monday morning, in the cavernous main hall of the conference centre, the prime minister declared he was "not wedded" to the Victoria amending formula, but he defended it on the grounds that it provided the regions with an important voice with respect to future amendments. Based on their actual populations, western Canada and Atlantic Canada would have greater control of amendments since, for example, four million people in the West could block an amendment equally as eight million in Ontario.[7] Trudeau also argued that the referendum was vital to the constitutional resolution because, if discussions failed to yield a unanimous agreement on an amending formula, the people could ultimately decide. The prime minister again rejected the provincial patriation plan because it might be used to deny "the national will" and, when coupled with the provision on fiscal compensation, would permit "incremental separatism." Turning to the charter, Trudeau described it as a constitutional guarantee of those rights and values that are accepted by all Canadians. As such, the federal government would only be prepared to consider the timing of the implementation of the charter but not the question of the principle of its entrenchment. Because the charter had been discussed even before Victoria, Trudeau argued that it was "made in Canada." Of course, this argument totally ignored the contention of the eight opposing provinces that both the charter and the other provisions of the Constitution should be "made in Canada" in the sense of receiving approval of the governments of Canada before being referred to Westminster.

In what appeared to be a well-orchestrated strategy, both Ontario and New Brunswick also indicated their flexibility. Although it continued to support the amending formula contained in the federal resolution, Ontario was "quite prepared to have a formula which does not give Ontario the veto."[8] However, such a new formula should take into account the interests of the regions of the country and "make sense." Ontario's abandonment of the veto was an important concession; most of the other provinces had repeatedly objected to any formula granting a veto over future constitutional amendments to some provinces and not to others. Some delegations interpreted this position as a decision by Ontario to put some distance between itself and the federal government. Perhaps Ontario's considerable influence might be directed to extract important concessions from the federal government. The extent to which this might be possible was widely debated among some of the other delegations. In his opening statement, the other federal ally, Hatfield of New Brunswick, suggested a compromise on the issue of the entrenchment of the charter. He proposed a two-tier charter of rights in which fundamental freedoms, democratic rights, mobility, official languages, and minority language education rights would be immediately entrenched and made applicable to both orders of government, while the balance of the proposed charter would be deferred for a three-year period, during which the governments would further negotiate their provisions. However, at the end of the three-year period, the balance, as originally proposed or as agreed upon, would become a part of the charter. Thus, the federal government, Ontario, and New Brunswick had all proposed significant concessions on two of the most contentious issues before the conference. Tactically, they scored a victory by appearing to be flexible and willing to negotiate.

Each of the dissenting provinces had its own message, notwithstanding the agreement reached the evening before to advance the provisions of the provincial patriation plan and the unconventionality of the process, as determined by the Supreme Court of Canada. For example, Saskatchewan's Blakeney stated that he supported the eight provinces' accord because "we prefer it to the amending provisions before Parliament with their elaborate one-sided referendum arrangement and their perpetual veto for the Senate."[9] However, Blakeney was prepared to consider other proposals and declared that "our preferred amending formula is the one we set out before the Parliamentary committee last December."[10] Quebec reminded the conference that its National Assembly had approved a resolution on 2 October 1981 which demanded the federal government "renounce its unilateral course of action"[11] and expressed its opposition to any action which would impair the rights and powers of the National Assembly. Like Manitoba, however, it stressed the provincial patriation plan as the basis of possible agreement; but, unlike Manitoba, it hinted that it might consider a limited charter of rights that could "adapt and grow." British Columbia repeated its theme that governments must settle their differences and proceed to a consideration of urgent economic matters. Prince Edward Island's statement expressed the hope that the Constitution would ensure that smaller provinces were not trampled upon by the larger ones. However, the central position of the dissenting provinces was set out by Lougheed of Alberta in his opening statement:

> From the perspective of Alberta, any amending formula that is devised must incorporate the principle of provincial equality and reflect the need to protect existing provincial legislative powers, rights and privileges. . . . Once an agreement on an amending formula has been reached, the conference can then decide whether it wishes to add other matters. . . .[12]

This was a strong restatement of the fundamentals contained in the April provincial patriation plan, but it was more than that: it was the clue to discovering a compromise.

The first private session Monday afternoon involved only the prime minister and premiers. After approximately one and one-half hours, the first ministers decided to invite one minister and one official from each delegation to join them in their fifth floor conference room. The prime minister described the preceding discussion amongst the first ministers as one that concentrated on the various amending formulas, with specific attention to the ones proposed in the federal resolution and the provincial patriation plan. Each side had rebutted the other, and it was apparent that there had not been movement in either of the positions. Quoting Saskatchewan's Premier Blakeney, Trudeau stated that, in searching for an amending formula, the conference was unable to "square the circle."

A new amending formula had to reflect the national will and, therefore, should result in constitutional uniformity throughout Canada. It also had to address the issue of a veto for Quebec. However, some provinces insisted that an amending formula must be based on the principle of equality. Although a formula might embrace two of the above principles, it was not likely to encompass all three of them. If one or more provinces were to possess the power to veto future constitutional amendments but all provinces were to be treated equally, the result would be that every province would possess the power to veto constitutional change or opt out of constitutional amendment. In this circumstance, Trudeau declared the federal government was back to "square one" since it opposed the "opting out with fiscal compensation" proposal of the provincial patriation plan.

At this point Lougheed cited Alberta's concerns about its ownership and jurisdiction over natural resources. Alberta had felt the power of the federal government in its various legislative and taxation measures; it was not inconceivable that provincial ownership and jurisdiction over natural resources might some day be constitutionally removed. Experience had convinced Lougheed that a future amending formula must protect provincial powers, rights, and privileges.

The Alberta premier also suggested that future amendments might be subject to approval from two-thirds of the members of a reconstituted second chamber, based on the 1980 discussions where all the members of such a new body would be appointed by provincial governments. The composition of the United States Senate granted the same power to the weakest of states as it did to the strongest and, in this regard, was dissimilar to the Canadian Senate. Trudeau replied that his government was considering instituting a system of proportional representation to the House of Commons in the near future.

In rejecting the opting-out provisions of the provincial patriation plan, Davis saw it as a potential weapon to frustrate the wishes of the entire country. As an alternative to both the opting-out and veto formulas, Davis suggested in general terms a "mathematical formula" based on a certain number of provincial governments with a specific percentage of the overall population. Bennett, acknowledging the problem of opting out, suggested yet another amending formula. Matters considered to be in the national interest would be listed and would require unanimity; matters not so listed would be subject to amendment based on approval of seven provinces with 50 percent of the population. The list might include natural resources, language provisions, provincial boundaries, and provincial proprietary rights. In effect, this model resembled the Toronto consensus of 1978–79. However, both Lougheed and Lévesque rejected this idea since the unanimity list would be very long and, in any event, unlikely to be agreed upon by the governments. In the words of Lévesque, "If we open up the list, you go right back to unanimity." Lougheed then asked if Ontario would accept an amending formula which was not tied to a certain percentage of the population. Trudeau interjected that Quebec had to be specifically designated as one of the seven provinces, at which point Lévesque objected to the singling out of Quebec. Davis responded that this kind of a formula would present certain problems for Ontario but might be accepted "if all else falls into place."

Blakeney then suggested an amending formula, similar to Bennett's proposal, but the difference was that the formula would include a "specialty list" of those issues which affected only one province and which could be amended on a bilateral basis by both the federal government and the province concerned. An example was the 1949 Terms of Union, involving only the province of Newfoundland. As will be seen later, this proposal was later presented to the entire conference in the form of a specific draft which also included the other outstanding issues.

Trudeau then requested the participants to direct their attention to the entrenchment of the charter. After a long silence, described by Trudeau as being "deafening," Blakeney stated that Saskatchewan could accept entrenchment of the provisions of language and democratic rights and fundamental freedoms. All of the other rights should be made subject to a legislative override provision. Blakeney argued that the mobility provision was too wide and would lead to judicial interference with necessary provincial legislation. The prime minister reiterated that he would be prepared to consider some changes in the wording of the charter, including the mobility section, and to delay implementation of parts of the charter; he was adamant, however, that an entrenched charter would form part of the constitutional package. Apart from this exchange, little else was discussed with respect to the charter.

At the end of Monday, the conference adjourned as it began—with the same competing proposals. The Victoria Charter amending formula, with a referendum, and the provincial opting-out plan, with full fiscal compensation, each commanded support from the same camps that existed before the conference began. Although there was some indication that new suggestions might be forthcoming, the overwhelming mood was that neither side was prepared to adopt the other's solution or another alternative to the impasse.

Tuesday

Tuesday morning's private session began with a review of the charter of rights but was soon diverted to another debate on the amending formula. The prime minister initiated the discussion on the charter by indicating that Hatfield's proposal was acceptable to the federal government if "there was a larger consensus." Without rejecting the entrenchment of at least some rights such as fundamental freedoms and democratic rights, both Lougheed and Bennett expressed their concern with the "phraseology" of the democratic rights portion of the charter. They objected to the inclusion of specific limitations upon the life of provincial legislatures and Parliament in a section intended to reflect higher notions of democratic ideals. These interventions failed to address the other issues of the charter, such as language guarantees or the legal and non-discrimination rights. Bennett then directed his concerns to the proposed section on equalization and reduction of regional disparities. His argument with this section was the same as that articulated throughout the summer of 1980 by his ministers and officials, namely, that a constitution should not set out the specific mode of payment of equalization. In some ways, it was incredible and depressing that, at that stage of the process, the section on equalization was still an outstanding issue.

The discussion gravitated to the question of the amending formula and specifically the referendum provision in the federal resolution before the House of Commons. Lougheed contended that either the resolution should specifically identify the two competing formulas, opting out and Victoria, or it should be silent on the issue. Blakeney dismissed any suggestion that he would agree to a referendum to settle this issue, especially since the federal resolution permitted "a straight majority" of the population in Canada to select the formula. Lévesque objected to the description of the proposed provincial amending formulas as amounting, for Quebec, to an "opt out of Canada" since it significantly restricted the area of opting out. He then endorsed, in general terms, Lougheed's suggestion that a referendum on the amending formula should not specifically identify only the Victoria Charter model.

Although the discussion focused on the concept of the referendum to break the impasse over the amending formula, it was clear that the referendum was gaining prominence as a possible mechanism to resolve the entire issue of patriation and the charter of rights. Debate over the referendum provision centred on the amending formula, but use of the referendum was applicable to patriation and entrenchment of a charter as well. To focus the debate, Blakeney identified four important questions with respect to the deployment of a referendum. First, since the federal resolution permitted Ottawa to substitute the Victoria amending formula for another one, had the provinces also the right to advocate an alternative to the opting-out formula? His answer was that there should be a limited period of time for such substitution by the provinces before the referendum was placed before the people. Second, how should the outcome of a referendum be determined? In this regard, Lougheed had urged that a referendum had to obtain the support of a majority of the people within each province, based on the principle of equality of the provinces, before it was effective. Trudeau, on the other hand, favoured acceptance of the majority of the people within a region defined by the Victoria Charter as the means by which the outcome could be ascertained. Third, how could an alternative amending formula of the provinces be determined? According to the proposed federal resolution, it could only be submitted by those provinces which comprised 80 percent of the population of Canada; provincial consensus, however, suggested that any formula developed by a majority of the provincial governments could be advanced. Finally, in the absence of agreement, what rule would apply to future constitutional amendments? Blakeney stated that Canadians would revert to the rule of unanimity, a rule recently rejected by the Supreme Court of Canada. If the "tyranny of unanimity" had been eliminated by the Supreme Court, why, Blakeney asked, is the conference "considering a path which might lead Canadians back to constitutional paralysis?" Trudeau answered that the constitutional deadlock must be broken somehow. If the governments were incapable of resolving the dilemma, as had been the situation for over half a century, the people would have to choose. Furthermore, the ultimate sovereignty over the Constitution resided with the people, not governments, and, as a result, they should determine these outstanding issues.

A heated debate ensued over whether the federal government had a mandate from the people to proceed with constitutional reform in the way it had. Lévesque argued that Trudeau's government had not campaigned during the preceding general federal election on the basis of its proposed unilateral patriation of the Constitution. If it had, Lévesque asserted, the electoral result in Quebec would have been very different. Trudeau replied that the outcome of the sovereignty-association referendum in Quebec had mandated all governments to act quickly and decisively to resolve outstanding constitutional issues. The two Quebec foes then again challenged each other's interpretation of the meaning of the Quebec referendum. Lévesque strongly intimated that a new campaign might produce different results in the light of the federal government's actions. The notion of a referendum as a mechanism to resolve the entire impasse had now risen to such prominence that at least two of the participants, Trudeau and Lévesque, appeared to agree in principle that it might be necessary once more to fight a referendum, this time to settle the constitutional issues.

Referendum and mandate were not the only areas of sharp exchange between Trudeau and Lévesque. The entrenchment of minority language education provisions prompted vigorous debate, as it had throughout the 1980 summer activities of the CCMC. Trudeau argued that, over a period of time, the nation would divide into two linguistic solitudes with separation being the inevitable outcome if language guarantees for English- and French-speaking Canadians were not entrenched in the Constitution and made available throughout the nation. On the other hand, Lévesque claimed that Quebec was the homeland for French language and culture in Canada and faced the constant threat of assimilation by North America. This threat could only be overcome if the Constitution acknowledged Quebec's unquestioned authority to legislate to protect the minority. The reaction of the other provinces ranged from support of entrenchment of the language rights, as advocated by Blakeney and Hatfield, to skepticism and, even, rejection. The debate had demonstrated there was no common ground on this issue between Lévesque and Trudeau.

Later in the morning, both Ontario and New Brunswick suggested further compromises with respect to the amending formula and the charter of rights. Davis raised the prospect of acceptance of the provincial patriation plan, "with some refinements," on the condition that the opposing provinces adopt the Charter of Rights and Freedoms. When questioned by some premiers about the need for a charter, in the face of Canadians' highly developed system of human rights, Davis argued that a charter was "a statement of nationhood." Most new nations would entrench rights in a new constitution, and, in patriating the Constitution, Canada was like a new nation. Blakeney once more urged consideration of a legislative override as a way to overcome the objections of those governments that saw an entrenched charter as a threat to the parliamentary system of government. Picking up on Davis's suggestion, Blakeney suggested that his government would agree to such a proposal if the other matters, such as resources, were also included. Both Bennett and Buchanan of Nova Scotia also voiced their willingness to consider a limited charter under these circumstances. However, the refinement of the provincial patriation plan proposed by Davis was the removal of the provision for fiscal compensation to the opting-out provinces. Most of the members of the defensive alliance objected and, once again, the conference regrouped around its two opposing camps.

When the conference finally adjourned for lunch, it did not reconvene that day, a fact which reflected the gravity of the situation. The eight dissenting premiers continued their hastily convened luncheon meeting beyond the starting time for the afternoon session. Davis was asked to join the meeting to discuss frankly all of the options that he and Trudeau might accept. It was decided that a committee of the dissenting premiers would submit a new proposal directly to Trudeau later in the afternoon. Originally, that group was to include Bennett, as chairman of the premiers' conference, Lougheed, as a representative of the hard-line opponents to the federal constitutional resolution, and Blakeney, as a representative of the soft-line opponents. However, since this committee would be comprised entirely of western premiers, the group decided that Buchanan of Nova Scotia should replace Blakeney.

The essential ingredients of the new proposal, called the B.C. compromise in recognition of the prominence of British Columbia's view in its formation, were: patriation; the provincial patriation plan amending formula; full fiscal compensation; immediate entrenchment of democratic rights and official language guarantees; a legislative override for fundamental freedoms; an opt-in provision for section 23, dealing with minority language education provisions; a new equalization provision which re-sembled British Columbia's earlier proposal; and a new and expanded section on provincial jurisdiction over natural resources, reflecting British Columbia's desire that "water" be included; and, finally, the establishment of a royal commission to study the implications of the remaining sections of the proposed charter with no time limitation to complete its work. In light of the treatment of human and language rights, the outcome of the meeting with Trudeau was predictable. The compromise was emotionally rejected.

After the eight dissenting premiers had received the report from their committee with respect to the meeting with the prime minister, Blakeney notified the group that he intended to pursue two courses of action. First, he would contact Davis to determine Davis's impression of the meeting with Trudeau. Second, Saskatchewan would advance some specific new proposals to the conference when it reconvened Wednesday morning. Pursuant to the Sunday evening agreement, the other members of the dissenting group would first receive the details. Most of the other members of the defensive alliance objected to this approach because they believed the B.C. compromise, when publicly revealed, would demonstrate to Canadians that it was the prime minister, and not the dissenting premiers, who was inflexible. Furthermore, some feared that Saskatchewan's new proposal would be interpreted to mean that the alliance of the eight provinces was broken, thereby reducing the pressure upon the prime minister to accommodate or abandon his plan. However, Blakeney's con-tention was that the conference was in the unenviable position of having no fresh proposal to consider other than the ones that continued to divide the participants. A new set of suggestions had to be proposed if the con-ference was not to collapse.

Based partly on the ideas and comments advanced during the private sessions and motivated again by the desire to develop a "centre bloc" of provincial governments, Saskatchewan's proposal contained the following principles. The amending formula was based on a short list of matters, which required the unanimous approval of all governments, and a general amending formula, which required the approval of Parliament and seven of the provinces. Another list of matters could be dealt with bilaterally between the federal government and the province directly concerned. The charter of rights would entrench fundamental freedoms, democratic rights, official bilingualism, and mobility rights, the text of the latter being only slightly altered to accommodate the previously stated concerns of Sas-katchewan and Prince Edward Island regarding provincial laws restricting land ownership. Legal and equality rights would be entrenched imme-diately at the federal level but, as with the provisions of Bill C-60 in 1978, the provinces would be permitted to opt in at some future date. On the thorny problem of minority language education rights, Saskatchewan proposed to entrench a statement of principles which would parallel the section on equalization which the federal government had included in the federal resolution. In this way, it was hoped that a common ground for Ottawa and Quebec could be found. The rest of the sections of the proposed federal resolution—aboriginal rights, equalization, and resources—would remain in the same form as they appeared in the federal resolution.

Attempts to contact Davis or his ministers to explain the principles of Saskatchewan's draft failed but, as chance would have it, the two provincial delegations met early Tuesday evening at an Ottawa restaurant. The discussion revealed a willingness on the part of Ontario to pursue the details of this proposal, although it appeared that many of the Ontario delegates had given up any hope of a compromise, especially in the aftermath of the B.C. compromise. McMurtry, however, stated that the principle of a legislative override was more likely, in his opinion, to be accepted by the federal government than other rearrangements or limitations on the charter. Thus, much of the discussion focussed on the nature and extent of such a legislative override and the timing for its introduction in the negotiations. No agreements were concluded and the delegations never did review the Saskatchewan idea in detail. After an all-night drafting session, Saskatchewan's officials finally prepared a detailed constitutional resolution with explanatory notes.

The federal Cabinet was convened early Tuesday evening to receive a report from the prime minister. Undoubtedly, both Davis's proposal of accepting the provincial patriation plan amending formula in exchange for the charter of rights and the B.C. compromise were discussed.[13] Davis's idea had received some tentative support but foundered on the question of deletion of fiscal compensation. The B.C. compromise darkened the prospects of agreement because it meant that the eight dissenting provinces remained united in their opposition to the key elements of the federal resolution. A national referendum would require the consent of all the political parties in the House of Commons, an extremely unlikely prospect. Thus, the federal Cabinet was in a difficult position. It had the choice of proceeding with the resolution as it was drafted, over the opposition of the eight provinces; amending it to suit the dissenting eight, a position unacceptable to the federal government; or abandoning the goal of patriation, an even less palatable alternative than the others. The press reports which emanated from the meeting indicated that Cabinet, having considered its situation, had confirmed its intention to press ahead with the resolution even if it met with an uncertain fate. The situation was extremely grave and the prospect of a settlement was very bleak.

Wednesday
Blakeney presented Saskatchewan's proposal to the other members of the

defensive alliance at their early Wednesday morning breakfast. Bennett then, unexpectedly, informed the group that he was now ready to support the minority language education provisions, a clear departure from the position of Quebec. At the same time, Chrétien and Romanow met at the conference centre, at the request of Chrétien. McMurtry joined them. Four possible solutions were identified. The first of these was an agreement based on the adoption of the April provincial patriation plan amending formula, with fiscal compensation, in exchange for the entire charter of rights. The difficulty with this option was that Trudeau had totally rejected the opting-out feature of this formula, and the majority of the other provinces had rejected, just as emphatically, the adoption of the proposed charter without further modifications. A second option was to adopt the provincial opting-out amending formula without fiscal compensation in exchange for the Hatfield proposal. The difficulty here was that the majority of the dissenting provinces strongly supported the fiscal compensation feature of the formula. Further, the Hatfield proposal would merely delay the eventual imposition of the entire charter upon the provinces. The third option was to accept the opting-out formula without fiscal compensation in exchange for the Hatfield proposal with a legislative override to those rights which had been identified as the subject of further study. The fourth option was a national referendum if the governments failed to agree upon an amending formula, together with the immediate entrenchment of democratic rights, mobility rights, and minority language education rights; the rest would be subject to the legislative override. The chances were remote that this approach would succeed since most of the dissenting provinces, with the possible exception of Quebec, had firmly rejected the referendum idea. The three ministers concluded that the third option represented the best opportunity for agreement. They agreed once again to attempt to convince their colleagues that the conference was doomed unless some compromise, some third option, was found.

When the conference convened Wednesday morning, Lévesque raised the possibility that he would have to leave by noon in order to be present for the opening of the National Assembly the following day. Trudeau replied that the conference was "one final attempt at agreement" and the federal government would not be party to a waiting game. In response to a plea by Davis that the conference should continue to meet until there was an agreement, Lévesque allowed that he could return on Thursday evening or Friday if there was "any respectable chance" of an agreement.

At this point, discussion began on the various proposals, including those that had been advanced to Trudeau by British Columbia the previous day. At first Trudeau did not respond, but when Lévesque and Peckford supported the proposal as a reasonable compromise, he forcefully stated that his government would not accept an opting-out formula with fiscal compensation and an emasculated charter of rights. He advocated patriation with a referendum to decide between the two competing amending formulas: the provincial patriation plan amending formula, with the complete charter; and the opting-out formula, without fiscal compensation, in exchange for the Hatfield proposal on the charter. Trudeau then indicated that he would be prepared to accept the opting-out formula with fiscal compensation but only in exchange for the full charter. If the Hatfield proposal were adopted, fiscal compensation had to be deleted from the amending formula. If an agreement on this basis were impossible, both the amending formula and the charter of rights should be determined by a regionally based referendum. He announced that details of the referendum proposal would be presented to the conference later that day.

At this juncture Blakeney submitted his government's proposal. Lougheed welcomed the initiative but categorically rejected the proposed amending formula. Peckford indicated that he would be prepared to consider the proposal further. Lévesque pointed out that Blakeney himself, in stressing the problems of "squaring the circle," had previously referred to the need to protect Quebec's rights. Since the proposed amending formula did not contain this protection, it was a "non-starter." Blakeney explained that he perceived the veto to be less important than on previous occasions since both Quebec and Ontario had indicated their willingness to do away with it. The provincial patriation plan did not provide a veto for Quebec. Moreover, both provinces had significant representation in the House of Commons and the Senate, where their special interests would be protected. Trudeau interjected that his government preferred a veto for Quebec but was prepared to accept the Saskatchewan proposal if Quebec was. Both Bennett and Davis responded that the proposal was worthy of further consideration and the conference adjourned briefly.

During the coffee break Blakeney and Romanow were asked to meet with Trudeau, Davis, McMurtry, and Wells, who were meeting in an adjoining room. The prime minister predicted the conference would not likely accept Saskatchewan's proposal. Since no other proposal was likely to be adopted, his course of action was clear. The federal government would request Canadians to settle the entire issue of amending formula, patriation, and a charter of rights by referendum if, after a two-year period, there was no agreement. In this way, the governments might also be pressured to some agreement. Also, governments could explain to the Canadian public that the conference was not a total failure. Would the Saskatchewan premier agree to this solution? Blakeney reiterated his anxiety about the detrimental effect of a highly emotional and polarized debate in Canada over the Constitution, but, in light of the stalemate, he would consider it. This was the first and last time that Trudeau, Blakeney, and Davis met privately during this conference. Intergovernmental contacts could only be made through a chain in which Blakeney and Lougheed formed a link. Lougheed commanded the support of Lyon, Peckford, and Lévesque.

Blakeney was the key. He enjoyed the confidence of Davis who, in turn, could influence Trudeau and Hatfield. Without this connection, there could be no access to Trudeau. If communication did not follow this chain, there was little likelihood of compromise, given the depth of the emotions and positions of the participants. As subsequent events demonstrated, the chain was crucial in achieving the final accord.

Upon the resumption of the conference that morning, all of the dissenting premiers rejected the Saskatchewan proposal. Once more, the question of a national referendum was raised, but this time by Lougheed, who wanted to know whether voting would be measured by regional or provincial support and what the situation would be if it failed. Trudeau replied that the referendum would be conducted on a regional basis. Failure would mean that the governments would revert to the rule of unanimity.

From the somewhat tangential and belligerent remarks of that morning, an astonishing new alliance was suddenly formed when Lévesque accepted in principle Trudeau's idea of a referendum to decide the outstanding issues. To the other members of the defensive alliance, none of whom had received any prior notification of Quebec's intentions, it seemed that Ottawa and Quebec had agreed in principle to a solution they had rejected for various reasons. Quebec had apparently assessed the situation after Saskatchewan tabled its proposals and, fearful that they commanded a broad consensus among the other provinces, decided the referendum was its best fallback position. In fact, no such consensus had been formed notwithstanding the efforts by Saskatchewan in the weeks preceding the conference. The trust within the alliance, already severely strained, was finally shattered. Quebec desperately tried to extricate itself from its position on the referendum later that day, especially after the complicated details were revealed by Ottawa, but the injury to the alliance was fatal. Whatever the reasons for Quebec's actions, the result was that the constitutional conference was no longer divided into two discernible opposing camps. The stage was set for further compromise.

It is difficult to believe that the federal government had seriously thought through the notion of the referendum which, at one point, was described as "bizarre." There was an enormous potential for further aggravation of serious regional splits on such issues as language and resources. Furthermore, with Ottawa alone setting the rules, the perception of fairness was drastically curtailed. The fact that the details of the referendum were not available in written form until later that day was further proof that the idea was given prominence by Ottawa only in an attempt to salvage some "success" and to pressure the provinces for some agreement. Undoubtedly, some of the premiers suspected that Trudeau's unpredictability might produce just this sort of result. On the other hand, it was potentially divisive for the country, notwithstanding the strong philosophical justification for its existence. Few prime ministers would gamble the unity of the nation with a referendum in the political atmosphere in which the constitutional debate was being conducted. A further problem with a referendum was that the federal government would need the consent of all of the political parties in the House of Commons, a difficult and time-consuming task. Planned or not, however, the idea of a referendum resulted in the destruction of the defensive alliance, a major precondition to reaching an agreement. The threat to Canadian unity posed by the referendum, in the event the conference should fail, motivated a search for compromise.

In the afternoon session the participants again explored the possibility of using the referendum to settle outstanding issues. Manitoba's attorney general, Gerry Mercier, who was that province's chief spokesman when Lyon departed Tuesday to resume his provincial election campaign, cited the funding for "parochial schools" in his province as an issue where the referendum might prove extremely harmful by resurrecting old divisions. Trudeau replied that, if the nation's leaders chose to be divided on language, then the nation would divide on language. If the country divided on this important matter, it would be divided forever. Specifically, referring to the government of Quebec, Trudeau concluded that the Parti Québécois had given up on the protection of minority language rights. He warned that, if the conference failed to incorporate his provisions with respect to minority language rights, it will give the Parti Québécois "a first class tool to fight for independence."

Lévesque entered the debate at this point, as he had done so many times in the past, to challenge Trudeau's vision of the country. Claiming that Quebec was only "tolerated" in Canada's political and economic institutions, Lévesque explained that he was gradually forced to acknowledge that Quebec's special interests could only be protected and promoted in a new relationship with the rest of Canada: sovereignty-association. This relationship would provide the basis for a more mature, more healthy arrangement between French-speaking Canadians and the rest of the nation since it would acknowledge Quebec's uniqueness. Hatfield described an entrenched charter as a statement of ideals and rights for all Canadians. Lougheed then tentatively accepted the charter but conditioned his support with a request that three sections, fundamental freedoms, equality, and legal rights, be subjected to a "saving provision," or legislative override. In order to redirect the discussion from general statements to a consideration of the specific provisions of the charter, Lougheed urged that the conference debate the charter "on an item-by-item basis."

Instead, Trudeau returned to a consideration of the opting-out amending formula. As an example of its potentially destructive effect, he pointed to the need to legislate portability of pensions through constitutional amendment. How would Canadians be guaranteed the right to transfer their pensions to any part of Canada if one or more of the provinces could opt out of the constitutional amendment? Fiscal compensation would only aggravate this undesirable situation. Moreover, the power legislatively to override some provisions of the charter gave the provinces another avenue of opting out.

Blakeney expressed his agreement with many of Prime Minister Trudeau's observations but stated that the provincial plan was preferable to the federal resolution, which granted the Senate a permanent veto over future constitutional change. It was also better than a formula based on the rule of unanimity. Even though a province could opt out, the rest of the nation would not be deprived of the constitutional amendment. However, since he also harboured some doubts about the precise effect of fiscal compensation, Blakeney declared his willingness to remove this provision from the formula. As for the legislative override, Blakeney observed that, although Britain was considering enactment of a bill of rights, there would always be a *non obstante* clause for the whole charter because Parliament in Westminster was supreme.

Since it appeared there was no agreement, the prime minister informed the conference that he would recommend to his Cabinet that notice be given to renew the debate on the resolution and that the federal government reserved the right to introduce changes to it. Then Trudeau requested the provinces to state their position on a national referendum. Only Ontario and New Brunswick supported it. Quebec, anxious to escape its previous acceptance of the idea, stated that it would adopt the referendum if the majority of the other provinces did. Again, it appeared that failure was inevitable.

Breakthrough

During a coffee break in the late afternoon, a flurry of informal, private meetings among the delegates occurred. At one of these a general outline of a possible accord was sketched; Chrétien and Romanow met and concluded that the situation was extremely serious. Referring to their discussions early that morning, Romanow agreed to contact his ministerial counterparts in Nova Scotia and British Columbia to seek their support for opting out without fiscal compensation and the Hatfield proposal with a legislative override. Both Ottawa and Saskatchewan had earlier expressed general support for the idea. Upon receiving a report of this conversation from Romanow, Blakeney asked that Romanow obtain in writing from Chrétien the key elements of such a compromise. It seemed that perhaps Ottawa might be willing to make a major compromise on the amending formula. Blakeney would, in turn, outline this development to Lougheed and Peckford and request them to delegate an official to meet with Saskatchewan later in the evening to elaborate upon the details. Lougheed was crucial if the other dissenting premiers were to agree. Peckford had earlier indicated an apparent willingness to compromise.

Chrétien and Romanow, joined later by McMurtry, a strong proponent of the legislative override and influential with Davis, then met in a small, secluded room away from the conference room to attempt to define more precisely what the "third option" really was. In private conversations with Gerald Ottenheimer, Newfoundland's attorney general, Romanow was told that the province's main concern was to ensure that the proposed provision on mobility did not prohibit Newfoundland's employment policies designed to favour its workers. Also, Newfoundland was sympathetic to a referendum on minority language education rights in those provinces that chose not to be bound by the proposed provisions of the charter within two years. These views were reported at the meeting and were considered for inclusion in the new compromise position. The meeting produced the "kitchen accord" hastily scribbled on a notepad. It included patriation; the opting-out amending formula without fiscal compensation; entrenchment of the charter with a provision for legislative override of the "second half" as identified by Hatfield on Monday; mobility rights limited when a province's employment rate was below the national average; a provincial referendum where there had been no acceptance of the minority language education provisions after two years; and the federal resolution dealing with natural resources and equalization. Chrétien stated that the prime minister might be convinced to accept this with one exception: the federal government would not agree to a referendum solely for minority language education. As for himself, Chrétien emphatically declared that he had had "enough of referendums to last a lifetime." Chrétien would meet with the prime minister to discuss the proposal. Romanow indicated that Blakeney would be asking Lougheed and Peckford to send officials to his hotel suite later that evening in order to study the proposed package in detail and prepare a draft of a possible accord.

Pressured by the prospects of failure and freed from the constraints of the alliance with the eight dissenting provinces, officials from four provinces met in Blakeney's suite: Howard Leeson and John Whyte from Saskatchewan, Peter Meekison from Alberta, Cyril Abery and Ronald Penney from Newfoundland, and Mel Smith from British Columbia. Just shortly before the meeting Romanow had seen Garde Gardom, British Columbia's minister of intergovernmental affairs, and invited him to send an official. Abery and Penney brought a brief written proposal to the meeting. Saskatchewan's George Peacock and Lionel Bonneville had been asked by Blakeney to draft detailed provisions based on the Romanow-Chrétien discussions. Since these were not ready as the meeting began, it was decided to work from a Newfoundland document, despite the fact that it contained references to a referendum on minority language rights, something explicitly rejected by Chrétien earlier. Discussions proceeded rapidly and easily, and the document soon reflected the afternoon's discussions. Meekison stated that Lougheed would insist that the legislative override apply to fundamental freedoms as well as to legal and equality rights. This change was agreed to.

In their meeting that late Wednesday afternoon, the three provincial ministers had discussed whether aboriginal rights should be included in the accord. The provision which had been added to the federal resolution by the joint parliamentary committee was now under heavy criticism from most of the aboriginal groups. At the meeting of officials Leeson, knowing Blakeney's views on this issue, urged that the officials should recommend to the premiers that aboriginal rights be maintained in the accord in the form set out in the federal resolution. Smith said that his government had strong reservations because almost none of British Columbia had been ceded by the Indians to the province through treaties. There was an uncertainty about the legal effect of this historical fact; the other provinces reluctantly acquiesced to this argument.

The officials were joined by Blakeney, who clarified some of their questions. He then called Premiers Peckford, MacLean, and Buchanan; Nova Scotia's intergovernmental affairs minister, Edmund Morris; Prince Edward Island's attorney general, Horace Carver; and Romanow to join the discussions. What emerged was a two-page document which set out the principles of patriation, the provincial opting-out formula without fiscal compensation, the entrenchment of a charter with a legislative override for fundamental freedoms, legal, and equality rights, and an amendment to the mobility rights provision to take into account Newfoundland's special concerns. On the issue of minority language education, the group proposed a section which would immediately bind the provinces which consented and would permit other provinces to opt in at a later time. It was agreed that Premier Peckford should present his proposal to the full conference the next day on behalf of the group.

The group then discussed how the proposal should be presented to Quebec. They wondered whether it would be possible to make changes that would garner Quebec's approval while still maintaining the apparent support of the federal government. In the end, all agreed that the issues of fiscal compensation and minority language education were two areas where Quebec City and Ottawa were irrevocably at odds. The proposal would be submitted to Lévesque at Thursday's breakfast meeting of the eight. Lougheed would be requested to inform Lyon, campaigning in Manitoba, of the developments. Blakeney would communicate with Davis, and Romanow would advise Chrétien early next morning.

Accord Day
When the premiers of the dissenting provinces met for breakfast, Lévesque

vigorously objected to the proposed accord. He criticized the others for not requesting him to join the meeting held during the night. He strongly disagreed with the concerns of the other premiers about the effects of an unseemly fight in Westminster, and he minimized the impact upon Canada as a whole if the constitutional issues remained unsolved. When the others remained committed to the new proposal, Lévesque requested them to reinstate the fiscal compensation section. Of course, if this occurred, both Trudeau and Davis would certainly reject the proposal and the conference would fail. Lévesque then advised the group that his government would never agree to the proposed accord.

The proposed opt-in provision for minority language education rights and the legislative override for fundamental freedoms were rejected by Chrétien when he was informed by Romanow of the previous evening's developments in an early Thursday morning telephone conversation. Chrétien, arguing that Quebec would still reject the proposed accord, even if it were granted an opting-in provision (as was subsequently confirmed by Lévesque during that morning's final closed session), insisted that the minority language education rights be immediately entrenched for every Canadian. The federal government wanted the immediate application of the so-called "clause Canada" provision of section 23. Furthermore, Chrétien claimed that the legislative override, as discussed late Wednesday afternoon, was intended to apply only to legal and equality rights in recognition of the special problems these provisions might create for provincial governments. Since fundamental freedoms were basic to all, there could be no legislative override with respect to them. Listening to Chrétien, it seemed as though the accord had not, in fact, bridged the gulf between the federal government and the dissenting provinces and that more negotiations might stall the momentum for agreement.

When the first ministers reconvened in the fifth floor conference room, both the expectation and the fear of the momentous occasion dominated the atmosphere. In one final attempt to derail the impending agreement, Lévesque returned to the notion of having a referendum after two years of discussion to resolve the issues. Trudeau again explained his position that a referendum, as an integral part of constitutional amendment, was still desirable. His main objection to the proposed accord was that it did not contain a provision whereby the people of Canada could be directly involved in the amending process, as was the situation with the federal resolution. However, the failure to accommodate his preference had to be weighed against the fact that a constitutional accord, at long last, seemed probable.

Peckford then introduced the proposed accord. Lévesque objected to the process, the removal of fiscal compensation, and linkage of mobility rights to "Statistics Canada," in reference to the special employment provisions of the accord. He also requested the conference to reinstate either fiscal compensation or the veto for Quebec. The prime minister stated that a federal government would have to assess carefully each instance where a province opted out and, in some special circumstances, arrangements could be made for fiscal compensation. However, to obligate the federal government to do so in each and every case would be undesirable. Trudeau concluded that he too regretted the failure of the conference to adopt a veto for Quebec, as had been proposed by his government, but he noted that Quebec had already abandoned the veto when it signed the provincial patriation plan in April. In any event, it was clear that most of the other provinces no longer accepted the notion of speciality in the Constitution for some provinces. But, the proposed opt-in provision for minority language education prevented Trudeau from accepting the proposed accord, as did the legislative override for fundamental freedoms. It was clear from Lévesque's earlier remarks that his opposition ranged over a number of issues, in addition to section 23, and opting out would not lessen his government's objections to the accord. For his part, Chrétien urged the provinces to grant the federal government freedom to propose changes to section 23, at a later date, to accommodate some of the concerns of both Quebec and the other provinces. Gradually this position was accepted.

The sole hurdle to an accord was the extension of the legislative override to fundamental freedoms. In a classic example of raw bargaining, Trudeau was persuaded to accept the override on fundamental freedoms on the condition that the entire override mechanism be limited to a five-year period, if exercised, after which a new legislative resolution would be enacted. After some debate on this suggestion, the premiers agreed.

The question of the dropping of aboriginal rights had been noted by Trudeau earlier but not discussed. However, just as the premiers were rising to leave the meeting Trudeau suggested that the proposal be amended to contain an agreement to constitutionalize further consultations with aboriginal native organizations. The premiers agreed. Thus, ten out of the eleven governments had fashioned a Canadian compromise.

It remained only for the first ministers to reconvene in public session to announce the compromise to the Canadian people. A wide variety of reactions and emotions characterized the delegations prior to the reconvening, but a certain degree of apprehension pervaded the conference centre.

As the various first ministers took their seats, most participants waited to see if the Quebec delegation would return. There was, after all, a chance that they would not. Empty chairs would speak their position as loudly as any words. Quebec had planned well for a constitutional war, but not at all for a constitutional peace. They were left with few options.

When Premier Lévesque arrived, and the conference resumed, there was a collective sigh of relief. It was easier to deal with a Quebec that was present than a Quebec that was not. In forceful terms he denounced the package and the "betrayal." He vowed to continue the fight. But it was not vintage Lévesque. The enormity of his political loss was all too apparent.

The remainder of the public conference was predictable. There was much rhetoric about compromise, and the prime minister gave an eloquent summary of the agreement. The conference was adjourned, and politicians left for the press conferences. The participants realized that they had been part of a profound event, that they had helped to shape a new ship of state that would now sail on different seas. There was, for once, a sense of accomplishment.

Improving the Accord
In the period immediately following the 5 November accord, several issues arose which required further consideration. The federal government made two proposals, with which the provinces agreed, designed to meet Quebec's objections. First, there was to be a partial restoration of fiscal compensation for education and cultural matters, and, second, there was to be a partial opting in for Quebec with respect to minority education language rights. In general terms, all the governments had granted the federal government the freedom to negotiate additional matters in this area in an attempt to mitigate the complaints of Quebec with respect to the accord. Apart from this delegation, it was agreed by the first ministers that the balance of the accord would be treated as a "package agreement" and would not be amendable. The reason was clear: if there were to be subsequent amendments to accommodate certain special concerns and not others, most governments would demand additional changes which they had abandoned in the interest of compromise. Simply stated, the "package" was a fragile compromise, embracing only some of the concerns of the governments, attained only after difficult negotiations. New matters would endanger its durability.

Aboriginal Rights
The events surrounding the Joint Parliamentary Committee's acceptance of section 35 in the proposed federal resolution, recognizing aboriginal and treaty rights, become relevant during the November First Ministers' Conference. The reaction of native groups to the decision to include section 35 was widely interpreted by governments to mean that the section was either of no value or no interest to the Indian organizations. In the last hours of the November meeting, the question of the scope and meaning of aboriginal rights, which had become more pressing because of the ongoing political and legal actions in London by native organizations, influenced many of the participants to exclude the provisions of section 35 from the embryonic accord. Entrenchment of those rights in the form of the proposed section appeared to be against the wishes of most aboriginal organizations.

This was not the only reason for the deletion of the section. The constitutional demands of native organizations were not fully understood by the participants since they had never had the careful consideration by ministers and officials that the other issues had received. Some of the provinces were particularly worried about the possible implications of such constitutional rights upon traditional provincial legislative jurisdiction. In addition to the uncertainty generated within the governments with respect to these objectives, the first ministers, ministers, and officials were mesmerized by the tantalizing prospect of achieving a constitutional accord, at long last. The nature of the last minute negotiations—complex, occasionally bitter and hurried—militated against any careful consideration of the entrenchment of aboriginal rights.

Equal Rights

When the conference considered the legislative override provision on Thursday morning, all the participants had agreed that section 33, the notwithstanding clause, should apply to section 28, which guarantees rights and freedoms equally to male and female persons. Since the equality rights section was made subject to the legislative override, it was logical to apply the same provision to section 28.

On 10 November the federal government contacted the provinces and requested the removal of the application of section 33 to section 28. In effect, their proposal meant that sexual equality in section 15 could not be overridden. On 16 November the subject of a free-standing section 28 was raised in a conversation between Chrétien and Blakeney. Blakeney expressed his government's concern that a free-standing section 28 might be interpreted by the courts to thwart affirmative action programs for women. Moreover, the process might lead to requests from other special interest groups or provinces to amend further the 5 November accord. On 17 November the federal deputy minister of justice, Roger Tasse, advised Leeson that every province had agreed to the new wording with the exception of Prince Edward Island and Nova Scotia, both of which desired more time to consider the matter. An earlier draft amendment, which would have taken Saskatchewan's concerns into account with respect to affirmative actions, was discarded by the federal government. Later that same evening Saskatchewan was told that all the provinces had now agreed to a free-standing section 28. Although there were valid legal concerns over the effect of a preeminent section 28, placing sexual equality above fundamental freedoms, racial equality, and democratic rights, events quickly forced all governments away from the substantive considerations. The political pressure on the government of Saskatchewan from women's groups and the press to adopt the change built very rapidly. Saskatchewan's position had been misrepresented in the Commons and elsewhere as being opposed to equality; in reality, concern for the process and the impact of change on other charter provisions had been uppermost in Saskatchewan's considerations.

If this were to be the new method by which the constitutional negotiations were to be conducted, Blakeney reasoned that other, less privileged and less powerful interests in society should have their rights also protected. Saskatchewan had consistently offered the aboriginal people support for their constitutional demands. While appearing before the Joint Parliamentary Committee studying the Constitution, Blakeney had argued for adequate constitutional guarantees for Indians and Métis. Saskatchewan was the only provincial government to do so. Saskatchewan had consistently submitted to the conference a constitutional provision dealing with aboriginal rights. On 12 November the Saskatchewan premier promised leaders of the Saskatchewan Indian organizations that, if the accord were reopened, he would resurrect the original section on aboriginal rights. The commitment was made, however, without any expectation that the accord would, in fact, be reopened so quickly. In agreeing to the proposed new wording for section 28, Saskatchewan insisted that constitutional recognition of aboriginal rights be also included. Some of the other provinces, particularly British Columbia and Alberta, were neither prepared for nor desired this position. But now the political pressure was mounting for them to incorporate this measure. Lougheed, after several days of silence, acquiesced to the change if the word "existing" were added to the constitutional provision that aboriginal and treaty rights "are hereby recognized and affirmed." On 23 November Chrétien announced to the House of Commons that all of the signatory provinces had agreed to changes to women's and aboriginal rights.[14] Thus, the unsettling period of bilateral negotiations over long-distance telephone ended. It was a strange way by which to settle important and complex legal and social questions, and consider their long-term ramifications but, perhaps, no less perplexing than many of the other decisions and events which transpired during this momentous period of Canada's history.

Notes

1. J. Langdon, *The Guardian* (London), 23 October 1981, at 1.
2. Transcript of a press conference with Prime Minister Trudeau in Seoul, Korea, 29 September 1981.
3. *Debates of the Quebec National Assembly*, 2 October 1981.
4. Transcript of press conference with W. Bennett, premier of British Columbia, following the Supreme Court's decision on the Constitution in Ottawa, 28 September 1981, at 5.
5. *Ibid.*
6. The meeting with Tom Wells and Roy McMurtry, of Ontario, Garde Gardom and Brian Smith, of British Columbia, Harry How, of Nova Scotia, and Roy Roma-

now, of Saskatchewan, took place in Toronto on 28 and 29 October 1981 upon the completion of the meeting of the ministers of the eight dissenting provinces.

7. *Federal–Provincial Conference of First Ministers on the Constitution, Verbatim Transcript—Opening Statement of P.E. Trudeau, Prime Minister*, Ottawa, 2–5 November 1981, C.I.C.S. Doc. 800-15/014. The actual figures of the populations of Ontario and the West were approximately 9 million and 6 million respectively.

8. *Ibid., Opening Address of W. Davis, Premier of Ontario.*

9. *Ibid., Opening Address of A. Blakeney, Premier of Saskatchewan.*

10. *Ibid.*

11. *Ibid., Opening Address of R. Lévesque, Premier of Quebec.*

12. *Ibid., Opening Address of P. Lougheed, Premier of Alberta.*

13. For a version of the events of federal Cabinet meetings, see R. Sheppard and M. Valpy, *The National Deal* (Toronto: Fleet Books, 1982).

14. *House of Commons Debates*, 32nd Parliament, 1st Session (23 November 1981).

Chapter 8
The Charter of Rights and Freedoms

Introduction

Nothing in the whole episode of constitutional transformation between 1978 and 1982 was as visible as the creation of the Charter of Rights and Freedoms. The prime minister, throughout the period of constitutional struggle, coupled reform and patriation with an undoubted ambition to entrench basic human and language rights for all Canadians. He was the most apparent political actor in remaking Canada's Constitution. His strategy of tying constitutional renewal, a subject of public indifference, to the appealing idea of protecting individuals from governmental oppression was displayed in his opening comments at the First Ministers' Conference in September 1980.

On the first morning of that conference the prime minister, after chiding the premiers (and, in his usual self-deprecating way, himself) for once again refusing to agree with each other, even on the question of how they should proceed to talk about constitutional reform, invited them to make opening statements. As for himself, he said, he preferred getting down to business without opening statements. At noon, when the premiers had finished, Trudeau admitted that there were a few remarks he wished to make. Speaking eloquently and forcefully, and never turning away from the television camera pointing at him from the other end of the conference horseshoe, the prime minister spoke, not to the assembled politicians and officials, but to the people of Canada. He reminded them that the vastly larger part of the conference agenda dealt with the desire of provinces to expand provincial powers and reduce federal powers. The remnant of the agenda, which was there on his insistence, dealt with matters for the benefit of the people of Canada. Foremost amongst these items was a charter of rights. He said:

> There are some powers that shouldn't be touched by Government, that should belong to the people, and that is why we call it the people's package because it isn't a quarrel or a quibbling of who can exercise what jurisdiction. It is a question of what basic fundamental rights of the

people are so sacred that none of us should have jurisdiction in order to infringe those rights.[1]

In concluding his plea to place individual rights in the Constitution, he said that the first ministers should not attempt to "trade more powers for governments and politicians" against something that the people really want, "the right to have a Canadian Constitution made in Canada and which protects all their fundamental rights."

Apart from the pride of place on the constitutional agenda which the charter was assigned by Prime Minister Trudeau, the idea of entrenched individual rights and liberties commanded public attention for a number of subsidiary reasons.

First, the charter was associated not only with traditional civil rights (the rights which, it was argued, accrue to a person merely by virtue of being a citizen and an individual of inherent worth), but also with language rights. Language rights have loomed large in the Canadian political consciousness because they are the focus of the debate over constitutional recognition of Canada's composition as two founding nations. More precisely, language rights have been the focus of the debate as it has been created by Prime Minister Trudeau. For twenty years Quebec's political leaders have consistently found other means of achieving constitutional recognition of Canada's dual colonial origin: the transfer to provinces of powers appropriate to give vent to cultural distinctiveness, the recognition of the French–English duality in central institutions, and, most recently, the creation of a special constitutional arrangement between Quebec and the rest of Canada. Trudeau has believed that, if Canadian francophones and, in particular, Quebec francophones were given a genuinely equal opportunity to hold national public sector jobs, if francophones could deal with their national government in their own language, and if francophones could travel throughout the country and receive public services, including education, in their mother tongue, they would believe themselves to be as much a part of Canada and be as deeply committed to Canada as any other Canadian, of whatever background. These ideas have motivated both the Pearson and Trudeau governments' language policy, as well as a major part of their constitutional policy towards Quebec.

The public profile of the federal government's language policy has been vastly enhanced, first, by the hostility with which the program of bilingualism has been received in various parts of English Canada and, second, by the lack of sympathy for it expressed by Quebec's political leaders. Since the election of the Parti Québécois in 1976, the Quebec government has preferred a policy of linguistically discrete regions. This policy would allow Quebec to become a French-speaking province with no official role for English, and an increasingly suppressed unofficial role for English. The other nine provinces would be free to pursue whichever language policies they preferred including, of course, militant English unilingualism. Conflict with federal language policies, created by the enemies of the French language as well as by the Quebec government, has meant that language rights has been as bitter an issue as any faced during the period of constitutional reform. Placement in the charter of language rights for individuals brought it into the centre of the political debate.

Second, the charter has been visible because it has been seen as the one aspect of constitutional reform giving individuals direct access to some public decisions affecting their lives. Whether or not in the public interest, there can be no doubt that entrenchment of rights has an immediacy which no other aspect of constitutional reform can match. A charter of rights deals in values which are rooted in the claims of individuals, as opposed to the needs and interests of governments and bureaucracies; consequently, the idea of a charter has genuine popular appeal. With growth of government has grown the realization that government rules our lives extensively: from what we eat, to what we study, what we pay to keep warm, what we earn, what we keep of what we earn, how we will be looked after when things go wrong. A parallel growth in the sense of each individual's worth and power in the political process has not, however, occurred. Elected bodies are not truly in control of the vast bulk of governmental activity, and, in any event, electors do not have immediate control of those issues which do get dealt with by the elected representatives. One antidote to the frustration and alienation that this produces is a charter of rights, a constitutional document that lets everyone know, at least in respect of some governmental activities, that the interests of individuals are to be controlling. Of all the justifications for constitutional reform—the need to patriate Canada's Constitution, the need to find a domestic amending authority, the need to respond to the shift of power to the West, the need to rearrange federalism to better protect the interests of the francophone minority—none were as responsive to widely shared anxieties as the proposal to entrench in the Constitution a list of fundamental rights.

Third, the charter loomed large in constitutional talks because of the vehemence of provincial opposition to it. Not only were most of the provinces against an entrenched charter, they expressed their opposition in ways which made the debate about entrenchment important and vital. Provincial premiers were not merely engaging in nay-saying, or in self-protection and defensiveness; they were promoting a set of political ideas, drawn from Canada's history, which matched Canada's traditional constitutional values. Furthermore, opposition to an entrenched charter of rights was not based on a lack of commitment to human rights, or on a disrespect for individual interests; it was based on a genuine disagreement on how best to secure the interests of all the people.

Of course, the arguments against entrenchment were sometimes overstated. A charter of rights is not, as suggested by Premier Sterling Lyon at the September 1980 First Ministers' Conference, inconsistent with democratic theory or even with the principles of a parliamentary system of government.[2] Entrenchment increases the range of issues over which legislatures and governmental administrators may be brought to account by the judiciary for ignoring values which are important for personal fulfillment and individual autonomy. In this sense it partially removes from the realm of political debate the process of mediating between claims made on behalf of individuals and claims made for the benefit of the whole community. Under a charter of rights there are more instances in which persons can resort to courts to press their claims. There are more instances in which individualistic claims can be entertained in the judicial process—a process in which governmental interests do not prevail merely because they are supported by government or a majority of the people.

It would, however, be a mistake to think that before the charter there was no room for bringing the government to account before a court. There was in place a lively system of judicial control of government in the sense that legislatures, governments, and administrators were required by courts to act within their assigned jurisdiction, and public decision makers were required to make decisions which affected individuals through fair processes. At the same time, the charter has not judicialized all legislative and public administration issues. There are many instances where insufficient respect is paid to the interests and concerns of individuals or groups which do not fall within the terms of the charter. Furthermore, the individual interests which are not covered by the charter, and which the courts cannot protect, relate to some of the most significant social concerns: health care, housing, employment, and income maintenance. The charter does not change the way that important political accommodations are made, nor does it subordinate the role of politics in the conflict between the state and the individual.

Provinces argued that the charter would not, in the long run, serve the interests of the public. They argued that courts were far less adept than legislatures or governmental departments in striking the right balance between the interests of individuals and the need for effective governmental programs which may proceed at the expense of individual interests. In making this claim, premiers had on their side not only the historical constitutional arrangement in Canada, but also the historical constitutional arrangement of the United Kingdom. Since neither country has an appalling record in respect of human rights, the premiers advanced the notion that real respect for human rights is a product of a much deeper phenomenon in the nation than a constitutional text; constitutionally entrenching rights could disrupt our tradition of respect for rights and, in the end, do more harm than good.

The debate between those who favoured entrenchment and those who opposed it was lively and serious. This factor placed the issue of the entrenchment of rights in the forefront of Canada's constitutional debate.

Early Attempts at Putting Rights in the Constitution

Although Prime Minister Trudeau became so closely associated with the entrenchment of a charter of rights that it looked as if the charter formed the chief part of his political raison d'etre, his interest in this matter accords with an older constitutional reformist tradition. The desire for governments to be active in the protection of human rights has been expressed in Canada since, at least, the last days of the Second World War. There is little doubt that the enemy which was beaten in that war was not so much Germany as a political program based on the idea of the inherent inferiority of classes of humans owing to racial or national distinction. The callousness shown to fellow humans, as well as the total state of tyranny under which this bureaucratically administered extermination was brought about without significant demur from within the nation, clearly lent poignancy to the battle and moral force to what is usually the most morally ambiguous of human enterprises, the waging of war. As the war effort moved towards its close, there arose in Canada political claims which matched exactly the purposes behind the fighting. What was sought was the eradication of human denigration. First, in 1944, Ontario began with its limited, but symbolically important, Racial Discrimination Act.[3] Then in 1947, Saskatchewan, under a CCF government, enacted its Bill of Rights,[4] an extensive statute giving recognition to civil liberties. It dealt with the fundamental freedoms commonly known as political civil liberties—the freedoms of speech, press, assembly, religion, and association. Companion bills prohibited racial and religious discrimination with respect to accommodation, employment, occupation, land transactions, education, businesses, and enterprises.

Both of these early attempts to protect basic human dignity did so by criminalizing the discriminatory conduct or, in the case of Saskatchewan's legislation, the repressive conduct. Criminal legislation did not work well; those discriminated against, as well as the public officials responsible for the Act's administration, were reluctant to charge persons who had engaged in acts of discrimination and, in any event, obtaining convictions was difficult. Furthermore, since the object of the Act was not only to punish the persons who discriminated, but also to redress those who suffered from discrimination, the social control mechanism of criminal law was not particularly suitable. In due course, provinces established schemes of regulation involving inquiry, conciliation, formal adjudication, and the awarding of damages. More and more provinces adopted this sort of legislation, so that by the 1970s all ten provinces had human rights schemes in operation.

Provincial concern for human rights was again made evident at the constitutional conference of the federal and provincial governments in January 1950. Again, it was Saskatchewan, through Premier T.C. Douglas, which actively promoted the entrenchment of rights. He said, in the context of stating which new matters should be entrenched in an amended Canadian Constitution:

> We would go even further and urge that the entrenched clauses should include a Bill of Rights, guaranteeing to every Canadian citizen freedom of worship, freedom from arbitrary arrest and imprisonment, and those other basic liberties which are fundamental to a free and democratic society. Having guaranteed certain minority rights and basic human freedoms against change with unanimous consent we will then be in a position to deal more dispassionately with a more flexible procedure for amending those areas of the Constitution which are of joint concern to the Dominion and the Provinces.[5]

Premier Douglas was, however, alone in advancing the idea of entrenchment of rights at that conference, and the idea was not pursued.

In the federal Parliament the same ideas were being promoted. In 1945 the CCF member of Parliament Alistair Stewart moved in the House of Commons that:

> . . . there should be incorporated in the constitution a bill of rights protecting minority rights, civil and religious liberties, freedom of speech and freedom of assembly; establishing equal treatment before the law of all citizens, irrespective of race, nationality or religious or political beliefs; and providing the necessary democratic powers to eliminate racial discrimination in all its forms.[6]

It is noteworthy that the earliest initiatives at the federal level in aid of protecting human rights were couched in the language of constitutional entrenchment, whereas the provinces had been content simply to pass legislation which brought immediate protection but did not immunize those protections from subsequent repeal. Indeed, they would have been powerless to do so. However, it is clear that, from the earliest days of the post-war period of concern for human rights, the preferred mode of protection has been placement of human rights beyond the reach of legislative majorities.

The Stewart motion sat on the order paper until 1946 when he agreed to drop it because the sentiments it contained were found in the new Citizenship Act, which had been introduced by Prime Minister Mackenzie King.[7] Obviously the recognition of equality within the citizenship bill and the constitutional entrenchment of rights are vastly different matters, but presumably Stewart was content at having performed the traditional CCF role of introducing ideas into the political consciousness of parliamentarians.

In 1946, during debate on the citizenship bill, John Diefenbaker moved that the bill "be not now read for the third time but that it be referred back to committee of the whole" to consider adding a subsection requiring Parliament to adopt "a bill of rights so as to assure the maintenance and preservation of democratic and traditional processes of liberty and equality under the law of all Canadian citizens without regard to race, creed or colour. . . .[8] The government took the line that these rights were already protected by the Magna Carta, the Quebec Act, the Constitutional Act, 1790, and the British North America Act, 1867 and resisted the amendment.[9]

In April 1947 the government moved to set up a joint committee to consider fundamental freedoms and the manner in which those obligations, accepted by all members of the United Nations, might best be implemented, with particular emphasis on the Canadian constitutional situation.[10]

John Diefenbaker drafted another bill of rights which he wanted to form the basis of consideration by the joint committee. In addition to the normal political freedoms, Mr. Diefenbaker wished to include in his bill what he labelled the "social freedoms," assuring educational, property, and social security rights.[11] A charter of such broad conception had not been advanced before, nor has it been accepted, or even seriously considered, at any time since. Yet there was a great deal of public support for Diefenbaker's proposal and on 18 June 1947, just a few weeks after the creation of the joint committee, he tabled in the House of Commons a petition in support of his proposal with 500,966 names.

An early concern of the joint committee was the question of the power of Parliament to enact legislation with respect to human rights and fundamental freedoms. In 1947 the committee wrote to all provincial attorneys general and the deans of Canadian law schools requesting their views and opinions on the question of the power of Parliament to enact a comprehensive bill of rights. There were not many responses, and those that there were were not of high quality.[12] With the exception of Saskatchewan, all the respondents claimed that Parliament was not competent to enact a bill of rights applicable against all Canadian governments. Saskatchewan did not disagree that there would be jurisdictional problems, but it was so wholeheartedly in support of a federal bill of rights that it offered to work out any jurisdictional problems that might arise.

In early 1948 Diefenbaker again took an active role in the debate by suggesting that a reference be submitted to the Supreme Court of Canada to determine the extent to which the preservation of fundamental freedoms was under the jurisdiction of Parliament. He saw the need to pursue this course because the opponents to a bill of rights were "shadow-boxing, going through motions, postponing and procrastinating, with the government forever hiding behind the constitutional position."[13] The Diefenbaker position was ruled to be out of order on the ground that the same legislative matter cannot be before two public bodies at the same time. The CCF member Stanley Knowles then reworded the motion so that the joint committee would simply be empowered to recommend that a reference be sent to the Court. The government accepted this change and the motion was carried,[14] but no such reference was ever sent to the Court.

During this period there was a great deal of confusion among proponents of a bill of rights about whether they were seeking constitutional entrenchment or merely the passage of a federal bill protecting rights in respect of matters within federal jurisdiction. The CCF leader, M.J. Coldwell, continued to urge writing into the Constitution a bill of rights, but the majority of parliamentary supporters of a bill of rights preferred Diefenbaker's strategy of enacting a bill of rights and simultaneously asking the Supreme Court of Canada the extent to which it could operate. In the final report of the joint committee there were two findings: first, the power of Parliament to enact a comprehensive bill of rights of general application was dubious; and, second, the committee favoured the constitutional entrenchment of rights. The result of these recommendations was that the committee "was unable to recommend that the Government give favourable consideration to the enactment of a Bill of Rights in the form of a federal statute."[15]

Parliamentary preoccupation with securing human rights continued in 1949. Again Diefenbaker attempted to keep alive the issue by introducing on 26 October 1949 a motion to consider the advisability of introducing a declaration or a bill of rights and, as well, the requirement that the minister of justice submit to the Supreme Court a bill of rights so that it could determine to what extent fundamental freedoms were under federal jurisdiction.[16] This motion was ruled out of order by the Speaker. In the meantime, public interest in a bill of rights was increasing. In 1948 a Citizens' Committee for a Bill of Rights was formed, and in 1949 a further petition with 625,510 signatures in support of a bill of rights was presented to the House of Commons. Senator Arthur Roebuck entered the fray at this point, insisting that a draft amendment to the British North America Act containing a bill of rights be submitted before the upcoming dominion–provincial conference.[17] He was informed that this matter was not appropriate for the agenda of that conference although, as we have seen, at least one provincial premier would have welcomed debate on this matter. On 20 March 1950 he moved to establish a Senate committee to determine the precise nature of the fundamental freedoms of Canadians and how they could be protected and preserved.[18] Unlike the previous joint committee, which had heard only from civil servants, the new Senate Committee on Human Rights and Fundamental Freedoms heard oral representations from a wide variety of interest groups. In June 1950 the committee made two recommendations.[19] First, it was necessary to wait until a dominion–provincial conference decided on a process for amending the Constitution before a bill of rights could be added to the Constitution. Second, until there was constitutional patriation and entrenchment of a bill in Canada by Canadians, the committee recommended that the government adopt a declaration of human rights limited to its own legislative jurisdiction. The Senate committee's report did not stop the agitation for a bill of rights. Coldwell moved a bill which was meant to cause entrenched rights to be written into the Constitution. In this way, he argued, the rights became "more valuable to the people of Canada and much more certain."[20] David Croll, in seconding Coldwell's motion, argued that a bill of rights should be in the Constitution:

> I urge there is a need for a formal restatement of the fundamental princi-
> ples of individual freedom. The people of Canada want to know their
> rights. They have a right to know that.[21]

The federal minister of justice spoke against the motion on the ground that it was desirable to reform the Constitution, making substantive amendments possible within Canada, without recourse to the Parliament at Westminster, before dealing with a bill of rights. The Coldwell motion was talked out.

On 24 March 1952 Diefenbaker again moved a resolution that imme-diate consideration be given to the advisability of introducing a bill or declaration of rights; he also moved, once again, that the government submit, for the opinion of the Supreme Court of Canada, the question of the degree to which fundamental freedoms of religion, speech, and the press and the preservation of the constitutional rights of the individual are matters of federal or provincial jurisdiction.[22] In 1952 he moved a resolu-tion to adopt the declaration of human rights[23] and in 1955 he introduced a draft bill of rights.[24] The persistence of John Diefenbaker in keeping this matter before the House meant that, of the two strategies—entrenchment or ordinary federal enactment—the latter gained ascendancy; during the 1950s, the main focus for securing rights was on the parliamentary enact-ment of rights, which would extend to federal jurisdiction only.

When the Progressive Conservatives came to power in 1957, under the leadership of John Diefenbaker, the future of an enacted bill of rights was assured. In September 1958 Diefenbaker introduced Bill C-60,[25] the fore-runner of the 1960 Canadian Bill of Rights. The bill was to be given first reading and then withdrawn and reintroduced in order to give interested individuals and organizations a chance to study the proposed bill and state their objections or criticisms. In 1959 Premier Douglas of Saskatchewan suggested that there be further federal–provincial discussions with a view to devising amendments to the British North America Act including a bill of rights which would be binding on all the governments. This suggestion was not pursued. In 1960 the House of Commons established a special committee to study Diefenbaker's bill but, by today's standards, the committee's hearings were not extensive. In any event, as a result of the committee's work, some changes were made to the bill before it was given third reading on 4 August, 1960.[26] The Canadian Bill of Rights came into force on 10 August 1960.[27]

This, of course, was not the constitutional entrenchment of human rights which had been so earnestly sought since the end of the Second World War. Nevertheless, it was an act of minor political bravery. It placed legislative and administrative action at the federal level under the control of the judiciary in respect of certain fundamental values. It carried the potential of inconvenience and disruption for federal political programs. The Canadian Bill of Rights was not frequently invoked by individuals (a fact resulting, in part, from the widespread lack of inventiveness of members of the Canadian legal profession), nor was it given a fair interpretation by the courts. In contrast to the two instances where federal legislation was struck down by the Supreme Court of Canada because of conflict with the Canadian Bill of Rights, there are large numbers of other cases in which the Supreme Court, through casuistic intellectual processes, avoided the application of the bill. Cases in which there were powerful claims of racial discrimination, sexual discrimination, suppression of freedom of religion, inequality before the law, cruel and unusual punishment, and denial of due process were all decided by the Supreme Court, often on implausible grounds, against persons who invoked the Canadian Bill of Rights.

Perhaps those who, at the next stage of constitutional development, took up the cause of entrenched rights should be grateful to the Supreme Court of Canada for demonstrating consistently through two decades that rights documents need be nothing more than hortatory and innocuous. Certainly, the experience of the Canadian Bill of Rights did not prepare Canadians for the kind of transformation in the role of courts which has been produced by the Canadian Charter of Rights and Freedoms.

The Liberals Get Religion

Trudeau's Influence

It seems clear that the Liberal government's consistent advocacy since 1967 of entrenching individual rights in the Constitution is a consequence of Trudeau's coming to Ottawa in 1965 as one of Pearson's "Three Wise Men" from Quebec. Certainly Trudeau's commitment to entrenched rights long predates that of the Liberal party, and probably stems from the experience of World War II. Richard Gwyn, in his biography of Trudeau, describes the aetiology of Trudeau's commitment to rights in this piece of only partially inventive scholarship:

The sign "Pierre Trudeau, Citizen of the World" that Trudeau hung on his door at Harvard in 1945 mirrored the mood of the times. The war had proven that liberal democracy was the best of all systems. Having triumphed over irrational racism, the best and the brightest of that era set out to establish a new, rational, democratic order in which men, no matter their colour, creed, or language, would count for more than race, religion, or what George Orwell called "the nasty little isms of ideology." World student movements, movements to promote world federalism, institutions dedicated to espousing the rule of law all exemplified the new, rational utopianism. Nothing exemplified it more eloquently than the 1948 Universal Declaration of Human Rights enshrined in the United Nations Charter. "Recognition of the inherent dignity and of the equal and inalienable rights of all members of the human family is the foundation of freedom, justice and peace in the world." Between that brave espousal of the conviction that out of legal equalities all other equalities would flow, and Trudeau's decade-long attempt to incorporate a Bill of Rights into the Canadian Constitution the line is unbroken.[28]

Whatever the precise nature of Trudeau's intellectual roots, his view that democratic theory included constitutional limitations on governments in favour of basic civil liberties was eloquently proclaimed in his 1958 article in the *Canadian Journal of Economics and Political Science*, "Some Obstacles to Democracy in Quebec." The article begins with panache: "Historically French-Canadians have not really believed in democracy for themselves; and English speaking Canadians have not really wanted it for others. Such are the foundations upon which our two ethnic groups have absurdly pretended to be building democratic forms of government. No wonder the ensuing structure has turned out to be rather flimsy."[29] One of the instances of failure of democracy in Quebec is what Trudeau considered to be the consistent disregard of the Duplessis government for civil liberties and the almost total acquiesence in this conduct by the French-Canadian press. The evidence that he mustered "proving that French-Canadians fundamentally do not believe in democracy" are instances of the suppression of speech and religious exercise and the creation of inequalities. The nexus between the requirements of democracy and the rights of individuals is found in these two observations:

> Democracy cannot be made to work in a country where a large part of the citizens are by status condemned to a perpetual state of domination, economic or otherwise.[30]

> Essentially a true democracy must permit the periodic transformation of political minorities into majorities.[31]

In 1955 Trudeau had proposed to the Quebec Royal Commission of Inquiry on Constitutional Problems (the Tremblay commission) that Quebec should take the side of promoting the incorporation of human rights in the Canadian Constitution.[32]

In April 1967 Prime Minister Pearson appointed Trudeau as the minister of justice and attorney general of Canada. Almost immediately, the issue of an entrenched bill of rights appeared on the federal political agenda. Within a month of Trudeau's joining the Cabinet, Pearson announced in the House of Commons his hope that all the Canadian governments, provincial as well as federal, would adopt a bill of rights for all Canadians, which would be enshrined not only in federal law but also in provincial law. He suggested that such a bill should even precede specific constitutional reforms because "before we can seriously hope to agree on structural changes, we should endeavour to agree, federally and provincially, on a statement of common values and on a declaration of our basic individual and collective rights as Canadians."[33] He announced that an interdepartmental committee would be set up within the department of justice to look at constitutional matters. Later in May 1967 Carl Goldenberg, of Montreal, and Ivan Head, of the University of Alberta, were appointed as special constitutional advisors to the minister of justice to examine the entrenchment of a bill of rights. In July 1967 the prime minister announced that he would be calling provincial premiers to a conference to discuss enshrining a bill of rights.[34]

Set against this sudden renaissance of constitutional reform, which must surely have been prompted by the appointment of Trudeau as the minister of justice, is the paradoxical theme repeatedly advanced by Trudeau that constitutional reform is of limited utility. In his long research paper, "Quebec and the Constitutional Problem," prepared at the Institut de Recherche en Droit Public at the University of Montreal in the spring of 1965, shortly before he became a member of Parliament, Trudeau advanced an extremely limited set of constitutional proposals relating only to language rights.[35] In 1964, as a member of the Committee for Political Realism, he was the joint author of a manifesto which labelled the building of a new constitutional structure as "futile as a huge game of blocks."[36] Again, in the House of Commons in January 1968, Trudeau stood by his earlier statement that the Constitution was "not very high on the list of priorities as things that this country must do."[37]

In the meantime, in September 1967, speaking at the annual meeting of the Canadian Bar Association, Trudeau explicitly tied constitutional reform to the entrenchment of rights. For him the beginning of constitutional reform was the definition of the purposes of law, and these purposes were the preservation of traditions and pursuit of the ideals which Canadian society cherishes. The most basic ideals were freedom and dignity of the individual. He said, "if we, as individuals, do not have the opportunity to stand erect, to retain our self-respect, to move freely throughout our country unhindered by any artificial impediment, then we have not created in this land the political climate that we are capable of creating, we will not have made of the law as we should."[38] He went on to announce the proposal for a charter of human rights which was meant to reflect the government's view that the most fundamental of our social values must be available to every Canadian in a permanent "and that means constitutional" fashion.

This enumeration of the steps of constitutional reform was repeated by Trudeau at the first constitutional conference held in February 1968. At that conference the federal government advanced its plan for reviewing the Constitution. The first stage was to be discussion of the protection of human rights through constitutional entrenchment. As Donald Smiley had noted, introduction of the idea of protecting rights as a central feature of the "rational approach" to constitutional reform reflected Trudeau's theory of politics. The idea was to agree upon general principles about the nature of the Canadian community and to embody them in the constitutional document. This, as Smiley has noted, gave constitutional reform a symbolic new role in capturing Canadian political allegiance.[39] Perhaps this function of constitutional reform was a legacy of Expo '67, during which it was demonstrated that Canadians could muster national pride when the enterprise in which the nation engaged was sufficiently vast and imaginative.

In any event, as a result of the federal initiative the entrenchment of rights was firmly on the constitutional agenda. It is, however, somewhat ironic that the Confederation of Tomorrow Conference, convened by the government of Ontario in November 1967 and generally credited with providing the initial thrust for modern constitutional reform, did not discuss the entrenchment of rights, although the document appeared on the proposed agenda.

For the first meeting of the constitutional conference in February 1968, Prime Minister Pearson issued a paper, *Federalism for the Future.*[40] It was a statement of the constitutional policy which would be pursued by the federal government. In this document the details of the proposed charter of human rights were set out. It was to consist of four parts. The first part would guarantee freedom of speech, freedom of conscience and religion, freedom of assembly and association, and freedom of the press. It would also assure the right of every individual to life, liberty, security of the person, and enjoyment of property and would guarantee to every individual equality before the law and equal protection of the law. The second part of the charter would protect the remedy of habeas corpus against legislative encroachment, and would assure such rights as the presumption of innocence, the right to be represented by counsel, and the right to a fair hearing. The third part would prohibit discrimination on the basis of sex, race, national or ethnic origin, colour, or religion. It was proposed that this prohibition extend to both private action and state action, whether federal or provincial. Finally the charter would contain a fourth part designed to protect linguistic rights. By breaking the provisions of the charter into classes, the federal government began a process, which has continued to the present time, of placing rights in various categories. One of the purposes of this exercise is to make it clear to the people of Canada what sorts of rights are protected by entrenched provisions. Undoubtedly one of the unintended consequences of this classification has been the creation of blocks of rights, facilitating bargaining for exclusion or inclusion. The 1968 conference resulted in the agreement that the matter of entrenching fundamental rights should form part of the future constitutional debate.

A year later, in February 1969, with Trudeau now the prime minister, the federal government issued a further book, *The Constitution and the People of Canada*,[41] which again set out federal proposals for entrenched rights. The proposed text, included in the book, matched the four-part categorization proposed the previous year in the rights document. It was noteworthy for three features. First, the language of the document was spare and, even, elegant; there were no phrases, as there were a decade later, designed to blunt the impact of entrenchment of rights upon the doctrine of parliamentary supremacy. Second, although the charter spoke only of traditional rights and not of the new social rights, relating to social and economic welfare, the rights protected were, for the most part, generously phrased. For instance, in this early draft both freedom of conscience and freedom of religion were included, as was a limited form of the right to property. Third, the charter not only contained the usual clause guaranteeing equal protection of the law, it also contained anti-discrimination provisions in relation to employment, property ownership, and obtainment of public accommodation, facilities, and services. Since this provision was designed to apply to the actions of private citizens, it would have replicated, if not rendered obsolete, the developed regimes of provincial human rights legislation.

The Victoria Charter

While the second meeting of the constitutional conference did not adopt the proposed charter of human rights, it did establish a committee of ministers, which was given the mandate to study all matters relating to fundamental rights, including the question of entrenchment. The committee met twice and established a subcommittee of officials and experts to consider the protection of rights further. Although all representatives at these meetings proclaimed themselves to be in favour of protecting human rights, differences arose in all aspects of the discussion. Saskatchewan, then under a Liberal government, argued strenuously against placing rights in the Constitution on the ground that it was alien to the principle of the supremacy of Parliament. The province made what was to become, over the years, the familiar argument that elected representatives, not the courts, have the ultimate responsibility for the protection of citizens.

With respect to political rights, some provinces argued against inclusion of the right to universal suffrage and free democratic elections at least every five years. The rights to freedom of conscience and religion, expression, assembly, and association were generally agreed upon, subject to the feeling in some quarters that the concepts required further definition. There were sharp disagreements over the inclusion of legal rights. Some provinces expressed major doubts about the advantages of entrenching legal rights and, as well, were alarmed at the prospect of a due process clause. There were, of course, some provinces who maintained that any modification in the Canadian system of protecting rights was unnecessary. Straying somewhat outside its territory, the committee also observed that agreement on rights to be entrenched would be enhanced by agreement on an amendment formula for the Constitution; no entrenchment of rights was possible, it claimed, in the absence of patriation and an amending formula.

The lack of widespread consensus in the committee of ministers was matched in the wider constitutional renewal process. The third meeting of the constitutional conference did not discuss fundamental rights at all but focused on the distribution of powers in relation to income security and social services, the spending power, and the regional disparities. Discussions on these topics did not go smoothly and, by the fall of 1970, the constitutional reform process had almost come apart. There was a constitutional working session in September 1970, which focused almost entirely on intergovernmental problems which were not, in fact, constitutional. However, the election in April 1970 of Robert Bourassa as the premier of Quebec altered the political context. Bourassa had run on a federalist platform and, as Donald Smiley has observed, "the new Liberal Government, was not disposed to advance the Quebec position through nationalist rhetoric or abstract and doctrinaire statements of principle."[42] As a result, it appeared that there was some hope for constitutional accommodation with Quebec on the basis that Quebec would support a new amending formula in exchange for provincial powers over social policy. With that basis for renewed hope, the federal and provincial governments met in working sessions throughout the winter of 1970–71 with the bulk of attention being paid to discussing an arrangement for the devolution of social security areas to the provinces. This effort was not successful but, nevertheless, the first ministers held a fourth constitutional conference in Victoria in June 1971. Agreement was reached on six matters, one of which was an amending formula, which had been accepted as feasible in February 1971, and another of which was the entrenchment of certain human rights. What was not included was the provision which Quebec had wanted with respect to provincial jurisdiction over income security. Although there appeared to be general acceptance of this limited package, in fact neither Saskatchewan nor Quebec gave formal agreement while in Victoria. It was decided that there would be an eleven-day waiting period following Victoria, during which provinces could indicate their support of the package. Six days after the conference, Premier Bourassa issued a statement saying that Quebec could not accept the Victoria Charter. It stated: "the texts dealing with income security have an uncertainty that meshes badly with the objectives inherent in any idea of constitutional revision. If this uncertainty were eliminated, our conclusion could be different."[43] In other words, the failure to include constitutional reform over income support systems proved to be fatal to the Victoria plan for patriation, including the bill of rights. The Saskatchewan government was locked in an election battle with the NDP and it, too, never signified its support.

Nevertheless, the terms of the Victoria Charter in relation to entrenched rights are worth examining; they are the closest that the governments in Canada have ever come to agreeing to a fully entrenched rights document, not subject in any way to legislative control. Under the rights portion of the Victoria Charter, freedom of thought, conscience, and religion, freedom of opinion and expression, and freedom of peaceful assembly and association were guaranteed. However, these rights were subject to qualification:

> Nothing in this part shall be construed as preventing such limitations on the exercise of the fundamental freedoms as are reasonably justifiable in a democratic society in the interests of public safety, order, health or morals, of national security, or of the rights and freedoms of others, whether imposed by the Parliament of Canada or the Legislature of a Province, within the limits of their respective legislative powers, or by the construction or application of any law.

This type of qualification has become standard in discussions in Canada on entrenching rights. It is born, no doubt, of the fear that courts will read literally the terms of a rights document, and not mediate between the rights which are stated to be guaranteed and the valid interests of the general public.

The Victoria Charter also contained clauses relating to the holding of elections and the length of parliamentary and legislative sessions. There were a series of provisions relating to language rights, in particular to the use of English and French in Parliament and the provincial legislatures; the publication of statutes, records, and journals; and the use of French and English in courts and in communications with governmental agencies. Each requirement attached to some, but not all, governments; governments affected by a particular provision varied according to the provision.

The Victoria Charter did not address property rights; rights relating to life, liberty, and security of the person; legal rights arising on arrest or detention; equality rights, or minority language education rights. It was, therefore, a modest proposal for constitutional entrenchment. In some ways, however, it offered greater protection for rights than the new Canadian Charter of Rights and Freedoms because fundamental rights were not made subject to parliamentary or legislative override.

The experience of the Victoria conference, of coming so close to constitutional resolution and yet failing, stalled the constitutional reform movement but did not stop it entirely. Even before Victoria the Senate and the House of Commons had established a Joint Parliamentary Committee to look into reform of the Constitution. This committee (known as the Molgat–MacGuigan committee) conducted an extensive enquiry, through the holding of public meetings, into the need for constitutional reform. Its report,[44] issued in March 1972, favoured a constitutionally entrenched bill of rights, and the rights it proposed for inclusion went far beyond those contained in the Victoria Charter. They were, in fact, very close to the rights which had been contained in the February 1969 document of the federal government and even went beyond the 1969 proposals in relation to language, economic, and social rights. It suggested that under the Constitution provinces should be competent to give official language status to languages other than French and English. It also suggested that the preamble to the Constitution should state the objective of promoting "economic, social and cultural equality for all Canadians as individuals." Notwithstanding the thoroughness of this inquiry, and the extent of its proposals, constitutional reform hardly acquired new life upon its publication.

The Trudeau Government Keeps Trying

Unwilling to let disappointment over the Victoria Charter long dissuade it from pursuing constitutional reform, the federal government some two and a half years later again took up the task. In the period between the speech from the throne in October 1974 and the election victory of the Parti Québécois in November 1976, federal initiatives and provincial responses, in respect of amending the Constitution included federal–provincial meetings, the sending of a federal emissary to provincial capitals, and the exchange of telexes. The goal of this activity was more to discover the scope of any potential constitutional agreement on matters other than simply the charter. Debate over precise terms regarding rights, or any other matter, did not take place.

The Task Force on Canadian Unity

The election in Quebec in late 1976 of a government whose program was to take Quebec out of Canada gave constitutional reform an intensity and public interest it had never before enjoyed. The first responses to the 1976 election were not, however, intergovernmental; a number of provinces and other agencies, such as the Canadian Bar Association, instituted close examinations of how the Constitution should be reformed. As already noted, the federal government established a Task Force on Canadian Unity under the chairmanship of former Liberal Cabinet minister Jean-Luc Pepin and former Ontario premier John Robarts. Although the report of the task force was almost diffident in its recommendations on human rights and language rights, it clearly favoured entrenchment:

> On balance we have concluded that some key individual and collective rights should be entrenched in a new Constitution.[45]

In keeping with its overall sensitivity to the role and interests of provinces, the report noted the considerable problems that would be encountered in seeking provincial concurrence in a bill of rights. It set out three options for overcoming this opposition. First was the enactment of federal legislation establishing a rights charter which would apply only to the federal level, but which would allow provinces individually to commit themselves to being bound by its terms. When all provinces opted in to the charter of rights, it would then become an entrenched constitutional document. Second, the Constitution could contain an extremely limited range of rights to which all governments would agree. Third, the rights document could contain a clause permitting provincial legislative overrides so that when provinces did not wish to be bound by a particular right, or when a province wished to avoid the result of a particular constitutional decision, it could simply pass legislation stating that the right did not apply in that circumstance. Perhaps it is because the device of a *non obstante* clause is described in the report as being responsive to provincial objections that the present similar provision in the Canadian Charter of Rights and Freedoms is often referred to as the "provincial override." In fact it is a power which is held by both the federal Parliament and the provinces.

As for language rights the report, again, set out options. At the provincial level the Constitution could be amended to extend the guarantees presently within it, in section 133, to every province or, at least, to some additional provinces. Alternatively, the Constitution could contain no explicit guarantees, and language rights would flow only from a general invitation to the provinces to legislate appropriate safeguards for their minorities. In the report it is stated that over time these provincial arrangements may coincide sufficiently to result in general agreement for entrenchment. In the words of the report, "each provincial legislature should have the right to determine an official language or official languages for the province within its sphere of jurisdiction."[46] This non-coercive form, indeed non-constitutional form, of responding to what had been generally considered a constitutional issue was also carried forward with respect to the rights of language minorities to education in their own language:

> We suggest that the provinces review existing methods and procedures
> for the teaching and learning of French and English and make greater
> efforts to improve the quality and availability of instruction in these lan-
> guages at all levels of education.[47]

This recommendation matched the view taken by all the provincial premiers at a meeting in Montreal in early 1978, at which they said that
minority language education rights should be recognized simply through
ordinary provincial legislation so that each child of a French-speaking or
English-speaking minority would be entitled to primary and secondary
school education in his or her language, "wherever numbers warrant."

Apart from whatever virtues the report of the Task Force on Canadian
Unity may have had (and, indeed, it represents a serious attempt to be
both thoughtful and inspiring), it was doomed to oblivion on the strength
of its recommendations on language rights alone. The vision in the report
of the gradual perfecting of language tolerance and language protection
through incremental provincial improvements was not what the federal
government had in mind. Entrenched minimum language provisions, im-
mune from the ebb and flow of tolerance for language minorities, at both
the federal and provincial levels, was what the Trudeau government expected to achieve and achieve soon. The goodwill and optimism which
permeates the report of the task force was thought by the federal government to be far too transient a thing on which to build an enduring policy
of bilingualism.

The members of the task force were euphoric about the experience of
travelling across Canada, meeting many hundreds of Canadians, discussing
every political issue under the sun, appearing on radio and television,
speaking to journalists and service clubs, consulting with experts in uni-
versities, meeting an impressive array of researchers, and, finally, converg-
ing to hammer out a report which they felt would make a real contribution
to the creation of Canadian unity. It was, they said, "an extraordinary
experience—something that we will carry with us for the rest of our
days."[48] But, on the question of human rights and language rights, it
offended the federal government. What it produced undoubtedly appealed
to provinces and may have made them more eager to participate in finding
the solutions to Canada's constitutional shortcomings. If so, the task force
made a contribution to the process of constitutional reform in Canada. But
it did not even approach the minimum federal position on rights, and,
consequently, its role in the subsequent history of constitutional reform
became virtually nonexistent.

Bill C-60

The kind of specific protections that the federal government had in mind
were revealed some months before the report of the task force, in June

1978, when Bill C-60 was introduced. Since this was a federal bill, intended to be enacted by Parliament, the part of it entitled "Rights and Freedoms Within the Canadian Federation" did not apply to provinces, and the enumerated rights would not have constrained provincial legislatures. The idea behind Bill C-60 was to constitutionalize certain arrangements, including individual rights. The mode of constitutionalization contemplated was through enactment by Parliament. The federal government drew a distinction in its proposal between constitutionalization which was, in effect, labelling the legislation as a constitutional Act, and entrenchment, which would come about only through formal amendment of the British North America Act with the concurrence of the provinces. The portion of Bill C-60 dealing with human rights would not, of course, be entrenched until such time as the provinces agreed to having its terms apply to them also. But it could be enacted by Parliament and apply at the federal level only. Individual provinces would be free at any time to adopt its provisions and declare themselves to be bound. It would become entrenched and, thereby, put beyond subsequent unilateral amendment by Parliament, or provincial legislatures, when enough provincial consents had been given for entrenchment to satisfy the requirement of the constitutional amending formula which would, in due course, be developed and entrenched.

The Bill C-60 mode of constitutional transformation did not proceed because the federal government, although pursuing a modest ambition, was insufficiently modest in defining what it might do unilaterally; its provisions relating to reform of the Senate were found to be beyond the competence of Parliament and required formal constitutional amendment.[49]

Bill C-60 included freedom of thought, conscience, and religion; freedom of opinion and expression; freedom of peaceful assembly and of association; freedom of the press and other media for the dissemination of news and the expression of opinion and belief; the right of the individual to life and to the liberty and security of his or her person, and the right not to be deprived thereof except by due process of law; the right of the individual to the use and enjoyment of property and the right not to be deprived thereof except in accordance with law; the right of the individual to equality before the law and to the equal protection of the law; a wide range of legal rights arising in connection with the administration of criminal justice; mobility rights, including the right to justice, to acquire and hold property, and to pursue a livelihood in any province or territory of Canada. It included a series of rights in connection with elections and required the holding of annual meetings of elected legislative bodies.

It also included a non-discrimination clause, which said that the rights and freedoms listed above were to be enjoyed without discrimination on the basis of race, national or ethnic origin, language, colour, religion, age, or sex. This sort of clause, stating that enumerated rights are to be available without discrimination, parallels the structure of section 1 of the Canadian Bill of Rights. It is a perplexing sort of provision in that it appears to be a general guarantee of non-discrimination on certain proscribed bases, but, in fact, it is not. It merely states that the rights listed in the charter cannot be limited in a discriminatory way. This is arguably a redundant provision since, presumably, rights are not meant to be abridged in any event. The listing of certain bases upon which inequality cannot be created makes sense in understanding a clause which generally guarantees equality before the law: it indicates that, while some inequalities—those, for example, between persons with high incomes and low incomes—are tolerable, other inequalities—those, for example, based on race—are not. It seems that, in Bill C-60 and the Canadian Bill of Rights, the guarantee of equal enjoyment of rights was to be tantamount to a general right to equal treatment.

As for language rights, Bill C-60 contained a complete list of instances in which both languages would be officially recognized; it also granted minority language education rights in both French and English wherever there were sufficient numbers of anglophones or francophones to warrant such a provision. These rights were, of course, contingent upon provinces' willingness to adopt the provision since education was a provincial matter.

The 1978–79 First Ministers' Conferences

Before the end of 1978 the federal government had entered into negotiations with the provinces for broad constitutional reform, including an entrenched charter of rights. In these discussions the issue of rights did not loom nearly as large as other topics, most notably provisions leading to jurisdiction over non-renewable resources; but, during the period of intensive negotiations in late 1978 and early 1979, elements of a charter of rights were developed. This is not to say that at the February 1979 First Ministers' Conference all the provinces agreed to a charter with these elements; in fact, a majority were extremely reluctant to accept such a charter. At most, the draft[50] represented a proposed resolution, conditional on agreements satisfactory to the provinces being reached on a significant number of the thirteen items discussed. Since, however, just what settlements would have to have been made on other items to secure provincial acceptance of this particular draft is not known, this episode of charter formulation is not terribly illuminating of the political will to entrench. The 1979 draft contained the same language rights and minority language education rights as did Bill C-60. It also contained the same fundamental freedoms relating to freedom of conscience, religion, thought, opinion, expression, peaceful assembly, and association. It contained similar democratic rights relating to voting and the holding of annual meetings of legislative bodies. With respect to legal rights, including the due process clause and rights on arrest and detention, and rights to equality, the "best efforts draft" allowed provinces to opt into these provisions; upon opting in provinces would also have a general override power to exempt themselves from the operation of the provisions from time to time. The "best efforts draft" also contained modified, and limited, mobility and property rights.

What is interesting about this document is its restructuring of rights. The rights are organized under headings which became the model for subsequent constitutional negotiations. The draft identified five categories of basic human rights and two categories of language rights. The human rights were fundamental freedoms, including the rights to religion, speech, and assembly; democratic rights, relating to voting and the holding of legislative sessions; mobility rights; legal rights, including the general right not to be deprived of life, liberty and security of the person (and, at that time, enjoyment of property) except by due process of law; and equality rights. The categories of language rights consisted of rights relating to the conduct of government business and rights relating to minority language education. A further clarification of the best efforts draft was the dropping of the non-discrimination clause and the combining of the guarantee against discrimination on the basis of race, etc., with the general requirement that governments do not deny equality before the law.

The organization of rights in the 1979 best efforts draft had an effect. Since there were so many categories, it became easier for the participants to denote which category of rights they could accept and with what conditions; placement of entrenched rights in small packages eased the process of negotiation. In the minds of some, this latter effect debased the idea of fundamental rights since they more readily became counters in a vast political bargaining session. However, when there is a conflict of values, as that created by the idea of entrenching rights and the importance of the various rights, political bargaining is inevitable and even desirable. In the end, the best-effort drafts facilitated that process of bargaining and moved the participants away from overly general positions from which no consensus was likely.

Apart from conflict over particular provisions and, in particular, the provisions guaranteeing freedom of choice in the language of education, the attempt to achieve constitutional agreement in February 1979 took place too late in the parliamentary term of the fading Liberals. The largely Conservative provincial premiers were not about to hand Prime Minister Trudeau the diplomatic coup of an agreement on the terms of patriation.

... And So Does Clark

The federal election in May 1979 brought into power the Clark government with its new minister of federal–provincial relations, William Jarvis. In late

October he convened in Halifax a federal–provincial meeting of ministers responsible for the Constitution. Although the discussion on most of the topics for constitutional reform was desultory, on the question of a charter of rights the federal government came with a new draft designed to meet most of the objections raised by provinces during the 1978–79 process. Federal officials unveiled the new charter to their provincial counterparts with great optimism. It was presented as a charter "you can't refuse." The new charter covered five categories of rights: fundamental freedoms, democratic rights, legal rights, general language rights, and minority language education rights. The provisions relating to fundamental freedoms carried a variation of the limitation clause which had been first introduced in Bill C-60 and was also part of the 1979 best efforts draft. Jarvis's draft stated that the freedoms declared in the section were "subject only to such limitations prescribed by law as are reasonably justifiable in a free and democratic society in the interests of morals, or the rights and freedoms of others." Although this is a very strongly expressed limitation clause, it would not quite have rendered the fundamental freedoms section of the charter a nullity; these clauses do not require complete deference to legislative choices. That limitation clause does, however, anticipate a significant balancing of interests between the rights of individuals and the needs of the whole community and permits legislatures and courts to be very sensitive to the latter interests.

In Halifax growing provincial concern over legal rights was expressed. Led by Ontario and Quebec, the provinces insisted that legal rights (or due process rights) apply only in the administration of criminal justice and not to provincial civil administration. Owing to the strength of opposition to a general due process clause, the federal government, in preparation for an officials' meeting in Toronto in November, rewrote the section stating that due process rights arose only in criminal or penal matters. Even then, the provinces were reluctant to accept the legal rights section. They argued that their capacity to develop efficient new modes of administering provincial offences could be limited by the section. This was, of course, a completely accurate reading of the section. In expressing their concern, provinces were simply advancing the philosophy that regimes of provincial criminal law, or any provincial administration whatsoever, should not be subject to judicially enforceable standards of due process. In other words, behind the attack on the limited provisions of the Jarvis charter was a general opposition to the idea of entrenched rights.

The provisions of the charter relating to language rights reflect the Clark government's constant attempt to meet provincial concerns while at the same time giving constitutional recognition to both the French and English languages. The language provisions of the charter relating to the publication of official records and the use of French or English in courts or other proceedings are granted in these terms: "to the greatest extent practicable accordingly as the legislature of the province prescribes." Governmental communication in French or English is provided in the charter as well but only "to the extent to which and in the areas of the province in which it is determined, in such manner as may be prescribed or authorized by the legislature of the province, that the rights shall pertain having regard to the practicability and necessity of providing such services."

Likewise, in respect of minority language education rights, Jarvis's opening statement at the Halifax conference reveals the Clark government's ambition to achieve two self-contradictory goals at the same time:

> What I am asking you today is whether you could take your agreement on minority language education rights, the Montreal Agreement of 1978, and see whether you could devise a form of words using agreement which could be entrenched in the Constitution, and which could be enforceable by the courts at the behest of any citizen or group of citizens who are able to establish that a province was clearly not making an adequate effort to apply the principle that is set out in the first paragraph of that Agreement.[51]

Since the fundamental feature of the Montreal agreement is that minority language education should be dealt with only through statutory provisions and not be constitutionalized, Jarvis was asking for the impossible. The language of Jarvis's draft was more direct. Most of the provinces rejected the proposed text, stating that this right was not appropriate for entrenchment.

At both the Halifax and Toronto officials' meetings, the new federal government showed remarkable resilience. It neither abandoned its attempts to entrench any of the five categories of rights, nor shut its ears to any of the provincial objections. It is entirely conceivable that federal officials would have come up with language which met the bulk of provincial objections and still have left a judicially enforceable charter, at least with respect to fundamental freedoms, democratic rights, and a portion of legal rights. How useful a rights document produced by the Clark government's process of conciliation and adaptation would have been is not clear and will never be known. The February 1980 election brought an end to the era of flexible charter formation.

The Liberals Return

The Summer of 1980

When Jean Chrétien made his whirlwind tour of the provincial capitals forty-eight hours after the result of the Quebec referendum, the only element of a charter included in his plan for instantaneous patriation related to language rights. Whatever gratitude the provinces may have felt for Chrétien and the federal Liberals for contributing to the defeat of the separatist cause in Quebec, it did not translate into a softened stand on entrenched bilingualism in the provinces or entrenched minority language education rights. Provincial reluctance to accept this point and the other elements of the plan brought an end to what was a poorly conceived and opportunistic strategy for achieving patriation. Instead, the eleven governments of Canada embarked on a summer-long, twelve-item agenda to put together a package of constitutional reforms which would attract general, and possibly unanimous, support.

An irony of the constitutional talks during the summer of 1980 is that, although a charter of rights was known to be central to any package that was to be formed, and that bargaining on its terms would be intense, the ministers and officials who travelled across the country in July and August, and the first ministers who met in Ottawa in September, gave the charter remarkably little attention. During the summer the subcommittee of officials responsible for discussing the charter did not meet at all in Montreal or Toronto. By and large, the officials who specialized in the charter were also responsible for discussions on the form of entrenchment of the Supreme Court of Canada, and many were also involved in the negotiations over a transfer of jurisdiction in family law; these other matters initially occupied the officials. Although it was quickly apparent that there was broad agreement in both these areas, the two subcommittees continued to meet in order to hear, out of an absurd level of tolerance, the few provinces who dissented from the consensus. Not only did officials not move to charter discussions quickly, the ministers at plenary sessions were largely preoccupied with new federal positions—the new federal position on powers over the economy, and the new hard line from Ottawa on the matter of jurisdiction over non-renewable resources. Apart from brief theoretical statements from Roy Romanow of Saskatchewan and Claude Morin from Quebec on the general question of entrenchment, the charter did not receive ministerial attention.

In Vancouver and Ottawa officials finally began to discuss a new draft charter which the federal government had tabled. Except for Ontario and New Brunswick, all the provincial respresentatives stated they had no mandate to agree to the entrenchment of any parts of the draft or to discuss any of its terms. Notwithstanding this serious constraint, discussions did go forward; provincial officials were drawn into discussion of the merits of the various clauses to a sufficient degree to enable the federal government to get a more precise idea of the provincial objections which were most intensely felt. Only Manitoba and Quebec carried their opposition to entrenchment to its logical conclusion and refused to participate in any discussion of the federal text. Nor, of course, did they indicate which changes would soften opposition.

The position taken by Ontario was particularly interesting. Although it was one of the provinces which officially supported a charter of rights, its officials opposed almost all aspects of the federal draft which would have presented the judiciary with a powerful weapon for controlling legislative action. In particular, it preferred that legal rights not confer the general due process protection on civil provincial administration and that particular guarantees be expressed largely in hortatory form. For example, Ontario preferred a search and seizure clause to confer the right to be secure against search and seizure "except on grounds provided by law and in accordance with prescribed procedures." No standard of the reasonableness of a challenged search and seizure would be available for court enforcement.

The September First Ministers' Conference

At the First Ministers' Conference in September, the morning that was devoted to debate on the charter of rights consisted entirely of theoretical debate on the question of entrenchment. Little discussion took place regarding the rights to be included or the mechanisms to be placed in the charter to secure provincial concurrence. The theoretical debate began well, with thoughtful speeches from Premiers Lyon and Blakeney, but it soon degenerated into mere assertion by federal Cabinet ministers and provincial premiers that Canadians placed greater trust in courts or in politicians. This was not the sort of debate which could produce resolution or even reveal any middle ground. At one point, the federal minister of environment, John Roberts, stated the issue in terms of whether people would prefer to litigate or to lobby and singled out women as an interest group which would prefer to litigate under a charter rather than lobby for political reform. In light of the fate of women's rights cases in the Supreme Court of Canada during the decade preceding the First Ministers' Conference, this claim seemed incredible and, indeed, led Premier Peckford to say to Prime Minister Trudeau: "I was trying to get your eye because I wanted to lend a little support to some of the things your were saying, that your government was saying and the longer it went on, not because you did not recognize me, but the more I heard from Mr. Roberts the less eager I was to give my support."[52]

Before the charter discussion was concluded at the First Ministers' Conference, the prime minister attempted to take a poll of provincial support for the various categories of rights in the federal draft. This poll taking, however, was merely a reiteration of well-known positions, and with one exception there was no discussion and no real attempt to find a compromise. The exception was Premier Blakeney's suggestion that Saskatchewan, and perhaps other provinces, would be comfortable with the entrenchment of legal rights if it were accompanied with a *non obstante* clause. This comment did not lead to an exploration of whether that device would, in fact, obtain provincial concurrence over a larger group of rights. Since this was precisely the device that brought agreement on a charter some fourteen months later, it is, perhaps, a pity that the combination of entrenched rights and legislative overrides did not receive more assiduous examination at the September meeting.

This statement of regret, however, is only appropriate on the assumption that the September 1980 First Minsiters' Conference was a serious attempt to find a common ground on which to proceed with patriation of the Constitution. This is not, however, an assumption which the evidence bears out. In fact, the discussion of the charter during the summer of 1980, including the discussion of the First Ministers' Conference, as much as any other evidence, supports the proposition that the federal government had, at the time of these constitutional negotiations, already turned its mind to proceeding unilaterally to patriate the Constitution. Additionally, most provinces did not show a generous spirit during the summer of 1980, when the issue of creating a charter of rights came up.

The Federal Drafts and the Provincial Drafts

During the summer of 1980 there were three different federal drafts. The first was distributed at the beginning of the summer and formed the basis of discussions at the subcommittee of officials. This document closely followed the provisions of the "best efforts draft" of February 1979. It did not, of course, contain a provincial discretion to opt in or enact legislative overrides in respect of legal rights and non-discrimination rights. In addition, the July 1980 draft included, for the first time, a section on mobility rights. This addition was part of the package of proposals put forth by the federal government in connection with Canadian economic union. Other elements relating to the free movement of goods, services, and capital were promoted through a different set of texts which were designed to form amendments to section 121 of the British North America Act. The federal government considered the free movement of people to be a basic right of citizenship and not merely an element of a policy in favour of economic efficiency. The mobility rights provisions not only conferred the right to move and take up residence in any province but also granted the right to acquire and hold property in any province and the right to pursue a livelihood in any province. What started as a human right acquired an aspect of free movement of capital; for this reason the mobility rights provisions were especially resisted by Saskatchewan and Prince Edward Island, both of which had enacted legislation placing restrictions on the ownership of land by persons living outside the province.

The July federal draft perpetuated the very broadly expressed limitation clause which had appeared in the best efforts draft of 1979. Another feature carried forward from that earlier draft was the phrasing of non-discrimination rights in general terms rather than referring to specific classes of discrimination which would not be permitted. The section provided that everyone would have the right to equality before the law and equal protection of the law without distinction "other than any distinction or restriction provided by law that is fair and reasonable having regard to the object of the law." This provision would allow the courts to review any categorization of persons in legislation in order to determine whether the classes created were reasonably related to the purposes of the legislative scheme. This form of non-discrimination clause delegated very wide reviewing authority over legislation to courts, and for this reason it was strongly resisted by the provinces. The non-discrimination rights provision also contained, as did the best efforts draft, an exemption for affirmative action programs which were designed to ameliorate the condition of disadvantaged persons or groups.

On 22 August the federal government issued its second draft of the summer. A major change in this draft was the deletion of the limitation clause as it appeared in various places in the earlier draft. Instead, a new section 1 was inserted, which stated that the rights recognized by the charter were "subject only to such reasonable limits as are generally accepted in a free and democratic society." This was the beginning of the general limitation clause which ultimately found its way into the final version of the charter of rights. Clearly the clause was designed to encourage judicial deference to legislative choices even though they affected civil liberties. From the perspective of those who were opposed to entrenchment, the limitation clause was, in some ways, superior to a *non obstante* clause. Under it there was no need for an explicit legislative expression of intent to override the charter in order to benefit from the limitation. On the other hand, the limitation clause hardly guaranteed complete judicial deference. A court would need to be convinced that the legislation that limited the rights was, in fact, generally accepted. This standard would certainly not help a province that designed innovative social legislation which imposed burdens on the civil liberties of individuals. Another feature of this general limitation clause was the abandonment for the first time of a limitation based on national security. The consequence of this was that Parliament and the federal government were not in a superior position to the provinces in invoking limitations; a limitation power based on national security would not normally be available to provinces but would have been of great use to the federal government. To some extent, then, the dropping of the national security limitation was a sign of good faith by the federal government; it signalled its willingness to live with the same impediments to free legislative choice as were imposed against provinces.

There were four other limiting features of the 22 August draft. The first was that property rights were deleted. The second was that legal rights were restructured in an attempt to restrict them to criminal and penal matters. The attempt would not, however, have been successful and the impact of the provisions on civil administration would not have been lessened. Third, the non-discrimination rights provision was rewritten to guarantee equality before the law without discrimination "because of race, national or ethnic origin, colour, religion, age or sex." Although these represent the most obvious categories of legislative inequality, the restriction of the section to these categories had the advantage, from the provinces' point of view, of limiting to a great extent the instances in which legislation could be challenged for creating inequalities.

Finally, the July draft had contained the right of witnesses to be heard in English or French through interpreters in any court in Canada in any criminal or serious provincial proceeding, and this provision was deleted in the draft. This was not too significant a concession since the legal rights provisions provided that anybody, of any language background, had the right to the assistance of an interpreter, if needed, in any proceedings.

Six days after the second federal draft, the provinces issued a proposal for a charter of rights. It was contingently presented in that the provinces would agree to their proposed charter only if there were an overall agreement in favour of the entrenchment of rights. In other words, the provinces did not commit themselves to entrenching rights in the Constitution but issued a document stating that, if it were decided in the context of the entire constitutional package that rights should be entrenched, then these were the ones they could accept. Their draft included fundamental freedoms, democratic rights, and some very weakly expressed legal rights. Given the limited nature of this document, there was no need for it to contain a *non obstante* clause. The protection of fundamental freedoms in the provincial document was couched with a limitation clause which stated that the rights were subject to limits "as are generally accepted in a free society living under a parliamentary democracy." This particular formulation of limitation was designed to produce even greater judicial deference than that produced by the federal draft's limitation clause. The idea behind the provincial text was that, if Parliament or a legislative assembly enacted a provision which was thought to infringe rights, it would in most instances, simply by virtue of being enacted, be considered to be generally accepted in a free society living under a parliamentary democracy. It was, of course, not absolutely certain that courts would accept this interpretation of the provincial limitation clause. It was, in any event, clear that the phrase that appeared in the latest federal draft "a free and democratic society" was designed to remind courts that the dominant constitutional idea in this country is parliamentary supremacy. The attempt may have been futile; theoretically parliamentary supremacy is not an inexorable aspect of parliamentary democracy. Under the provincial draft courts could well have held that an enactment of Parliament, or a legislative assembly, limited rights in a way which undermined democratic values.

The legal rights provisions of the provincial draft contained the confining phrases much favoured by Ontario. The rights were conditioned by the phrase, "except on grounds provided by law and in accordance with prescribed procedures." As noted earlier, this allows for no judicial check against legislative encroachments on legal rights. More noteworthy, the provincial draft did not include a general provision guaranteeing "life, liberty and the security of the person and the right not to be deprived thereof except in accordance with the due process of law." In this way the provincial draft contained no risk whatsoever that the legal rights would apply in other than criminal and penal matters.

The provincial draft did not contain mobility rights, non-discrimination rights, property rights, rights pertaining to the use of official languages, or minority language education rights. Needless to say, the federal government did not indicate to the provinces that it found their draft a useful basis for further discussions.

Between the final meeting of ministers responsible for the Constitution in late August and the First Ministers' Conference in September, the federal government issued yet another draft. Although this draft was not substantially different from the August one, there were two important changes. First, the limitation clause was rewritten to state that the rights in the charter were subject to reasonable limits "as are generally accepted in a free and democratic society with a parliamentary system of government." This was a further concession by the federal government to the interest of the provinces in building into the charter as large an element of judicial deference to legislative choices as possible.

The second innovation was the alteration of the basic legal rights section from the guarantee of life, liberty, and security of the person and the right not to be deprived of these "except by due process of law" to a new concluding phrase, "except in accordance with the principles of fundamental justice." During the summer's meetings provincial officials repeatedly raised the concern that the courts would read the "due process of law" phrase as guaranteeing substantive due process. What was meant by this phrase was that courts would have authority not only to determine whether the processes by which the essential interests of individuals were adversely affected were appropriate or fair but would also have responsibility for determining whether the idea behind the law was a sound one. The concept of "substantive due process" is self-contradictory and, therefore, it would have been reasonable to assume that courts would read due process as invoking only procedural standards; provincial officials, however, pointed to the development of a body of American law in which the due process clause in the United States Constitution had provided the justification for judicial review of the substantive merits of legislation. Provincial officials concluded that the due process clause could be read to create a greater scope of review than permissible under the mere constitutional protection of minimal procedural standards. Due process could lead to the most intrusive form of review of all—review by courts of the ethical propriety of legislation.

This analysis of the due process clause was prompted by reference to American cases from the first three decades of this century, a period in which there was indeed full-scale substantive review under the Fourteenth Amendment. In particular, provincial officials noted the famous case of *Lochner v. New York*,[53] a case in which the United States Supreme Court invalidated maximum hours of labour legislation on the ground that it unfairly took away employers' liberty to contract. Generally speaking, in this period the Supreme Court of the United States did apply the Fourteenth Amendment to strike down progressive and redistributive social and economic legislation. The due process clause was used to allow the judiciary to protect freedom of contract and to prevent deprivations of common law liberty, most notably the liberty to enjoy property without confiscation through regulatory burdens imposed by the state. But what seems to have been ignored in this desperate desire not to create a *Lochner* situation in Canada is that, since the 1930s, the Supreme Court of the United States had virtually abandoned these sorts of applications of the due process clause and had adopted an attitude of deference to legislative choices which imposed substantive burdens on individual property interests. In other areas, most notably in the protection of privacy, the United States Supreme Court has continued the concept of substantive review. In order to respond to this provincial concern, however, the language of the basic legal rights section was altered. It is arguable that the textual change did not address the concerns which prompted it.

Unilateral Action and the Joint Parliamentary Committee

Involving the People

The First Ministers' Conference was a resounding failure. The acrimony of the public sessions was matched only by the acrimony of the private meetings and dinners. Less than three weeks later the federal government tabled in the House of Commons[54] the resolution which it proposed to send unilaterally to Great Britain requesting that the United Kingdom Parliament change the terms of the British North America Act, 1867. The resolution contained a charter of rights which was almost identical to the charter which had been tabled by the federal government at the first ministers' meeting. Westminster would be asked to legislate into existence the complete charter. Regardless of provincial views on the question of entrenchment, or on any of the particular rights, the charter would be entrenched and would be applicable to all Canadian governments. No doubt unilateral action of any sort would have been unacceptable to the majority of the provinces; what most intensified opposition, however, was the imposition of a charter over which there had been such intense debate and such deep division of views.

The provinces were not alone in attempting to stop the strategy of unilateral patriation. While the federal NDP supported Trudeau's move, the federal Progressive Conservative party decided to oppose it. They were not, of course, opposed to a constitutional charter of rights but only to Canada's obtaining one in the way proposed by the government. Largely through the efforts of the Conservatives, the government was forced to support the establishment of a Joint Parliamentary Committee to consider the report on the proposed resolution. The Liberals hoped that the Joint Parliamentary Committee would conduct its review quickly so that the matter could be placed before the House of Commons and Senate and transmitted to Britain as soon as possible. The committee had other ideas. It wished to do a thorough job and, in any event, it was inundated with requests by groups and citizens to appear before it to comment on the terms of the resolution. In the end, the Joint Parliamentary Committee had 106 meetings on 56 hearing days. It sat for 270 hours and heard presentations from six governments, ninety-three groups and five individuals. In fact, there were many, many more requests to appear before the committee which had to be denied. In total the committee received over twelve hundred submissions and letters.[55] Since it was the nation's Constitution which was being revised, it is not surprising that there was widespread interest in the resolution, nor that the review by the Joint Parliamentary Committee ultimately took up so many hours and pages of testimony. What is interesting is that the great majority of the time spent by the committee was spent on considering the charter of rights and most of the groups and persons who came before the committee to make submissions did so in order to address to the charter issue. These persons, as well as senators and members of Parliament, were faced with the dilemma of proposing improvements to the charter, while at the same time confronting the morality of amending the Constitution of a federal state and thereby impinging on provincial powers through a process in which provinces had no role. Undoubtedly, the Conservative members of the committee felt this tension acutely. So did some of the witnesses, most notably, Archbishop Edward Scott of the Anglican Church of Canada. He said, "I have some deep concerns about the process we are now involved in in seeking to develop a Constitution for Canada focusing primarily on patriation."[56] His concern, however, went beyond the role of provinces and extended to what he considered to be the inadequate participation of all Canadians in the constitutional process. On the other hand, Doris Anderson, president of the Advisory Council on the Status of Women, had no such misgivings. In a statement which shocked those who, in the provincial capitals, followed the proceedings of the Joint Parliamentary Committee, Anderson replied to a question on entrenchment by saying, "most countries do not get the chance to rewrite their Constitution, unless they have a war or a revolution, and here we have a heaven-sent opportunity to entrench a Charter of Rights in our Constitution."[57]

The version of the charter which the Joint Parliamentary Committee and its witnesses considered was essentially the same as the one the federal government had prepared for the First Ministers' Conference. However, since the versions of the charter which had been circulated during the summer and in September were not public documents, the resolution provided Canadians with the first opportunity to see what sort of charter of rights was being considered. The reaction from most groups that appeared before the committee was hostile. The vast majority of the groups that were chosen to appear before the committee were organizations whose goal was to promote the rights of citizens or of special interest groups within society. They all wanted a charter, and they all wanted a charter which protected the interests of their members. The result was that the testimony which the committee received was overwhelmingly in favour of a charter with terms which were as broad and potent as they could be. The committee heard neither the arguments against entrenchment, nor did it hear the debate on the appropriate limits of constitutionalization. It was not presented with the view that some interests, although deserving of attention, should not be removed from political debate for all time by transforming them into entrenched rights. There was no doubt that the nature of the testimony which the committee heard was orchestrated by the government in order to isolate provincial opposition and to create a movement for an even more extensive charter than the one contained in the resolution. The plan was successful. The members of the committee were generally effusive in their praise of the contribution made by the various witnesses and undertook in many cases to reform the document to reflect what was said to them. Although the committee's reforms were largely determined by the amendments to the charter submitted to it by the minister of justice, Jean Chrétien, on 12 January 1981, Chrétien's proposed amendments reflected the evidence presented to the committee and the committee's positive reaction to it. On 13 February 1981 the committee submitted to the House of Commons its revised version of the charter, which the government also supported. It contained only a few changes from Chrétien's version of 12 January, but these changes continued the pattern of broadening the scope of the charter.

The Charter in the Resolution of 2 October

The 2 October 1980 version of the charter, although minimally altered from the immediately previous version, did contain three noteworthy changes. First, the federal government continued to attempt to meet the misgivings expressed by provinces, particularly Ontario, with respect to legal rights. Although Ontario supported unilateral patriation of the Constitution with a charter, it did not abandon its vocal opposition to legal rights. This opposition was reflected in the activities of Rod McLeod, a senior official in the Ministry of the Attorney General, who had dominated legal rights discussions during the summer's meeting and who took his campaign against legal rights before various audiences and to the press. The 2 October draft picked up on the weak provincial draft of 22 August and stated that the rights not to be subjected to search and seizure, not to be detained or imprisoned, and to obtain bail were subject to derogation "in accordance with procedures established by law." As noted before, this sort of clause foreclosed judicial control of legislation which impinged on those rights.

The second change was made in relation to minority language education rights. Earlier versions had given a general right to citizens of Canada who were members of an English-speaking or French-speaking minority to have their children educated in their minority language. In the 2 October draft this right was limited. Only those citizens of Canada whose language first learned and still understood was in a minority would have the right to have their children educated in that language. This seemingly minor alteration had the effect of removing from non-French or non-English-speaking immigrants, who became members of a French or English language minority, the right to have their children educated in the minority language.

Finally, the charter which formed part of the resolution contained for the first time a new application section. Of course, previous versions of the charter had stated that any law, order, regulation, or rule that was inconsistent with the provisions of the charter were, to the extent of the inconsistency, of no force or effect. This clause did two important things. First, it made the charter enforceable; persons whose rights were denied through governmental action could go to court to get an order limiting or nullifying the legislation or executive action. Second, it made clear that the charter provided a set of constitutional constraints which operated against governments. The charter contained in the resolution added a section which said that the charter would apply:

a. to the Parliament and Government of Canada all matters within the authority of Parliament including all matters relating to the Yukon Territory and NorthWest Territories; and

b. to the Legislature and Government of each province and to all matters within the authority of the Legislature of each province.

This was a dramatic addition. It made the charter applicable not only to governmental action but, by stating that all matters within the legislative jurisdiction of Parliament or the provinces were also subject to the terms of the charter, it gave the charter control over all private conduct. Since all the things that private citizens do are within the legislative jurisdiction of one level of government or another, the wording of the new application section turned the charter not only into a constitutional document which restrained government, but a constitutional set of norms relating to the whole of social activity within the country. This was a radical transformation of the nature of the charter. Although this problem was repeatedly brought to the attention of federal officials by the provinces, it was not raised at the hearings of the Joint Parliamentary Committee. As a result the version of the charter which was reported back to Parliament contained this clause. It was not until the constitutional accord was reached on 5 November 1981 that the problem was dealt with. At a lawyers' drafting session that took place long into the night following the signing of the accord by first ministers, the wording of the application section was changed so that the charter again reached governmental action.[58]

The Work of the Joint Parliamentary Committee

The Joint Parliamentary Committee was responsible for a significant number of minor alterations to the charter, but its most significant effects were in relation to modifying section 1 (the general limitation clause), the legal rights sections, and section 15 (the equality, or non-discrimination, clause).

The Limitation Clause. Section 1 received almost universal condemnation from the civil rights groups which appeared before the committee in its early hearings. The consequence of almost complete judicial deference to legislative choice, which would be produced by section 1, would, they argued, make a mockery of the charter. In response to this attack on section 1, the Department of Justice altered the section to remove the reference to a parliamentary system of government and thereby removed the potential for a tautological interpretation: that which legislative bodies enact is, by definition, generally accepted in a parliamentary form of government. In addition, the clause which said that limitations needed to be generally accepted was changed to "demonstrably justified." This change seemed to impose a burden on governments to produce actual evidence of the need to limit rights instead of relying on a more abstract claim that the legislation under challenge was within a range of acceptable responses to the social situation. The consequence of this alteration could well be that, unless governments show the exact cost of not controlling behaviour otherwise protected by the charter, the legislation, albeit motivated by a desire to make social improvements, would not pass the scrutiny of the courts.

A third alteration to section 1 was the introduction of the phrase that the limitations must be "prescribed by law." This would prevent the court from engaging in a balancing process whereby the incidental limiting effects of legislation are tolerated because of the general benefit conferred by the scheme. Under this language if the administration of the law does infringe a person's rights, even if the infringement is consonant with a free and democratic society, it will not be allowed unless the legislation expressly empowers those who administer the law to effect the infringement. If these changes to section 1 were applied literally, claims by governments that their limitation on individual rights were reasonable would face a tough test.

Legal Rights. Civil liberties groups also attacked the watered-down version of the legal rights provisions and the Department of Justice was quick to revert to its preferred language as, for example, in relation to search and seizure: "Everyone has the right to be secure against unreasonable search and seizure." This alteration, of course, gave the courts full scope to determine whether both the administration of the law and the legislation being administered took proper account of the property and personal integrity of the suspected person. In the version of the charter which the minister of justice submitted to the House of Commons in February 1981, that clause was further changed to protect citizens against unreasonable search *or* seizure. This change did not alter the intent of the original section, but is evidence of the continuing attempt to remove words which might limit the protections granted in the charter.

In the Joint Parliamentary Committee a great deal of interest was expressed in the basic legal rights section protecting life, liberty, and security of the person. In the first place, the Conservative members of the committee wished to have "enjoyment of property" added to this list in order to secure property rights. In fact the Conservative proposal was agreed to by the solicitor general, Robert Kaplan,[59] when he was sitting in for Jean Chrétien who, because of exhaustion, spent a week in hospital. When Chrétien returned, he announced to the committee that the government could not agree with the inclusion of property rights.[60] The federal government feared loss of the support of its NDP allies in Parliament as well as alienation of the Saskatchewan government, which seemed to be on the verge of agreeing to support the resolution. Chrétien's announcement that enjoyment of property would not be added to the section produced debate over questions of privilege and rules of order which took up most of the three days which the committee devoted to an examination of the legal rights section.

Toward the end of the committee's debate on the legal rights section, the members finally turned their attention to the troublesome phrase "and the right not to be deprived thereof except in accordance with the principles of fundamental justice." Members of the committee were not sure what this meant but were alert to the possibility that it might invite substantive review by the courts. Barry Strayer, the assistant deputy minister of public law, advanced this view of the meaning of the concluding words:

> It was our belief that the words "fundamental justice" would cover the same thing as what is called procedural due process, that is the meaning of due process in relation to requiring fair procedure. However, it in our view does not cover the concept of what is called substantive due process, which would impose substantive requirements as to the policy of the law in question.[61]

In response to the suggestion of Svend Robinson, an NDP member of the committee, that fundamental justice might well invite substantive review, officials from the Department of Justice replied that there was no distinction between the principles of fundamental justice and the rules of natural justice. Conservative member David Crombie also pressed Strayer on the meaning of the proposed wording and his dialogue concluded with this exchange:

> Mr. Crombie: Natural justice and fundamental justice do not deal with substantive matters, only procedural fairness, that is the difference between those two and due process?
>
> Mr. Strayer: Yes.[62]

The reason for the confidence of officials that fundamental justice precluded judicial review of the substantive policy of enactments was that the phrase had been used in section 2(e) of the Canadian Bill of Rights. The officials referred members of the joint committee to the treatment of that section by the Supreme Court of Canada in the previous case of *Duke v. R.* In that case the court said, in applying section 2(e), that a "tribunal which adjudicates upon a person's rights must act fairly, in good faith, without bias and in a judicial temper, and must give to him the opportunity adequately to state his case."[63]

In fact the officials' testimony, as well as their reference to the *Duke* case should not have convinced the members of the committee. The test of section 2(e) of the Canadian Bill of Rights, to which they were referred, states that no law of Canada "shall be construed or applied so as to deprive a person of the right to a fair hearing in accordance with the principles of fundamental justice for the determination of rights and obligations." In this clause the "fundamental justice" phrase is placed so squarely in the context of procedural guarantees that it is inconceivable that a substantive standard could have been intended. The section of the charter which the committee was considering is not placed in that same context. As it appears in the charter, the phrase "the principles of fundamental justice" seemed very much to carry substantive meaning. This was especially true in light of the political rhetoric and political philosophy during the last half century. In that time the idea of doing justice has come to mean not only dealing with a person's claims in a procedurally fair way, but also in assessing those claims in accordance with policies which are substantively appropriate in terms of both punishment and redistribution. Furthermore, the philosophy that has grown up around the modern activist state has universally considered political behaviour in light of this substantive notion of justice. It has become counter-intuitive to think of the principles of fundamental justice as being simply procedural standards.

In fairness to the officials of the Department of Justice, there is one sense in which reference to the language of the Canadian Bill of Rights might have led to a belief that the phrase would have a restricted meaning. The drafters of the section in the 1960 bill were referring to a concept known in law as "the rules of natural justice." This concept has a relatively fixed and limited meaning confined to procedural fairness. By substituting the phrase "rules of natural justice" in a context where the phrase "principles of fundamental justice" would have been appropriate, it could be argued that the new phrase was equivalent to the earlier phrase and likewise limited to the natural justice ideas. In truth, however, this does not seem to be a convincing justification for the assurances given by justice officials. The fundamental justice terminology has neither the tradition of a term of art enjoyed by the earlier phrase nor is it, on its face, uniquely suggestive of procedural concerns. As it appears in the bill, it is highly ambiguous, but that ambiguity is controlled by placing it within the context of a right to a fair hearing; no such contextual control of the phrase is present in the proposed charter. Furthermore, the careful and contextual way in which the "principles of fundamental justice" is used in the 1960 bill suggests that it is inherently indeterminate and, when taken out of that context as in the charter, has a much broader meaning.

Equality Rights. One of the more organized onslaughts on the provisions of the draft charter was that on section 15, the provision guaranteeing equality before the law. This onslaught was led by women's rights groups, most effectively by the Advisory Council on the Status of Women. Their claim was not that the draft ignored the issue of sexual equality. In fact, section 15 states that persons are entitled to equal protection of the law without discrimination because of, among other things, sex. Nor was it that the women's rights groups took the position that the nation would have a better charter if it contained a general right to equality before the law of the sort that would subject any legislative classification to challenge in the courts on the basis that that classification was irrational and needlessly burdensome to some classes of persons.

The concern of the advisory council was that, regardless of the recognition of sexual equality in the Constitution, the courts would not strike down legislation which created sex-based inequalities unless the section were drafted in a manner which made judicial revisionism impossible. The council's ambition was, in short, to create an equality provision which would force governments and courts to be "sex-blind." There were two main reasons why the version of section 15 which appeared in the 2 October charter did not achieve this goal. First, was the experience of the Canadian Bill of Rights: it also precluded legislative discrimination on the basis of sex, but in two notorious cases in the 1970s, *Lavell*[64] and *Bliss*,[65] the Supreme Court of Canada had no trouble in finding that federal legislation which was indeed sex-based and discriminatory did not violate the 1960 bill. Second, the draft listed among the prohibited categories of discrimination not only race and sex but also age. Since it is apparent that legislation frequently makes distinctions on the basis of age without violating our conception of equality, women's rights groups recognized that courts could not interpret section 15 to foreclose absolutely the use of the listed categories. Once the categories were seen as only presumptively suspect, the courts, if they followed the pattern established by the Supreme Court of Canada in the 1970s, would probably find the use of sex-based categories in legislation to be appropriate for the purpose of the legislative scheme (even though significant burdens might be placed upon women); they would, therefore, refuse to declare them unconstitutional.

The strategy employed by the Advisory Council on the Status of Women was suggested in an article prepared for it by Professor Beverly Baines, legal advisor to the council.[66] Baines suggested creation in section 15 of a two-tiered system. The first tier guaranteed the right to equality in a general sense so that any legislative classifications, regardless of the category used, could be challenged if irrationally related to the purposes of the statute. The second tier would list certain categories which would be more than suspect: they would be virtually impermissible. In that list the advisory council hoped to place sex. The submission to the committee by the advisory council was technical and effective, and the committee indicated that it was willing to make this sort of change to section 15. However, the ambitions for the text held by the advisory council were thwarted to the extent that they did not feel able to advocate the deletion of age, and neither the committee nor the Department of Justice was willing to drop it from the list. In fact, Saskatchewan a year before, in one of the early meetings of the Ottawa–Saskatchewan bilateral negotiations, had suggested that age be dropped from the resolution's equality provision. Its reason for making the suggestion was identical to the concerns of the Advisory Council on the Status of Women: inclusion would weaken the force of the listed categories. Federal officials told the Saskatchewan delegation that dropping age from section 15 at that point would be impossible for political reasons.

To weaken the case for women's rights even further, there was a tremendous push on behalf of mentally and physically handicapped persons to have the equality provision prohibit discrimination on the basis of these features. Clearly legislation and administrative action will frequently make distinctions on the basis of physical and intellectual capacity or disability; inclusion in the list of categories of "mental or physical disability" would make the categories merely suspect, subject to judicial scrutiny to ensure their use was, in the circumstance, reasonable. This is precisely the sort of judicial inquiry which women's rights groups hoped to avoid.

It is possible that, when section 15 comes into force on 17 April 1985, courts will not treat all the categories in exactly the same way; instead, they may identify some categories, such as race or sex, as not generally available in devising legislative schemes and others, such as age and physical and mental disability, as acceptable in some instances. But, this interpretive discretion is precisely what women's rights groups sought to avoid. They achieved a remarkable expansion of the scope of the equality rights, but they did not achieve, at least through amendments to section 15, the absolute barrier to sex-based legislative categories that they sought. For this reason women's rights groups felt it necessary to continue their lobby to change the terms of the charter even after the Joint Parliamentary Committee had tendered its report. In April the minister of justice proposed further amendments, which were approved in the House of Commons on 23 April and the Senate on 24 April 1981. The only significant amendment at that time was the introduction of section 28, which stated, "Notwithstanding anything in this Charter, the rights and freedoms referred to in it are guaranteed equally to male and female persons." It is not clear whether this provision will achieve what was sought by women's rights groups. What is guaranteed to be equally available are the rights of the charter and not the benefits and burdens of governmental schemes. It might be argued that any time a sex-based classification appears in legislation, there is a presumptive violation of the rights to equality under section 15 read literally, and, since that right is now guaranteed to be equally available on the basis of sex, section 28 will be violated. This, however, is not a compelling view of the effect of sections 28 and 15. The right that is guaranteed in section 15 is the right to equal treatment on the basis of, amongst other things, sex. There is no necessary infringement on that right simply by the use of sex-based categories in the legislation. Only if, at the end of the day, a court concludes that the sex-based category imposes an unwarranted burden on one sex or the other will section 15 be violated. Until that conclusion is reached, there has been no violation of a charter right, and there is nothing for section 28 to operate on.

The other purpose behind section 28 was to counter the inclusion in the charter of the guarantee that the rights and freedoms would not be construed to derogate from rights pertaining to the aboriginal peoples of Canada. Women's rights groups, including organizations of Indian women, feared that the exemption to the application of the charter's provisions would permit the continuation of Indian membership rules which discriminate against women. It was sought to trump this exception to the provisions of the charter with a section which would not allow aboriginal rights to be more important than sexual equality. The opening phrase in section 28, "notwithstanding anything in this Charter," is meant precisely to indicate that the exemption in favour of the rights of aboriginal people is to be subordinate to it.

Other Changes. The Joint Parliamentary Committee recommended other improvements. For example, it approved further changes to the minority language education rights provision. The draft that it originally considered, as has already been noted, guaranteed minority language education only for children of persons whose mother tongue was either French or English. The committee's further amendment extended the guarantee to the children of persons who had received their primary school education in Canada in either French or English. Under the amendment, this right seems to accrue even though the person claiming the right on the basis of having received his or her primary education in the minority language was not, in fact, a member of the language minority in the province where the primary education was given.

The committee added a new subsection to the enforcement section which permitted courts to exclude evidence obtained in contravention of the charter (normally in violation of legal rights) if it were shown that admission of the evidence would bring the administration of justice into disrepute. The exclusion of evidence was a matter hotly contested during the federal–provincial meetings in the summer of 1980. The provinces were keen that any remedial powers given in the charter expressly exclude the power of the courts to exclude evidence which was wrongfully obtained. Again, Ontario took a leading role in fighting against the development of an exclusionary rule. In keeping with the general tendency of the 2 October draft to meet some of the provincial concerns, that text included a clause which said that the terms of the charter would not affect the laws respecting the admissibility of evidence or the authority of any legislative body to make laws relating to admissibility. That immunization of legislative authority in relation to admissibility was another matter which was critically addressed by witnesses before the Joint Parliamentary Committee. As a result, the Department of Justice, in recognition of the committee's agreement with the witnesses' complaint, suggested a wording which would allow the exclusion of evidence.

The wording does not compel the exclusion of evidence. An early draft by the Department of Justice said that courts may exclude evidence when the administration of justice was brought into disrepute but the committee forced the government to change the wording to "shall." This change, of course, did not create mandatory exclusion, which was dependent upon an affirmative answer by the courts that the admission of evidence would be harmful to the reputation of the justice system. The courts have more than enough discretion in deciding that question.

The charter, beefed up by the committee process during the winter of 1980–81, was approved by the House of Commons and Senate in late April 1981 just four days before the commencement of the Supreme Court of Canada's hearing into the constitutional validity of the federal government's strategy of unilateral patriation. By this time, largely because of the provincial victory in the Newfoundland court of appeal, it was apparent that the federal government could not proceed to send its resolution to Great Britain before the Supreme Court of Canada issued its decision. Consequently, further discussion of the text of the resolution was pointless.

Federal-Provincial Bargaining Again

In the weeks between the decision of the Supreme Court of Canada in late September and the meeting between the prime minister and the provincial premiers in early November, all governments were required to do some hard thinking about which elements of a patriation package they could support. One thing was clear: failure to agree would not result in the abandonment of the patriation plan in anticipation that constitutional diplomacy would be taken up at a later date. The Supreme Court of Canada's decision meant that the federal government could legally proceed to London if the talks in November failed. One of the elements in a patriation agreement would be some form of a charter, and when the first ministers met in November, there were only two provinces which were irrevocably opposed to any charter: Manitoba and Quebec. Ontario and New Brunswick had always been in favour of the federal charter; Newfoundland had never been opposed to the entrenchment of some rights; and British Columbia, Alberta, Prince Edward Island, Nova Scotia, and Saskatchewan, all went to the November meeting in the knowledge that they would accept some form of the charter.

There were a number of options other than accepting the version of the charter which the House of Commons and Senate had approved in April. At a meeting in October between Prime Minister Trudeau and Premier Bennett of British Columbia, Trudeau had suggested that the provinces might accept a "small" charter to come into effect now with the guarantee that the balance of it would come into effect later. Another option being considered was inclusion in the charter of a clause granting a general legislative override. A third option limited such a legislative override to only some portions of the charter. Gordon Robertson, the former clerk of the Privy Council and Mr. Trudeau's chief constitutional advisor until 1979, had suggested a fourth option. His proposal was that the charter be passed but not be binding on any provincial legislature for a period of four years. During that time a legislature could become bound by the charter by declaring its wish to be bound. At the end of the four-year period, the charter would automatically become binding in all provinces except those whose legislatures had passed a resolution declaring that the charter would not apply to it. In other words, if a provincial legislature did not want the province to be bound by the charter, it would have to pass a resolution rejecting the entire charter. The virtue of Robertson's scheme was that, in the four-year period, the chances were high that a provincial election would be fought on the basis of whether the government supported the charter. Robertson's proposal, then, contained a reasonable substitute for constitutionalization by referendum.

Yet another option was to enact a charter but allow the provinces to opt out of certain sections of it during the following four years only. Other conditions could be built into the scheme: opting out could be permitted only by a resolution passed by, for example, 60 percent of the members of the legislative body; alternatively, opting out could be made contingent upon the holding of a provincial referendum. The sixth option was to have the charter in its present form enacted by the U.K. Parliament but apply only to the federal government and any province, which, by resolution of its legislative assembly, indicated its desire to be bound. Once such a resolution were passed and the charter applied to a province, its application could not be revoked. A further suggestion was that the patriation package include only an amending formula and that there be a collateral agreement between the provinces that they dedicate themselves to two years of negotiations designed to write a charter which would be acceptable to everyone. Finally, there were a series of options which would entrench and make applicable to provinces various parts, but not all, of the charter. The ones most commonly favoured for inclusion under this option were fundamental freedoms, democratic rights, mobility rights, and language rights.

With respect to minority language education rights, Quebec was not alone in its concerns about including this in the charter; therefore, in this area too there were a series of options. These were: entrenching the minority language education provision and making it binding in all provinces; entrenching it with a legislative override clause; entrenching it with an opt-out clause; entrenching it with an opt-in clause; or, finally, entrenching the principle of minority language education without creating a judicially enforceable right.

It is fair to say that all governments went to the November conference without a clear idea about which of these options would be likely to succeed. As we know, a halfway proposal was chosen, and the story of how that came about has already been told.

Conclusion

The choice by ten of the governments of Canada to include in the Charter of Rights and Freedoms a provision enabling legislative bodies to override the protections of the charter has been said to destroy the very idea of entrenchment. To the extent that constitutional rights are viewed as claims which, in every instance, can prevail over the wish of legislative majorities, the charter does not provide rights, at least in respect of fundamental freedoms, legal rights, and equality rights. In the absence of use of the legislative override, however, the terms of the charter operate with full force; so long as there is no legislative override to suppress that operation, individuals clearly have rights which prevail over the wishes of Parliament, the legislatures and the actions of governmental administration. The charter of rights does create rights, and rights have clearly been placed in the Constitution. However, the override clause means that the values which are found in the charter may not, in every case, be saved from attack by determined majorities.

There can be no doubt that, since 1945, Canada has come a long way in giving legal recognition to basic human rights. It has not gone as far as it could have, either in framing the form or the scope of those rights. Canada has not, therefore, carried the political idea of entrenchment to its logical conclusion. But it is also true that in 1867 Canada did not carry the idea of federalism to *its* logical conclusion. It would not be consistent with the Canadian experience for Canada's Constitution to be based on the whole-hearted adoption of a single political idea. What is truly Canadian is to tamper, to modify, to dilute, and to reflect the ambivalence that exists about the nature of the nation. Just as the 1867 Constitution contained both the principle of federalism and an array of centralizing powers, which over time would produce national fusion, so the Constitution Act, 1982, contains both the general and unifying standards of the Charter of Rights and Freedoms as well as the legislative power allowing provinces to take themselves outside the norms of the charter. The tension between the desire to create a nation state, while honouring the diversity of its various communities, is reflected in the 1867 Act. It continues to be reflected in our current Constitution making. The charter may, however, produce such a strong national political identity that the tension between the idea of nation and the idea of community will gradually lose its force and, in the end Canada, because of the Charter of Rights and Freedoms, will become something different.

Notes

1. *Federal-Provincial Conference of First Ministers on the Constitution, Verbatim*

Transcript—Opening Statement by P.E. Trudeau, Prime Minister, Ottawa, 8–13 September 1980, C.I.C.S. Doc. 800-14/050, at 4.

2. *Notes for a Statement on the Entrenchment of a Charter of Rights*, Ottawa, 9 September 1980, C.I.C.S. Doc. 800-14/072.

3. Racial Discrimination Act, 1944, S.O. 1944, c. 51.

4. Saskatchewan Bill of Rights Act, 1947, S.S. 1947, c. 35.

5. *Proceedings of the Dominion–Provincial Conference*, Ottawa, 10–12 January 1950, at 36.

6. *House of Commons Debates*, 20th Parliament, 2nd Session, 1:900 (10 October 1945).

7. *House of Commons Debates*, 20th Parliament, 2nd Session, 1:1047–49 (30 April 1946), 2:1300–1315 (7 May 1946), 2:1328–44 (8 May 1946), 2:1575–79 (16 May 1946).

8. *House of Commons Debates*, 20th Parliament, 2nd Session 2:1575–76 (16 May 1946).

9. *Ibid.*, at 1579.

10. *House of Commons Debates*, 20th Parliament, 3rd Session, 4:3189 (15 May 1947).

11. *Ibid.*, at 3152 (16 May 1947).

12. For an account of the responses, see "The Joint Committee on Human Rights and Fundamental Freedoms" (1948), 26 *Canadian Bar Review* 706.

13. *House of Commons Debates*, 20th Parliament, 4th Session, 3:2846–47 (9 April 1948).

14. *Ibid.*, at 2887.

15. *Second and Final Report of the Special Joint Committee on Human Rights and Fundamental Freedoms*, June 1948, at 728–31.

16. *House of Commons Debates*, 21st Parliament, 2nd Session, 2:1173 (26 October 1949).

17. *Senate Debates*, 21st Parliament, 1st Session, 215 (3 November 1949).

18. *Senate Debates*, 21st Parliament, 2nd Session, (20 March 1950), at 94.

19. The Special Committee on Human Rights and Fundamental Freedoms reported on 27 June 1950. *Senate Debates*, 21st Parliament, 2nd Session (27 June 1950), at 585–90.

20. *House of Commons Debates*, 21st Parliament, 2nd Session, 1:919 (20 March 1950).

21. *Ibid.*, at 950.

22. *House of Commons Debates*, 21st Parliament, 6th Session, 1:714–722 (24 March 1952).

23. *Ibid.*, at 720 (24 March 1952).

24. *House of Commons Debate*, 22nd Parliament, 2nd Session, 1:894–933 (7 February 1955).

25. House of Commons of Canada, 24th Parliament, 1st Session, 7 Elizabeth 2, 1958, 1st Reading 5 September 1958.

26. *House of Commons Debates*, 24th Parliament, 3rd Session, 7:7553 (4 August 1960).

27. Canadian Bill of Rights, S.C. 1960, c. 44.

28. R. Gwyn, *The Northern Magus: Pierre Trudeau and Canadians* (Toronto: McClelland and Stewart, 1980), 53. Used by permission of The Canadian Publishers, McClelland and Stewart Limited, Toronto.

29. P.E. Trudeau, "Some Obstacles to Democracy in Quebec" (1958), 24 *Canadian Journal of Economics and Political Science* 297.

30. *Ibid.*, at 304.

31. *Ibid.*

32. See P.E. Trudeau, minister of justice, "A Constitutional Declaration of Rights," an address to the Canadian Bar Association, Quebec, 4 September 1967, reprinted in P.E. Trudeau, *Federalism and the French Canadians* (Toronto: Macmillan of Canada, 1968), 52 at 53.

33. *House of Commons Debates*, 27th Parliament, 2nd Session, 1:55 (10 May 1967).

34. *House of Commons Debates*, 27th Parliament, 2nd Session, 2:2299 (6 July 1967).

35. *Supra*, note 32, at 3.

36. "Manifesto," (May, 1964) *Canadian Forum* 29. One of the members of the Committee for Political Realism with Trudeau was Marc Lalonde, the present minister of finance in the Trudeau government.

37. *House of Commons Debates*, 27th Parliament, 2nd Session, 6:6137 (30 January 1968).

38. P.E. Trudeau, "Constitutional Reform and Individual Freedoms, Exerpts from Speeches" (1969), 8 *University of Western Ontario Law Review* 1, at 3.

39. D. Smiley, *Canada in Question: Federalism in the Seventies*, 2d ed. (Toronto: McGraw-Hill Ryerson, 1976), 42.

40. L.B. Pearson, *Federalism for the Future* (Ottawa: Queen's Printer, 1968).

41. P.E. Trudeau, prime minister, *The Constitution and the People of Canada* (Ottawa: Queen's Printer, 1969).

42. *Supra*, note 39, at 44.

43. Communiqué from the office of R. Bourassa, premier of Quebec, 23 June 1971.

44. *Report of the Special Joint Committee of the Senate and of the House of Commons on the Constitution of Canada Report*, 28th Parliament, 4th Session, 1972.

45. Task Force on Canadian Unity, *A Future Together*, (January 1979), Chapter 7, "A Restructured Federalism," at 108.

46. *Ibid.*, at Chapter 9, "Specific Recommendations," at 121.

47. *Ibid.*, at 122.

48. *Ibid.*, at 3.

49. *Reference Re Legislative Authority of Parliament in Relation to the Upper House*, [1980] 1 S.C.R. 54, 102 D.L.R. (3d) 1.

50. *Best Efforts Draft of Charter of Rights and Freedoms*, Ottawa, 5–6 February 1979, C.I.C.S. Doc. 800-10/010.
51. *Opening Address to the First Ministers' Conference on the Constitution by William Jarvis*, Halifax, 22–23 October 1979, C.I.C.S. Doc. 830-74/010.
52. *Federal–Provincial Conference of First Ministers on the Constitution, Verbatim Transcript*, Ottawa, 8–13 September 1980, C.I.C.S. Doc. 800-14/042, at 574. Extract from an unverified and unofficial verbatim transcript.
53. *Lochner v. New York* (1905), 198 U.S. 45.
54. *House of Commons Debates*, 32nd Parliament, 1st Session, 3:3274 (6 October 1980).
55. *Minutes of Proceedings and Evidence of the Special Joint Committee of the Senate and the House of Commons on the Constitution of Canada*, 32nd Parliament, 1st Session, 57: (13 February 1981).
56. *Ibid.*, 33:7 (7 January 1981).
57. *Ibid.*, 9:133 (20 November 1980).
58. Section 32(1) reads as follows: This Charter applies: a. to the Parliament and government of Canada in respect of all matters within the authority of Parliament including all matters relating to the Yukon Territory and Northwest Territories; and b. to the legislature and government of each province in respect of all matters within the authority of the legislature of each province.
59. *Supra*, note 55, 43:59 (22 January 1981).
60. *Ibid.*, 45:9–10 (26 January 1981).
61. *Ibid.*, 46:32 (27 January 1981).
62. *Ibid.*, at 46:42.
63. *Duke v. R.*, [1972] S.C.R. 917, 28 D.L.R. (3d) 129.
64. *Lavell v. Attorney General of Canada*, [1974] S.C.R. 1349, 38 D.L.R. (3d) 481.
65. *Bliss v. Attorney General of Canada* [1979] 1 S.C.R. 183, [1978] 6 W.W.R. 711.
66. B. Baines, "Women, Human Rights and the Constitution," in A. Doerr and M. Carrier, *Women and the Constitution in Canada* (Ottawa: Canadian Advisory Council on the Status of Women, 1981), 29.

Chapter 9
Looking Back, Looking Ahead

An Evaluation

The November accord and the ensuing political manoeuvering to obtain revisions and additions to it produced a constitutional text which effected four significant changes in Canada's constitutional arrangements. First, individual and language rights were entrenched; second, aboriginal rights were recognized; third, rules for amending the Constitution were created; and, finally, new authority was allocated to the provinces in respect of non-renewable resources. In all cases the text which was ultimately arrived at was the product of compromises made in order to obtain agreement, with the result that none of the governments, or groups of governments, which initially made the proposals for change were truly satisfied by the outcome. Virtually no government got what it wanted on any of the terms in the Constitution Act, 1982 except, perhaps, with respect to the provisions relating to equalization and regional disparities. The extent of political accommodation at work in the making of a new Constitution was impressive, and the precise nature of that accommodation needs to be explored.

One government, however, did not adjust its demands and did not concur in the political bargain that was reached. Formal implementation of the Constitution was proceeded with notwithstanding Quebec's objection. As a result, a Canadian Constitution applying to all parts of Canada is in force. Quebec's involuntary loss of its preferences is more profound than that of any other province, if only by virtue of the fact it did not acquiesce in the concessions imposed on it. In fact, its loss in the process is made even more poignant when it is realized that Quebec's needs for constitutional reform have always been a significant impetus for reform and, in fact, have been the sole impetus throughout much of the period since 1960. Quebec's commitment to substantive reform preceding constitutional patriation has always been more firmly stated than that of any other province. It is appropriate then to start our analysis of the accord with an assessment of how constitutional reform went ahead without Quebec's concurrence.

Quebec

In the last hours of the November conference everyone acknowledged that no proposal on minority language education rights and an amending formula would be acceptable both to Ottawa and Quebec City. In the end an accord was reached with Ottawa and Quebec rejected it. Quebec's angry denunciation of the compromises and the process by which they came about is a source of continuing concern. But how accurate are the arguments of the government of Quebec that the processes of the November conference were unfair to it? In order to assess this, one must examine the true nature of the eight provinces' defensive alliance to which Quebec attaches so much importance in its denunciation of the other provinces.

What united provincial governments of different political philosophies and different notions of federalism was a common opposition to Ottawa's constitutional actions. The alliance's ability to embrace such divergent views as the separatism of Quebec, the compact theory of Prince Edward Island, and the "substantial consent" concept of Saskatchewan resulted from the nature of the alliance as a defensive pact established to stop Ottawa's initiatives. While adhering to differing philosophies, their alliance was a pragmatic expression of protest against the federal government's denial of their differences.

Although the government of Quebec must have realized the truth of this view, it also hoped for more. It came to the November First Ministers' Conference on the ground that it would not depart in any substantive way from the April provincial patriation plan. But, if Quebec's understanding of the alliance was that it was other than a true defensive pact, such understanding would have arisen as a result of willful blindness. Many other members of the alliance clearly did not see the provincial patriation plan as the only possible basis of negotiation. After all, the plan had already been publicly and forcefully rejected by Ottawa. There would be little sense in convening yet another constitutional conference if that were the only proposal which could be advanced.

Saskatchewan in the weeks before the First Ministers' Conference had repeatedly said that it would continue its search for compromise; so had British Columbia. On the Wednesday morning of the conference, Saskatchewan's indication that it would submit a compromise text again demonstrated the depth of Saskatchewan's commitment to a negotiated settlement. Blakeney made it absolutely clear, however, that Saskatchewan would not consent to any proposal that did not receive the support of the federal government and of a majority of the provinces. The Wednesday morning proposal failed, receiving neither the support of Ottawa nor the support of members of the defensive alliance. Thus, the impasse continued throughout the day.

What shattered the sense of there being a common position of the

Gang of Eight to which all would adhere in the absence of another proposal which attracted adequate support, was Quebec's rapid acceptance of Trudeau's referendum plan to break the impasse. Some Quebec officials have described Quebec's statements with respect to the referendum as the product of only a "momentary interest," adopted because the common front no longer existed. However, since every other alternative to the provincial patriation plan and the federal resolution had been swept away, Quebec was not correct in concluding that the common front no longer existed. Quebec's decision to adopt the referendum proposal was a surprise to the other provinces. When the details of the referendum were distributed late that day, it was apparent how favourable to federal interests the proposal was. The negative reaction to the referendum proposal of the other provinces was confirmed once the details were available. Quebec, while reversing its position of acceptance of the referendum, did not totally reject it, notwithstanding that it had the support of no other province. At the end of the session on Wednesday the common front had ceased to exist.

What most caused the sense of callous isolation of Quebec by the other nine provinces was the failure to invite Quebec to participate in gathering provincial support for the compromise proposal worked out between Ottawa and Saskatchewan on Wednesday afternoon. Should Quebec have been invited to participate in the Wednesday night discussions? Clearly, if there were to be a resolution of the conflict over the terms of patriation, it would lie in something like the compromise proposal and not in the provincial patriation plan. A referendum had proven to be unacceptable to everyone except Ottawa and Quebec. Quebec had repeatedly emphasized that it would not go beyond the essential elements of the April accord. Now the federal government was prepared to move a long way towards a common ground on which general agreement could be reached, although not agreement which could include Quebec. In this context it made little sense to invite Quebec to participate unless the provinces took the position that they would agree to nothing that Quebec was not able to agree to, in which case confirmation should have been sought of Quebec's anticipated negative reaction to the proposal. But no province had taken the position that it would never agree to a settlement which did not include Quebec, and Quebec could hardly have expected such an agreement. It may certainly have wished the provinces would join in such an alliance, but that had not happened, and Quebec's subsequent claims of betrayal lacked factual basis.

In the final analysis the difference between Quebec's actions and those of the majority were their goals. Quebec's sole objective at this stage of the negotiations was to wreck Ottawa's plan for patriation. A defeat of the federal resolution represented a "successful" conference for Quebec.

The other provinces refused to equate the defeat of the federal resolution with the success of the conference. Saskatchewan felt it was imperative to stop Ottawa's unilateral action; however, merely stopping such action was not thought to be sufficient since the collapse of the November conference would not lead to a healthier climate for future negotiations. Failure to achieve any agreement on the questions of patriation and renewal was anticipated to result in devastating consequences for Canadian unity and for Canada.

Thus, the paramount objective late Wednesday, as it had been throughout the conference, was to settle Canada's constitutional differences in Canada, even if it meant a limitation of provincial powers through the entrenchment of human and language rights.

Quebec's isolation was also caused by the substance of the provisions of the accord as they affected that province. The new Constitution embraced some of the province's demands. For one thing the compromise brought to an end the referendum mechanism which was to be wielded by only one level of government, an arrangement which was of deep concern to Quebec. As well, the principle of the amending formula included in the accord is the one agreed to by the government of Quebec in April 1981. The amending formula grants provinces the authority to withdraw from general amendments which "derogate" from their powers and privileges. Quebec is thereby guaranteed that none of its existing legislative powers will be diminished. While this capacity is less than a veto power, it is a guarantee that no future amendments diminishing Quebec's legislative powers will apply to it.

Quebec has argued that its waiver of the full veto was conditional upon the provision of fiscal compensation for provinces which exercise the opt-out clause of the amending formula. With the removal of this section, the true value of the amending formula was lost. The merits of this argument need to be carefully assessed. First, subsequent amendments to the November accord restored fiscal compensation for opt outs in respect of education and "other cultural matters," two extremely important fields of provincial concern. In this way, the impact of the total removal of the general fiscal compensation section has been mitigated. Second, as the prime minister argued in the course of the debate in November 1981, it is probable that most federal governments would arrange fiscal compensation to a province that opted out. Special fiscal arrangements, especially with Quebec, comprise much of the current federal–provincial relationship. Third, most governments were uncertain as to the kinds of circumstances which would dictate the payment of fiscal compensation since it was felt that most constitutional amendments which transferred jurisdiction, such as the granting of new regulatory powers, would not entail large governmental expenditures.

Nevertheless, it must be granted that the new amending formula will permit constitutional amendments to be made which are contrary to Quebec's interests and to which the opt-out provision will not apply. For instance, an amendment creating a new Senate with greatly increased representation from the West could not be opted out of by Quebec and, of course, could not be vetoed by Quebec.

Where does this leave Quebec and the rest of Canada in the endless struggle to find lasting constitutional accommodation? The opt-out provisions do not satisfactorily answer the claim that both the process and the substance of the constitutional accord destroyed Quebec's constitutional equality with the rest of Canada. Moreover, the plain fact is that the province's government refused to accept the accord and will continue to do so until such time as Quebec's special place in the constitutional arrangement is recognized. This dictates a further round of constitutional negotiations that will produce alterations to the amending formula. This will be a herculean task under the best of conditions. And it will simply be impossible so long as most provincial governments refuse to deviate from the principle of the equality of governments, or so long as the federal government refuses to expand the scope of the fiscal compensation clause. In fact, the polarization of positions, as acute nearly three years after the signing of the accord as it was at the time it was made, means that the task of finding constitutional accommodation is as daunting as ever. Yet the situation of one of Canada's founding partners refusing to accept the nation's constitution is totally unacceptable and cannot remain. All the ingenuity and capacity to construct legitimate compromises that Canadians have demonstrated in the past will need to be summoned once again as the people and governments of Canada consider the options of veto, full fiscal compensation and, perhaps, referendum mechanisms.

One crucial question remains: should the governments have entered into the accord of November 1981 without Quebec? An answer to this question requires an examination of the options. After a full year of bitter political and legal conflict over the patriation plan of the Trudeau government, the option of no provincial participation without Quebec (and in November 1981 this was the only other option available since, beyond doubt, the negotiations had brought Quebec and the federal government to such an impasse on fundamental principles that there was simply no negotiating room left) would have produced a federal–provincial constitutional war that Canada would have paid for dearly and from which it would have long borne the scars.

Was that prospect less threatening to the nation than the course chosen—signing an accord which did not include Quebec? Obviously the participants in the agreement thought not. Moreover, the substance of the agreement properly reflected their idea of the Canadian federal nation. To their minds, and ours, the decision taken in November 1981 was correct— the crisis that faced Canada at that moment had to be met.

But as Canada's history demonstrates, no single constitutional pact is adequate to meet all of the country's challenges; constitutional arrangements require constant re-evaluation and re-wording. Quebec, with its special linguistic and cultural place in Canada, presents a constitutional challenge that has not been met, and this is the major part of Canada's unfinished constitutional business.

Aboriginal Rights

Section 35 of the Constitutional Act says that "existing aboriginal and treaty rights of the aboriginal peoples of Canada are hereby recognized and affirmed." For much of the period of constitutional negotiations between 1978 and 1981, the federal government was reluctant to include such a provision. Initially the recognition of aboriginal rights was the result of intense lobbying by the federal NDP with the government and the Joint Parliamentary Committee which sat during 1980–81. Many provinces were also concerned about the consequences of including the recognition of aboriginal rights since they were not clear what the consequence of such a provision would be for provincial lands and provincial legislative authority.

The aboriginal peoples would have preferred aboriginal rights to be accompanied with an enforcement section which matched the enforcement section included in the charter of rights. Of greater concern to these groups was the addition of the word "existing" to the phrase "aboriginal and treaty rights" in late November 1981 when section 35 was, with some reluctance, being accepted by the provinces. Both these concerns may be groundless. The recognition of aboriginal rights is contained in the new Constitution. Section 52 of that document says that any law that is inconsistent with the Constitution is, to the extent of the inconsistency, of no force or effect, and this general provision will certainly give courts scope to enforce aboriginal rights. It is not likely that that word "existing" will preclude the courts from upholding rights which had not been judicially recognized by the time the Constitution Act came into force in 1982. However, some have argued that that will be the precise effect and, so, the apprehension is legitimate. Clearly, these two features of the provision diminish the political victory for aboriginal groups. Furthermore, a significant problem remains: the absence of any definition of aboriginal or treaty rights will raise acute problems when attempts are made to vindicate those rights against governments. Finally, it must be recognized that the failure to include in the new Constitution new rights for aboriginal groups, such as the right to self-government, means that aboriginal groups failed to achieve many of their objectives.

In recognition of how far the constitutional agreement fell short of the long-term political goals of the aboriginal groups in Canada, a provision was placed in the Constitution which guaranteed that, within one year of its coming into force, there would be a further First Ministers' Conference at which the matter of aboriginal rights would be discussed. That conference took place eleven months after patriation day on 17 April 1982, and a slight expansion of the clause recognizing aboriginal rights was agreed upon. As well, that conference agreed that there would be further meetings to deal with the claims of aboriginal peoples—a satisfactory compromise only if, at some future time, the governments in Canada address the issues with the same sense of urgency they had in November 1981. It is doubtful that that political climate will be replicated, and the sense of lost opportunity felt by aboriginal leaders may be correct.

Amending Formula
Ottawa's acceptance of the provincial patriation plan, which allowed provincial opting out and was based on the principle of equality of all provinces, was fundamental in obtaining a final agreement. Considering the imperatives which the various governments have brought to the struggle to find an amending formula over the years, agreement on this subject was a minor miracle.

The general amending provision, set out in section 38 of the Constitution Act, 1982, provides that resolutions by the Senate and House of Commons and at least two-thirds of the provinces representing at least 50 percent of the population must be enacted to effect an amendment. Five items are identified in section 41 as requiring the unanimous consent of Parliament and all of the provinces. Included on this list are the office of the queen, the office of the governor general and each lieutenant governor of a province, the rights of a province pertaining to the use of English and French language, the composition of the Supreme Court of Canada, and the amending formula itself.

With respect to any general amendment that "derogates from the legislative powers, the proprietary rights or any other rights or privileges of the legislature or government of a province," if a legislature expresses its dissent by a resolution supported by a majority of its members prior to its proclamation, then the amendment will have no effect in that province. Dissent to amendments may be withdrawn at any time. "Reasonable compensation" is provided to any province which has dissented from a general amendment which tranfers provincial legislative powers pertaining to "education or other cultural matters from provincial legislatures to Parliament. . . ."

Section 42 makes special mention of some matters to which the general amending formula applies, thus precluding the claim that these matters are either within the sole authority of Parliament to amend or are amendable on a bilateral basis. These matters concern representation in the

House of Commons, the powers of the Senate, the appointment of senators, the level of provincial representation in the Senate, most matters
respecting the Supreme Court, the extension of provinces, and the creation
of new provinces.

Section 43 permits a constitutional amendment to "any provision that
applies to one or more but not all of the provinces" upon passage of
resolutions in Parliament and the province to which the amendment per-
tains. Specifically included in this section are amendments to boundaries
between provinces and to the use of French or English within a province.

The Senate has a suspensive veto of 180 days with respect to any
amendment made under the provisions of sections 38, 41, 42, or 43; after
this time, if the Senate has not approved the amendment, the House of
Commons can again adopt the resolution and the amendment will take
effect. Sections 44 and 45 deal with the limited exclusive powers of the
federal Parliament and the provinces, respectively, to amend the Constitution.

The search for an appropriate amending formula, which, in a small,
culturally and regionally diverse nation such as Canada, has always been
difficult, was made particularly difficult by the political context of recent
constitutional negotiations. The western provinces insisted that any
amending formula not contain a provision which would legally permit the
rest of the nation to restrict or to remove provincial jurisdiction over
ownership of natural resources. Furthermore, only a formula which was
based on the equality of provinces was acceptable to Alberta. The demand
for equality had earlier been a strong theme of provincial governments. At
the dominion–provincial conference of 1927 and at the meeting of the
Continuing Committee on Constitutional Questions in 1936, the principle
of equality was assumed. A provision for limited opting out,[1] considered
in 1936, was consistent with this objective. However, from the time of
Duplessis to the Victoria conference of 1971, the demands of Quebec
grew in importance and the principle of equality of provinces gradually
gave way to the principle of speciality. By the time of the Victoria conference, most governments were prepared to constitutionalize a special position for Quebec with respect to the amending formula, in recognition of
its concern about amendments that could, without its consent, affect things
it considered vital to its different culture and character.

When viewed from the longer historical perspective, the new formula
cannot be seen as novel. It represents a confirmation of one of the most
important traditional objectives of most of the provinces. When contrasted
to the rigidity of unanimity, the present amending formula is much to be
preferred.

It is claimed that the major flaw with the amending formula is that the
opting-out feature means that some parts of a federal state are able to
escape some constitutional amendments. Federalism is premised on the

two orders of government being equal, each in its own legislative sphere. Neither the federal government nor the provinces may act for the whole of Canada on all matters, and certainly not with respect to constitutional reform. Sovereignty belongs to the nation that has been created and does not vest in any order of government. This normally means that, when the two orders of government exercise their collective sovereignty, those provinces which dissent cannot excuse themselves from the effects of constitutional decisions endorsed by the majority. Opting-out provisions are not part of the normal understanding of the federal sovereign state.

However, the amending formula fits Canada's brand of federalism, which regularly has had to adjust to the nation's diverse and conflicting nature. Even before the constitutional accord, Canada's intergovernmental and constitutional arrangements could be characterized as a "checkerboard." Quebec was the only province bound by the language provisions of section 133. French-speaking Canadians have a special status in Manitoba. Administratively, a multitude of federal and provincial cost-sharing arrangements give special recognition to the various needs and demands of the various regions of the nation. The proposed Victoria amending formula would have constitutionalized the different nature of provinces and regions. Viewed from this perspective, the amending formula attempts to accommodate Canada's vast regional and provincial diversities within a strong, united nation.

The amending formula will not enhance provincial legislative authority and weaken the central authority. The function of the opting-out provisions is to prevent a province from having its current powers diminished without its consent. It applies only to future amendments which derogate from provincial powers by transferring provincial jurisdiction to the federal government. Since Ottawa holds a permanent veto over all constitutional amendments, it can refuse those in respect of which the level of opting out is sufficient to create intolerable unevenness. Most significantly, the opt-out provisions have a ratchet effect: a province which has opted out may, at a future time, choose to bind itself to an amendment but, once bound, a province may never again exempt itself from that amendment.

The new amending formula contains no mechanism for the people to participate directly in remaking the Constitution. It has been described as a confirmation of the supremacy of governments and a denial of the ultimate sovereignty of the people. In August 1978 Ottawa issued a background paper, *The Canadian Constitution and Constitutional Amendment*, which advanced the idea of a referendum both as a mechanism to break the deadlock over an amending formula and as an alternative method of amending the Constitution. The background paper described two instances in which a referendum would serve to break a deadlock. First, it could be held within any region which had rejected a proposed constitutional amendment that had been accepted elsewhere. Second, a national referendum could be held to override parliamentary disapproval of a constitutional amendment if four provinces, one from each of the regions, so desired.[2]

The difficult and important question of referendums was not seriously considered during the ministerial deliberations in 1978–79 or 1980. In each period negotiations had emphasized examination of the various previous formulas. Thus, in the course of the 1978–79 deliberations, governments considered the Victoria formula, favoured by Ottawa; the Toronto consensus, supported by Saskatchewan; and the opt-out formula, prepared and supported by Alberta. In 1980 this last formula, by then known as the Vancouver formula, received the most attention because Ottawa indicated that it might adopt it, with modifications, in exchange for acceptance by the provinces of an entrenched charter of rights. The idea of the referendum was never debated. The notion of a referendum, both as a mechanism to amend the Constitution and as a method to break an impasse, surfaced for the first time as a serious proposal when it appeared in the federal resolution of 2 October 1980.

The resolution provided that a referendum needed to be approved by both houses of Parliament. In order to succeed, the referendum would need approval by a majority of voters in the same combination of provinces whose consent was required by the Victoria amending formula, that is, a majority in Ontario, Quebec, and two provinces in the East and two provinces in the West, whose population in each case represented 50 percent of the population of the East or West.

Most of the provinces opposed both the principle and the details of the referendum. In a regionally diverse country such as Canada, the referendum was seen as potentially divisive, pitting one region against another. Some, like Premier Blakeney, saw the referendum as a weapon for conservatism since, invariably, it would be easier to defend the status quo than the proposed constitutional reform. All provinces feared, in varying degrees, that difficulties in framing appropriate wording for a referendum would be insurmountable. In Saskatchewan's bilateral negotiations with Ottawa it urged that, if there was to be a referendum, it should be available to the provinces in circumstances where Parliament was blocking a constitutional amendment. The federal government could not accept the idea of a provincially initiated referendum but did agree to a mechanism which would allow seven provinces to prevent a referendum by passing legislative resolutions to that effect. The federal government steadfastly turned away "reciprocity" suggestions for the referendum; it was a weapon to be used exclusively by the federal government. All of the important issues— the referendum question, the establishment of rules for the debate, and the decision required to trigger the process—were assigned exclusively to the federal government. The federal government had discovered the power of the referendum in strengthening the direct relationship between Parliament and the people of Canada, even in respect of matters which entailed provincial powers. It was not about to dilute this effect by agreeing to provincial referendums.

Provincial opposition to the referendum was aggravated by its introduction to the constitutional debate after the breakdown of federal and provincial negotiations in September 1980 and without prior notice or discussion with the provinces. This contributed to the view that the motivation behind it was to strengthen federal power.

From another perspective, however, the failure to include a referendum mechanism in the Constitution Act, 1982, and the denial of direct participation by citizens in forming the arrangements under which they are governed violates one vision of the proper relationship between the individual and the state. Prime Minister Trudeau, in his closing remarks at the November 1981 conference, said, "The Constitution will only truly belong to the nation when the people have the opportunity to endorse it through constitutional amendment."[3]

Non-renewable Resources

Surprisingly, in light of the history of recent constitutional negotiations the question of jurisdiction to regulate non-renewable resources received little attention at the November 1981 First Ministers' Conference. In the absence of debate it is hard to know why Alberta acquiesced in the resources provisions of the federal resolution. For Saskatchewan the provisions, particularly the conferral of jurisdiction to levy indirect taxes, were of significant benefit; however, as was the case for Alberta, the absence of protection for the international trade aspects of its resources policies in the new section 92A was a disappointment. To some extent these provinces viewed the resource provision as a bonus since, notwithstanding the five-year struggle to avoid precisely this result, the agenda of the conference was to discuss patriation and the amending formula. For Alberta, there was another consideration. It viewed the opting-out formula in the amending provisions as a major gain in its ongoing struggle with Ottawa over resources. Alberta had harboured suspicions that the majority of Canada might choose to alter existing constitutional provisions with respect to natural resources to get clear access to Alberta's resource wealth. With the new amending formula this concern was alleviated since it would be able to opt out of any amendments which would allow this strategy. Furthermore, the energy-pricing agreement which had been concluded between Ottawa and Edmonton just weeks before the November conference removed a substantial irritant in the relationship between those two governments with respect to energy resources. Finally, the mounting pressure from the Canadian public on governments to settle the protracted constitutional debate restrained any attempt by resource-rich provinces to frustrate the agreement through revival of the demands of the 1978–79 period.

What assessment can be made of the legal and political significance of section 92A? The section gives the provinces concurrent jurisdiction over interprovincial trade and commerce, and the federal government is now at least obligated to enact a specific statute before provincial legislation is found to be ineffective. It is noteworthy that in the case of oil and natural gas the federal Petroleum Administration Act[4] now occupies the trade and commerce field and would overrule any provincial legislation with which it conflicted. It stands as a potent reminder of the limited benefit of the admission of provinces to the interprovincial trade and commerce field.

The granting of power to impose indirect tax is of particular significance to Saskatchewan. About 40 percent of Saskatchewan's resources has been transferred to private interests; recovery of economic rents from the sale of these resources can only be by way of taxation and not by the imposition of royalties. Relieving Saskatchewan from the need to frame its taxation legislation in the form of direct taxation is undoubtedly important. However, this provision is of less value to Alberta since the great proportion of its resources are owned by the crown, and economic rents are recoverable through royalties.

For Alberta the continued presence of the federal general power, "peace, order and good government," represents a serious and unresolved threat to provincial ownership and jurisdictional authority over natural resources. During negotiations in 1978–79 Alberta demanded that this power be diminished. The power has an uncertain meaning, its scope waning and waxing with the passage of time. In three recent instances, the *Anti-Inflation* case,[5] the *Hauser* case,[6] and the minority judgment in the *Alberta Gas Tax Reference*,[7] the power has been interpreted expansively. In light of this judicial development, provincial governments which enact legislation with respect to energy resources should be mindful that federal legislation manifesting conflicting policies could be sustained under this power.

Admittedly section 92A has enhanced the scope of provincial legislative jurisdiction over non-renewable resources. Still, apart from a more liberal approach to taxation, the scope for provincial regulation where a resource is exported remains limited. The possibility of invasion of the provincial domain of development, conservation, and management of non-renewable resources through the use of the federal peace, order, and good government power and the trade and commerce clause remains unchecked.

The history of negotiation for a new category of provincial power over resources shows the complexity of the conflict. The interrelatedness of the questions of distribution of revenue, regional aspiration, equalization amongst provinces, and federal economic strategies suggests that the attempt to achieve reconciliation through constitutional reform is probably unworkable. It may be that the system of federal–provincial consultations and negotiations will yield far more satisfactory compromises. For example, intergovernmental negotiation has produced agreements with respect to energy pricing and the implementation of the national energy program. Likewise, conflict over offshore resources in Nova Scotia and the taxation of provincial crown corporations have been solved through agreement. For a country as regionally diverse as Canada, intergovernmental negotiation leading to specific agreements may reflect more suitable compromise than constitutional amendment.

The Future

The constitutional agreement of November 1981 did not resolve the nation's outstanding problems. A review of its specific provisions demonstrates the limited nature of the agreement. For those who focussed on the linguistic cleavage in Canada, the results seem meagre indeed. Worse, without the concurrence of Quebec, the agreement leaves open the likelihood of future confrontation. For those whose concerns were resources and regional economic wealth, there are only unsatisfactory, halfway solutions. The role of Indians, Inuit and Métis in a restructured Canada was postponed, and nothing was done about reform of central institutions. After a long and numbing process, how do we know whether there was really anything to cheer about?

Perhaps we are wrong in posing the question. Like work horses plodding daily to the same watering hole, our analysis continues down the familiar intellectual paths, evaluating events by the old, and seemingly, useful measuring sticks. The importance of November 1981 lies not in an evaluation of its specific changes, and their relevance to the forces that generated them; it lies in setting the agreement in the context of a process which began in the mid-seventies, and in the larger context of the history of this nation.

Residents of Quebec, and French Canadians generally, had never been asked if they wished to be part of Canada. Their fierce loyalty to language, culture, and religion was born of the need to preserve a heritage within a relationship that seemed designed first to subordinate and then to destroy it. They fought the battle for survival with what means were available. Their lack of consent remained a source of tension within Canada, a source of strength for organic communitarian conceptions of the nation. As long as the citizens of Quebec were not called upon to say yes or no to Canada, they could be counted amongst the ranks of those opposed to the centralizing conceptions of the nation. Only after 1976 did that situation change. Only then did the process begin which would end the ambiguity of their position. In the spring of 1980, Quebec residents were asked a question about their primary loyalties. A majority chose the larger nation and, for the first time, Quebec could not be counted upon to support the organic view of Canada. A majority was now willing to take its chances within the larger nation-state.

In the same way western Canadians had never been given the opportunity to pass judgment on their role and continued presence in Canada. Born as colonies of Ottawa, kept in a subordinate position in confederation until 1930, and plagued by their obvious political powerlessness, they seethed their way through the twentieth century, alternately blaming "the East" for its policies of economic domination, and themselves for their inability to come together to "do something" about their fate. Whatever the problem, it could be blamed on "the enemy without." Whatever the circumstance, it had to be overcome despite the opposition of a self-centred central Canada. These attitudes, so typical of the weaker members of any union, were forced into sharp relief in the 1970s. As long as the West was clearly a weaker partner, the sense of alienation was sustained. But, by the 1980s, the facts no longer fitted the myth. Western Canada was economically powerful: it could obviously exercise an influence which it had never before possessed. And it did. But in so doing, it forced western Canadians, as it had Quebeckers, to choose. To choose between compromise and Canada, or no compromise and something else. They chose Canada. In one sense, the newly acquired strength was a blessing, but, in another, it signalled the beginning of the end of an era of regional alienation. In the West also, the signing of the oil-pricing agreements and the constitutional accord heralded a new relationship between individual western Canadians and their nation.

The charter of rights, the rest of the constitutional agreement of 1981, the oil-pricing arrangements agreed to in the same year, and the defeat by referendum of sovereignty-association in 1980 formed a series of events which marked a watershed in the direction of political history in Canada. In that two-year period, the organic forces of Canada lost ground to the more individualistic liberal conception of the country.[8]

Some would wholeheartedly applaud this new direction. They point to new freedom and to new initiatives that Canada would be able to undertake unencumbered by regional division. A new sense of national purpose, they argue, would accompany this transformation and enrich each Canadian. But others are not so convinced. They lament the passing of a unique society that had learned to balance centralizing forces and liberal individualism with cooperative and organic values.

Canada's recent experience in constitutional renewal reveals two conflicting facts. First, where widely varying political goals prevail from region to region, the conjunction of factors conducive to constitutional change is not commonplace. Second, the need for constitutional reform has not been lessened by the limited success of 1981. Significant numbers of unresolved constitutional dilemmas await attention. Quebec has still not gained authority over those matters which are directly related to shaping its cultural and social environment. The aboriginal peoples have received no constitutional recognition of either the structures or the rights which would allow them to develop societies which are neither subordinate nor marginal. The Senate remains both a theoretical and political embarass-ment for Canada. Apart from the question of the appointment of its members, it has reached a point of complete failure in representing at the centre the regional interests of Canada. Parliament requires an institution by which it can respond to the diversities in Canada, as they bear on matters within its jurisdiction, and a restructured upper chamber is likely the answer. The Supreme Court of Canada has, with the coming into force of the charter of rights, assumed an ever more powerful role in the regula-tion of governmental activity. Yet of all the governments that it controls by setting jurisdictional limits, only one has any influence in appointing the persons who form it. The Supreme Court must be transformed into an institution the structure of which legitimates its role as enforcer of the norms of Canadian society. Finally, conflict between the federal and pro-vincial governments over their respective roles in forming and implement-ing policies of economic development must be ameliorated. New consti-tutional arrangements must permit the rationalization of economic regu-lation without, at the same time, destroying the ability of provinces to perform their responsibility of improving economic and social conditions within the province.

In all the areas of necessary constitutional reform there is a basic tension. On the one hand, there is the desire to make changes which reduce the centres of power and facilitate the development of uniform and coherent national policies and standards. On the other hand, there is the view that Canada's strength derives from its promotion of communities, provinces, and of racial, ethnic, and distinctive language groups, each with the self-confidence and autonomy to make innovations which improve the quality of life. Social experimentation, economic innovation, and intra-national competition have given the nation its special flavour and allowed its people to feel at home.

These values are in danger. Perhaps we will not have the political energy to readdress Quebec's need for additional jurisdiction. We may not be able to admit the distinct cultural and ideological values of aboriginal groups into our constitutional order; we may, for instance, be reluctant to abandon our present preoccupation with individual rights to allow for the collectivism necessary to sustain the Indians, the Métis, and the Inuit, as distinct peoples. It may be that Senate reform ranks too low in the priorities of the country to be reached or, if reached, that the national political parties will be unwilling to advocate changes in the Senate that would lessen their power over its membership, whether elected or appointed. It may be that the view of the Supreme Court as representative of both orders of governments and of the regions will be said to flow from a debased idea of the legal process and the administration of justice; we may avoid reform on the grounds that concerns relevant to political legitimacy are irrelevant to judicial legitimacy and that the neutrality and uniformity of our legal system make constitutional reform unnecessary.

Other constitutional reforms may be more likely. Pressures of international competition from Japan, Germany, and the United States, of chronic unemployment, of technological developments, and of securing development capital may all produce the cry for wide federal powers to promote economic efficiency. Deep economic anxiety may induce the nation to adopt a course of centralization.

Uncertainties about the effect of what we have wrought and about the resolution of our unsolved problems are the uncertainties of life. We can never be sure of the meaning of our history or of how our future will unfold, yet, in the story of the Canadian nation, the events of 1976 to 1982 were more than ordinarily important. We now face a future in which we are not sure that our national cohesion will continue to be based on an appreciation of our rich diversities. We have reinvented Canada. Did we lose its soul?

Notes

1. Guy Favreau, *The Amendment of the Constitution of Canada* (Ottawa, 1965), 22.
2. Marc Lalonde and Ron Basford. *The Canadian Constitution and Constitutional Amendment* (Ottawa, 1978), 20–21. See also, Canadian Bar Association, *Towards a New Canada* (Montreal, 1978). Referendums were considered by the CBA's Committee on the Constitution at 145: "We also considered a variation involving a national majority that was sufficiently large to require a high degree of regional acceptance. In the end, however, we abandoned these attempts as impractical for a number of reasons. Among these was that there was such diversity in size in the provinces that a workable formula could not be arrived at, particularly one that would take into account population changes. Morever, we think that any such formula should give the French speaking majority of Quebec adequate weight, and this would require an unacceptably high percentage of agreement to a proposed change in that province. However, a province should, if it so desires, be free to call a referendum to determine from the electorate whether it should consent to a constitutional proposal." The Task Force on Canadian Unity, in *A Future Together* (Ottawa, 1979), also considered referendums at 177: "While we support the continuation of federal–provincial conferences as the forum for constitutional discussion, we believe that there should be a popular ratification of the results. . . . This would mean that, after an agreement on a new constitution arrived at by the federal and

provincial governments, a Canada-wide referendum would be held, and approval of the new constitution or the set of constitutional amendments would require a majority vote in each of four regions of Canada—the Atlantic Region, Quebec, Ontario and the western provinces. Thus, final responsibility for constitutional change would rest with the people themselves."

3. P.E. Trudeau, *Closing Remarks*, Ottawa, 5 November 1981, C.I.C.S. Doc. 800-15/014.

4. S.C. 1974-75-76, c. 47. Renamed by S.C. 1980-81-82, c. 114, s.1, the Energy Administration Act.

5. *Reference Re Anti-Inflation Act*, [1976] 2 S.C.R. 373, 68 D.L.R. (3d) 452.

6. *R. v. Hauser*, [1979] 1 S.C.R. 984, [1977] 5 W.W.R. 1.

7. (1982), 136 D.L.R. (3d) 385.

8. Some have argued that the legislative override of portions of the charter and the provision for provincial opting out on some constitutional amendments are of more importance in assessing the balance of regionalist and centralist forces in Canada. They may be right. We do not think so. Provisions for constitutional amendment, as evidenced in other federal states, have not been central to the direction of centrifugal and centripetal movement. Of greater import have been bills of rights and the enhanced role of the national judiciary. In any event, under the new amendment provisions, the ratchet effect of the opt-out provision will mean that over time any centralizing amendments will likely come into force generally. As for the legislative override, even if it were to be frequently used, which is unlikely, the day-to-day impact of the charter on the life of Canadians will be persistent and significant.

Index

Abery, Cyril, 208
Aboriginal rights, 66, 77, 121-22, 202,
    209, 211, 212-13, 268-69, 275, 277
Alberta:
  on amending formula, 49, 50, 87-88,
    195
  on charter of rights, 257
  on economic powers, 74
  and federal government, xviii, 93,
    108, 115-16, 130, 158
  and natural resources, 14, 24-25, 27-
    28, 51, 52, 63, 64, 196
  and oil, xvii, xviii, 89, 115-16, 129
  vs. Ontario, xviii, 49, 55, 56, 107
  on patriation, 52, 195
  and regional wealth, xvii
  and Saskatchewan, 23, 116
  on Senate reform, 34
  on Supreme Court reform, 36-37, 38
  and Trudeau, 23, 89
  urbanization of, xviii
  see also Western Canada
Alternatives Canada (Banff, 1978), 11
Amending formula, 51-52, 63-65, 86-
    88, 230-31, 269-73;
  provinces', 5, 48-50, 87-88, 117, 172,
    173, 193-214
Anderson, Doris, 247-48
Anti-Inflation Reference, 35
Atlantic provinces:
  regional disparity of, 54, 64
  on fisheries, 39-41, 51, 75
  on offshore resources, 41-42, 51, 74
  see also individual provinces

Bennett, Bill, 33, 52, 190-91, 192, 196,

197, 200, 203, 204, 257
Bill C-60 (1978), 7-10, 11, 13-14, 16,
    25-26, 32-33, 34, 36, 42, 51, 79,
    126, 157, 210, 234-36, 238
Bill of Rights, Canadian, 36, 77, 221-
    25, 226-27, 236
Bilingualism, 9, 77, 107, 201, 217
Blakeney, Allan, 34, 50, 52, 55, 62, 63,
    65, 98, 100, 109, 110, 117-18, 119-
    20, 123-29, 177-78, 180, 192, 195,
    197-214, 241
Bonneville, Lione, 208
Bourassa, Henri, 32
Bourassa, Robert, 2, 3-4, 12, 21, 230,
    231
British Columbia:
  on charter of rights, 257
  on economy, 191, 195
  on equalization payments, 84
  on federal spending, 46
  on fisheries, 40, 76
  on offshore resources, 75
  on patriation, 52, 129, 130, 131, 158,
    190-91, 193
  and regional interests, xix, 42-43,
    50, 51, 108
  on resources, 27, 210
  on Senate reform, 5, 33, 64
  and Supreme Court reform, 37
  and veto power, 5, 49
  see also Western Canada
British North America Act:
  amendment of, 134, 166-71, 182,
    259
  court decisions on, 166-71
  patriation of, 85, 109, 259